ALSO BY AMERICA'S TEST KITCHEN

FOR A FULL LISTING OF ALL OUR BOOKS

CooksIllustrated.com

AmericasTestKitchen.com

PRAISE FOR AMERICA'S TEST KITCHEN TITLES

"With their bounty of photos and information, ATK cookbooks are great for meeting readers right where they are, and while all home chefs can find a pie recipe here tailored to the skills they already have, they're bound to pick up more along the way."

BOOKLIST ON *THE PERFECT PIE*

Selected as one of the 10 Best New Cookbooks of 2017

THE LA TIMES ON *THE PERFECT COOKIE*

"The editors at America's Test Kitchen pack decades of baking experience into this impressive volume of 250 recipes. . . . You'll find a wealth of keeper recipes within these pages."

LIBRARY JOURNAL (STARRED REVIEW) ON *THE PERFECT COOKIE*

"The book offers an impressive education for curious cake makers, new and experienced alike. A summation of 25 years of cake making at ATK, there are cakes for every taste."

THE WALL STREET JOURNAL ON *THE PERFECT CAKE*

Selected as the Cookbook Award Winner of 2017 in the Baking Category

INTERNATIONAL ASSOCIATION OF CULINARY PROFESSIONALS (IACP) ON *BREAD ILLUSTRATED*

"With 1,000 photos and the expertise of the America's Test Kitchen editors, this title might be the definitive book on bread baking."

PUBLISHERS WEEKLY ON *BREAD ILLUSTRATED*

"Cooks with a powerful sweet tooth should scoop up this well-researched recipe book for healthier takes on classic sweet treats."

BOOKLIST ON *NATURALLY SWEET*

"This book is a comprehensive, no-nonsense guide . . . a well-thought-out, clearly explained primer for every aspect of home baking."

THE WALL STREET JOURNAL ON *THE COOK'S ILLUSTRATED BAKING BOOK*

"The sum total of exhaustive experimentation . . . anyone interested in gluten-free cookery simply shouldn't be without it."

NIGELLA LAWSON ON *THE HOW CAN IT BE GLUTEN-FREE COOKBOOK*

"A one-volume kitchen seminar, addressing in one smart chapter after another the sometimes surprising whys behind a cook's best practices. . . . You get the myth, the theory, the science, and the proof, all rigorously interrogated as only America's Test Kitchen can do."

NPR ON *THE SCIENCE OF GOOD COOKING*

"Some books impress by the sheer audacity of their ambition. Backed up by the magazine's famed mission to test every recipe relentlessly until it is the best it can be, this nearly 900-page volume lands with an authoritative wallop."

CHICAGO TRIBUNE ON *THE COOK'S ILLUSTRATED COOKBOOK*

"The 21st-century *Fannie Farmer Cookbook* or *The Joy of Cooking*. If you had to have one cookbook and that's all you could have, this one would do it."

CBS SAN FRANCISCO ON *THE NEW FAMILY COOKBOOK*

"The go-to gift book for newlyweds, small families, or empty nesters."

ORLANDO SENTINEL ON *THE COMPLETE COOKING FOR TWO COOKBOOK*

"This book upgrades slow cooking for discriminating, 21st-century palates—that is indeed revolutionary."

THE DALLAS MORNING NEWS ON *SLOW COOKER REVOLUTION*

"Some 2,500 photos walk readers through 600 painstakingly tested recipes, leaving little room for error."

ASSOCIATED PRESS ON *THE AMERICA'S TEST KITCHEN COOKING SCHOOL COOKBOOK*

"This impressive installment from America's Test Kitchen equips readers with dozens of repertoire-worthy recipes. . . . This is a must-have for beginner cooks and more experienced ones who wish to sharpen their skills."

PUBLISHERS WEEKLY (STARRED REVIEW) ON *THE NEW ESSENTIALS COOKBOOK*

everything
CHOCOLATE

A Decadent Collection
of Morning Pastries, Nostalgic Sweets,
and Showstopping Desserts

AMERICA'S TEST KITCHEN

Library of Congress Cataloging-in-Publication Data has been applied for

ISBN 978-1-948703-08-6

AMERICA'S TEST KITCHEN
21 Drydock Avenue, Boston, MA 02210

Manufactured in the United States of America
10 9 8 7 6 5 4 3 2 1

Distributed by Penguin Random House Publisher Services
Tel: 800.733.3000

Pictured on front cover Chocolate Pound Cake (page 149) with All-Purpose Chocolate Glaze (page 378)

Pictured on back cover Vegan Dark Chocolate Cupcakes (page 119), Chocolate-Hazelnut Biscotti (page 224), Milk Chocolate Revel Bars (page 136), Chocolate Shortbread (page 102), Chocolate Brioche Buns (page 84), Bergers-Style Cookies (page 38), Homemade Chocolate Cannoli (page 142), Chocolate Sorbet (page 306), Chocolate Pecan Pie (page 209)

Editorial Director, Books **Adam Kowit**

Executive Food Editor **Dan Zuccarello**

Project Editors **Sacha Madadian and Elizabeth Wray Emery**

Senior Editors **Leah Colins and Sara Mayer**

Assistant Editor **Brenna Donovan**

Editorial Assistant **Sara Zatopek**

Test Cook **Samantha Block**

Recipe Development **Sandra Wu**

Art Director, Books **Lindsey Timko Chandler**

Deputy Art Director **Courtney Lentz**

Photography Director **Julie Bozzo Cote**

Photography Producer **Meredith Mulcahy**

Senior Staff Photographers **Steve Klise and Daniel J. van Ackere**

Staff Photographer **Kevin White**

Additional Photography **Keller + Keller**

Food Styling **Catrine Kelty, Chantal Lambeth, Ashley Moore, Elle Simone Scott, and Kendra Smith**

Photoshoot Kitchen Team

    Photo Team Manager **Timothy McQuinn**

    Lead Test Cook **Eric Haessler**

    Assistant Test Cooks **Sarah Ewald, Hannah Fenton, and Jacqueline Gochenouer**

Senior Manager, Publishing Operations **Taylor Argenzio**

Imaging Manager **Lauren Robbins**

Production and Imaging Specialists **Tricia Neumyer, Dennis Noble, Jessica Voas, and Amanda Yong**

Copy Editor **Deri Reed**

Proofreader **Patricia Jalbert-Levine**

Indexer **Elizabeth Parson**

Chief Creative Officer **Jack Bishop**

Executive Editorial Directors **Julia Collin Davison and Bridget Lancaster**

contents

welcome to
AMERICA'S TEST KITCHEN

This book has been tested, written, and edited by the folks at America's Test Kitchen. Located in Boston's Seaport District in the historic Innovation and Design Building, it features 15,000 square feet of kitchen space, including multiple photography and video studios. It is the home of *Cook's Illustrated* magazine and *Cook's Country* magazine and is the workday destination for more than 60 test cooks, editors, and cookware specialists. Our mission is to test recipes over and over again until we understand how and why they work and until we arrive at the best version.

We start the process of testing a recipe with a complete lack of preconceptions, which means that we accept no claim, no technique, and no recipe at face value. We simply assemble as many variations as possible, test a half-dozen of the most promising, and taste the results blind. We then construct our own recipe and continue to test it, varying ingredients, techniques, and cooking times until we reach a consensus. As we like to say in the test kitchen, "We make the mistakes so you don't have to." The result, we hope, is the best version of a particular recipe, but we realize that only you can be the final judge of our success (or failure). We use the same rigorous approach when we test equipment and taste ingredients.

All of this would not be possible without a belief that good cooking, much like good music, is based on a foundation of objective technique. Some people like spicy foods and others don't, but there is a right way to sauté, there is a best way to cook a pot roast, and there are measurable scientific principles involved in producing perfectly beaten, stable egg whites. Our ultimate goal is to investigate the fundamental principles of cooking to give you the techniques, tools, and ingredients you need to become a better cook. It is as simple as that.

To see what goes on behind the scenes at America's Test Kitchen, check out our social media channels for kitchen snapshots, exclusive content, video tips, and much more. You can watch us work (in our actual test kitchen) by tuning in to *America's Test Kitchen* or *Cook's Country* on public television or on our websites. Download our award-winning podcast *Proof*, which goes beyond recipes to solve food mysteries (AmericasTestKitchen.com/proof), or listen in to test kitchen experts on public radio (SplendidTable.org) to hear insights that illuminate the truth about real home cooking. Want to hone your cooking skills or finally learn how to bake—with an America's Test Kitchen test cook? Enroll in one of our online cooking classes. And you can engage the next generation of home cooks with kid-tested recipes from America's Test Kitchen Kids.

However you choose to visit us, we welcome you into our kitchen, where you can stand by our side as we test our way to the best recipes in America.

- facebook.com/AmericasTestKitchen
- twitter.com/TestKitchen
- youtube.com/AmericasTestKitchen
- instagram.com/TestKitchen
- pinterest.com/TestKitchen

AmericasTestKitchen.com
CooksIllustrated.com
CooksCountry.com
OnlineCookingSchool.com
AmericasTestKitchen.com/kids

getting STARTED

INTRODUCTION

Chocolate: It's almost universally loved and craved, and a treasured ingredient that transcends trend. While savory sweets might be en vogue one day and cotton-candy plays on childhood treats another, chocolate *anything* never goes out of style. There isn't a baking book, bakery case, or restaurant menu without it. We're programmed to love chocolate from a young age as bars and novelties made just about any occasion—from Halloween to Valentine's Day—special. For adults, it's a welcome luxury—a savored square of the deepest dark chocolate bar or a salted caramel, or the filling for a sleek tart for dinner party guests.

Yes, anything chocolate dipped, chocolate filled, or chocolate chipped is sure to please all, so we've fully indulged in our first book devoted to the ingredient, from white to milk to dark, for breakfast (wake up with Chocolate Brioche Buns), a snack (Chocolate Peanut Butter Candies will get you through the 3 p.m. slump), or dessert (where do we begin?) as well as how to work with it, how to bake with it, how to decorate with it, how to enjoy it.

Tapping into nostalgia, we open the book with perfected versions of recipes that will take you back: gooey, chocolate-enrobed (and superlatively easy to make) Chocolate Fluff Cookies to Ultimate Chocolate Milkshakes (using intense chocolate sorbet makes them outshine the soda fountain special). Kids will have fun screwing the tops off Chocolate Sandwich Cookies, our recreation of Oreos, while adults will appreciate their upgraded midnight cocoa flavor (bolstered by black cocoa, which you'll learn more about, and a bit of espresso powder). A chapter of bakery favorites will similarly delight with homey classics like Black-Bottom Cupcakes (with a luscious cream cheese center) or specialty sweets like Homemade Chocolate Cannoli. Quick Candy Clusters and Chocolate Toffee make confections doable at home.

While we recall chocolate memories, there's no shortage of the exquisite and modern here: Layer upon layer of flaky buttery pastry surround bands of chocolate for Chocolate Croissants that take you to Paris (pair them with a steaming cup of our Make-Ahead Hot Chocolate and you have the very best Sunday breakfast). White Chocolate Macadamia Nut Cake with Mango is a chocolate-frosted masterpiece that has just as much place under your cake dome as Old-Fashioned Chocolate Cake. And your celebrations are set with sleek Chocolate-Pecan Torte (take it up a notch with our decorating tips), light-and-lovely Chocolate Pavlova with Whipped Cream and Berries, and hot fudge–draped Chocolate Profiteroles (you can go the extra mile and fill them with our Milk Chocolate No-Churn Ice Cream).

Whether chocolate is the main event like in our Rich Chocolate Tart with a deep chocolate shortbread crust, filling, and glaze, or the supporting player, like the thin coating on Millionaire's Shortbread, we want its flavor—the sweet, caramel notes of dairy-rich milk chocolate or the bitter complexity of dark chocolate—to be clear, resonant, and at its best. We've explored how to manipulate chocolate to achieve these results, and you'll uncover tidbits in the book's introduction as well as throughout the chapters. The best chocolate flavor starts with buying the best product, and you'll learn our taste-tested winners for chips, baking bars, and cocoa powder. You can achieve a shiny, snappy tempered DIY Candy Bar with the microwave. Unsweetened chocolate is the right choice when you want the deepest flavor but also a moist, fudgy texture, as with S'mores Brownies. Caramelizing white chocolate can give the sweet variety butterscotch-like complexity. And a sprinkle of salt uncovers interesting flavor notes. This collection has everything covered—in chocolate.

FROM WHITE TO DARK: THE WORLD OF CHOCOLATE VARIETIES

We all know what chocolate tastes like. It's rich. It melts on the tongue. It can be creamy and sweet or brash and bold with a complex flavor profile. But chocolate isn't a simple confection: What *is* this food we crave?

Chocolate begins as something you wouldn't have any interest in eating raw: cacao beans. These very floral, bitter beans are found in large pods that grow on cacao trees. How do beans become bars? The beans are fermented, dried, and roasted and then the inner meat (or nib) of the bean is removed from the shell and ground into a paste called chocolate liquor—the base of all the chocolate we eat. Chocolate liquor consists of about 55 percent cocoa butter and 45 percent cocoa solids. Cocoa butter is the edible, natural fat in the dried beans; it provides a silky texture, while the cocoa solids are the source of chocolate flavor. The combination of cocoa butter and cocoa solids makes up the cacao percentage in processed chocolate. (This is manipulated by the addition of more cocoa butter as well as the presence of extra ingredients such as sugar and milk.) White chocolate is made from just the cocoa butter and doesn't contain any cocoa solids. Milk and dark chocolates go through a refining process known as conching, in which the liquor and the other ingredients are smeared against rollers until smooth. Here are the types of chocolate we use most in the test kitchen, along with our carefully vetted taste test winners.

Unsweetened Chocolate

Unsweetened chocolate is simply chocolate liquor formed into bars. It's used for recipes in which we want a bold hit of chocolate and a not-too-sweet flavor. But why not skip the step of melting bar chocolate and simply use cocoa powder instead? Cocoa powder has been largely defatted, while unsweetened chocolate still contains the cocoa butter from the cacao bean. (For more information on cocoa powder, see page 8.) We use some unsweetened chocolate in baked goods and confections where extra fat contributes to the dense, fudgy texture we're looking for, like S'mores Brownies (page 127), Chocolate Chess Pie (page 205), and Hot Fudge Sauce (page 340). If a recipe calls for unsweetened chocolate but you don't have any on hand, you can replace 1 ounce of unsweetened chocolate with 3 tablespoons of cocoa powder and 1 tablespoon of butter or oil. This substitution is best for small quantities, as it ignores the important differences between butter, oil, and cocoa butter.

The flavor of unsweetened chocolate puts the variety and origin of the cacao beans on display—but manufacturers of unsweetened chocolate generally don't disclose where they come from. If an unsweetened chocolate has sour, overly tropical, or overly vanilla notes, you can presume they come from the mystery beans and how they're roasted. Our winner, American-classic **Baker's Unsweetened Baking Chocolate Bar 100% Cacao**, has no off flavors and tastes familiar, rich, and deeply cocoa-y in desserts.

Dark Chocolate: The Semi- and the Bittersweet

There is some confusion surrounding the world of dark chocolate. Is what's labeled "bittersweet chocolate" the same thing as dark chocolate? What about "semisweet?" What's the difference between the two? We associate semisweet chocolate with the chips found in chocolate chip cookies but, legally speaking, both bittersweet and semisweet are considered dark chocolate, which is made when chocolate liquor is blended with additional cocoa butter and mixed with sugar. The FDA doesn't set an identity for dark chocolate except that "bittersweet" *and* "semisweet" chocolate must contain at least 35 percent cacao—although most contain more than 50 percent and some go as high as 99 percent.

That said, we specify semisweet or bittersweet in our recipes' ingredient lists. Why? Most manufacturers use the term "bittersweet" for chocolates that are higher in cacao (and hence less sweet) than their "semisweet" offering. Thus, "bittersweet" and "semisweet" can be useful terms for comparing products within one brand even if they are imprecise across different brands. So if one of our recipes, such as our Thin Chocolate Mint Cookies (page 35) or Double Chocolate Dessert Waffles (page 303), calls for semisweet chocolate, you can assume we want a friendlier-to-all dark chocolate flavor than one calling for generally bolder bittersweet chocolate. That's not to say you can't use bars labeled "bittersweet" in these places—you absolutely can. In fact, our overall favorite dark chocolate is **Ghirardelli 60% Cacao Bittersweet Chocolate Premium Baking Bar**, which will work in every recipe calling for semisweet or bittersweet chocolate in this book. It has a complex flavor that combines the tart fruitiness of cherries and wine with a slight smokiness. Its level of cocoa solids is high enough to give desserts a dark, bold chocolate flavor, but not so high that it's difficult to work with: It consistently turns out creamy, satiny custards and ganaches. The only thing you *shouldn't* do when choosing dark chocolate for baking recipes that call for semisweet or bittersweet is choose a chocolate that's 85 percent cacao or higher; you are likely to experience compromised texture and in some cases a too-bitter flavor.

You can replace 1 ounce of semisweet or bittersweet chocolate with ⅔ ounce of unsweetened chocolate and 2 teaspoons of granulated sugar—but because the unsweetened chocolate has not been conched it will not provide the same smooth, creamy texture and your desserts will be starchier.

Milk Chocolate

In the chocolate world, dark chocolates frequently hog all the glory, but milk chocolates can display an impressive range of nuances in texture and flavor, too. Milk chocolate is created when milk and sugar are processed with chocolate liquor. Milk chocolate must contain at least 10 percent chocolate liquor and 12 percent milk solids. The result is a smooth but mellow flavor (milk chocolate is usually more than 50 percent sugar), so we use it only in very specific applications such as Milk Chocolate Cheesecake (page 214), where a creamy texture is desired and a more bitter chocolate flavor would overwhelm the subtle tang of the cream cheese, or in the frosting for our Chocolate Malted Cake (page 183), which has a rich, milky flavor that counterbalances the deep chocolate of the cake. Still, our favorite milk chocolates are on the higher end of the cacao percentage range, with our winner, **Endangered Species Chocolate Smooth + Creamy Milk Chocolate**, containing 48 percent. The higher percentage helps creamy desserts set up better because there are more cocoa solids to thicken them and also more fat from cocoa rather than from milk (cocoa fat stiffens better). But many milk chocolate wrappers leave off this important information, so how can you tell if your milk chocolate has a high cacao percentage? We recommend purchasing a product that lists "chocolate" as the first ingredient over products listing milk and sugar first.

White Chocolate

White chocolate is made from cocoa butter alone and not cocoa solids, the element responsible for milk and dark chocolate's characteristic brown color and nutty roasted flavor. We couldn't possibly leave this confection out of a chocolate book— it's made from part of the cacao bean, after all. Plus, it has chocolate in its name—and is delicious.

Authentic white chocolate must contain at least 20 percent cocoa butter. Many products rely on palm oil in place of some or all of the cocoa butter—often to keep costs down—and so can't be labeled "chocolate." Instead, these are labeled "white chips" or "white confection." We're not too picky, however: White chocolate derives its flavor from milk and sugar, not from the fat, so we find this distinction makes little difference in recipes since both styles offer a milky sweetness and meltingly smooth texture. The chocolate that worked in all our recipes was **Guittard Choc-Au-Lait White Chips**. (Yes, a chip: It can be used in any recipe calling for chopped chocolate— but not for curls and shavings.) Their silky, creamy texture is ideal for the white chocolate mousse in our Triple Chocolate Mousse Cake (page 258). These chips contain a mixture of palm kernel oil and cocoa butter.

BEAN-TO-BAR: EXPLORING CRAFT CHOCOLATE

Our favorite chocolates listed in the preceding pages perform admirably in baked goods and, of course, they're good to eat on their own, too. But in the past decade, Americans have gotten serious about dark chocolate. Rich, complex, and bitter (sometimes bracingly so), its flavor transcends the mild, sugar-laden milk chocolate that many of us grew up snacking on. As a result, ever-climbing cacao percentages are now posted prominently on packaging, and chocophiles have come to describe bars with the same level of detail that they'd use for a fine Cabernet. Now-hot "bean to bar" chocolate is handcrafted and small-batch; unlike commercial producers (chocolatiers) who make bars and confections from already-processed couverture chocolate that they purchase, bean-to-bar producers (chocolate makers) control every aspect of working with the chocolate, from sourcing beans to production. Single-origin bars, those made from just one variety of bean, are trendy, too, showcasing distinct regional characteristics such as the intensely floral flavor of beans from the mountains of Peru or the dried mint overtones of beans from Trinidad.

Almost all of these pricey chocolates are meant to be eaten plain, savored by the sliver, rather than used for cooking. It seems wasteful to cook with them (although you can), as many of their more delicate notes won't survive a hot oven. (You know the irresistible fragrance that pervades the kitchen when you're baking chocolate cake or brownies? Those are flavor and aroma volatiles driven out of the baked goods by the heat.) Since all of these bean-to-bar chocolates are unique, we've outlined the characteristics that bring them together to help you understand these tasty treats.

High Cacao Percentages

Chocolate made by big companies in big batches often contains additional ingredients such as sugar, vanillin, cocoa butter, and emulsifiers for creaminess. Bean-to-bar chocolate makers source whole cocoa beans and most add just enough sugar to bring out the beans' sweetness and no additional cocoa butter. (Some makers have started to include add-ins such as vanilla or sea salt.) With so few ingredients and the focus on cocoa beans, bean-to-bar chocolate almost always contains a high cacao percentage.

Direct-Trade Model

Direct trade removes any barriers between the farmers and the chocolate maker. Think fair trade, but without the middle-person. Craft chocolate makers communicate with the farmers themselves instead of paying someone else to do it. This means the makers get to see their cocoa beans before they buy them, and the farmers get paid more for their product.

Made in America

Bean-to-bar chocolate made in the United States is different than the European-style, which is known for its even, rounded flavor thanks to additions like extra cocoa butter and vanilla. American craft chocolatiers usually eschew extra ingredients, so the chocolate flavor tends to be bolder, tasting more like the cocoa beans the chocolate is made from—and that flavor can vary depending on where the beans were grown.

Regions of Flavor

In the same way that grapes' region of origin influences the flavor of a resulting wine, cocoa beans from different regions have their own distinctive flavors. This has to do with terroir—that is, the effect that the soil, landscape, and environment have on the flavor of the beans. So if you're shopping for a single-origin chocolate bar, here is a cheat sheet for the predominant flavors in bars from just a few areas around the world:

Bright and Fruity Hawaii, Costa Rica, Belize, Dominican Republic, Brazil, Madagascar, Vietnam

Nutty Nicaragua, Venezuela, Grenada

Earthy Tanzania, Philippines

Floral Ecuador

Smoky Papua New Guinea (the cocoa beans are dried inside with a fire because it's too rainy to do it outside)

THE ALOHA CHOCOLATE

Sure, the American bean-to-bar chocolate market is bustling as is locavorism, but you won't find beans from Omaha. Hawaii is the only state in the country that grows its own cocoa beans. That's because it's the only state whose ecosystem allows cocoa beans to grow. But they're not native to the state. Cacao trees were brought and planted there in the 1850s by German physician William Hillebrand and they grew there for 100 years before anyone used them to make chocolate.

CHIPPING CHOCOLATE

You might think chocolate chips are simply miniature versions of bar chocolate, but that isn't the case. Chocolate chips have a similar cacao percentage but less cocoa butter (i.e., fat) than bar chocolate, which makes them cheaper to produce and more able to maintain their shape when baked. (They also tend to have higher levels of emulsifiers, which further helps them hold their shape.) The chocolate chip cookie actually precedes the chocolate chip. Yes—the original Toll House cookie from 1938 called for chopping chocolate and became so famous that in 1941 the company began making the teardrop-shape chips that are ubiquitous today.

Bar versus Chip

To find out if the differences between bars and chips would matter when the chips were melted and put to use, we gathered several of our recipes that call for melted chopped semisweet or bittersweet chocolate, including Dark Chocolate No-Churn Ice Cream (page 305), Pots de Crème (page 289), and German Chocolate Cake (page 172), and made one batch of each with bar chocolate and another with chips. In the ice cream and pots de crème, the chips produced a slightly grainy, overly thick, and viscous texture, while the bar versions were light and silky. However, the crumb of the cake seemed to mask any textural difference between the two versions. (Tasters did notice that the cake made with chips was slightly sweeter.) We'll turn to chips for simple recipes to avoid chopping chocolate, but if your sights are set on something custardy, head to the store for bar chocolate.

While this was the exception and not the rule, we did find that chips are actually a better choice in a few applications that need a little extra stability, such as Creamy Vegan Chocolate Frosting (page 347) or the topping for Bergers-Style Cookies (page 38). (Recipes will specify when to use chips.) The impact of emulsifiers makes a particular difference in the two-ingredient (plus salt) vegan frosting. The frosting we made with chopped bar chocolate and coconut milk broke and curdled. But when we used chocolate chips, the frosting turned out ultracreamy and smooth, and it held its peaks. And of course, chips are perfect for countless baked goods such as Chocolate Chip Cookies (page 101) and Chocolate Zucchini Cake (page 68) where a treat studded with distinct morsels is the goal.

The Best Dark Chocolate Chips

While fresh, homemade chocolate chip cookies really can't fail, our winning chips will give yours an advantage. With the highest percentage of cacao in the lineup in our testing—60 percent, comparable to bar chocolate—and the most cocoa butter by far, **Ghirardelli 60% Premium Baking Chips** hit all the right notes. With more cacao than sugar, they ensure a milder sweetness that balances sugary desserts like cookies; the generous amount of cocoa butter gives them a creamy texture.

The Best Milk Chocolate Chips

Though decadent dark chocolate chips may find their way into most desserts, milk chocolate chips deserve some attention, too. After all, a good milk chocolate is creamy, delicate, and sweet, with a melt-in-your-mouth smoothness you just don't get from dark chocolate. Our rankings depended on the flavor of the chips alone and as a stand-in in our Chocolate Chip Cookies (page 101). Despite differences in the amount of sugar or type of milk, we found flavor differences among brands of milk chocolate chips to be minimal. In fact, we liked all the milk chocolate chips we tried. But our favorite is **Hershey's Kitchens Milk Chocolate Chips**, which pack a punch, boasting deep chocolate flavor with fruity notes and classic creaminess.

WHAT ARE CHOCOLATE CALLETS?

We call for chocolate chips in our Chocolate Chip Cookies (page 101), but there's another chocolate product on the market that's sometimes used for the same purpose: chocolate callets, which are formulated for melting. We thought these disks might create appealing puddles of chocolate throughout our cookies so we gave them a try—but the cookies that emerged were flat, with indistinguishable layers rather than distinct morsels. That's because callets contain more fat than chips—enough more to change the composition of the dough so that they bake differently and spread too thin. If you're using bits of chocolate for a melted application, callets will work just fine; but for recipes where you want distinct morsels, such as for cookies, make sure you use true chocolate chips.

DECODING COCOA

When you think of chocolate, you probably think of the bar stuff—the choppable, the meltable, the snackable. But when we want big chocolate flavor in everything from cookies and cakes to puddings and pies, we often turn to cocoa powder. Cocoa powder has a higher proportion of flavorful cocoa solids than any other form of chocolate—including unsweetened chocolate—so ounce for ounce, it tastes more intensely chocolaty. It's made in two styles, Dutch-processed and natural. And there's fierce debate in the baking world about which is best. But is choosing between Dutched and natural the most important decision you can make, or is there more to it than that?

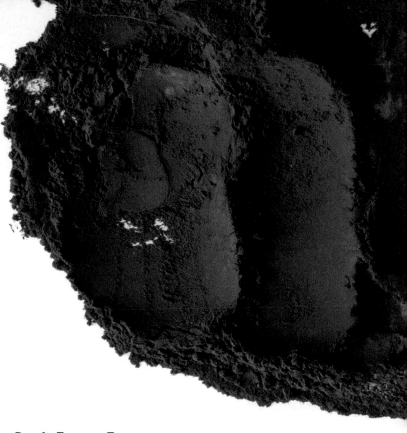

What is Dutching?

In a process developed in the 19th century by Dutch chemist and chocolatier Conrad Van Houten, cocoa powder is Dutched when an alkalizing agent is added to it. This optional step darkens the powder's color from a sandy, reddish brown to a velvety brown or near-black color and mellows its astringent notes, as chocolate is naturally acidic. (Compare the left-most shade of cocoa, a Dutch-processed cocoa, with the light natural cocoas on the right end of the spectrum in the image above.) Dutching raises the chocolate's pH from 5 to about 7. Manufacturers use a variety of alkalizing agents such as potassium carbonate or sodium carbonate. They can also adjust the temperature and time of the process and may opt to alkalize the nibs, the liquor, or the final powder.

What Does Dutching Do?

More acidic natural powders often produce taller, airier, and crumblier cookies and cakes, while most Dutched powders produce baked goods that don't rise quite as tall. This makes sense: Baking soda is a common ingredient in baked goods. The acidity level of a cocoa affects how it interacts with the baking soda; in general, less-acidic Dutched powders produce fudgier, moister desserts.

Don't Forget Fat

Despite the tendency for Dutched powders to create fudgier baked goods, pH doesn't predict all; fat is also an important variable. Fat adds richness and flavor to baked goods. Cocoa powder contains fat (generally between 10 and 24 percent) because, when the chocolate liquor is pressed before being dried and turned to powder, some cocoa butter remains with the solids. We prefer cocoa powders that contain at least 20 percent fat because they tend to ensure cookies and cakes bake up moist and tender. The less fat a cocoa powder has, the more starch it contains. These starches are very absorbent—capable of soaking up 100 percent of their weight in moisture—so lower-fat cocoa powders result in drier, crumblier cakes and cookies. You can tell the difference in fudginess just from the images below; to zero in on the differences, we performed a test with cocoa powder–water mixtures that we cooked on the stove to exactly the same temperature.

Chocolate Crinkle Cookies Made with Natural Cocoa Powder

Chocolate Crinkle Cookies Made with Dutched Cocoa Powder

High Starch, Low Fat Cocoa Powder

Low Starch, High Fat Cocoa Powder

Best of All Worlds

If our recipe calls for "unsweetened cocoa powder," it will work with either Dutched or natural powders. Sometimes, when lift and lightness are of paramount importance in a baked good, we'll call for natural powder. A majority of the time, however, we use our favorite cocoa powder, **Droste Cacao**, which is Dutched. Use this when an ultramoist texture and rich, dark color are top priorities; it's high in fat and therefore low in moisture-absorbing starch. (If the nutrition label is all you have to go by, seek out a product with at least 1 gram of fat per 5-gram serving.) If we're using natural cocoa, we turn to Hershey's Natural Unsweetened Cocoa for its familiar, straightforward chocolate flavor.

What Is Black Cocoa Powder?

For Chocolate Sandwich Cookies (page 28) with the authentic color of the commercial version and big chocolate flavor, we used black cocoa powder. Black cocoa has been heavily Dutched, which causes the color to darken even more. It contains very little fat, however, so to avoid a crumbly texture in our cookies, we cut it with some regular Dutch-processed cocoa and then add a little espresso powder to deepen the chocolate flavor. You can buy true black cocoa powder from kingarthurflour.com or use Hershey's Special Dark cocoa powder, which is also heavily Dutched.

Cocoa Cabinet Life

Wondering if cocoa spoils or loses its flavor over time as spices do, we made our Holiday Chocolate Butter Cookies (page 220) with cocoas two years past their expiration date, comparing them with samples made with fresh cocoa. Tasters couldn't differentiate between the samples. The compounds that give cocoa powder its flavor are less volatile than those in ground spices, which lose much of their flavor and aroma after about a year.

PUMPING UP THE POWDER WITH POWDER

Sometimes we call for espresso powder in chocolate recipes even when coffee flavor isn't the goal. Why? Just a pinch amplifies chocolate flavor considerably, making it more intense and complex without imparting a noticeable coffee presence. Our favorite instant espresso powder for brewing a demitasse or baking brownies is **Cafe D'Vita Imported Premium Instant Espresso**, which contributes dark, deep, fruity, roasty notes to baked goods such as our Chocolate Financiers (page 74).

STORING CHOCOLATE

Chocolate is a prized commodity—store it right. Unopened chocolate should be stored in a zipper-lock bag in a cool, dry place (such as a kitchen cabinet or pantry). Opened bars of chocolate should be wrapped tightly in plastic wrap and given the same treatment. Avoid the refrigerator or freezer, as cocoa butter easily absorbs off-flavors from other foods and temperature changes can alter its crystal structure so it behaves differently in recipes. Stored properly, unsweetened and dark chocolate will last about 2 years. The milk solids in white and milk chocolate give them a shorter shelf life of about 6 months.

Bloomed Chocolate

Storing chocolate at temperatures that are either too warm or too cool will cause a harmless white film, or bloom, to develop on the surface. One type of bloom occurs when cocoa butter crystals melt and migrate to the surface. Another type happens in humid conditions when water condenses on bittersweet and milk chocolate, dissolving some of the sugar before evaporating and leaving behind a fine layer of sugar crystals.

In tests, we found that bloomed chocolate of either type was fine for baking. But when we dipped cookies in melted chocolate with cocoa butter bloom, the chocolate took longer to set up and the bloom reappeared. This is because the chocolate's fat structure had changed. Also, the sugar crystals in the melted sugar–bloomed chocolate never dissolved, resulting in a grainy coating.

Bar Chocolate with Bloom

Chocolate Coating Made from Bloomed Chocolate

"BLOOMING" ISN'T ALWAYS BAD

The word "blooming" has another meaning: It's a technique that we use in many of our chocolate recipes —especially those including cocoa powder—when we want the chocolate flavor to go the extra mile. To bloom cocoa powder, we either combine it with hot water (or coffee, milk, even beer) as in our Old-Fashioned Chocolate Cake (page 156), or with melted butter as in Chocolate Sandwich Cookies (page 28) to awaken dormant flavor compounds for a fuller, richer cocoa flavor. This process also helps make the cocoa easy to blend with the other ingredients in the recipe. In our Chocolate Pound Cake (page 149), we use both cocoa powder and bar chocolate; we microwave the cocoa powder with the bar chocolate rather than whisking it with the other dry ingredients to apply heat and bloom the cocoa powder.

OTHER CHOCOLATE PRODUCTS

The three main chocolate ingredients we use in our recipes are bar chocolate, chocolate chips, and cocoa powder. But there are some other chocolate products worth knowing.

Cacao Nibs

Cacao nibs are the fermented, roasted, and cracked pieces of cacao beans that manufacturers process to make chocolate. They are dry and crunchy and have the bitterness of unsweetened chocolate or coffee, tempered by a slightly fruity acidity. Cacao nibs don't melt when heated, but their cocoa butter comes to the surface. Sprinkled over the top, they're a great way to upgrade common breakfasts or snacks such as oatmeal or yogurt. If you want to bake them into treats, we've found that they are best suited to applications like banana bread where there aren't a lot of other competing flavors (or textures), although we love them in our Chewy Granola Bars with Hazelnuts, Cherries, and Cacao Nibs (page 65). Likewise, they also are nice in granola. Use ½ to ⅔ cup of cacao nibs per 9-cup batch of granola, loaf of quick bread, or dozen muffins.

Chocolate Extract

Vanilla extract is a staple in every baker's pantry, so why not chocolate extract? Like vanilla, chocolate extract uses alcohol to draw out the bean's flavor. Chocolate extract gave our brownie batter richer, more complex chocolate flavor. Try substituting chocolate extract for half of the vanilla in recipes for chocolate cake or brownies. (Vanilla is still necessary for its rounding notes.) It costs about as much as vanilla.

Mexican-Style Chocolate

Much Mexican chocolate is stone-ground in the traditional manner, which gives it a pleasantly gritty, substantial texture—it seems less like confection. (Other chocolate is conched, a process invented in the late 19th century to smooth and refine it; see page 3.) Our tasters found that sweetened Mexican chocolate (which is often ground with cinnamon) has notes of molasses, dried fruit, and/or coffee. In the United States, look for Taza, Abuelita, or Ibarra brands.

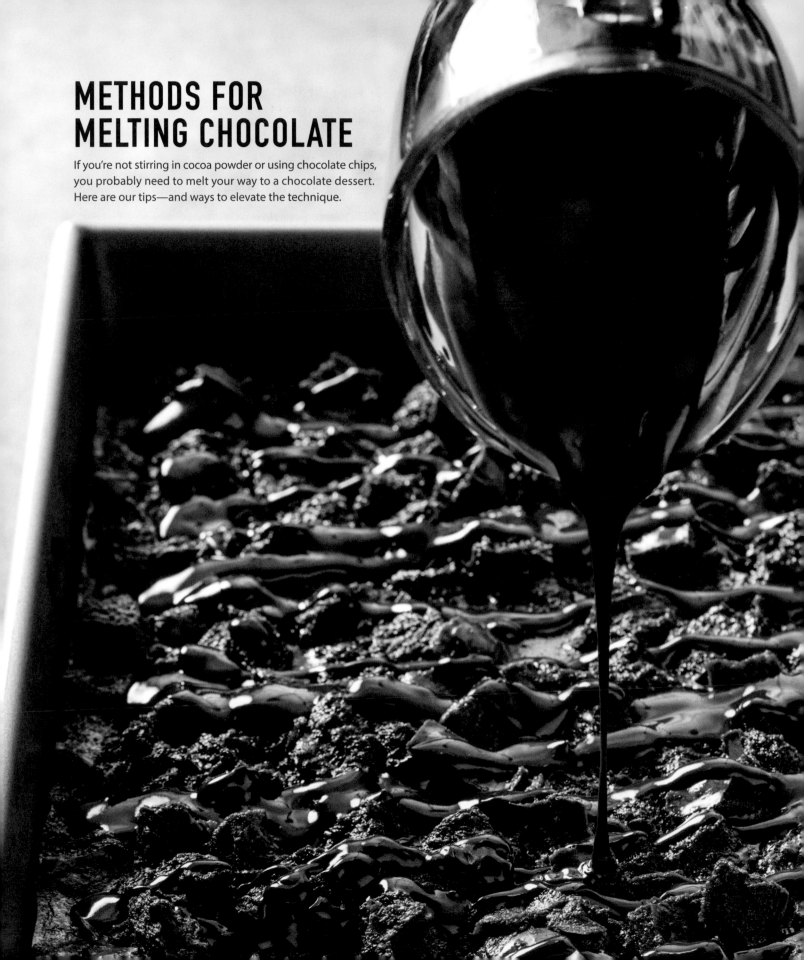

METHODS FOR MELTING CHOCOLATE

If you're not stirring in cocoa powder or using chocolate chips, you probably need to melt your way to a chocolate dessert. Here are our tips—and ways to elevate the technique.

Melting Chocolate

Chocolate can burn easily, so it's best to use a gentle approach for melting. Our preferred method for melting chocolate is to use the microwave, whether it's to simply liquefy it (for a frosting or a cake) or to temper it (so it hardens into a shiny, snappy glaze; for more information on tempering see page 14). The microwave is far less fussy than the old-fashioned method of warming chopped chocolate in a bowl set over a saucepan of simmering water, and it's also a lot quicker. (That said, we still use this method for some stovetop desserts or for recipes that include other ingredients that need gentler heat.) The microwave method is more efficient because heat surrounds the chocolate completely, while in the stovetop method the heat is concentrated at the bottom of the bowl.

Melting in the Microwave

Microwave the chopped chocolate in a bowl at 50 percent power. (The time will depend on the amount.) Stir the chocolate (so the chocolate liquifies evenly) as directed in the recipe, and continue microwaving until melted.

Melting on the Stovetop

Place chopped chocolate in a heatproof bowl set over a saucepan filled with 1 inch of barely simmering water. (Be sure the bowl is not touching the water or the chocolate could scorch.) Stir as directed in the recipe.

Melted Mistake

Seizing—the nearly instantaneous transformation of melted chocolate from a fluid state to a stiff, grainy one—is usually the result of a tiny amount of moisture being introduced. To prevent this from happening in recipes that contain no liquid, keep the area and tools dry. Even a tiny drop of water will form a syrup with the sugar in the chocolate to which the cocoa particles will cling, creating grainy clumps. In recipes containing liquids such as melted butter, liqueur, or water, always melt the chocolate along with these ingredients.

But what if your melted chocolate does seize? Do you need to throw away an expensive ingredient? Although it may seem counterintuitive, the solution to fix seized chocolate is to add more liquid to return the chocolate to a fluid state, as the liquid dissolves seized sugar and cocoa particles. Add boiling water to the chocolate, 1 teaspoon at a time, stirring vigorously after each addition, until smooth. But don't use the diluted chocolate for baking; use it for chocolate sauce or hot chocolate.

Tempering Chocolate

Chocolate takes on various characteristics when melted and rehardened due to cocoa butter's crystalline structure. If you're melting chocolate to mix with other ingredients, you just need to do it gently enough that it doesn't burn. But if you're melting it for candy (as with our Pomegranate and Nut Chocolate Coins on page 329) or for a coating (such as for our Thin Chocolate Mint Cookies on page 35) and are aiming for a professional finish—shiny, with the snap of the bar you melted it from—you'll want to temper it. Otherwise it will look soft, blotchy, and/or dull-looking and will melt in your fingers.

Chocolate Not in Temper   **Chocolate in Temper**

Why the difference? In short, the crystal structure of the cocoa butter in the chocolate changes when chocolate is melted. Cocoa butter can solidify into any of six different types of crystals, each of which forms at a specific temperature. But only one type—beta crystals—sets up dense and shiny and stays that way even at temperatures well above room temperature. When a chocolate is made up of beta crystals, it is said to be in temper. So how do you get melted chocolate back in temper? The traditional way is a painstaking process known as, unsurprisingly, tempering. First, the chocolate is melted so that all its fat crystals dissolve. It's then cooled slightly, which allows new "starter" crystals to form. Finally, it's gently reheated to a temperature high enough to melt the less stable crystals and allow only the desirable beta crystals to remain (both of these occur at 88 degrees), triggering the formation of more beta crystals that form a dense, hard, glossy network. Phew.

WE PREFER A FAR SIMPLER APPROACH: Finely chop three-quarters of the chocolate and grate the remainder into fine shards (you can do this on the small holes of a box grater). Microwave the chopped chocolate at 50 percent power until it's about two-thirds melted. Add the grated chocolate and stir until it melts, returning it to the microwave for no more than 5 seconds at a time to complete the melting. This easy-tempered chocolate will have a nice luster and decent snap once it has cooled and set. This method works because it keeps the temperature of the chocolate close enough to 88 degrees that mostly stable beta crystals form and act as seed crystals.

1. Microwave the finely chopped chocolate in a bowl at 50 percent power, stirring often, until about two-thirds melted, 2 to 4 minutes. (Melted chocolate should not be much warmer than body temperature; check by holding the bowl in the palm of your hand.)

2. Add the grated chocolate portion and stir until smooth.

3. Return the bowl of chocolate to the microwave for no more than 5 seconds at a time to finish melting (if necessary).

Melt It, then Dip It

Once you melt chocolate—especially if you've tempered it—it's time to dig, or more often, dip in. Dipping or coating cookies, fruit, or other foods in melted chocolate should result in a tidy, snappy, shiny coat—not a dribbly mess.

If dipping a delight such as our Chocolate-Dipped Potato Chip Cookies (page 32) or a piece of fruit half- or partway in regular melted chocolate, dip the item into the chocolate, scrape off the excess with your finger or on the edge of the bowl (this prevents a thick "foot" of hardened chocolate from forming beneath the item), and place it on a parchment paper–lined baking sheet. Refrigerate or let sit until set.

If you're coating something more cautiously, perhaps with tempered chocolate for a candy, such as for Needhams (page 330) (depicted below), we employ two simple instruments: forks. The tines allow us to touch the item minimally when dipping it and transferring it to a baking sheet or plate to set up, and excess chocolate falls through them.

1. Drop the candy into the chocolate. Using 2 forks, gently flip the candy to coat all over.

2. Lift 1 candy from the bowl with a fork. Tap the fork against the side of the bowl and then wipe the underside of the fork on the edge of the bowl to remove excess chocolate from the bottom of the candy.

3. Use a second fork to slide the candy onto a parchment paper–lined baking sheet.

COVERING WITH COUVERTURE

No matter how well you melt them, milk and dark chocolate have body to them—you can't coat items in a paper-thin layer. That's where couverture chocolate (also known as chocolate callets; see page 7) comes in. It's manufactured specifically for dipping cookies and truffles and coating molds. It's ideal for the job because it produces a thinner layer of chocolate that's shinier and snappier than regular chocolate when set. It can also be costly—up to $20 per pound. If you'd like a scant coating of chocolate on a delicate treat, we found a cheaper way to that result. Melt regular chocolate (we used our favorite dark chocolate, Ghirardelli 60% Cacao Bittersweet Chocolate Premium Baking Bar) with a small amount of white chocolate. Here's why the combination works: When chocolate melts, the cocoa butter becomes liquid; all its other components are insoluble and are suspended in the liquid. Because white chocolate contains cocoa butter but no cocoa solids, it creates a more fluid product that allows for a thinner coating. Also, the more cocoa butter there is, the more rigid (snappy) and glossy the final coating will be. Avoid white chocolate chips and any bars that contain partially hydrogenated palm oil, palm kernel oil, soybean oil, or cottonseed oil, as these are added in lieu of some or all of the cocoa butter and thus, while these products taste good and work best in other desserts, they won't work as well to thin out the chocolate.

HERE'S OUR CHEATER METHOD: Finely chop 4 ounces of dark chocolate and ¼ ounce of pure white chocolate (we like Ghirardelli White Chocolate Premium Baking Bar here). Microwave 3 ounces of the dark chocolate at 50 percent power until it is mostly melted, stirring frequently. Then add the remaining 1 ounce of dark chocolate and the white chocolate and stir it until melted, returning it to the microwave for no more than 5 seconds at a time to complete the melting.

Cookie Dipped in Cheater's Couverture

GANACHE: THE ALL-PURPOSE CHOCOLATE INGREDIENT

At its most basic, ganache is simply equal parts chocolate and cream melted together to create a decadent mixture. Tweak the ratio or temperature, or add other ingredients, however, and it turns truly versatile—able to serve as filling, frosting, glaze, or even candy. Here's a visual representation of ganache in every state and form.

1 Good Ol' Ganache

Equal parts cream and chocolate (generally, the cream is gently heated and then poured over chopped chocolate to melt) create a creamy-smooth mixture for glazing Chocolate Raspberry Torte (page 216) or any number of cakes, cupcakes, or even brownies (for extra decadence) if used shortly after being mixed. It will set up and thicken as its temperature drops.

2 Room Temperature Ganache

Let your standard ganache sit at room temperature for 15 to 30 minutes and it becomes a spreadable filling between cake layers, as in Chocolate-Espresso Dacquoise (page 276); it also works as a swirlable topping or a dip that won't drip.

3 Chilled Ganache

Transfer standard ganache to the refrigerator for 45 minutes or longer and it becomes a scoopable mixture, perfect for dropping in the center of sandwich cookies and pressing to the edges, or whipping into Ganache Frosting (page 346).

4 Ganache + Confectioners' Sugar

A little bit of the superfine sweet stuff thickens ganache just enough to make it a rich, creamy filling for our Ultimate Chocolate Cupcakes (page 115). Use this trick when you need a ganache that stays put no matter the room's temperature.

5 Ganache + Corn Syrup

When you add a couple tablespoons of corn syrup to ganache, you can achieve the mirrored effect of bakery-case goods. This glossy sheen makes the glazes for our Boston Cream Pie (page 166) and Tunnel of Fudge Cake (page 184)—or anything else you like—striking and easily pourable.

6 Ganache + Butter

The addition of a small amount, a tablespoon or two, of butter will give your ganache a flavor boost—more depth and unmatchable richness. Enriched ganache is perfect as spreadable ganache, as for our Yule Log (page 236); whip in a generous amount of butter, sticks worth, and ganache becomes a frosting for our Chocolate Sheet Cake with Milk Chocolate Frosting (page 150).

7 Double-the-Chocolate Ganache

When you tweak the ratio so that there's double the amount of chocolate than of cream and then let that sit and chill, you can roll out a confection—Chocolate Truffles (page 312)!

CREAMLESS GANACHE FILLING

In the 1990s, French chemist Hervé This developed a technique for a cream-free whipped chocolate—and not because he wanted a dairy-free alternative to traditional ganache. He found that by melting chocolate with an abundant amount of water (equaling as much as 90 percent of the weight of the chocolate in some cases) and then whipping it to achieve a mousse-like texture, he could make ganache with incredibly clear chocolate flavor. Without the cream found in a classic ganache to mask the deep chocolate notes, the result is something intensely chocolaty and decadent yet simultaneously not too dense in texture. We use this technique in our Chocolate-Hazelnut Tart (page 192) and our Chocolate, Matcha, and Pomegranate Tart (page 270).

TOOLS FOR WORKING WITH CHOCOLATE

There are certain pieces of equipment that make working with chocolate neater, easier, and more precise. These are the basic tools you'll need and the specialty items you'll want for chocolate desserts and candies.

Digital Kitchen Scale

Chocolate isn't something to waste; we want all our desserts featuring this regal ingredient to come out just right. That's why we weigh dry ingredients to ensure consistent results. We prefer digital scales for their readability and precision. Look for one that has a large weight range and that can be zeroed. The **OXO Good Grips 11 lb Food Scale with Pull Out Display** ($50) has clear buttons, and its display can be pulled out from the platform for easy viewing when weighing bulky items.

Glass Bowls

Many of our recipes call for melting chocolate using our easy microwave method (see page 13), and a glass mixing bowl is the ideal vessel. With their shallow, gently curved walls and easy-to-grip rims, the **Pyrex Smart Essentials Mixing Bowl Set with Colored Lids** ($19.88) are our top choice. Bonus: Tight-fitting lids make these versatile bowls great for storage as well.

Chef's Knife

A sharp-bladed chef's knife isn't just for savory cooking; this kitchen staple is essential for lots of baking prep steps, such as chopping bar chocolate and nuts. We think the best knife for this or any job is the inexpensive **Victorinox 8" Swiss Army Fibrox Pro Chef's Knife** ($34); it has been a test kitchen favorite for more than 20 years. We find that it maintains its edge long after its competitors have gone dull. Its textured grip feels secure for a wide range of hand sizes and is comfortable for a variety of different grips. You'll use it for everything.

Rubber Spatula

For scraping bowls, stirring melted chocolate, smoothing batter, softening chocolate ice cream, and combining the ingredients for chocolate truffles, you'll want the no-nonsense **Rubbermaid Professional 13.5" High-Heat Scraper** ($13) and the **Di Oro Living Seamless Silicone Spatula—Large** ($16). The large head on the Rubbermaid spatula makes it easy to properly fold ingredients; the Di Oro Living spatula is a good multipurpose tool.

Serrated Knife

There are many uses for a serrated knife in the kitchen when baking: It can be used to cut cake layers horizontally, chop chocolate with ease, or score and trim the meringue layers for our Chocolate-Espresso Dacquoise (page 276). A long blade is essential; with the fewest, widest, and deepest serrations as well as a grippy handle, the **Mercer Culinary Millennia 10" Wide Bread Knife** ($22) is a standout.

Vegetable Peeler

A vegetable peeler for baking? If you want to make chocolate curls to garnish your fanciful creation (see how on page 266), this is the tool you'll need. The Y-shaped **Kuhn Rikon Original Swiss Peeler** ($8) easily tackles every task, thanks to a razor-sharp blade and a ridged guide, which ensures a smooth ride with minimal surface drag.

Small Offset Spatula

Mini offset spatulas provide the control you need when spreading batter or melted chocolate in a cake pan or frosting smaller treats such as cupcakes. The **Wilton 9-Inch Angled Spatula** ($11) offers great control for these tasks. Sleek, sturdy, and comfortable, the 4.5-inch blade is just about flawless.

Large Offset Spatula

For frosting a cake, there's no better tool than a large offset spatula. The long, narrow blade on the **OXO Good Grips Bent Icing Knife** ($10) is ideal for scooping and spreading frosting, and it bends like a stairstep where it meets the handle for better leverage. The 6.5-inch blade is sturdy but nimble and very comfortable.

Baking Sheet

Baking sheets aren't just for cookies. We bake our Texas Sheet Cake (page 153) in one, and they can hold multiple ramekins of chocolaty goodness, catch drips from glazing, serve as a vessel for making chocolate shingles, and make transferring pies to and from the oven a breeze. The **Nordic Ware Baker's Half Sheet** ($14.97) performs flawlessly.

Wire Cooling Rack

A wire rack is an indispensable kitchen tool: Properly cooling baked goods is an essential step that shouldn't be overlooked, and a wire rack allows air to circulate all around cookies, cakes, and more. And when set in a rimmed baking sheet, a wire rack is ideal for drizzling chocolate and glazes over desserts. The **Checkered Chef Cooling Rack** ($17) is our favorite.

Parchment Paper

Lining your cake pans and baking sheets with parchment paper is a simple way to make sure all of your cakes, cookies, and chocolate confections release effortlessly. We like **King Arthur Flour's Baking Parchment Paper** ($19.95 per package), a commercial-inspired home product we're not sure how we lived without. After tearing, trimming, and flattening paper in our testing, we appreciated that this product contains precut sheets that you can store flat.

Liquid Measuring Cup

We turn to the industry-standard durable, accurate **Pyrex Measuring Cups** (in multiple sizes) for measuring milk, buttermilk, water, and coffee. We like to whisk our wet ingredients in these cups when a recipe calls for adding them gradually to the mixer—and, of course, they're ideal for pouring melted chocolate over anything.

Cake Stand

While you can frost and decorate cakes on any surface you like—such as a cutting board, platter, or cake pedestal—it's much easier to get smooth coatings on a rotating cake stand. The **Winco Revolving Cake Decorating Stand** ($37) is tall and provides excellent visibility and comfort. It rotates quickly and smoothly, and it has three shallow circles etched onto its surface for easy cake centering.

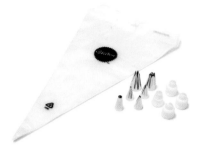

Piping Sets

Floppy cloth pastry bags can stain or hold on to smells. Canvas bags tend to be too stiff. We prefer disposable plastic bags; they're easy to handle for neat dessert decorating and effortless to clean if you do want to reuse them. In addition, we consider a mix of a few different round, petal, closed star, and open star tips appropriate for covering a range of piping needs. You'll also want four couplers—plastic nozzles that adhere the tip to the bag. We like **Wilton** supplies.

Instant-Read Thermometer

When it comes to sweet tasks, thermometers aren't just for candy making. They're also incredibly helpful for judging the doneness of breads such as Chocolate Babka (page 90) and custard-based desserts such as Magic Chocolate Flan Cake (page 180). Using an accurate thermometer is essential for the caramel—a confection that must reach a specific temperature to achieve the proper consistency—in our Ultimate Turtle Brownies on page 128 and for fillings such as the one for Millionaire's Shortbread (page 135). A digital instant-read thermometer—rather than a slow-registering stick candy thermometer—will provide you with an accurate reading almost immediately. Thermometers with long probes easily reach into deep pots. The **ThermoWorks Thermapen Mk4** ($99) has every bell and whistle.

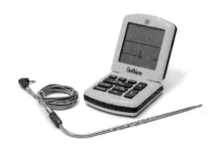

Clip-On Probe Thermometer

We highly recommend owning the **ThermoWorks Thermapen Mk4** ($99), which is a great all-purpose thermometer for kitchen tasks. But if you want to expand on this essential tool, there's another thermometer that makes projects such as candy making and deep frying particularly easy, and it's also made by ThermoWorks: the **ThermoWorks ChefAlarm** ($59). The clip-on digital thermometer allows for hands-free temperature checking, providing the temperature of oil (for frying our Chocolate Cake Doughnuts on page 81), bubbling caramel (for Chocolate-Covered Caramels on page 334), or toffee (for Chocolate Toffee on page 315) every second of the way. The super-accurate thermometer can be calibrated and features programmable high- and low-temperature alarms, adjustable brightness and volume, an on/off switch, and a small knob on the probe that stays cool for over-the-pot adjustments.

nostalgic
TREATS

CHOCOLATE FLUFF COOKIES

MAKES 12 COOKIES

12 Carr's Whole Wheat Crackers

5 ounces marshmallow crème

8 ounces bittersweet chocolate, chopped fine

2 tablespoons vegetable oil

Why This Recipe Works The union of rich chocolate, crisp graham crackers, and gooey marshmallows is one that is beloved far and wide: From MoonPies and Mallomars in this country to tea cakes in Britain and Dream Puffs in Canada, this magical trio is sure to stir up fond childhood memories no matter where you're from. For our version, we ditched the graham crackers and replaced them with Carr's Whole Wheat Crackers, which provided a more substantial base for our cookie. We also liked Carr's crackers for their round shape, crisp texture, and gentle sweetness. Opting for bittersweet chocolate further ensured the sweetness of the marshmallow was kept in check. We wanted a cookie that would be simple to prepare, so rather than make marshmallows from scratch, we simply scooped rounded portions of marshmallow crème right from the container. Briefly freezing the fluff-topped cookies made coating them with chocolate a much neater process. Adding a little vegetable oil to the melted chocolate helped it spread smoothly and stay shiny. You can use a spoon or a liquid measuring cup to pour the chocolate evenly over each cookie.

1 Set wire rack in rimmed baking sheet. Distribute crackers evenly on top of rack. Top each cracker with 1 heaping tablespoon marshmallow crème. Place baking sheet in freezer until marshmallow crème has firmed up, about 10 minutes.

2 Microwave chocolate and oil in bowl at 50 percent power, stirring occasionally, until melted and smooth, 2 to 4 minutes. Let cool completely.

3 Spoon chocolate mixture over each cookie to cover marshmallow crème completely. Return baking sheet to freezer until chocolate is set, about 10 minutes. Transfer sheet to refrigerator until cookies are completely firm, about 1 hour, before serving. (Cookies can be refrigerated for up to 2 days.)

NUTELLA AND HAZELNUT CRISPY RICE CEREAL TREATS

MAKES 15 BARS

Why This Recipe Works Crispy rice cereal treats may first capture hearts as an after-school snack, but grown-ups also find the chewy, tender bars hard to resist. We wanted to put a chocolaty spin on rice cereal treats with the addition of another universally loved treat: Nutella. To achieve just the right texture, we first needed to determine the proper ratio of ingredients. We melted 8 tablespoons of butter along with two 10-ounce packages of marshmallows, ½ cup of Nutella, a couple of teaspoons of vanilla, and salt. A small amount of espresso powder enhanced the chocolate flavor of the Nutella. To ensure maximum chew, we limited the evaporation of water from the melting butter and marshmallows by stirring in the crispy rice cereal just as the marshmallows were fully melted. Dampening our hands before pressing the mixture into the pan helped prevent sticking. A sprinkling of chopped hazelnuts added welcome crunch and a drizzle of milk chocolate was a special finishing touch. Do not use mini marshmallows here. For the best results, weigh the cereal.

8 tablespoons unsalted butter

2 (10-ounce) packages large marshmallows

½ cup Nutella

2 teaspoons vanilla extract

¼ teaspoon instant espresso powder

¼ teaspoon table salt

10 cups (10 ounces) crisped rice cereal

½ cup hazelnuts, toasted, skinned, and chopped

3 ounces milk chocolate, chopped

1 Spray rubber spatula and 13 by 9-inch baking pan with vegetable oil spray. Melt butter in Dutch oven over medium heat. Add marshmallows, Nutella, vanilla, espresso powder, and salt and cook, stirring often with prepared spatula, until marshmallows are just melted, about 3 minutes (some marshmallows may not be fully melted; this is OK). Off heat, stir in cereal until fully combined.

2 Transfer cereal mixture to prepared pan. Sprinkle hazelnuts over cereal mixture. Using your dampened hands, press cereal mixture into even layer. Let sit for 1 hour to set. Run knife around edge of pan to loosen treats, then turn out onto cutting board. Flip treats right side up.

3 Microwave chocolate in bowl at 50 percent power, stirring occasionally, until melted, 1 to 2 minutes. Drizzle melted chocolate over cooled treats and let chocolate set for 15 minutes. Cut into 15 pieces. Serve.

CHOCOLATE SANDWICH COOKIES

MAKES ABOUT 40 SANDWICH COOKIES

COOKIES

- 3 tablespoons unsalted butter, melted and cooled, plus 5 tablespoons softened, divided
- ¼ cup (¾ ounce) black cocoa powder
- 2 tablespoons Dutch-processed cocoa powder
- ½ teaspoon instant espresso powder
- ½ cup (3½ ounces) granulated sugar
- ¼ teaspoon table salt
- 1 large egg yolk
- 1½ teaspoons vanilla extract
- 1 cup (5 ounces) all-purpose flour

FILLING

- 2 tablespoons unsalted butter, softened
- 2 tablespoons vegetable shortening
- 1 cup (4 ounces) confectioners' sugar
- ½ teaspoon vanilla extract
- Pinch table salt

Why This Recipe Works Given the tagline "milk's favorite cookie," it's no surprise Oreos unfailingly appeal to the kid in everyone, ourselves included. But we have to admit that nostalgia may have clouded our memory, as we've come to realize that the flavor of Oreos is, in fact, pretty bland and only mildly chocolaty. We set out to re-create—and improve—these iconic cookies. For that midnight-black Oreo color, we turned to specialty black cocoa powder (a heavily Dutched cocoa powder). Black cocoa has almost no fat, so we cut it with some standard Dutch-processed cocoa to prevent our cookies from crumbling. To achieve the rich flavor and melt-away texture of classic Oreo filling, we used a combination of butter and shortening. Whether you're a dunker or you prefer to twist and lick, you'll find these homemade cookies have supreme flavor and texture that make the effort worthwhile. It is important to slice the cookies exactly to size so they are thin enough to have the classic Oreo snap. You can order black cocoa powder online.

1 For the cookies Stir melted butter, black cocoa, Dutch-processed cocoa, and espresso powder in bowl until combined and smooth.

2 Using stand mixer fitted with paddle, beat softened butter, sugar, salt, and cocoa mixture on medium-high speed until fluffy, about 2 minutes, scraping down bowl as needed. Add egg yolk and vanilla and beat until combined, about 30 seconds. Reduce speed to low and slowly add flour in 3 additions, mixing well after each addition and scraping down bowl as needed. Continue to mix until dough forms cohesive ball, about 30 seconds.

3 Divide dough in half. Roll each half into 6-inch log. Wrap logs tightly in plastic wrap, twisting ends to firmly compact dough into tight cylinder, and refrigerate until firm, at least 1 hour or up to 3 days.

4 Adjust oven racks to upper-middle and lower-middle positions and heat oven to 325 degrees. Line 2 baking sheets with parchment paper. Trim ends of dough logs, then slice into ⅛-inch-thick rounds and space them ½ inch apart on prepared sheets.

5 Bake until cookies are firm and reveal slight indentation when pressed with your finger, 14 to 16 minutes, switching and rotating sheets halfway through baking. Let cookies cool on sheets for 5 minutes, then transfer to wire rack. Let cookies cool completely.

6 For the filling Using clean, dry mixer bowl and paddle, mix butter, shortening, sugar, vanilla, and salt on medium-low speed until combined, about 1 minute. Increase speed to medium-high and beat until light and fluffy, about 2 minutes.

7 Place rounded ½ teaspoon filling in center of bottom of half of cookies, then top with remaining cookies, pressing gently until filling spreads to edges. Serve. (Cookies can be stored at room temperature for up to 1 week.)

PEANUT BUTTER SANDWICH COOKIES WITH MILK CHOCOLATE FILLING

MAKES 24 SANDWICH COOKIES

Why This Recipe Works Chocolate and peanut butter is a much-loved combination that stands the test of time. But in cookie form the chocolate is often an afterthought—a sprinkling of chips mixed into a peanut butter dough. We wanted to create a sandwich cookie that would give chocolate its share of the spotlight in the form of a creamy filling layered between thin, crunchy peanut butter cookies. Focusing first on the cookies, we found that a combination of peanut butter and finely chopped peanuts contributed big flavor. The addition of some milk helped the dough spread during baking while a full teaspoon of baking soda created air bubbles that burst before the cookies set, resulting in thin, crisp cookies. For the filling, we started with a base of peanut butter and confectioners' sugar; after mixing in a variety of chocolates we settled on milk chocolate for its comforting familiarity and sweet dairy notes. We heated the peanut butter in the microwave before adding the chocolate; the warm peanut butter melted the chocolate and made the filling easy to spread. Do not use unsalted peanut butter. Take care when processing the peanuts—you want to chop them, not turn them into a paste.

1 For the cookies Adjust oven racks to upper-middle and lower-middle positions and heat oven to 350 degrees. Line 2 baking sheets with parchment paper. Pulse peanuts in food processor until finely chopped, about 8 pulses. Whisk flour, baking soda, and salt together in bowl. Whisk melted butter, peanut butter, granulated sugar, brown sugar, milk, and egg together in second bowl. Using rubber spatula, stir flour mixture into peanut butter mixture until combined. Stir in chopped peanuts until evenly distributed.

2 Using 1-tablespoon measure or #60 scoop, drop 12 mounds evenly onto each prepared sheet. Using your dampened hand, press each mound until 2 inches in diameter.

3 Bake cookies until deep golden brown and firm to touch, 15 to 18 minutes, switching and rotating sheets halfway through baking. Let cookies cool on sheets for 5 minutes, then transfer to wire rack. Let baking sheets cool completely and repeat with remaining dough. Let cookies cool completely.

4 For the filling Microwave peanut butter until melted and warm, about 40 seconds. Stir chocolate into warm peanut butter until melted, microwaving for 10 seconds at a time if necessary. Using rubber spatula, stir in confectioners' sugar until combined.

5 Place 1 tablespoon (or #60 scoop) warm filling in center of bottom of half of cookies, then top with remaining cookies, pressing gently until filling spreads to edges. Let filling set for 1 hour before serving. (Cookies can be stored at room temperature for up to 3 days.)

COOKIES

- 1¼ cups raw or dry-roasted peanuts, toasted and cooled
- ¾ cup (3¾ ounces) all-purpose flour
- 1 teaspoon baking soda
- ½ teaspoon table salt
- 3 tablespoons unsalted butter, melted
- ½ cup creamy peanut butter
- ½ cup (3½ ounces) granulated sugar
- ½ cup (3½ ounces) light brown sugar
- 3 tablespoons whole milk
- 1 large egg

FILLING

- ½ cup creamy peanut butter
- 6 ounces milk chocolate, chopped fine
- 1 cup (4 ounces) confectioners' sugar

CHOCOLATE-DIPPED POTATO CHIP COOKIES

MAKES 24 COOKIES

¾ cup (3¾ ounces) all-purpose flour

1½ ounces reduced-fat potato chips, crushed fine (½ cup)

¼ cup pecans, toasted and chopped fine

¼ teaspoon table salt

8 tablespoons unsalted butter, cut into 8 pieces, softened but still cool

¼ cup (1¾ ounces) granulated sugar

¼ cup (1 ounce) confectioners' sugar

1 large egg yolk

½ teaspoon vanilla extract

10 ounces bittersweet chocolate, chopped fine

Flake sea salt

Why This Recipe Works The potato chip cookie is one in a long line of recipes invented by manufacturers to push their products on consumers—and, in this case, we're totally fine with that. This retro treat brings together sugar, salt, and crunch for an addictive combination of flavors and textures. We wanted to take these old-fashioned cookies to the next level by dipping them in chocolate for a sophisticated finishing touch. The cookie itself should be multi-textured, with the right balance of shortness and chew. Using half granulated sugar and half confectioners' sugar gave us a cookie that was tender without being too delicate. Tasters preferred potato chip crumbs to the shards found in many recipes—all of the crunch without the sharp edges. Using reduced-fat chips eliminated greasiness and prevented the edges of the cookies from darkening too much. Chopped pecans—a common addition—provided a nice nutty crunch. For the coating, we opted for bittersweet chocolate, which we simply melted in the microwave. After dipping our cookies in the rich, dark chocolate, we added a sprinkle of sea salt for a final flourish. Cape Cod 40% Reduced Fat Potato Chips are the test kitchen favorite among reduced-fat chips.

1 Adjust oven rack to middle position and heat oven to 350 degrees. Line 2 baking sheets with parchment paper. Combine flour, potato chips, pecans, and table salt in bowl.

2 Using stand mixer fitted with paddle, beat butter, granulated sugar, and confectioners' sugar on medium-high speed until pale and fluffy, about 3 minutes. Add egg yolk and vanilla and beat until combined. Reduce speed to low and slowly add flour mixture in 3 additions. Roll dough into 1-inch balls and space them 3 inches apart on prepared sheets. Using floured dry measuring cup, press each ball to ¼-inch thickness.

3 Bake cookies, 1 sheet at a time, until just set and lightly browned on bottom, 10 to 13 minutes, rotating sheet halfway through baking. Let cookies cool completely on sheet, about 15 minutes.

4 Microwave chocolate in bowl at 50 percent power, stirring occasionally, until melted, 2 to 4 minutes. Carefully dip half of each cooled cookie in chocolate, scraping off excess with finger, and place on parchment paper–lined baking sheet. Sprinkle sea salt over warm chocolate and refrigerate until chocolate is set, about 15 minutes. Serve. (Cookies can be stored at room temperature for up to 2 days.)

THIN CHOCOLATE MINT COOKIES

MAKES ABOUT 70 COOKIES

Why This Recipe Works Thin Mints—the best-selling Girl Scout cookies with a crisp chocolate coating and just the right amount of cool mint flavor—are a favorite of children and adults alike. No longer wanting to count the days until the cookie season arrives, we decided to re-create them. To keep the mint flavor in check, we used peppermint oil in the chocolate coating only and omitted it from the cookie itself. Thin Mints get their crisp, short texture from palm kernel oil but we found that coconut oil, which is in the same family, did the trick. Baking the cookies until they were thoroughly dry ensured the proper crunch. For the shell, we knew we would need to temper the chocolate. We turned to our easy microwave method, which yielded a chocolate coating that was every bit as attractive and crisp as one made by the traditional method. (For more information on tempering chocolate, see page 14.) Our spin on Thin Mints doesn't just live up to our expectations; it exceeds them—Scout's honor.

1 For the cookies Whisk flour, cocoa, salt, baking powder, and baking soda together in bowl; set aside. Using stand mixer fitted with paddle, beat oil and sugar on medium-high speed until fluffy, about 2 minutes. Reduce speed to low; add milk, egg, and vanilla; and beat until combined, about 30 seconds. Slowly add flour mixture and beat until just combined, about 1 minute, scraping down bowl as needed. Divide dough in half. Form each half into 4-inch disk, wrap disks tightly in plastic wrap, and refrigerate until dough is firm yet malleable, about 45 minutes.

2 Adjust oven racks to upper-middle and lower-middle positions and heat oven to 350 degrees. Line 2 baking sheets with parchment paper. Working with 1 disk of dough at a time, roll into 11-inch circle, about ⅛ inch thick, between 2 large sheets of lightly floured parchment paper. Remove top piece of parchment. Using 1¾-inch round cookie cutter, cut dough into rounds; space rounds ½ inch apart on prepared sheets. Gently reroll scraps ⅛ inch thick, cut into rounds, and transfer to prepared sheets. Bake until cookies are very firm, 16 to 18 minutes, switching and rotating sheets halfway through baking. Let cookies cool on sheets for 5 minutes, then transfer to wire rack. Let cookies cool completely.

3 For the chocolate coating Line baking sheet with parchment paper. Microwave finely chopped chocolate and oil in bowl at 50 percent power, stirring often, until about two-thirds melted, 2 to 4 minutes. (Melted chocolate should not be much warmer than body temperature; check by holding bowl in palm of your hand.) Add grated chocolate and stir until smooth, returning to microwave for no more than 5 seconds at a time to finish melting if necessary.

4 Working with 1 cookie at a time, place cookie on fork and dip bottom of cookie in chocolate. Using offset spatula, spread chocolate over top of cookie, creating thin coating. Transfer cookie to prepared baking sheet and repeat with remaining cookies. Let cookies sit until chocolate sets, about 15 minutes, before serving. (Cookies can be stored at room temperature for up to 2 weeks.)

COOKIES

- 1½ cups (7½ ounces) all-purpose flour
- ½ cup (1½ ounces) unsweetened cocoa powder
- ½ teaspoon table salt
- ¼ teaspoon baking powder
- ¼ teaspoon baking soda
- ½ cup refined coconut oil, chilled
- ¾ cup (5¼ ounces) sugar
- 2 tablespoons milk
- 1 large egg
- 1 teaspoon vanilla extract

CHOCOLATE COATING

- 1 pound semisweet chocolate (12 ounces chopped fine, 4 ounces grated), divided
- ⅛ teaspoon peppermint oil

CHOCOLATE TURTLE COOKIES

MAKES ABOUT 30 COOKIES

1 cup (5 ounces) all-purpose flour

⅓ cup (1 ounce) unsweetened cocoa powder

¼ teaspoon table salt

8 tablespoons unsalted butter, softened

⅔ cup (4⅔ ounces) sugar

1 large egg, separated, plus 1 large white, divided

2 tablespoons milk

1 teaspoon vanilla extract

1¼ cups pecans, chopped fine

14 soft caramels

3 tablespoons heavy cream

Why This Recipe Works Pecan turtles are so good because they pack multiple flavors and textures into every bite: Crunchy, buttery pecans are held together by chewy, sweet caramel, and the whole thing is coated with rich chocolate. We wanted to translate this irresistible combination into an equally satisfying cookie. A thumbprint cookie was the ideal choice; its hollowed-out center could conveniently hold a pour of gooey caramel. Cocoa powder gave the base of our cookie—a rich chocolate dough—its deep flavor; since cocoa powder contains no sugar, it kept our cookies from being too sweet when paired with the caramel. For a dense, tender cookie, we omitted the egg white (and saved it for the coating) and added just one yolk. Rolling the balls of dough in chopped pecans provided all-around crunch. To keep things simple, we used store-bought caramel candies for the filling and melted them down with heavy cream. We filled the cookie divots with caramel when the cookies were done baking so it set without becoming too hard or chewy. Be sure to microwave the caramel and cream in a bowl large enough to contain the mixture, and stir occasionally to prevent the mixture from bubbling over or scorching.

1 Whisk flour, cocoa, and salt together in bowl. Using stand mixer fitted with paddle, beat butter and sugar on medium-high speed until pale and fluffy, about 2 minutes. Add egg yolk, milk, and vanilla and beat until incorporated. Reduce speed to low, add flour mixture, and mix until just combined. Cover bowl tightly with plastic wrap and refrigerate until firm, about 1 hour.

2 Adjust oven racks to upper-middle and lower-middle positions and heat oven to 350 degrees. Line 2 baking sheets with parchment paper. Whisk egg whites in bowl until frothy. Place pecans in second bowl. Roll dough into 1-inch balls, dip in egg whites, then roll in pecans; space balls 2 inches apart on prepared sheets. Using greased rounded ½-teaspoon measure, make indentation in center of each dough ball. Bake until cookies are set, about 12 minutes, switching and rotating sheets halfway through baking.

3 Meanwhile, microwave caramels and cream in bowl, stirring occasionally, until melted and smooth, 1 to 2 minutes. When cookies are done baking, gently reshape indentation with ½-teaspoon measure. Fill each indentation with ½ teaspoon caramel mixture. Let cookies cool on sheets for 10 minutes, then transfer to wire rack and let cool completely before serving. (Cookies can be stored at room temperature for up to 3 days.)

BERGERS-STYLE COOKIES

MAKES 24 COOKIES

Why This Recipe Works For those from Baltimore, Bergers cookies are a familiar treat. Featuring a lightly sweet, softly crumbly, dome-shaped vanilla cookie base and—the real draw—a ½-inch layer of fudgy chocolate frosting that sits proudly on top, these cookies appeal no matter what region you're from. For a tender yet sturdy cookie that could support a generous spread of frosting, we nixed the yolk and used only the egg white. Moving on to the topping, we made a ganache by microwaving chocolate chips and cream and then stirred in confectioners' sugar; when spread over the cookies while still warm it naturally cascaded over the cookies and set up into a smooth, dense frosting as it cooled. Semisweet chips made the frosting a tad too bitter, but switching to milk chocolate chips improved matters. Swapping some of the confectioners' sugar for Dutch-processed cocoa powder added complexity and the requisite dark color. Finished with some vanilla and salt to intensify the chocolate flavor, we had a dead ringer for the original Bergers frosting. If the frosting's temperature drops below 90 degrees, it may become too thick to spread. To bring it back to its proper consistency, simply microwave it at 50 percent power in 5-second intervals, whisking after each interval.

1 **For the cookies** Adjust oven rack to middle position and heat oven to 350 degrees. Line 2 baking sheets with parchment paper. Whisk flour, baking powder, and salt together in bowl; set aside. Using stand mixer fitted with paddle, beat butter and sugar on medium-high speed until pale and fluffy, about 3 minutes.

2 Add egg white, cream, and vanilla and beat until combined. Reduce speed to low and add flour mixture in 3 additions until incorporated, scraping down bowl as needed.

3 Working with 1 heaping tablespoon dough at a time, roll into balls and space 2 inches apart on prepared sheets, 12 per sheet. Using your moistened fingers, press dough balls to form disks about ¼ inch thick and 2 inches in diameter. Bake, 1 sheet at a time, until cookies are just beginning to brown around edges, 8 to 10 minutes, rotating sheet halfway through baking. Let cookies cool completely on sheet.

4 **For the frosting** Once cookies have cooled, combine chocolate chips, cream, and salt in large bowl. Microwave chocolate mixture at 50 percent power, stirring occasionally, until melted and smooth, 1 to 3 minutes. Whisk cocoa, sugar, and vanilla into chocolate mixture until smooth. (Frosting should be texture of thick brownie batter and register about 95 degrees.)

5 Flip cookies on sheets. Spoon 2 tablespoons frosting over flat side of each cookie to form mound. Let cookies sit at room temperature until frosting is set, about 3 hours. Serve. (Cookies can be stored at room temperature for up to 2 days.)

COOKIES

- 2 cups (8 ounces) cake flour
- 1½ teaspoons baking powder
- ¼ teaspoon table salt
- 8 tablespoons unsalted butter, softened
- ¾ cup (5¼ ounces) granulated sugar
- 1 large egg white
- 1½ tablespoons heavy cream
- 1½ teaspoons vanilla extract

FROSTING

- 3 cups (18 ounces) milk chocolate chips
- 1¼ cups heavy cream
- ¼ teaspoon table salt
- 1⅔ cups (5 ounces) Dutch-processed cocoa powder
- 1¼ cups (5 ounces) confectioners' sugar
- 1½ teaspoons vanilla extract

WHOOPIE PIES

MAKES 6 SANDWICH COOKIES

CAKES

- 2 cups (10 ounces) all-purpose flour
- ½ cup (1½ ounces) Dutch-processed cocoa powder
- 1 teaspoon baking soda
- ½ teaspoon table salt
- 8 tablespoons unsalted butter, softened
- 1 cup packed (7 ounces) light brown sugar
- 1 large egg, room temperature
- 1 teaspoon vanilla extract
- 1 cup buttermilk

FILLING

- 12 tablespoons unsalted butter, softened
- 1¼ cups (5 ounces) confectioners' sugar
- 1½ teaspoons vanilla extract
- ⅛ teaspoon table salt
- 2½ cups marshmallow crème

Why This Recipe Works Consisting of two cakelike chocolate cookies stuffed to the gills with fluffy vanilla filling, the whoopie pie is a sweet indulgence. For the cake portion, we drew inspiration from devil's food cake, creaming butter with sugar, adding eggs and buttermilk for tenderness, and using all-purpose flour and baking soda for the right amount of structure. For the chocolate component, we preferred the darker color and deeper flavor that Dutch-processed cocoa provided. One-half cup of cocoa delivered a balanced flavor, especially when boosted with a splash of vanilla extract. We tried replacing some of the granulated sugar with brown sugar, and found that it deepened the cakes' flavor and added moisture. In fact, we liked the results so much we switched to using all brown sugar. Using a ⅓-cup dry measuring cup, we portioned the batter onto two baking sheets to give the cakes plenty of room to spread. For the filling, we eschewed the traditional sugar and lard in favor of marshmallow crème, which we enriched with butter for a mixture that was fluffy yet firm. Don't be tempted to bake all the cakes on one baking sheet; the batter needs room to spread while it bakes.

1 For the cakes Adjust oven racks to upper-middle and lower-middle positions and heat oven to 350 degrees. Line 2 baking sheets with parchment paper. Whisk flour, cocoa, baking soda, and salt together in bowl.

2 Using stand mixer fitted with paddle, beat butter and sugar on medium speed until pale and fluffy, about 3 minutes. Add egg and beat until incorporated, scraping down bowl as needed. Add vanilla and mix until incorporated. Reduce speed to low and add flour mixture in 3 additions, alternating with buttermilk in 2 additions. Give batter final stir by hand to ensure that no flour pockets remain. Using ⅓-cup dry measuring cup, scoop 6 mounds of batter onto each prepared sheet, spaced about 3 inches apart. Bake until centers spring back when lightly pressed, 15 to 18 minutes, switching and rotating sheets halfway through baking. Let cakes cool completely on sheets.

3 For the filling Using stand mixer fitted with paddle, beat butter and sugar on medium speed until fluffy, about 3 minutes. Beat in vanilla and salt. Add marshmallow crème and mix until combined, about 2 minutes. Refrigerate until slightly firm, about 30 minutes. (Filling can be refrigerated for up to 2 days.) Place ⅓ cup filling on bottom of half of cakes, then top with remaining cakes, pressing to spread filling to edge. Serve. (Whoopie pies can be refrigerated for up to 3 days.)

NANAIMO BARS

MAKES 18 BARS

Why This Recipe Works Named after a city just a few miles from Washington State, Nanaimo bars have been a Canadian favorite for ages. Featuring three layers—a chocolate-coconut cookie base, custardy center, and dark chocolate ganache top—these no-bake bars have a spectrum of flavors and textures guaranteed to satisfy any sweet tooth. For our version, we blitzed graham crackers, coconut, pecans, and cocoa powder in the food processor and bound them with melted dark chocolate and corn syrup to create a fudgy and chewy yet sturdy base. The soft middle layer is traditionally made by creaming butter, confectioners' sugar, vanilla, and custard powder, an ingredient common in Canadian kitchens but not readily available stateside. Fortunately, we found that nonfat dry milk powder made an ideal replacement—it contributed a sweet-salty flavor and gave the filling its signature soft yet set texture. A quick ganache of melted bittersweet chocolate chips, butter, and corn syrup slathered over the chilled filling helped these Nanaimo bars shine.

1 For the crust Make foil sling for 8-inch square baking pan by folding 2 long sheets of aluminum foil so each is 8 inches wide. Lay sheets of foil in pan perpendicular to each other, with extra foil hanging over edges of pan. Push foil into corners and up sides of pan, smoothing foil flush to pan. Spray foil with vegetable oil spray.

2 Microwave chocolate chips in bowl at 50 percent power, stirring occasionally, until melted, 1 to 2 minutes. Process cracker pieces, coconut, pecans, cocoa, and salt in food processor until cracker pieces are finely ground, about 30 seconds. Add corn syrup and melted chocolate and pulse until combined, 8 to 10 pulses (mixture should hold together when pinched with your fingers). Transfer to prepared pan. Using bottom of greased measuring cup, press crumbs into even layer in bottom of pan. Refrigerate while making filling.

3 For the filling In clean, dry food processor, process sugar, butter, milk powder, and salt until smooth, about 30 seconds, scraping down sides of bowl as needed. Add cream and vanilla and process until fully combined, about 15 seconds. Spread filling evenly over crust. Cover pan with plastic wrap and refrigerate until filling is set and firm, about 2 hours.

4 For the topping Microwave chocolate chips, butter, and corn syrup in bowl at 50 percent power, stirring occasionally, until melted and smooth, 1 to 2 minutes. Using offset spatula, spread chocolate mixture evenly over set filling. Refrigerate until topping is set, about 30 minutes.

5 Using foil overhang, remove bars from pan. Slide foil out from under bars. Using chef's knife, trim outer ¼ inch of square to make neat edges (wipe knife clean with dish towel after each cut). Cut square into thirds to create 3 rectangles. Cut each rectangle crosswise into 6 equal pieces. Let bars sit at room temperature for 20 minutes before serving. (Bars can be refrigerated for up to 2 days.)

CRUST

- ½ cup (3 ounces) bittersweet chocolate chips
- 6 whole graham crackers, broken into 1-inch pieces
- ⅔ cup (2 ounces) sweetened shredded coconut
- ½ cup pecans, toasted
- ¼ cup (¾ ounce) unsweetened cocoa powder
- ⅛ teaspoon table salt
- ⅓ cup light corn syrup

FILLING

- 1¼ cups (5 ounces) confectioners' sugar
- 8 tablespoons unsalted butter, softened
- ¼ cup (¾ ounce) nonfat dry milk powder
- ⅛ teaspoon table salt
- ¼ cup heavy cream
- 2 teaspoons vanilla extract

TOPPING

- ⅔ cup (4 ounces) bittersweet chocolate chips
- 2 tablespoons unsalted butter
- 1 tablespoon light corn syrup

MIDNIGHT CHOCOLATE CAKE

SERVES 16

2 cups (10 ounces) all-purpose flour

¼ cup (¾ ounce) natural unsweetened cocoa powder

2 teaspoons baking soda

1 cup mayonnaise

1 cup (7 ounces) sugar

1 teaspoon vanilla extract

1 cup water

Why This Recipe Works Sometimes, the craving for a piece of rich, moist chocolate cake strikes without warning. When we need chocolate cake now, this old-fashioned snack cake comes to the rescue: Made from pantry ingredients you're likely to have on hand, it has surprisingly deep chocolate flavor and couldn't be easier to prepare thanks to one clever ingredient and a super simple mixing process. Using mayonnaise in place of the usual eggs and butter (or oil) meant we could skip the step of pulling out the mixer to cream butter and sugar. The eggs in the mayo provided plenty of structure (a key role of whole eggs in most cake recipes), while the mayo's oil contributed enough fat to make for an incredibly moist cake. Whisking the dry ingredients into the mayonnaise in three additions—alternating with water—helped minimize clumping. We found that this cake needed a bit more baking soda than most, as the emulsified eggs in the mayonnaise didn't provide any leavening the way regular whole eggs would. Cocoa powder gave our cake plenty of chocolate flavor, but this was one instance where we found it essential to use natural rather than Dutch-processed; the acidity of natural cocoa helped maximize the baking soda's leavening potential and gave our cake the proper rise. Dust with confectioners' sugar to serve.

1 Adjust oven rack to middle position and heat oven to 350 degrees. Grease and flour 13 by 9-inch baking pan. Whisk flour, cocoa, and baking soda together in bowl. Whisk mayonnaise, sugar, and vanilla in large bowl until smooth. Whisk flour mixture into mayonnaise mixture in 3 additions, alternating with 2 additions of water, until incorporated.

2 Transfer batter to prepared pan and bake until toothpick inserted in center comes out with few crumbs attached, about 25 minutes. Let cake cool completely in pan on wire rack, about 2 hours. Serve. (Cake can stored at room temperature for up to 2 days.)

CHOCOLATE CREAM CUPCAKES

MAKES 12 CUPCAKES

Why This Recipe Works Cream-filled Hostess cupcakes conjure memories of lunch box envy and beloved after-school snacks. But fond reminiscing aside, we knew America's most iconic cupcake could stand some improvement—starting with the weak chocolate flavor. For the cake, we found that blooming cocoa powder in boiling water was an easy way to intensify the chocolate flavor, and the addition of semisweet chips and espresso powder added further complexity. Moving on to the filling, we wanted it to be substantial enough that it wouldn't dribble out, and we wanted rich, creamy flavor. Combining marshmallow crème—as well as some butter for richness—with a small amount of gelatin gave us a perfectly creamy filling that stayed put. Injecting the filling into the cupcakes caused them to crumble and tear, so we cut inverted cones from the tops of the cupcakes instead. We prefer stiffer marshmallow crème in this filling; do not use marshmallow sauce. For an accurate measurement of boiling water, bring a full kettle of water to a boil and then measure out the desired amount.

1 For the cupcakes Adjust oven rack to middle position and heat oven to 325 degrees. Grease and flour 12-cup muffin tin.

2 Whisk flour, baking soda, and salt together in bowl. Whisk boiling water, cocoa, chocolate chips, and espresso powder in large bowl until smooth. Whisk sugar, sour cream, oil, eggs, and vanilla into cocoa mixture until combined. Whisk in flour mixture until just incorporated. Divide batter evenly among prepared muffin cups. Bake until toothpick inserted in center comes out with few crumbs attached, 18 to 22 minutes, rotating muffin tin halfway through baking. Let cupcakes cool in muffin tin on wire rack for 10 minutes. Remove cupcakes from muffin tin and let cool completely on rack, about 1 hour.

3 For the filling Sprinkle gelatin over water in large bowl and let sit until gelatin softens, about 5 minutes. Microwave until mixture is bubbling around edges and gelatin dissolves, about 30 seconds. Whisk in butter, vanilla, and salt until combined. Let mixture cool until just warm to touch, about 5 minutes, then whisk in marshmallow crème until smooth. Refrigerate filling until set, about 30 minutes. Transfer ⅓ cup filling to pastry bag fitted with small plain tip; set aside remaining mixture for filling cupcakes.

4 For the glaze Microwave chocolate chips and butter in small bowl at 50 percent power, stirring occasionally, until melted and smooth, 1 to 2 minutes. Let glaze cool completely, about 10 minutes.

5 Insert tip of paring knife at 45-degree angle ¼ inch from edge of each cupcake and cut cone from top of cupcake. Slice off bottom ½ inch from each cone and discard. Place 1 tablespoon filling inside each cupcake and place tops on filling, pressing to adhere. Spread each cupcake with 2 teaspoons cooled glaze and let sit for 10 minutes. Using pastry bag, pipe curlicues across tops of glazed cupcakes. Serve. (Cupcakes can be stored at room temperature for up to 2 days.)

CUPCAKES

- 1 cup (5 ounces) all-purpose flour
- ½ teaspoon baking soda
- ¼ teaspoon table salt
- ½ cup boiling water
- ⅓ cup (1 ounce) unsweetened cocoa powder
- ⅓ cup (2 ounces) semisweet chocolate chips
- 1 tablespoon instant espresso powder
- ¾ cup (5¼ ounces) sugar
- ½ cup sour cream
- ½ cup vegetable oil
- 2 large eggs
- 1 teaspoon vanilla extract

FILLING

- ¾ teaspoon unflavored gelatin
- 3 tablespoons water
- 4 tablespoons unsalted butter, softened
- 1 teaspoon vanilla extract
  Pinch table salt
- 1¼ cups marshmallow crème

GLAZE

- ½ cup (3 ounces) semisweet chocolate chips
- 3 tablespoons unsalted butter

HOT FUDGE PUDDING CAKE

SERVES 6 TO 8

- 6 tablespoons unsalted butter, cut into 6 pieces
- 2 ounces bittersweet chocolate, chopped
- ⅔ cup (2 ounces) unsweetened cocoa powder, divided
- ¾ cup (3¾ ounces) all-purpose flour
- 2 teaspoons baking powder
- ¼ teaspoon table salt
- ⅓ cup packed (2⅓ ounces) light brown sugar
- 1 cup (7 ounces) granulated sugar, divided
- 1 cup brewed coffee
- ½ cup water
- ⅓ cup whole milk
- 1 tablespoon vanilla extract
- 1 large egg yolk

Why This Recipe Works Hot fudge pudding cake begins with a simple yet magical concoction that is transformed upon baking into a decadent two-layer dessert. It starts with a fairly standard chocolate cake batter that is sprinkled with a sugar-cocoa layer, followed by liquid poured over the top. As the batter bakes, the cake rises to the top and what's left on the bottom turns into a puddinglike chocolate sauce. Unfortunately, while most hot fudge pudding cakes look rich and fudgy, all too often they are lacking in actual chocolate flavor. To make sure ours delivered on flavor as well as looks, we used a combination of cocoa powder and bittersweet chocolate for multiple layers of chocolate flavor. Most recipes call for water in the pudding layer, but we found that replacing some of the water with coffee deepened the chocolate flavor further (without making the pudding taste like coffee). We made this treat in a cast-iron skillet because hot fudge pudding cake is meant to be served hot: Cast iron does a great job of holding onto heat, so there was no worry that the dessert would cool down before it was time to eat. Serve with Whipped Cream (page 340) or ice cream.

1 Adjust oven rack to middle position and heat oven to 325 degrees. Melt butter, chocolate, and ⅓ cup cocoa together in 10-inch cast-iron skillet over low heat, stirring often, until smooth, 2 to 4 minutes. Set aside to cool slightly.

2 Whisk flour, baking powder, and salt together in bowl. Whisk brown sugar, ⅓ cup granulated sugar, and remaining ⅓ cup cocoa together in second bowl, breaking up any large clumps of brown sugar with fingers. Combine coffee and water in third bowl.

3 Whisk milk, vanilla, egg yolk, and remaining ⅔ cup granulated sugar into cooled chocolate mixture. Whisk in flour mixture until just combined. Sprinkle brown sugar mixture evenly over top, covering entire surface of batter. Pour coffee mixture gently over brown sugar mixture.

4 Transfer skillet to oven and bake until cake is puffed and bubbling and just beginning to pull away from sides of skillet, about 35 minutes, rotating skillet halfway through baking. Using potholders, transfer skillet to wire rack and let cake cool for 15 minutes. Serve.

CHOCOLATE ÉCLAIR CAKE

SERVES 15

Why This Recipe Works Icebox cake is a somewhat old-fashioned creation—a cool, creamy dessert that is chilled rather than baked. At its simplest, it features nothing more than whipped cream and chocolate wafers, which soften and meld into cakelike layers. But variations abound. One such variation is a chocolate éclair cake, which features layers of store-bought vanilla pudding and Cool Whip sandwiched between graham crackers and topped off with chocolate frosting. As the graham crackers soften, the whole thing melds into a creamy, sliceable cake. While we loved the ease of these convenience items in theory, our enthusiasm waned when confronted by their flavor. Fortunately, with a couple of easy techniques and very little active time, we produced a from-scratch version that easily trumped its inspiration. Since the cake layers required no more work than lining a pan with graham crackers, we made the effort to prepare a quick stovetop vanilla pudding, folding in whipped cream to lighten it. And no éclair is complete without the all-important chocolate topping; for ours we created a simple microwave-and-stir glaze from semisweet chocolate chips, corn syrup, and heavy cream.

1¼ cups (8¾ ounces) sugar

6 tablespoons cornstarch

1 teaspoon salt

5 cups whole milk

4 tablespoons unsalted butter, cut into 4 pieces

5 teaspoons vanilla extract

1¼ teaspoons unflavored gelatin

2 tablespoons water

2¾ cups heavy cream, chilled, divided

14 ounces graham crackers

1 cup (6 ounces) semisweet chocolate chips

5 tablespoons light corn syrup

1 Combine sugar, cornstarch, and salt in large saucepan. Whisk milk into sugar mixture until smooth and bring to boil over medium-high heat, scraping bottom of pan with heatproof rubber spatula. Immediately reduce heat to medium-low and cook, continuing to scrape bottom, until thickened and large bubbles appear on surface, 4 to 6 minutes. Off heat, whisk in butter and vanilla. Transfer pudding to large bowl and place plastic wrap directly on surface of pudding. Refrigerate until cool, about 2 hours.

2 Sprinkle gelatin over water in bowl and let sit until gelatin softens, about 5 minutes. Microwave until mixture is bubbling around edges and gelatin dissolves, 15 to 30 seconds. Using stand mixer fitted with whisk attachment, whip 2 cups cream on medium-low speed until foamy, about 1 minute. Increase speed to high and whip until soft peaks form, 1 to 3 minutes. Add gelatin mixture and whip until stiff peaks form, about 1 minute.

3 Whisk one-third of whipped cream into chilled pudding, then gently fold in remaining whipped cream, 1 scoop at a time, until combined. Cover bottom of 13 by 9-inch baking dish with layer of graham crackers, breaking crackers as necessary to line bottom of pan. Top with half of pudding–whipped cream mixture (about 5½ cups) and another layer of graham crackers. Repeat with remaining pudding–whipped cream mixture and remaining graham crackers.

4 Combine chocolate chips, corn syrup, and remaining ¾ cup cream in bowl and microwave at 50 percent power, stirring occasionally, until melted and smooth, 1 to 2 minutes. Let glaze cool completely, about 10 minutes. Spread glaze evenly over graham crackers and refrigerate cake for at least 6 hours or up to 2 days before serving.

CREAMY CHOCOLATE PUDDING

SERVES 6

2 teaspoons vanilla extract

½ teaspoon instant espresso powder

½ cup (3½ ounces) sugar

3 tablespoons unsweetened cocoa powder

2 tablespoons cornstarch

¼ teaspoon table salt

½ cup heavy cream

3 large egg yolks

2½ cups whole milk

5 tablespoons unsalted butter, cut into 8 pieces

4 ounces bittersweet chocolate, chopped fine

Why This Recipe Works We love the comforting simplicity of a bowl of chocolate pudding, but the boxed versions of our childhood fail to impress our grown-up palates with their lackluster chocolate flavor, overwhelming sweetness, and grainy texture. Since nostalgia alone isn't enough to make this dessert worthwhile, we wanted to create a recipe for homemade chocolate pudding that would satisfy our cravings for this homey treat. We were surprised to learn that graininess is caused by too much cocoa butter rather than by too many cocoa solids. Using a moderate amount of bittersweet chocolate in combination with unsweetened cocoa and espresso powder gave us the best of both worlds: potent chocolate flavor and a supremely smooth texture. For thickening, cornstarch proved the right choice, and using mostly milk, along with half a cup of heavy cream and three egg yolks, ensured that our pudding had a silky, smooth texture. We prefer this recipe made with 60 percent bittersweet chocolate; using a chocolate with a higher cacao percentage will result in a thicker pudding. One or 2 percent low-fat milk may be substituted for the whole milk with a small sacrifice in richness. Do not substitute skim milk. We like to top the pudding with Whipped Cream (page 340).

1 Stir vanilla and espresso powder together in bowl; set aside. Whisk sugar, cocoa, cornstarch, and salt together in large saucepan. Whisk in cream and egg yolks until fully incorporated, making sure to scrape corners of saucepan. Whisk in milk until incorporated.

2 Place saucepan over medium heat; cook, whisking constantly, until mixture is thickened and bubbling over entire surface, 5 to 8 minutes. Cook for 30 seconds longer, remove from heat, add butter and chocolate, and whisk until melted and fully incorporated. Whisk in vanilla mixture.

3 Strain pudding through fine-mesh strainer into bowl. Place lightly greased parchment paper against surface of pudding and refrigerate for at least 4 hours or up to 2 days. Serve.

Mexican Chocolate Pudding

Add ½ teaspoon cinnamon, ¼ teaspoon chipotle chile powder, and pinch cayenne pepper to saucepan along with cocoa powder.

Mocha Pudding

Increase espresso powder to 1 teaspoon. Add 1 tablespoon Kahlúa to vanilla mixture. Substitute ¼ cup brewed coffee for ¼ cup milk.

S'MORES MOLTEN MICROWAVE MUG CAKES

MAKES 2 MUG CAKES

Why This Recipe Works S'mores may be a favorite summertime treat, but we crave their flavors all year long. We wanted to incorporate the classic s'mores elements of marshmallow and graham crackers into chocolate mug cakes—individual cakes that are cooked in coffee mugs in the microwave—for a nearly instant dessert we could enjoy any time of year. To keep our cakes from overflowing, we found we had to supplement bittersweet chocolate with cocoa powder; because cocoa powder has less fat it produces less steam, thus decreasing the chance of an overflow. We tried making a graham cracker crust on the bottom of each mug, but it dissolved into the warm cake batter. Instead, we crushed the graham crackers and sprinkled the crumbs into an even layer for an attractive topping. Marshmallows grew pleasantly puffy in the microwave when placed atop the layer of cracker crumbs. For added decadence, we also pushed one into the center of each cake to create a molten core. Served with extra graham crackers as a fun garnish, our s'mores mug cakes were complete—no campfire required. We developed this recipe in a full-size, 1200-watt microwave. If you're using a compact microwave with 800 watts or fewer, increase the cooking time to 90 seconds for each interval. For either size microwave, reset to 50 percent power at each stage of cooking. Use a mug that holds at least 12 ounces, or the batter will overflow.

4 tablespoons unsalted butter

1 ounce bittersweet chocolate, chopped

¼ cup (1¾ ounces) sugar

2 large eggs

2 tablespoons unsweetened cocoa powder

1 teaspoon vanilla extract

⅛ teaspoon table salt

¼ cup (1¼ ounces) all-purpose flour

½ teaspoon baking powder

6 marshmallows

2 whole graham crackers, crushed into crumbs, plus 1 whole graham cracker, broken into quarters, divided

1 Microwave butter and chocolate in large bowl at 50 percent power, stirring often, until melted and smooth, about 1 minute. Whisk sugar, eggs, cocoa, vanilla, and salt into chocolate mixture until smooth. Combine flour and baking powder in second bowl. Whisk flour mixture into chocolate mixture until combined. Divide batter evenly between 2 (12-ounce) coffee mugs.

2 Place mugs on opposite sides of microwave turntable. Microwave at 50 percent power for 45 seconds. Stir batter and microwave at 50 percent power for 45 seconds (batter will rise to just below rim of mug).

3 Press 1 marshmallow into center of each cake until top of marshmallow is flush with top of cake. Sprinkle each cake with 2 tablespoons graham cracker crumbs and top with remaining marshmallows, pressing to adhere to top of cake. Microwave at 50 percent power for 30 seconds to 1 minute (marshmallows should be softened and puffed). Let cakes sit for 2 minutes. Sprinkle with remaining graham cracker crumbs and garnish with graham cracker quarters. Serve.

CHOCOLATE ICE CREAM SANDWICHES

MAKES 8 ICE CREAM SANDWICHES

1 cup (5 ounces) all-purpose flour

½ cup (1½ ounces) Dutch-processed cocoa powder

¼ teaspoon table salt

⅛ teaspoon baking soda

2 large eggs

⅔ cup (4⅔ ounces) sugar

¼ cup (2¾ ounces) chocolate syrup

8 tablespoons unsalted butter, melted

2 pints ice cream

Why This Recipe Works While we have fond memories of unwrapping the white paper from a perfectly rectangular ice cream sandwich, there's no escaping the reality that these store-bought confections are disappointing, consisting of subpar ice cream and tacky chocolate cookies that somehow manage to taste nothing like chocolate. We wanted to create a truly superior chocolate ice cream sandwich. For the cookie component, we turned to a basic chocolate batter made with flour, cocoa powder, eggs, and sugar. Using Dutch-processed cocoa gave our cookies a darker hue similar to that of store-bought sandwiches. The unusual addition of chocolate syrup not only heightened the chocolate flavor but also made for soft and chewy—not sticky—cookies. Rather than form individual portions prior to baking, we simply spread the batter onto a rimmed baking sheet; once it had baked and cooled, we cut out perfect rounds of cookies with a biscuit cutter. For the ice cream, we placed the pint container on its side and sliced it into rounds, then we stamped out evenly matched rounds of ice cream. The batter will be very thick; greasing the baking sheet before lining it with parchment paper will make it easier to spread the batter in an even layer. For a dressed-up dessert, roll the sides of the sandwiches in chopped nuts, sprinkles, or chocolate chips.

1 Adjust oven rack to middle position and heat oven to 350 degrees. Grease 18 by 13-inch rimmed baking sheet and line with parchment paper.

2 Whisk flour, cocoa, salt, and baking soda in bowl. Whisk eggs, sugar, and chocolate syrup in large bowl until mixture is combined and light brown. Add melted butter and whisk until fully incorporated.

3 Using rubber spatula, gradually incorporate flour mixture into egg mixture; stir until batter is evenly moistened and no dry streaks remain. Transfer batter to prepared sheet; using offset spatula, spread batter evenly in pan. Bake until cookie springs back when touched, 10 to 12 minutes, rotating sheet halfway through baking. Let cool in pan on wire rack for 5 minutes, then run paring knife around edges of sheet to loosen. Invert cookie onto large cutting board; carefully peel off parchment. Let cool completely, about 30 minutes.

4 Using 2¾- to 3-inch round biscuit cutter, cut 16 rounds from baked cookie. Using serrated knife, slice away bottoms of ice-cream containers. Dip knife in warm water, wipe clean, and slice four ¾-inch-thick rounds from each container, cutting through cardboard. Peel away and discard cardboard. Using same biscuit cutter, cut out rounds from each ice cream slice. Assemble ice cream sandwiches, placing ice cream round on cookie bottom, then topping with another cookie, shiny side up. Transfer ice cream sandwiches to aluminum foil–lined rimmed baking sheet, cover with foil, and freeze for 3 hours before serving. (Sandwiches can be frozen, wrapped individually in waxed paper, then in foil, for up to 1 week; let ice cream sandwiches sit at room temperature for 10 minutes before serving.)

ULTIMATE CHOCOLATE MILKSHAKES

SERVES 4

Why This Recipe Works Ordering a chocolate milkshake at the diner or soda shop should make the meal, but the typical shake arrives thin and soupy, and the flavor is no better: The chocolate always seems like an afterthought, most likely supplied by a meager squeeze of chocolate syrup into a shaker of vanilla ice cream. We set out to create our own thick, creamy, and superchocolaty milkshake that would always deliver. For the best consistency, we found that a whopping 4½ cups of ice cream and ½ cup whole milk gave us a shake that was thin enough to be enjoyed with a straw but thick enough to keep its chill while drinking. For the ultimate chocolate flavor, we tried replacing the usual vanilla ice cream with chocolate ice cream, but tasters found it contributed a sour flavor. Replacing a portion of the vanilla ice cream with chocolate sorbet—which packs pure chocolate punch—worked much better. Finally, we ditched the syrup, which contributed more sweetness than actual chocolate flavor. The bittersweet flavor of hot fudge was worlds better, and its thick texture made for a rich shake. You can use store-bought ingredients, but we love our homemade Chocolate Sorbet (page 306) if you have some in the freezer and our Classic Hot Fudge Sauce (page 340). Soften the ice cream and sorbet at room temperature for 5 minutes before scooping. If your hot fudge is refrigerated, microwave 2 tablespoons in a small dish for 5 seconds. Make sure to chill your glasses before making the milkshakes. Garnish with Whipped Cream (page 340) and your choice of toppings, if desired.

- 3 cups vanilla ice cream, cut into large pieces
- 1½ cups chocolate sorbet, cut into large pieces
- ½ cup whole milk
- 2 tablespoons hot fudge sauce, room temperature

Process all ingredients in food processor or blender until smooth, scraping down sides of bowl as needed, about 20 seconds. Pour into chilled glasses. Serve.

FROZEN SNICKERS ICE CREAM CAKE
SERVES 8

2 pints chocolate ice cream

1 cup chunky peanut butter

32 Nabisco Famous Chocolate Wafers

1½ cups Classic Caramel Sauce (page 342)

Why This Recipe Works It's hard not to love ice cream cake: Not only does it evoke fond memories of summertime birthday parties, but the appeal of two beloved desserts combined into one cold, creamy slice is far more satisfying than a scoop of ice cream haphazardly dolloped onto a slice of cake. We wanted to put our own spin on this classic, and thought that a Snickers-inspired version would be sure to please chocolate fans of any age. Rich, creamy chocolate ice cream was a must and served as our starting point. Softening the ice cream by stirring and folding it with a rubber spatula was essential so that it could be spread into even layers; this step also allowed us to easily incorporate a generous portion of chunky peanut butter for the requisite peanut element. We layered our ice cream mixture with classic chocolate wafers and rich, buttery caramel sauce for a satisfying combination of flavors and textures. Our favorite chocolate ice cream is Turkey Hill Premium Dutch Chocolate Ice Cream. You can use store-bought caramel sauce instead of homemade.

1 Line loaf pan with plastic wrap, letting ends of plastic wrap overhang pan by 6 inches. Scoop ice cream into large bowl. Using rubber spatula or wooden spoon, break up scoops of ice cream. Stir and fold ice cream to achieve smooth consistency. Fold peanut butter into ice cream until uniformly mixed.

2 Working quickly, arrange 8 chocolate wafers to cover bottom of pan (some overlapping is fine). Spread one-third of ice cream mixture evenly over wafers and smooth top. Spread ½ cup caramel sauce over ice cream. Wrap pan and bowl of ice cream with plastic and freeze until cake is just firm, about 15 minutes. Repeat with 8 chocolate wafers, one-third of ice cream mixture, and ½ cup caramel sauce; freeze for 15 minutes longer. Repeat layering one more time with 8 chocolate wafers, remaining ice cream, and remaining caramel sauce and top with remaining 8 chocolate wafers, pressing lightly. Wrap pan tightly in plastic and freeze cake until firm, about 6 hours.

3 Unwrap loaf pan and, using plastic overhang, gently lift cake from pan. (If necessary, briefly dip bottom of pan into hot water.) Using plastic wrap to handle loaf, invert onto serving platter. Discard plastic wrap. Let cake sit at room temperature for 5 minutes before slicing and serving.

wake up with
CHOCOLATE

THREE EASY WAYS TO GET YOUR MORNING CHOCOLATE JOLT

Dashing out the door in the morning? What better fuel is there than chocolate? In this chapter you'll find chocolate recipes that can be prepared mostly in advance or that don't take too much time on a lazy weekend morning. But here are three supersimple recipes for starting your day with chocolate, even if you have just a few minutes.

1

Chocolate–Hazelnut Spread
MAKES 1½ CUPS

The queen of nut butters, Nutella, is a morning-treat favorite that is just as satisfying slicked between crêpes as it is spread on top of on-the-go breakfasts. Use it to top toast, banana bread, or croissants or swirl it into your cup of overnight oats and go. (And a spoonful straight from the jar is always an option.) Once you taste homemade Nutella, you'll realize that what you've been eating from the store is a little plasticky and wan. You can make a deeply nutty, chocolaty spread that's not too sweet with freshly toasted hazelnuts and good cocoa powder. We blanch the hazelnuts in a baking soda solution before using them to easily remove every trace of skin, which can make the spread taste bitter. A whir in the food processor with the other ingredients creates a glossy paste. Hazelnut oil is available in high-end grocery stores and gourmet shops. Walnut oil also works well. If you cannot find either, use vegetable oil.

- 2 **cups hazelnuts**
- 6 **tablespoons baking soda**
- 1 **cup (4 ounces) confectioners' sugar**
- ⅓ **cup (1 ounce) unsweetened cocoa powder**
- 2 **tablespoons hazelnut oil**
- 1 **teaspoon vanilla extract**
- ⅛ **teaspoon table salt**

1. Fill large bowl halfway with ice and water. Bring 4 cups water to boil. Add hazelnuts and baking soda and boil for 3 minutes. Transfer hazelnuts to ice bath with slotted spoon, drain, and rub skins off with dish towel.

2. Adjust oven rack to middle position and heat oven to 375 degrees. Place hazelnuts in single layer on rimmed baking sheet and roast until fragrant and golden brown, 12 to 15 minutes, rotating sheet halfway through roasting.

3. Process hazelnuts in food processor until oil is released and smooth, loose paste forms, about 5 minutes, scraping down sides of bowl often.

4. Add sugar, cocoa, oil, vanilla, and salt and process until fully incorporated and mixture begins to loosen slightly and becomes glossy, about 2 minutes, scraping down sides of bowl as needed. (Spread can be stored at room temperature or refrigerated for up to 1 month.)

2 Chewy Granola Bars with Hazelnuts, Cherries, and Cacao Nibs

MAKES 24 BARS

Granola (see page 71) is a hearty, healthful vehicle for chocolate, but we like it best eaten with milk or topping yogurt—not practical when you're running out the door. Granola bars keep well and once they're made they're on hand to be eaten out of hand—en route to school or work. Here, the chocolate comes from a powerful source: crunchy, pleasantly bitter cacao nibs (just a half cup has impact). Their intensity is tempered by rich nuts and sweet dried fruit. We prefer Mediterranean or Turkish apricots in this recipe. Be sure to use apricots that are soft and moist, or the bars will not hold together well. Avoid using extra-thick rolled oats.

1½	cups blanched hazelnuts
2½	cups (7½ ounces) old-fashioned rolled oats
1	cup raw sunflower seeds
1	cup dried apricots
1	cup packed (7 ounces) brown sugar
¾	teaspoon table salt
½	cup vegetable oil
3	tablespoons water
1½	cups (1½ ounces) crisped rice cereal
1	cup dried cherries, chopped
½	cup cacao nibs

1. Adjust oven rack to middle position and heat oven to 350 degrees. Make foil sling for 13 by 9-inch baking pan by folding 2 long sheets of aluminum foil; first sheet should be 13 inches wide and second sheet should be 9 inches wide. Lay sheets of foil in pan perpendicular to each other, with extra foil hanging over edges of pan.

Push foil into corners and up sides of pan, smoothing foil flush to pan. Lightly spray foil with vegetable oil spray.

2. Pulse hazelnuts in food processor until finely chopped, 8 to 12 pulses. Spread hazelnuts, oats, and sunflower seeds on rimmed baking sheet and toast until lightly browned and fragrant, 12 to 15 minutes, stirring halfway through toasting. Reduce oven temperature to 300 degrees.

3. While oat mixture is toasting, process apricots, sugar, and salt in food processor until apricots are very finely ground, about 15 seconds. With processor running, add oil and water. Continue to process until homogeneous paste forms, about 1 minute longer. Transfer paste to large, wide bowl.

4. Add warm oat mixture to bowl and stir with rubber spatula until well coated. Add cereal, cherries, and cacao nibs and stir gently until ingredients are evenly mixed. Transfer mixture to prepared pan and spread into even layer. Place 14-inch sheet of parchment paper or waxed paper on top of granola and press and smooth very firmly with your hands, especially at edges and corners, until granola is level and compact. Remove parchment and bake granola until fragrant and just beginning to brown around edges, about 25 minutes. Transfer pan to wire rack and let cool for 1 hour. Using foil overhang, lift granola out of pan. Return to wire rack and let cool completely, about 1 hour.

5. Discard foil and transfer granola to cutting board. Using chef's knife, cut granola in half crosswise to create two 6½ by 9-inch rectangles. Cut each rectangle in half to make four 3¼ by 9-inch strips. Cut each strip crosswise into 6 equal pieces. (Granola bars can be stored at room temperature for up to 3 weeks.)

3 Make-Ahead Hot Chocolate

MAKES 10 CHOCOLATE BALLS; ENOUGH FOR TEN 1-CUP SERVINGS

You might think there are only two options for hot chocolate: a dusty packet or a luxurious cup of drinking chocolate that takes more time than you have in the morning to prepare. But with our make-ahead (who knew?) alternative you can have hot chocolate in your thermos just as easily as you can coffee or tea. How did we do it? We took inspiration from ganache frosting and combined semisweet chocolate chips (for crowd-pleasing flavor) with cream to create our base. We rolled this mixture into large truffle-like balls that can be kept in the refrigerator. When it's time to make a cup of cocoa, simply microwave one of our ganache balls with the appropriate amount of milk—2 minutes to bliss.

2	cups (12 ounces) semisweet chocolate chips
1	cup heavy cream
¼	teaspoon salt

1. Microwave chocolate chips, cream, and salt in large bowl at 50 percent power, stirring occasionally, until melted and smooth, about 2 minutes. Refrigerate until firm, about 2 hours.

2. Working with 3 tablespoons chilled chocolate mixture at a time, roll into 2-inch balls. Wrap balls individually in plastic wrap and transfer to zipper-lock bag. (Balls can be refrigerated for up to 5 days or frozen for up to 2 months.)

To make 1 cup of hot chocolate: Place 1 unwrapped chocolate ball and 1 cup milk in mug. Microwave, stirring occasionally, until smooth, about 2 minutes. Serve.

CHOCOLATE-WALNUT MUFFINS

MAKES 12 MUFFINS

Why This Recipe Works What makes a chocolate breakfast muffin different from a chocolate cupcake? Aside from technique (simply stirring wet and dry ingredients together rather than creaming butter and sugar as a first step), one big difference is that more rustic chocolate muffins don't have a tall crown of frosting or a swath of ganache to hide under—they're breakfast, after all. Our goal, then, was a moist, just-sweet-enough, generously sized muffin with plenty of rich chocolate flavor and a characteristically domed top—a decadent breakfast treat that would pair nicely with a cup of coffee. A combination of cocoa powder and bittersweet chocolate gave these muffins intense flavor. Folding in some more chopped chocolate provided little pockets of melted chocolate every few bites. We had three means of making our muffins moist: incorporating sour cream, using oil rather than butter, and swapping brown sugar for the granulated. Baking the muffins on a higher rack and at 375 degrees—a bit higher than the 350 degrees at which we'd bake cupcakes—initiated a quick rise to give them a nicely domed top. To solidify the muffin's place as breakfast, we added toasted chopped walnuts to the batter as well as topped the muffins with a walnut streusel. For an accurate measurement of boiling water, bring a full kettle of water to a boil and then measure out the desired amount.

1 Adjust oven rack to upper-middle position and heat oven to 375 degrees. Spray 12-cup muffin tin with vegetable oil spray.

2 **For the streusel** Pulse walnuts, flour, sugar, and salt in food processor until walnuts are coarsely chopped, about 4 pulses. Add butter and pulse until mixture resembles coarse sand, 4 to 5 pulses. Transfer to bowl; set aside.

3 **For the muffins** Whisk flour, baking soda, and salt together in large bowl. Whisk boiling water, cocoa, 2 ounces chocolate, and espresso powder in second bowl until smooth. Whisk in sugar, sour cream, oil, eggs, and vanilla until thoroughly combined. Gently fold chocolate mixture into flour mixture until just combined (do not overmix). Fold in remaining chocolate and walnuts.

4 Divide batter evenly among prepared muffin cups and sprinkle with streusel. Bake until toothpick inserted in center comes out with few moist crumbs attached, 25 to 27 minutes, rotating muffin tin halfway through baking. Let muffins cool in muffin tin on wire rack for 10 minutes. Remove muffins from muffin tin and let cool completely, about 1 hour. Serve.

STREUSEL

- ½ cup walnuts, toasted
- 3 tablespoons all-purpose flour
- 2 tablespoons packed light brown sugar
- Pinch table salt
- 2 tablespoons unsalted butter, cut into ½-inch pieces

MUFFINS

- 1¾ cups (8¾ ounces) all-purpose flour
- ¾ teaspoon baking soda
- ¾ teaspoon table salt
- ¾ cup boiling water
- ¾ cup (2¼ ounces) unsweetened cocoa powder
- 5 ounces bittersweet chocolate, chopped, divided
- 1 teaspoon instant espresso powder
- 1¼ cups packed (8¾ ounces) light brown sugar
- ¾ cup sour cream
- ¾ cup vegetable oil
- 3 large eggs, room temperature
- 1 teaspoon vanilla extract
- ¾ cup walnuts, toasted and chopped

CHOCOLATE ZUCCHINI CAKE

SERVES 12 TO 16

2½ cups (12½ ounces) all-purpose flour

¼ cup (¾ ounce) unsweetened cocoa powder

1 teaspoon baking soda

½ teaspoon baking powder

½ teaspoon table salt

½ teaspoon ground cinnamon

¼ teaspoon ground cloves

8 tablespoons unsalted butter, softened

½ cup vegetable oil

1¾ cups (12¼ ounces) sugar

2 large eggs

1 teaspoon vanilla extract

½ cup buttermilk

2 zucchini, seeded and shredded

¾ cup (4½ ounces) semisweet chocolate chips

Why This Recipe Works Zucchini cakes and breads are a familiar sight at the breakfast table. But while they're an easy way to incorporate one of summer's favorite (and definitely most abundant) vegetables into something sweet, with few exceptions we find their flavor a little bland. We wanted to add another dimension to zucchini cake by incorporating chocolate for an indulgent morning treat. Zucchini gave the cake nice moisture but that came, of course, with some heft. Using both baking soda and baking powder provided adequate lift to prevent the zucchini from making our cake too dense. Using the traditional creaming method—in which butter and sugar are beaten together until light and fluffy before adding the other ingredients—developed good structure and height in the cake, and replacing some of the butter with more neutral-flavored vegetable oil allowed the chocolate flavor to come through. A generous amount of semisweet chocolate chips sprinkled over the top before baking guaranteed pockets of chocolate throughout.

1 Adjust oven rack to middle position and heat oven to 325 degrees. Grease 13 by 9-inch baking pan. Whisk flour, cocoa, baking soda, baking powder, salt, cinnamon, and cloves together in bowl. Using stand mixer fitted with paddle, beat butter, oil, and sugar on medium speed until smooth, 1 to 2 minutes. Add eggs, vanilla, and buttermilk and mix until incorporated. Stir in flour mixture until combined. Stir in zucchini.

2 Transfer batter to prepared pan and top with chocolate chips. Bake until toothpick inserted in center comes out clean, about 45 minutes, rotating pan halfway through baking. Let cake cool completely in pan on wire rack, about 2 hours. Serve. (Cake can be stored at room temperature for up to 2 days.)

CHOCOLATE GRANOLA

MAKES ABOUT 9 CUPS

Why This Recipe Works Granola consisting of plain sweetened oats, nuts, and fruit is a standard in cereal bowls or atop yogurt, but it doesn't always excite us to eat breakfast. Chocolate granola, on the other hand, will make a morning person out of anyone. We knew simply stirring in chocolate wouldn't do: We whisked ⅓ cup of cocoa powder into the wet ingredients (maple syrup, brown sugar, vanilla, salt, and vegetable oil) that coat and clump the clusters before tossing in oats and walnuts. This ensured that every piece of granola had chocolate flavor. For satisfying clusters rather than the dusty bits you find in store-bought versions, we firmly packed the mixture into a rimmed baking sheet before baking. Since the granola was dark from the cocoa powder, we relied on other cues to tell when it was properly baked: It smelled fragrant and felt firm. Once it was baked, we had a granola "bark" that we could break into crunchy clumps of any size. We tossed in a liberal amount of chopped chocolate at this point so it would stay intact rather than melt during baking. Do not use quick oats. Chop the nuts and chocolate by hand for even texture.

½ cup vegetable oil

⅓ cup maple syrup

⅓ cup (1 ounce) unsweetened cocoa powder

⅓ cup packed (2⅓ ounces) light brown sugar

4 teaspoons vanilla extract

½ teaspoon table salt

5 cups (15 ounces) old-fashioned rolled oats

2 cups (8 ounces) walnuts, chopped

6 ounces bittersweet or semisweet chocolate, chopped

1 Adjust oven rack to upper-middle position and heat oven to 325 degrees. Line rimmed baking sheet with parchment paper and spray with vegetable oil spray.

2 Whisk oil, maple syrup, cocoa, sugar, vanilla, and salt together in large bowl. Fold in oats and walnuts until thoroughly combined.

3 Transfer oat mixture to prepared sheet and spread across entire surface of sheet in even layer. Using stiff metal spatula, press down firmly on oat mixture until very compact. Bake until fragrant and granola gives little resistance when pressed, 35 to 40 minutes, rotating sheet halfway through baking.

4 Transfer sheet to wire rack and let granola cool completely, about 1 hour. Break cooled granola into pieces of desired size and transfer to large bowl. Add chocolate and gently toss to combine. Serve. (Granola can be stored in airtight container at room temperature for up to 2 weeks.)

Cherry–Almond Chocolate Granola
Substitute whole almonds for walnuts. Add 1 cup chopped dried cherries to granola with chocolate.

Coconut–Cashew Chocolate Granola
Substitute raw cashews for walnuts. Add 1 cup unsweetened flaked coconut to granola with chocolate.

CHOCOLATE CHIP SCONES

MAKES 8 SCONES

8 tablespoons (1 stick) unsalted butter, frozen whole, plus 1 tablespoon melted

½ cup whole milk

½ cup sour cream

2 cups (10 ounces) all-purpose flour

¼ cup packed (1¾ ounces) light brown sugar

2 teaspoons baking powder

¼ teaspoon baking soda

½ teaspoon table salt

1½ cups (9 ounces) semisweet chocolate chips

1 tablespoon Demerara or turbinado sugar

Why This Recipe Works Behind glass, coffee shop chocolate chip scones look spectacular—substantial wedges dotted with chocolate beckon invitingly. But we know to resist the temptation because reality never meets expectation: The dough isn't buttery enough, the brick-like scones are dry, and the sparse chocolate mix-ins don't pack a flavor punch. We wanted a rich but not-too-heavy scone studded with plenty of chocolate that would go well with coffee—but wouldn't require it. To lighten the scones, we borrowed a technique from puff pastry where the dough is turned, rolled, and folded multiple times to create layers that are forced apart by steam when baked. In addition to preventing a dense, crumbly texture, this technique also kept abundant chocolate chips neatly packed and evenly distributed within the scones. Coarse sugar sprinkled on at the end provided a pleasing crunch. To ensure that the butter would stay as cold and as solid as possible within the dough, we froze it and then grated it into the dry ingredients using a coarse grater. Consider freezing two sticks of butter in step 1 and grating just half of each stick for a total of 8 tablespoons; this will help keep your fingertips safely away from the grater.

1 Adjust oven rack to middle position and heat oven to 425 degrees. Line baking sheet with parchment paper. Grate 8 tablespoons butter on large holes of box grater into bowl; transfer to freezer until needed. Whisk milk and sour cream together in second bowl and refrigerate until needed.

2 Whisk flour, brown sugar, baking powder, baking soda, and salt together in third bowl. Add frozen grated butter and toss with your fingers until thoroughly coated. Using rubber spatula, gently fold in chilled milk mixture until just combined.

3 Transfer dough and any floury bits to well-floured counter. Using your lightly floured hands, knead dough gently 6 to 8 times until it just holds together in ragged ball, adding flour as needed to prevent sticking.

4 Roll dough into 12-inch square. Gently fold top, bottom, and then sides of dough over center to form 4-inch square, loosening dough from counter with bench scraper if necessary. Transfer dough to lightly floured plate and freeze for 5 minutes; do not overchill.

5 Transfer dough to floured counter and roll again into 12-inch square. Sprinkle chocolate chips evenly over dough and press lightly to adhere. Loosen dough from counter with bench scraper, roll into tight log, and pinch seam closed. Turn dough seam side down and press flat into 12 by 4-inch rectangle. Using floured bench scraper, cut dough crosswise into 4 equal rectangles, then cut each rectangle on diagonal into 2 triangles. (Triangles can be refrigerated for up to 24 hours; bake as directed.)

6 Place scones on prepared sheet, brush tops with melted butter, and sprinkle with Demerara sugar. Bake until tops and bottoms are golden brown, 18 to 25 minutes, rotating sheet halfway through baking. Transfer scones to wire rack and let cool for at least 10 minutes. Serve warm or at room temperature.

Chocolate Chip–Ginger Scones
Reduce chocolate chips to 1 cup. Sprinkle dough with chocolate chips and ½ cup chopped crystallized ginger.

Chocolate Chip Scones with Hazelnuts and Coconut
Reduce chocolate chips to ¾ cup. Sprinkle dough with chocolate chips; ½ cup hazelnuts, toasted, skinned, and chopped; and ½ cup toasted unsweetened shredded coconut in step 5.

CHOCOLATE FINANCIERS

MAKES 16 TO 19 FINANCIERS

½ cup plus 1½ tablespoons (4¼ ounces) sugar

2 tablespoons plus 1 teaspoon all-purpose flour

1½ teaspoons instant espresso powder

½ teaspoon kosher salt

½ cup (2¼ ounces) almond flour

¼ cup (¾ ounce) Dutch-processed cocoa powder

3 large egg whites

8 tablespoons unsalted butter

1 ounce unsweetened chocolate

Why This Recipe Works Financiers are French *petit-four* cakes (*petit four* literally translates as "small oven" and refers to bite-size baked items that can be sweet or savory). They have a textural contrast—crisp and chewy at the edges and decadently soft and moist at the center—that is immensely appealing. With significantly less sugar than most baked goods, we think financiers are a justifiable breakfast treat alongside a hot cup of tea. Our goal was to add chocolate to the mix for a next-level financier. For intense chocolate flavor we used a combination of unsweetened chocolate and cocoa powder; using Dutch-processed cocoa ensured a moist interior crumb and provided a slightly bitter, more complex edge, which we underscored with the addition of a bit of espresso powder. Almond flour added substance to these nearly flourless petite cakes. With all that chocolate, the subtle nuttiness from browning the butter was lost, so we ditched this traditional extra step. Using a mini muffin tin gave the financiers a perfect ratio of crisp exterior to soft interior. Use a finely ground almond flour made from blanched almonds, like Bob's Red Mill Super-Fine Almond Flour. A pastry bag makes portioning this batter into the muffin tin a cinch. If you don't have one, place plastic wrap directly onto the surface of the batter in the bowl to prevent a skin from forming and portion the batter with a tablespoon measure.

1 Adjust oven rack to upper-middle position and heat oven to 375 degrees. Fit pastry bag with ½-inch round tip; set aside. Whisk sugar, all-purpose flour, espresso powder, and salt together in large bowl. Sift almond flour through fine-mesh strainer into bowl with sugar mixture; discard any coarse bits in strainer. Sift cocoa powder into bowl with sugar mixture; whisk to combine. Form well in center of sugar mixture. Pour egg whites into center of well, then whisk, gradually incorporating sugar mixture, until well combined and glossy, scraping down bowl as needed, about 1 minute. Set aside.

2 Bring butter and chocolate to simmer in small saucepan over medium-high heat, about 2 minutes. Working quickly, whisk hot butter mixture into bowl with batter until smooth and well incorporated, about 30 seconds. Transfer batter to pastry bag and let sit for at least 10 minutes, or up to 30 minutes.

3 Spray 24-cup mini muffin tin with vegetable oil spray. Pipe 1½ tablespoons batter into each muffin cup. (You will not fill every cup.) Bake until toothpick inserted in center of financier comes out clean, 13 to 15 minutes, rotating muffin tin halfway through baking. Let financiers cool in muffin tin for 5 minutes. Remove financiers from muffin tin and transfer to wire rack. Serve warm or at room temperature.

CHOCOLATE-ORANGE CRÊPES

SERVES 4

Why This Recipe Works Crêpes have a reputation for being temperamental, but the reality isn't quite so daunting. We wanted to make crêpes at home and add some chocolate in a manner that was a bit more refined than the typical spread of Nutella. The batter itself is simple: We found it didn't need to be made in a blender or rested as many recipes suggest. Instead, the real success of our crêpes relied on a few crucial cooking steps: heating the pan properly, using just enough batter to coat the bottom of the pan, and employing a tilt-and-shake method to distribute it. Sugared crêpes are a classic; for an elegant upgrade we flavored our sugar with orange zest and finely grated bittersweet chocolate. The crêpes will give off steam as they cook, but if the skillet begins to smoke, remove from the heat immediately and turn down the heat. Stacking the crêpes on a wire rack allows excess steam to escape so they won't stick together. To allow for practice, the recipe yields 10 crêpes; only eight are needed for the amount of filling. For more information on making crêpes, see page 261.

½ teaspoon vegetable oil

1 cup (5 ounces) all-purpose flour

¼ cup (1¾ ounces) plus 1 teaspoon sugar, divided

¼ teaspoon table salt

1½ cups whole milk

3 large eggs

2 tablespoons unsalted butter, melted and cooled

1 teaspoon finely grated orange zest

2 ounces bittersweet chocolate, grated fine

1 Heat oil in 12-inch nonstick skillet over low heat for at least 10 minutes.

2 While oil is heating, whisk flour, 1 teaspoon sugar, and salt together in bowl. Whisk milk and eggs together in second bowl. Add half of milk mixture to flour mixture and whisk until smooth. Add melted butter and whisk until incorporated. Whisk in remaining milk mixture until smooth.

3 Wipe out skillet with paper towels, leaving thin film of oil on bottom and sides of pan. Increase heat to medium and let skillet heat for 1 minute. After 1 minute, test heat of skillet by placing 1 teaspoon batter in center of pan and cooking for 20 seconds. If mini crêpe is golden brown on bottom, skillet is properly heated; if it is too light or too dark, adjust heat accordingly and retest.

4 Pour ¼ cup batter into far side of skillet and tilt and shake gently until batter evenly covers bottom of skillet. Cook crêpe without moving it until top surface is dry and edges are starting to brown, loosening crêpe from sides of skillet with heat-resistant rubber spatula, about 1 minute. Gently slide spatula underneath edge of crêpe, grasp edge with your fingertips, and flip crêpe. Cook until second side is lightly spotted, about 30 seconds. Transfer crêpe, spotted side up, to wire rack. Return skillet to heat and heat for 10 seconds before repeating with remaining batter. As crêpes are done, stack on wire rack. Using your fingertips, rub orange zest into remaining ¼ cup sugar. Stir in chocolate.

5 Transfer stack of crêpes to large plate and invert second plate over crêpes. Microwave until crêpes are warm, 30 to 45 seconds (45 to 60 seconds if crêpes have cooled completely). Remove top plate and wipe dry with paper towel. Sprinkle 1½ tablespoons sugar mixture over top half of top crêpe. Fold unsugared half over sugared half, then fold in half again. Transfer filled crêpe to second plate. Repeat with remaining crêpes. Serve immediately.

CHOCOLATE BREAD PUDDING

SERVES 12

1 (1-pound) loaf challah, cut into ½-inch cubes

4 cups heavy cream, divided

2 cups whole milk

½ cup (1½ ounces) unsweetened cocoa powder

1 tablespoon instant espresso powder

1 cup (7 ounces) sugar, divided

8 ounces semisweet chocolate, chopped

10 large egg yolks

Why This Recipe Works Bread pudding—with its rich, custardy base and pieces of bread that are at once crispy, chewy, and soft—is an immensely satisfying alternative to individual slices of French toast in the morning. We knew that adding chocolate to the mix would be a winning proposition. We started with a basic recipe that called for soaking cubed, toasted sandwich bread in egg yolks, cream, milk, and sugar. For well-rounded chocolate flavor, we knew a combination of cocoa powder and melted chocolate would be key. We preferred the richness of semisweet chocolate to milk chocolate (too sweet) or unsweetened (too grainy). Rich challah suited the chocolate base better than delicate sandwich bread, but we ran into a problem: The melted chocolate made the base too thick to fully soak into the bread. The solution was allowing the bread to soak in a warm mixture of cream, milk, cocoa, espresso powder, and sugar before adding the custard of melted chocolate, egg yolks, sugar, and cream. Once the bread cubes were fully saturated with our "hot cocoa" mixture, we poured the custard over the bread and baked our pudding until crisp on the outside but still soft on the inside. A generous drizzle of chocolate sauce provided the finishing touch.

1 Adjust oven rack to middle position and heat oven to 300 degrees. Toast challah cubes on rimmed baking sheet, stirring occasionally, until golden and crisp, about 30 minutes. Transfer to large bowl.

2 Increase oven temperature to 325 degrees. Grease 13 by 9-inch baking pan. Heat 1½ cups cream, milk, cocoa, espresso powder, and ½ cup sugar in small saucepan over medium-high heat, stirring occasionally, until steaming and sugar has completely dissolved. Pour warm cream mixture over toasted challah and let stand, tossing occasionally, until liquid has been absorbed, about 10 minutes.

3 Meanwhile, bring 1 cup cream to simmer in now-empty saucepan over medium-high heat. Remove from heat, add chocolate to hot cream, and stir until chocolate has melted and mixture is smooth. Transfer 1 cup chocolate mixture to bowl and let cool for 5 minutes (cover pan and set aside remaining chocolate mixture). Whisk egg yolks, remaining 1½ cups cream, and remaining ½ cup sugar into chocolate mixture in bowl until combined.

4 Transfer soaked challah mixture to prepared pan, distributing it evenly over bottom of pan. Pour chocolate custard mixture evenly over challah mixture. Bake until custard is just set and surface of pudding is slightly crisp, about 45 minutes, rotating pan halfway through baking. Transfer to wire rack and let cool for 30 minutes.

5 Warm reserved chocolate mixture over low heat, then pour over pudding. Serve. (Leftover bread pudding can be wrapped in plastic wrap and refrigerated for up to 3 days; reheat individual portions in microwave.)

CHOCOLATE CAKE DOUGHNUTS

MAKES 12 DOUGHNUTS AND 12 DOUGHNUT HOLES

Why This Recipe Works Whether you're surprised with a box of doughnut-shop treats on the breakfast table or encounter one in the work breakroom, there's a good chance you're going to rush to snatch the coveted chocolate cake doughnut. Some are great, but many taste good only due to nostalgia and are in fact dry, crumbly, and light in chocolate flavor—and supermarket options are even worse. We think if you're going to have a doughnut for breakfast, it should be tender, moist, and richly chocolaty. Fortunately, cake doughnuts are easy to make at home. To supercharge the flavor, we used a generous amount of intense unsweetened cocoa powder. Sour cream was the ticket to textural perfection: The acidic ingredient tenderized our dough by shortening the gluten chains (which create structure but also toughness), and we liked the richness and tang it added. The moist dough was now quite sticky, but a quick 30 minutes in the fridge made it much easier to cut out doughnuts. Use a Dutch oven that holds 6 quarts or more. If you don't have a 3-inch doughnut cutter, use a 3-inch round biscuit cutter and stamp out the holes with a 1½-inch biscuit cutter.

1 **For the doughnuts** Whisk flour, cocoa, baking powder, baking soda, and salt together in bowl; set aside. Using stand mixer fitted with paddle, beat butter and sugar on medium-high speed until pale and fluffy, about 3 minutes. Add egg and beat until combined. Add sour cream and beat until smooth. Reduce speed to low and add flour mixture in 3 additions, scraping down bowl as needed. Stir batter once or twice with rubber spatula to ensure no dry streaks remain. Transfer batter to lightly greased bowl, cover with plastic wrap, and refrigerate for 1 hour.

2 Transfer batter to floured counter and roll with heavily floured rolling pin into 10-inch round, about ½ inch thick. Using heavily floured 3-inch doughnut cutter, stamp out dough rings and holes, reflouring cutter between cuts. Gather scraps and gently press into disk; repeat rolling and stamping process until all dough is used. Transfer doughnuts and holes to lightly floured rimmed baking sheet, cover, and refrigerate for 30 minutes.

3 Set wire rack in second rimmed baking sheet and line with triple layer of paper towels. Add oil to large Dutch oven until it measures about 2 inches deep and heat over medium-high heat to 375 degrees. Carefully place 3 doughnuts and 3 doughnut holes into hot oil and fry until golden brown, about 45 seconds per side for holes and 60 seconds per side for doughnuts. Adjust burner, if necessary, to maintain oil temperature between 350 and 375 degrees. Using slotted spoon or wire skimmer, transfer doughnuts to prepared rack. Return oil to 375 degrees and repeat with remaining doughnuts and holes in 3 batches; let cool slightly.

4 **For the glaze** Whisk sugar, milk, and cocoa in bowl until combined. Once doughnuts are cool enough to handle, remove paper towels from rack. Dip both sides of each doughnut and doughnut hole into glaze, shaking off any excess, and return to wire rack. Let sit until glaze has set, about 10 minutes. Serve.

DOUGHNUTS

- 2¼ cups (11¼ ounces) all-purpose flour
- 1 cup (3 ounces) unsweetened cocoa powder
- 1 teaspoon baking powder
- ½ teaspoon baking soda
- ¾ teaspoon table salt
- 4 tablespoons unsalted butter, softened
- 1 cup (7 ounces) granulated sugar
- 1 large egg, room temperature
- 1½ cups sour cream
- 3 quarts peanut or vegetable oil for frying

GLAZE

- 3 cups (12 ounces) confectioners' sugar
- ½ cup whole milk
- ¼ cup (¾ ounce) unsweetened cocoa powder

CHURROS WITH MEXICAN CHOCOLATE SAUCE

MAKES 18 CHURROS

CHURROS

- 2 cups water
- 2 tablespoons unsalted butter
- 2 tablespoons sugar, plus ½ cup (3½ ounces), divided
- 1 teaspoon vanilla extract
- ½ teaspoon table salt
- 2 cups (10 ounces) all-purpose flour
- 2 large eggs
- 2 quarts vegetable oil
- ¾ teaspoon ground cinnamon

SAUCE

- 1¼ cups (8¾ ounces) sugar
- ⅔ cup whole milk
- ¼ teaspoon table salt
- ¼ teaspoon ground cinnamon
- ¼ teaspoon chipotle chile powder
- ⅓ cup (1 ounce) unsweetened cocoa powder, sifted
- 3 ounces unsweetened chocolate, chopped fine
- 4 tablespoons unsalted butter, cut into 8 pieces and chilled
- 1 teaspoon vanilla extract

Why This Recipe Works There's a lot to love about churros: These fluted pastries are fried until crisp on the outside and soft on the inside, at which point they're rolled in a cinnamon-sugar coating and served with a side of rich, warm chocolate sauce for dipping. A decadent breakfast treat for sure, but there's no denying that the lightly crisp pastry, inviting fragrance of cinnamon, and slightly bitter edge of chocolate pair perfectly with a steaming mug of coffee. Many recipes call for piping the cooled dough directly into hot oil, but we found this process to be hectic and dangerous. Instead, we piped the still-warm dough onto a baking sheet and refrigerated the churros for a few minutes to firm them up. This made the process of transferring them to the oil easy. A combination of cocoa powder and unsweetened chocolate kept the sweetness of our sauce in check, while a bit of chipotle chile powder added heat and a little cinnamon contributed warmth. We used a closed star #8 pastry tip, ⅝ inch in diameter, to create deeply grooved ridges in the churros. However, you can use any large closed star tip of similar diameter, though your yield may vary slightly. To keep the eggs from scrambling, it's important to mix the dough for 1 minute in step 2 before adding them. Use a Dutch oven that holds 6 quarts or more.

1 For the churros Line rimmed baking sheet with parchment paper and spray with vegetable oil spray. Combine water, butter, 2 tablespoons sugar, vanilla, and salt in large saucepan and bring to boil over medium-high heat. Off heat, add flour all at once and stir with rubber spatula until well combined with no streaks of flour remaining.

2 Transfer dough to bowl of stand mixer. Fit mixer with paddle and mix dough on low speed until cooled slightly, about 1 minute. Add eggs, increase speed to medium, and beat until fully incorporated, about 1 minute.

3 Transfer warm dough to piping bag fitted with ⅝-inch closed star pastry tip. Pipe 18 (6-inch) lengths of dough onto prepared sheet, using scissors to snip dough at tip. Refrigerate uncovered for at least 15 minutes or up to 1 hour.

4 For the sauce Meanwhile, heat sugar, milk, salt, cinnamon, and chile powder in medium saucepan over medium-low heat, whisking gently, until sugar has dissolved and liquid starts to bubble around edges of saucepan, about 6 minutes. Reduce heat to low, add cocoa, and whisk until smooth.

5 Off heat, stir in chocolate and let sit for 3 minutes. Whisk sauce until smooth and chocolate is fully melted. Whisk in butter and vanilla until fully incorporated and sauce thickens slightly. (Sauce can be refrigerated for up to 1 month; gently warm in microwave, stirring every 10 seconds, until pourable, before using.)

6 Adjust oven rack to middle position and heat oven to 200 degrees. Set wire rack in second rimmed baking sheet and place in oven. Line large plate with triple layer of paper towels. Add oil to large Dutch oven until it measures about 1½ inches deep and heat over medium-high heat to 375 degrees.

7 Gently drop 6 churros into hot oil and fry until dark golden brown on all sides, about 6 minutes, turning frequently for even cooking. Adjust burner, if necessary, to maintain oil temperature between 350 and 375 degrees. Transfer churros to prepared plate for 30 seconds to drain off excess oil, then transfer to wire rack in oven. Return oil to 375 degrees and repeat with remaining dough in 2 more batches.

8 Combine cinnamon and remaining ½ cup sugar in shallow dish. Roll churros in cinnamon sugar, tapping gently to remove excess. Transfer churros to platter and serve with sauce.

CHOCOLATE BRIOCHE BUNS

MAKES 12 BUNS

DOUGH

3⅔   cups (20⅛ ounces) bread flour

2¼   teaspoons instant or rapid-rise yeast

1½   teaspoons table salt

1   cup water, room temperature

2   large eggs, plus 1 large yolk

½   cup (3½ ounces) granulated sugar

12   tablespoons unsalted butter, cut into 12 pieces, softened

⅓   cup (1 ounce) unsweetened cocoa powder

FILLING

2   ounces bittersweet chocolate, chopped

4   tablespoons unsalted butter

3   tablespoons unsweetened cocoa powder

¼   cup (1 ounce) confectioners' sugar

1   large egg white

1   large egg, lightly beaten with 1 tablespoon water

Why This Recipe Works While we love frosted, glazed, and molten creations, chocolate decadence doesn't have to come in an ooey-gooey package—especially at breakfast time. We wanted a breakfast bun with some restraint, one that would make a beautiful addition to Sunday brunch and would be buttery, rich, and substantial yet tender. Our first thought was brioche: Enriched with eggs and butter, the bread is a perfectly rich pairing for our star ingredient. Sure, we could just add chocolate chips to a standard roll, but that seemed like an afterthought. We wanted a bun where chocolate was a truly integral part, so we shaped spirals of plain and chocolate-flavored doughs. Using bread flour ensured the dough would have enough structure to later fill and shape into scrolls. To make chocolate brioche dough, we added a generous ⅓ cup of cocoa powder to half of the dough. Shaping our impressive buns was easier than it looks. We rolled the separate plain and chocolate doughs into squares and stacked them with a filling of bittersweet chocolate, cocoa powder, butter, and confectioners' sugar (made tacky with an egg white) in the middle. We refrigerated the layered doughs so they would firm up before rolling, cutting, and coiling. We also refrigerated the shaped buns to proof overnight so we wouldn't have to wake up with the sun to enjoy them. When kneading the dough on medium-low speed, the mixer can wobble and move on the counter. Place a towel or shelf liner underneath it to keep it in place and watch it closely.

1 **For the dough** Whisk flour, yeast, and salt together in bowl of stand mixer. Whisk water, eggs and yolk, and sugar together in 4-cup liquid measuring cup. Using dough hook on low speed, slowly add water mixture to flour mixture and mix until cohesive dough starts to form and no dry flour remains, about 2 minutes, scraping down bowl as needed.

2 Increase speed to medium-low; add butter, 1 piece at a time; and knead until butter is fully incorporated, about 4 minutes. Continue to knead until dough is smooth and elastic and clears sides of bowl, 11 to 13 minutes.

3 Transfer dough to lightly floured counter and divide in half. Knead half of dough by hand to form smooth, round ball, about 30 seconds. Place dough seam side down in lightly greased large bowl or container. Return remaining half of dough to mixer, add cocoa, and knead on medium-low speed until cocoa is evenly incorporated, about 2 minutes. Transfer dough to lightly floured counter and knead by hand to form smooth, round ball, about 30 seconds. Place second dough ball seam side down in second lightly greased large bowl or container. Cover bowls tightly with plastic wrap and let rise at room temperature until increased in size by half, 45 minutes to 1 hour.

4 **For the filling** Microwave chocolate, butter, and cocoa in bowl at 50 percent power, stirring occasionally, until melted and smooth, about 2 minutes. Stir in sugar until combined and let cool completely, about 30 minutes. Whisk in egg white until fully combined and mixture turns glossy.

5 Line baking sheet with parchment paper and lightly flour. Transfer plain dough seam side down to prepared sheet and press into 6 by 6-inch square. Spread filling over dough, leaving ¼-inch border around edges. Press chocolate dough into 6 by 6-inch square on lightly floured counter. Place on top of filling and press gently to adhere. Cover loosely with greased plastic and refrigerate for 30 minutes.

6 Line 2 rimmed baking sheets with parchment paper. Transfer chilled dough square to lightly floured counter. Press and roll dough into 12 by 16-inch rectangle with short side parallel to counter edge. Using sharp pizza wheel or knife, starting at 1 short side, cut dough into twelve 16 by 1-inch strips. Working with 1 dough strip at a time, tightly coil ends of strip in

opposite directions to form tight S shape. Arrange buns on prepared sheets, six per sheet, spaced about 2½ inches apart. Cover loosely with greased plastic and refrigerate for at least 2 hours or up to 24 hours.

7 One hour before baking, remove buns from refrigerator and let sit at room temperature. Adjust oven racks to upper-middle and lower-middle positions and heat oven to 350 degrees. Gently brush buns with egg mixture and bake until golden brown, 18 to 22 minutes, switching and rotating sheets halfway through baking. Transfer buns to wire rack and let cool completely, about 30 minutes. Serve.

SHAPING CHOCOLATE BRIOCHE BUNS

1. Press plain dough into 6 by 6-inch square.

2. Spread filling over dough, leaving ¼-inch border around edges.

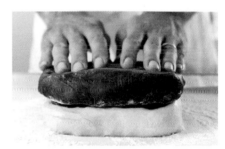

3. Press chocolate dough into 6 by 6-inch square. Place on top of filling and press gently to adhere. Cover loosely with greased plastic and refrigerate for 30 minutes.

4. Press and roll dough into 12 by 16-inch rectangle with short side parallel to counter edge.

5. Starting at 1 short side, cut dough into twelve 16 by 1-inch strips.

6. Working with 1 dough strip at a time, tightly coil ends in opposite directions to form tight S shape.

TRIPLE CHOCOLATE STICKY BUNS

MAKES 12 BUNS

FLOUR PASTE

⅔ cup whole milk

¼ cup (1¼ ounces) all-purpose flour

DOUGH

⅔ cup whole milk

1 large egg plus 1 large yolk

3¼ cups (16¼ ounces) all-purpose flour

2¼ teaspoons instant or rapid-rise yeast

3 tablespoons granulated sugar

1½ teaspoons table salt

6 tablespoons unsalted butter, cut into 6 pieces and softened

TOPPING

¾ cup packed (5¼ ounces) brown sugar

6 tablespoons unsalted butter, melted

¼ cup dark corn syrup

2 tablespoons water

1 tablespoon unsweetened cocoa powder

¼ teaspoon table salt

FILLING

4 ounces bittersweet chocolate, chopped fine

4 tablespoons unsalted butter

1 cup (6 ounces) milk chocolate chips

Why This Recipe Works Sticky buns are the ultimate, decadent breakfast treat. Could we—or should we—make them any better? Certainly. To really take sticky buns over the top, we wanted to give them a chocolate punch that would satisfy the most serious chocolate lover. For the dough, we used a Japanese bread-making technique called *tangzhong,* in which a portion of the flour and milk is microwaved before being added to the rest of the dough ingredients. This gel-like paste locked in moisture and produced ultratender buns. We loved the texture of the buns, so we decided to keep them chocolate-free and instead incorporate chocolate into the other elements. For our filling, we combined butter and bittersweet chocolate to form a ganache that we spread over the rolled-out dough (we ditched the traditional cinnamon, as it competed with the chocolate flavor). We then sprinkled on milk chocolate chips before rolling up the dough for delightfully creamy pockets of chocolate. Adding cocoa powder to our super easy caramel—which simply forms in the pan as the buns bake—provided a final dose of gooey chocolate. One packet of rapid-rise or instant yeast contains 2¼ teaspoons of yeast. Be sure to use a metal, not glass or ceramic, baking pan. The tackiness of the dough aids in flattening and stretching it in step 7, so resist the urge to use a lot of dusting flour. Rolling the dough cylinder too tightly in step 8 will result in misshapen rolls. Buns baked according to the make-ahead instructions will be shorter than buns baked after the second proofing.

1 For the flour paste Whisk milk and flour in small bowl until no lumps remain. Microwave, whisking every 25 seconds, until mixture thickens to stiff paste, 50 to 75 seconds. Whisk until smooth.

2 For the dough Whisk flour paste and milk in bowl of stand mixer until smooth. Add egg and yolk and whisk until incorporated. Add flour and yeast. Fit mixer with dough hook and mix on low speed until mass of dough forms and all flour is moistened, 1 to 2 minutes. Turn off mixer, cover bowl with dish towel or plastic wrap, and let dough stand for 15 minutes.

3 Add sugar and salt to dough. Knead on medium-low speed for 5 minutes. Add butter and continue to knead until incorporated, scraping down dough hook and bowl as needed (dough will be sticky), about 5 minutes longer.

4 Transfer dough to lightly floured counter and knead briefly by hand to form ball. Place dough seam side down in greased large bowl or container, cover tightly with plastic, and let rise until doubled in size, about 1 hour.

5 For the topping Meanwhile, whisk all ingredients in bowl until combined. Spray 13 by 9-inch metal baking pan with vegetable oil spray. Pour topping into prepared pan and use rubber spatula to spread to edges of pan; set aside.

6 **For the filling** About 30 minutes before dough is done rising, microwave bittersweet chocolate and butter in bowl at 50 percent power, stirring occasionally, until melted and smooth, about 2 minutes. Refrigerate until matte and firm, 30 to 40 minutes.

7 Transfer dough to lightly floured counter and lightly flour top of dough. Press and roll dough into 18 by 15-inch rectangle, with long side parallel to counter's edge. Stir bittersweet chocolate mixture with rubber spatula until smooth and spreadable (mixture should have similar texture to frosting). Using offset spatula, spread mixture over entire surface of dough, leaving 1-inch border along top edge. Sprinkle evenly with chocolate chips.

8 Beginning with long edge nearest you, loosely roll dough away from you into even log, pushing in ends to create even thickness. Pinch seam to seal. Roll log seam side down and slice into 12 equal portions. Place buns, cut side down, in prepared pan in 3 rows of 4, lightly reshaping buns into rounds as needed. Cover tightly with plastic and let rise until buns are puffy and touching one another, about 1 hour.

9 Adjust oven racks to lowest and lower-middle positions and heat oven to 375 degrees. Place rimmed baking sheet on lower rack to catch any drips. Discard plastic and bake buns on upper rack until golden brown on top, about 20 minutes. Cover loosely with aluminum foil and continue to bake until center buns register at least 200 degrees, about 15 minutes longer.

10 Carefully remove foil from pan (steam may escape) and immediately run paring knife around edge of pan. Place large platter or second rimmed baking sheet over pan and carefully invert pan and sheet. Remove pan and let buns cool for 15 minutes. Serve.

To make ahead Follow recipe through step 8, then refrigerate buns for at least 8 hours or up to 24 hours. When ready to bake, let buns sit on counter for 30 minutes before proceeding with step 9. Increase uncovered baking time by 10 minutes.

SHAPING TRIPLE CHOCOLATE STICKY BUNS

1. Using offset spatula, spread chocolate mixture over entire surface of dough rectangle, leaving 1-inch border along top edge. Sprinkle evenly with chocolate chips.

2. Loosely roll dough away from you into even log, pushing in ends to create even thickness. Pinch seam to seal.

3. Roll log seam side down and slice into 12 equal portions. Place buns, cut side down, in prepared pan in 3 rows of 4, lightly reshaping buns into rounds as needed.

CHOCOLATE BABKA

SERVES 12

DOUGH

2 cups (10 ounces) all-purpose flour

1½ teaspoons instant or rapid-rise yeast

½ teaspoon table salt

½ cup (4 ounces) whole milk, room temperature

¼ cup (1¾ ounces) granulated sugar

2 large egg yolks, room temperature

1 teaspoon vanilla extract

8 tablespoons unsalted butter, softened

FILLING

2 ounces bittersweet chocolate, chopped

4 tablespoons unsalted butter

3 tablespoons unsweetened cocoa powder

¼ cup (1 ounce) confectioners' sugar

1 large egg white

1 large egg, lightly beaten with 1 tablespoon water and pinch salt

Why This Recipe Works Cinnamon and sugar are nice, but we're bigger fans of chocolate babka and wanted our loaf to feature deep, dark spirals of decadent chocolate. By definition, babka dough is a rich and tender dough, akin to brioche. But go too far in that direction and the dough will collapse under the weight of the chocolate filling, leaving large gaps in the bread. To add richness yet preserve the loaf's structural integrity, we cut back on the butter found in most traditional recipes and substituted two egg yolks for one whole egg. For the filling, a combination of bittersweet chocolate and cocoa powder provided the full, rounded chocolate flavor and appealingly fudgy texture we were looking for. To make sure the filling stayed put and didn't sink to the bottom of the loaf, we also mixed in confectioners' sugar and an egg white, which helped stiffen it up. The test kitchen's preferred loaf pan measures 8½ by 4½ inches; if you use a 9 by 5-inch loaf pan, increase the shaped rising time by 20 to 30 minutes and start checking for doneness 10 minutes earlier than advised in the recipe. We do not recommend mixing this dough by hand. If the dough becomes too soft to work with at any point, refrigerate it until it's firm enough to easily handle.

1 For the dough Whisk flour, yeast, and salt together in bowl of stand mixer. Whisk milk, sugar, egg yolks, and vanilla in 4-cup liquid measuring cup until sugar has dissolved. Fit mixer with dough hook and mix on low speed, slowly adding milk mixture to flour mixture until cohesive dough starts to form and no dry flour remains, about 2 minutes, scraping down bowl as needed.

2 Increase speed to medium-low; add butter, 1 tablespoon at a time, and knead until butter is fully incorporated, about 4 minutes. Continue to knead until dough is smooth and elastic and clears sides of bowl, 10 to 12 minutes.

3 Transfer dough to lightly floured counter and knead by hand to form smooth, round ball, about 30 seconds. Place dough seam side down in lightly greased large bowl or container, cover tightly with plastic wrap, and let rise until increased in size by about half, 1½ to 2 hours. Place in refrigerator until dough is firm, at least 1 hour or up to 24 hours. (If dough is chilled longer than 1 hour, let rest at room temperature for 15 minutes before rolling out in step 5.)

4 For the filling Microwave chocolate, butter, and cocoa in bowl at 50 percent power, stirring occasionally, until melted and smooth, 1 to 2 minutes. Stir in sugar until combined; let cool completely. Whisk in egg white until fully combined and mixture turns glossy. Measure out and reserve 1 tablespoon filling.

5 Grease 8½ by 4½-inch loaf pan. Press down on dough to deflate, then transfer to lightly floured counter. Press and roll dough into 18 by 14-inch rectangle, with long side parallel to counter edge. Spread remaining filling over dough, leaving ½-inch border around edges.

6 Roll dough away from you into firm cylinder, keeping roll taut by tucking it under itself as you go. Pinch seam closed, then reshape cylinder as needed to be 18 inches in length with uniform thickness. Position cylinder seam side up and spread reserved filling over top. Fold cylinder on top of itself and pinch ends to seal.

7 Gently twist double cylinder twice to form double figure eight. Place loaf in prepared pan, pressing dough gently into corners. Cover loosely with greased plastic and let rise until loaf is level with lip of pan, 1½ to 2 hours.

8 Adjust oven rack to lower-middle position and heat oven to 350 degrees. Gently brush loaf with egg mixture and bake until deep golden brown and loaf registers 190 to 195 degrees, 40 to 45 minutes, rotating pan halfway through baking. Let loaf cool in pan for 15 minutes. Remove loaf from pan and let cool completely on wire rack, about 3 hours, before serving.

MAKING CHOCOLATE BABKA

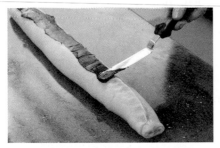

1. Transfer dough to lightly floured counter and knead by hand to form smooth, round ball, about 30 seconds. Let rise until increased in size by about half, 1½ to 2 hours. Refrigerate until dough is firm, at least 1 hour or up to 24 hours.

2. Microwave chocolate, butter, and cocoa at 50 percent power, stirring occasionally, until melted, 1 to 2 minutes. Stir in sugar until combined; let cool completely. Whisk in egg white until mixture turns glossy. Set aside 1 tablespoon filling.

3. Press and roll dough into 18 by 14-inch rectangle. Spread filling over dough, leaving ½-inch border around edges.

4. Roll dough away from you into firm cylinder. Pinch seam closed and spread reserved 1 tablespoon filling over top. Fold cylinder on top of itself and pinch ends to seal.

5. Gently twist double cylinder twice to form double figure eight. Place loaf in prepared pan, pressing dough gently into corners. Cover and let rise until loaf is level with lip of pan, 1½ to 2 hours.

6. Gently brush loaf with egg mixture and bake until deep golden brown and loaf registers 190 to 195 degrees, 40 to 45 minutes, rotating pan halfway through baking.

CHOCOLATE CROISSANTS

MAKES 16 CROISSANTS

27 tablespoons (13½ ounces) unsalted European-style butter, very cold, divided

1¾ cups whole milk

4 teaspoons instant or rapid-rise yeast

4¼ cups (21¼ ounces) King Arthur all-purpose flour

¼ cup (1¾ ounces) sugar

2 teaspoons table salt

3½ ounces bittersweet chocolate, chopped fine

1 large egg, beaten with 1 tablespoon water and pinch salt

Why This Recipe Works The only thing better than waking up to the smell of buttery pastries is waking up to the smell of buttery pastries filled with chocolate. We set out to make a crisp, flaky *pain au chocolat*: croissant dough wrapped around two dark chocolate batons. Making the dough—a process called lamination in which dough and butter are layered, folded, and rolled repeatedly to create flaky pastry—can be intimidating. To make it more feasible we built in a series of freezer chills. To avoid seeking out batons, we lined up finely chopped chocolate, which neither interrupted nor punctured the dough layers. If you can't find King Arthur all-purpose flour, substitute bread flour. Our favorite European-style butter is Plugrá. Do not attempt to make these croissants in a room that is warmer than 80 degrees. If at any time during rolling the dough retracts or softens, dust it lightly with flour, fold it loosely into thirds, cover it, and return it to the freezer to rest for 10 to 15 minutes. This recipe yields 8 baked croissants and 8 croissants for freezing and baking at a later time.

1 Melt 3 tablespoons butter in medium saucepan over low heat. Remove from heat and immediately stir in milk (temperature should be lower than 90 degrees). Whisk in yeast; transfer milk mixture to bowl of stand mixer. Add flour, sugar, and salt. Using dough hook, knead on low speed for 1 minute. Remove bowl from mixer and cover with plastic wrap. Let dough rest at room temperature for 30 minutes.

2 Transfer dough to parchment paper–lined rimmed baking sheet and shape into 10 by 7-inch rectangle, about 1 inch thick. Wrap tightly with plastic and refrigerate for 2 hours. While dough chills, fold 24-inch length of parchment in half to create 12-inch rectangle. Fold over 3 open sides of rectangle to form 8-inch square with enclosed sides. Crease folds firmly. Place 24 tablespoons cold butter directly on counter and beat with rolling pin for about 60 seconds until butter is just pliable but not warm, then fold butter in on itself using bench scraper. Beat into rough 6-inch square. Unfold parchment envelope. Using bench scraper, transfer butter to center of parchment, refolding at creases to enclose. Turn packet over so that flaps are underneath and gently roll until butter fills parchment square, taking care to achieve even thickness. Refrigerate for at least 45 minutes.

3 Transfer dough to freezer. After 30 minutes, transfer to lightly floured counter and roll into 17 by 8-inch rectangle with long side parallel to edge of counter. Unwrap butter and place in center of dough. Fold sides of dough over butter so they meet in center. Press seam together with your fingertips. Using rolling pin, press firmly on each open end of packet. Roll out lengthwise into 24 by 8-inch rectangle. Starting at bottom of dough, fold into thirds like business letter into 8-inch square. Turn dough 90 degrees counterclockwise. Roll out lengthwise again into 24 by 8-inch rectangle and fold into thirds. Place dough on sheet, wrap tightly with plastic, and return to freezer for 30 minutes. Transfer dough to lightly floured counter so that top flap opens on right. Roll out dough lengthwise into 24 by 8-inch rectangle and fold into thirds. Place dough on sheet, wrap tightly with plastic, and refrigerate for at least 2 hours or up to 24 hours.

4 Transfer dough to freezer. After 30 minutes, transfer to lightly floured counter and roll into 16 by 18-inch rectangle with short side of rectangle parallel to counter edge. Using sharp pizza wheel or knife, staring at 1 short side, cut dough into four 4 by 18-inch strips. Then cut dough crosswise into 4 by 4½ inch rectangles (16 rectangles total).

5 With short side of 1 dough rectangle facing you, spread 1 teaspoon chopped chocolate, end to end, in tidy row, ½ inch from bottom. Stretch and fold bottom third of dough over chocolate to center. Spread 1 more teaspoon chocolate end to end along dough seam. Brush top of folded dough with portion of egg wash. Stretch and fold top third of dough over chocolate until even with bottom edge of dough; gently press seam to seal. Repeat with remaining rectangles.

6 Place 4 croissants each, seam side down, on 2 parchment-lined rimmed baking sheets at least 3 inches apart. Cover loosely with greased plastic. Let rise at room temperature until nearly double in size, 2½ to 3 hours. (Shaped croissants can be refrigerated for up to 18 hours. Remove from refrigerator to rise and add at least 30 minutes to rising time). Place remaining 8 croissants on separate parchment-lined rimmed baking sheet, spaced about 1 inch apart. Wrap tightly with greased plastic and freeze until solid, about 2 hours. Transfer frozen croissants from baking sheet to zipper-lock bag and return to freezer. (Frozen croissants can be stored in freezer for up to 2 months. Arrange on 2 sheets as directed and increase rising time by 1 to 2 hours.)

7 After 2 hours of rising, adjust oven racks to upper-middle and lower-middle positions and heat oven to 425 degrees. Brush croissants with remaining egg wash. Place croissants in oven and reduce temperature to 400 degrees. Bake for 10 minutes, then switch and rotate baking sheets. Continue to bake until deep golden brown, 8 to 12 minutes. Transfer to wire rack and let cool completely, about 1 hour. Serve.

SHAPING CHOCOLATE CROISSANTS

1. With short side of 1 dough rectangle facing you, spread 1 teaspoon chopped chocolate, end to end, in tidy row, ½ inch from bottom.

2. Stretch and fold bottom third of dough over chocolate to center.

3. Spread 1 more teaspoon chocolate end to end along dough seam.

4. Brush top of folded dough with egg wash.

5. Stretch and fold top third of dough over chocolate until even with bottom edge of dough.

6. Gently press seam to seal.

bakery case
FAVORITES

CHOCOLATE CRINKLE COOKIES

MAKES 22 COOKIES

1 cup (5 ounces) all-purpose flour

½ cup (1½ ounces) unsweetened cocoa powder

1 teaspoon baking powder

¼ teaspoon baking soda

½ teaspoon table salt

1½ cups packed (10½ ounces) brown sugar

3 large eggs

4 teaspoons instant espresso powder (optional)

1 teaspoon vanilla extract

4 ounces unsweetened chocolate, chopped

4 tablespoons unsalted butter

½ cup granulated sugar

½ cup confectioners' sugar

Why This Recipe Works Rolled in powdered sugar before baking, chocolate crinkle cookies (often called earthquakes) feature chocolaty fissures that break through the bright white surface as the cookies spread in the oven. While striking in appearance, the cookies often fall short on chocolate flavor. Using a combination of cocoa powder and unsweetened chocolate rather than bittersweet (which contains sugar) certainly upped the intensity. The addition of some espresso powder further underscored the chocolate flavor, and replacing the granulated sugar with brown sugar created a complex sweetness. At this point, the cookies had deep, rich flavor, but the exterior cracks were too few and too wide, and the cookies weren't spreading enough. Using a combination of baking soda and baking powder helped—the bubbles produced by the leaveners rose to the surface and burst, leaving fissures—but the cracks gapped. We had been refrigerating this fluid dough overnight, but the cold dough didn't begin to spread very much until after that dried exterior had formed, forcing the cracks to open wide. The solution was to not refrigerate the dough, but simply bake the cookies after letting the dough sit at room temperature for 10 minutes, which was just enough time for the dough to firm up to a scoopable consistency.

1 Adjust oven rack to middle position and heat oven to 325 degrees. Line 2 baking sheets with parchment paper. Whisk flour, cocoa, baking powder, baking soda, and salt together in bowl.

2 Whisk brown sugar; eggs; espresso powder, if using; and vanilla together in large bowl. Microwave chocolate and butter in third bowl at 50 percent power, stirring occasionally, until melted and smooth, 2 to 3 minutes.

3 Whisk chocolate mixture into egg mixture until combined. Fold in flour mixture until no dry streaks remain. Let dough sit for 10 minutes.

4 Spread granulated sugar in shallow dish. Spread confectioners' sugar in second shallow dish. Working in batches, drop 2-tablespoon mounds of dough (or use #30 scoop) directly into granulated sugar and roll to coat. Transfer dough balls to confectioners' sugar and roll to coat; space dough balls evenly on prepared sheets, 11 per sheet.

5 Bake cookies, 1 sheet at a time, until they are puffed and cracked and edges have begun to set but centers are still soft (cookies will look raw between cracks and seem underdone), about 12 minutes, rotating sheet halfway through baking. Let cookies cool on sheet for 5 minutes, then transfer to wire rack. Let cookies cool completely before serving.

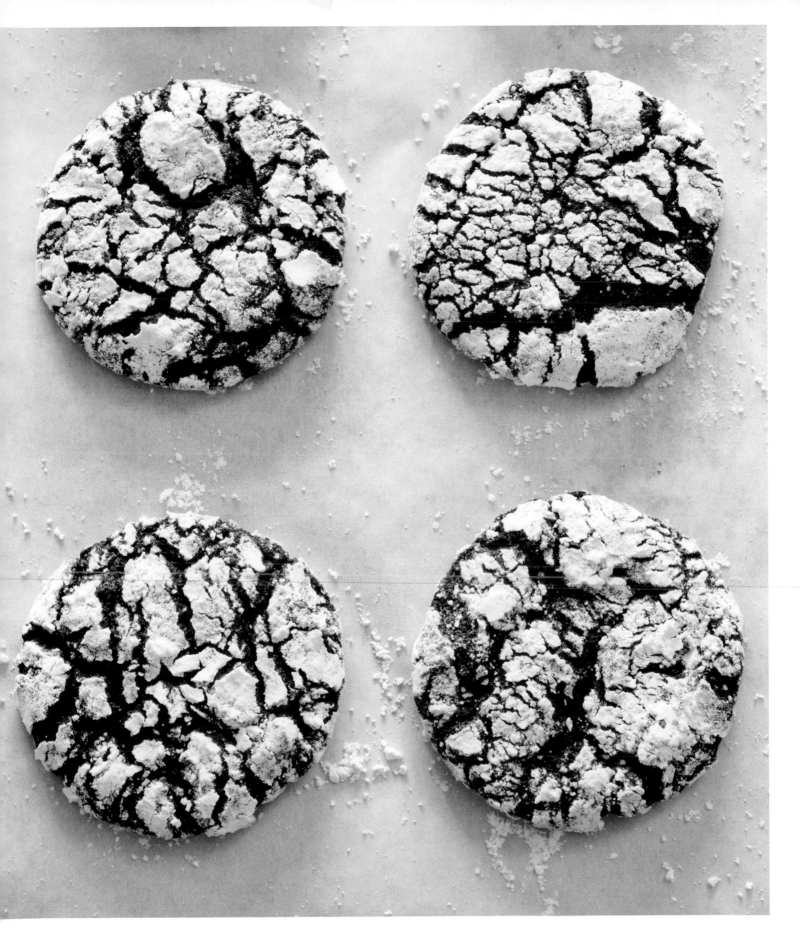

CHOCOLATE CHIP COOKIES

MAKES 16 COOKIES

Why This Recipe Works There's no question that the chocolate chip cookie is the most iconic American treat involving chocolate. We wanted a reliably moist and chewy cookie with crisp edges and deep butterscotch notes—and we wanted gooey chocolate bits in every bite. For the ideal texture, the key was melting the butter: When butter melts, its water content is readily available to interact with the flour, thus developing more gluten and a chewier texture. Continuing to cook the butter until it browned contributed deep caramel notes. (Since browning burns off some of the butter's moisture, we made sure not to brown all of it.) Using two egg yolks but only one white added richness without giving the cookies a cakey texture. And resting the batter briefly—along with a little whisking—allowed the sugar to more fully dissolve, resulting in crisp edges and full toffee flavor. Studded with almost half a pound of chocolate chips—semisweet and bittersweet worked equally well—and boasting complex flavor and ideal texture, these are chocolate chip cookies, perfected. Light brown sugar can be used in place of the dark, but the cookies won't be as full-flavored.

1¾ cups (8¾ ounces) all-purpose flour

½ teaspoon baking soda

14 tablespoons unsalted butter, divided

¾ cup packed (5¼ ounces) dark brown sugar

½ cup (3½ ounces) granulated sugar

2 teaspoons vanilla extract

1 teaspoon table salt

1 large egg plus 1 large yolk

1¼ cups (7½ ounces) semisweet or bittersweet chocolate chips

¾ cup pecans or walnuts, toasted and chopped (optional)

1 Adjust oven rack to middle position and heat oven to 375 degrees. Line 2 baking sheets with parchment paper. Whisk flour and baking soda together in bowl.

2 Melt 10 tablespoons butter in 10-inch skillet over medium-high heat. Continue to cook, swirling skillet constantly, until butter is dark golden brown and has nutty aroma, 1 to 3 minutes. Transfer browned butter to large bowl and stir in remaining 4 tablespoons butter until melted. Whisk in brown sugar, granulated sugar, vanilla, and salt until incorporated. Whisk in egg and yolk until smooth and no lumps remain, about 30 seconds.

3 Let mixture stand for 3 minutes, then whisk for 30 seconds. Repeat process of resting and whisking 2 more times until mixture is thick, smooth, and shiny. Using rubber spatula, stir in flour mixture until just combined, about 1 minute. Stir in chocolate chips and pecans, if using.

4 Working with 3 tablespoons dough at a time, roll into balls and space them 2 inches apart on prepared sheets. (Dough balls can be frozen for up to 1 month; bake frozen dough balls in 300-degree oven for 30 to 35 minutes.)

5 Bake cookies, 1 sheet at a time, until golden brown and edges have begun to set but centers are still soft and puffy, 10 to 14 minutes, rotating sheet halfway through baking. Transfer baking sheet to wire rack. Let cookies cool completely before serving.

CHOCOLATE SHORTBREAD

MAKES 16 WEDGES

2 cups (10 ounces) all-purpose flour

¼ cup (¾ ounce) unsweetened cocoa powder

½ teaspoon table salt

16 tablespoons unsalted butter, softened

½ cup (2 ounces) confectioners' sugar

1 tablespoon granulated sugar (optional)

Why This Recipe Works At its simplest, shortbread contains just four ingredients—flour, sugar, salt, and butter—and should feature an ultrafine, sandy texture. We had our sights set on a rich chocolate shortbread, but with so few ingredients we wondered if the addition of chocolate would throw off this careful balance. Indeed it did: When we tried mixing melted bittersweet chocolate into our standard shortbread dough, the dough became very soft and the baked cookie greasy. With so much butter in the recipe the chocolate's high fat content upset our carefully calibrated ratios. Substituting cocoa powder for a portion of the flour worked much better; with its high proportion of cocoa solids, ¼ cup cocoa powder was all we needed for intense chocolate flavor. Although baking the shortbread on a double layer of parchment isn't necessary, we found it helps absorb some of the butter from the dough during baking and cooling.

1 Whisk flour, cocoa, and salt together in bowl. Using handheld mixer set at medium speed, beat butter and confectioners' sugar in large bowl until light and fluffy, 3 to 6 minutes, scraping down bowl and beaters as needed. Reduce mixer speed to low and slowly add flour mixture until combined, about 30 seconds.

2 Using your hands, press dough into ball in bowl. Transfer dough to lightly floured counter and knead until very smooth, about 3 minutes. Press dough into disk. Roll dough into 9-inch round (about ½ inch thick) on sheet of parchment paper.

3 Transfer dough and parchment to parchment-lined baking sheet. Using your fingers, flute dough edge, then poke dough all over with fork and score into 16 wedges. Cover with plastic wrap and refrigerate dough for at least 20 minutes or up to 24 hours.

4 Adjust oven rack to middle position and heat oven to 300 degrees. Sprinkle granulated sugar, if using, evenly over dough. Bake shortbread until edges are firm and center springs back slightly when pressed, 40 to 45 minutes, rotating sheet halfway through baking.

5 Transfer sheet to wire rack and, using sharp knife, cut through scored marks to separate wedges. Let shortbread cool on sheet for 10 minutes, then transfer wedges to wire rack and let cool completely before serving, about 1 hour.

FORMING CHOCOLATE SHORTBREAD

1. Knead shortbread dough until very smooth, about 3 minutes.

2. Press dough into disk.

3. Roll dough into 9-inch round on sheet of parchment paper.

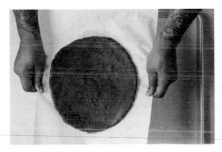

4. Transfer dough and parchment to parchment-lined baking sheet.

5. Using your fingers, flute edges of dough.

6. Poke dough all over with fork and score into 16 wedges.

CHOCOLATE-FILLED LACE SANDWICH COOKIES

MAKES ABOUT 18 SANDWICH COOKIES

4 tablespoons unsalted butter

6 tablespoons packed (2⅔ ounces) dark brown sugar

¼ cup light corn syrup

3 tablespoons all-purpose flour

1½ teaspoons heavy cream

½ teaspoon vanilla extract

⅛ teaspoon table salt

½ cup almonds, chopped fine

6 ounces semisweet chocolate, chopped fine

Why This Recipe Works Made from a dropped batter that spreads into crisp, gossamer-thin creations as they bake, lace cookies practically melt in your mouth. But these wafer-thin almond cookies have a reputation for being fussy and unpredictable. We wanted a recipe that would turn out perfect lace cookies every time, and we envisioned using them to form delicate sandwich cookies featuring a thin layer of chocolate for the filling. The amount and type of sugar is really what determines the thickness and spread of lace cookies, and after toying with every possible option we settled on a combination of light corn syrup and dark brown sugar. Less flour made for a more fluid batter that flowed easily onto the baking sheet. After letting the cookies cool briefly on the baking sheet, we transferred them to a wire rack to cool completely before spreading melted chocolate over the bottoms of half of the cookies and topping them with the remaining cookies. Semisweet chocolate provided plenty of rich chocolate flavor without overwhelming the delicate cookies the way bittersweet did. We recommend baking these fragile cookies on a reusable baking mat for easy release, although parchment paper can also be used. For best results, bake the cookies one sheet at a time. (It is not necessary to cool the baking sheet between batches.)

1 Adjust oven rack to upper-middle position and heat oven to 350 degrees. Line baking sheet with reusable baking mat.

2 Bring butter, sugar, and corn syrup just to boil in medium saucepan over medium heat, stirring frequently. Off heat, whisk in flour, cream, vanilla, and salt until smooth. Stir in almonds. (Bowl of lace cookie dough can be wrapped tightly with plastic wrap and refrigerated for up to 3 days; let soften at room temperature, then portion and bake as directed.)

3 Working in batches, drop teaspoons of batter onto prepared sheet spaced about 4 inches apart. Bake cookies until they spread thin, are no longer bubbling, and are deep golden brown, 5 to 7 minutes, rotating sheet halfway through baking.

4 Let cookies cool and firm up slightly on sheet for 1 to 2 minutes, then, using thin metal spatula, transfer to wire rack and let cool completely. Repeat with remaining dough.

5 Microwave chocolate in bowl at 50 percent power, stirring occasionally, until melted, 1 to 3 minutes. Spread about 2 teaspoons chocolate over bottom of 1 cookie, then gently cover with bottom of another cookie to make sandwich. Repeat with remaining cookies and chocolate. Serve.

MAKING CHOCOLATE-FILLED LACE SANDWICH COOKIES

1. Drop teaspoons of batter onto prepared sheet spaced about 4 inches apart.

2. Bake until the cookies spread thin, are no longer bubbling, and are deep golden brown, 5 to 7 minutes, rotating sheet halfway through baking.

3. Let cookies cool and firm up slightly on sheet for 1 to 2 minutes, then, using thin metal spatula, transfer to wire rack and let cool completely.

4. Spread about 2 teaspoons chocolate over bottom of 1 cookie.

5. Gently cover with bottom of another cookie to make sandwich. Repeat with remaining cookies and chocolate.

TRIPLE CHOCOLATE COOKIES

MAKES 26 COOKIES

Why This Recipe Works Triple-chocolate cookies shouldn't be a case of death by chocolate, but they should be rich and intense all the same. Balance is key in these soft and chewy cookies: Unsweetened chocolate adds deep, earthy notes; bittersweet chocolate contributes a sophisticated richness; and semisweet chocolate offsets the two more bitter chocolates. With more than a pound of chocolate in the recipe, our typical methods for mixing dough produced cookies that were too wet and didn't hold their shape. We got the best results by first beating the eggs and sugar together until fluffy; we then added the melted chocolate and butter and mixed in the dry ingredients last. The step of beating the eggs and sugar gave the dough more structure and resulted in cookies with a pleasantly crisp, meringue-like shell. A little coffee powder and vanilla bolstered the chocolate flavor even further. Allowing the cookies to cool completely on the baking sheet—rather than on a wire rack—ensured they retained their satisfyingly fudgy texture. Do not use bar chocolate in place of the bittersweet chocolate chips; the extra fat in the bar chocolate will make the cookies too rich and they won't hold their shape.

- 1½ cups (9 ounces) bittersweet chocolate chips
- 3 ounces unsweetened chocolate, chopped
- 7 tablespoons unsalted butter, cut into 7 pieces
- 2 teaspoons instant coffee powder
- 2 teaspoons vanilla extract
- 3 large eggs, room temperature
- 1 cup (7 ounces) sugar
- ½ cup (2½ ounces) all-purpose flour
- ½ teaspoon baking powder
- ½ teaspoon table salt
- 1½ cups (9 ounces) semisweet chocolate chips

1 Microwave bittersweet chocolate chips, unsweetened chocolate, and butter in large bowl at 50 percent power, stirring occasionally, until melted and smooth, 2 to 4 minutes; set aside to cool slightly.

2 Stir coffee powder and vanilla in small bowl until dissolved; set aside. Using stand mixer fitted with paddle, beat eggs and sugar at medium-high speed until mixture is very thick and pale, about 4 minutes. Add coffee mixture and continue to beat until fully incorporated, about 20 seconds. Reduce speed to low, add chocolate mixture, and mix until thoroughly combined, about 30 seconds.

3 Whisk flour, baking powder, and salt together in bowl. Using rubber spatula, fold flour mixture and semisweet chocolate chips into batter. Cover bowl with plastic wrap and let stand until batter firms up, 20 to 30 minutes (mixture will resemble thick brownie batter).

4 While batter rests, adjust oven racks to upper-middle and lower-middle positions and heat oven to 350 degrees. Line 2 baking sheets with parchment paper. Working with 1 heaping tablespoon dough at a time, roll into balls and space them 2 inches apart on prepared sheets. Bake until tops of cookies are shiny and tiny cracks appear evenly across surface, 11 to 14 minutes, switching and rotating sheets halfway through baking. Let cookies cool completely on sheets on wire racks before serving. (Cookies can be stored at room temperature for up to 3 days.)

CHOCOLATE CHUNK OATMEAL COOKIES

MAKES ABOUT 16 COOKIES

1¼ cups (6¼ ounces) all-purpose flour

¾ teaspoon baking powder

½ teaspoon baking soda

½ teaspoon table salt

1¼ cups (3¾ ounces) old-fashioned rolled oats

1 cup pecans, toasted and chopped

1 cup (4 ounces) dried sour cherries, chopped

4 ounces bittersweet chocolate, chopped into pieces about size of chocolate chips

12 tablespoons unsalted butter, softened

1½ cups packed (10½ ounces) dark brown sugar

1 large egg

1 teaspoon vanilla extract

Why This Recipe Works Adding chocolate to a chewy oatmeal cookie is always a good idea as far as we're concerned, but all too often recipes for this classic cookie are overloaded with a crazy jumble of extraneous ingredients. We wanted a chocolate-oatmeal cookie with just the right mix-ins that would complement, rather than overwhelm, the chocolate and oats. Focusing first on the basics of our cookie, we pitted semisweet chips against chopped dark and milk chocolates. The bitter edge and irregular distribution of the hand-chopped dark chocolate ensured it would retain the upper hand and remain the star ingredient. Using all brown sugar—and leveling up to dark brown—contributed deep molasses flavor and the chewiest texture. Making big cookies (a whopping ¼ cup of dough per cookie) and baking them just until set yet slightly underdone further ensured chewy cookies. For our carefully curated selection of mix-ins, we found that toasted pecans and tart dried cherries struck a perfect balance of flavors and textures. You can substitute walnuts or skinned hazelnuts for the pecans and dried cranberries for the cherries. Quick oats can be used in place of the old-fashioned oats, but they will yield a cookie with slightly less chew.

1 Adjust oven racks to upper-middle and lower-middle positions and heat oven to 350 degrees. Line 2 baking sheets with parchment paper. Whisk flour, baking powder, baking soda, and salt together in bowl. Stir oats, pecans, cherries, and chocolate together in second bowl.

2 Using stand mixer fitted with paddle, beat butter and sugar on medium speed until no sugar lumps remain, about 1 minute, scraping down bowl as needed. Reduce speed to medium-low, add egg and vanilla, and beat until fully incorporated, about 30 seconds, scraping down bowl as needed. Reduce speed to low, add flour mixture, and mix until just combined, about 30 seconds. Gradually add oat mixture until just incorporated. Give dough final stir by hand to ensure that no flour pockets remain and ingredients are evenly distributed.

3 Working with ¼ cup dough at a time, roll into balls and space them 2½ inches apart on prepared sheets. Using bottom of greased dry measuring cup, press each ball to 1-inch thickness.

4 Bake cookies until medium brown and edges have begun to set but centers are still soft (cookies will look raw between cracks and seem underdone), 20 to 22 minutes, switching and rotating sheets halfway through baking. Let cookies cool on sheets for 5 minutes, then transfer to wire rack. Let cookies cool completely before serving.

CHOCOLATE CROISSANT COOKIES

MAKES 20 COOKIES

1 cup (5 ounces) all-purpose flour

⅛ teaspoon table salt

8 tablespoons unsalted butter, softened

4 ounces cream cheese, softened

2 tablespoons granulated sugar

½ teaspoon vanilla extract

6 (1.55-ounce) Hershey's milk chocolate bars

1 large egg, lightly beaten

3 tablespoons white sanding sugar

Why This Recipe Works While the appeal of flaky, buttery pastry wrapped around a pocket of rich, creamy chocolate is undeniable, making Chocolate Croissants (page 94) at home is definitely a project. We wanted to capture their essence in an easy-to-prepare cookie form. To achieve the buttery richness of croissants, we started with an equally buttery and rich shortbread dough. The addition of some cream cheese added a subtle tang and made our dough easier to roll out. After we cut the cookie dough into 4 by 2-inch rectangles, we placed a rectangle of milk chocolate in the center and then folded the dough around it so that whole package resembled a mini chocolate croissant. Brushing the cookies with an egg wash and sprinkling them with sanding sugar before baking gave them a professional finish, while a drizzle of melted milk chocolate completed the look. It is essential to use Hershey's milk chocolate bars in this recipe: The cookies were engineered to work with three-rectangle blocks of this iconic chocolate.

1 Whisk flour and salt together in bowl. Using stand mixer fitted with paddle, beat butter, cream cheese, and granulated sugar on medium-high speed until fluffy, about 3 minutes. Add vanilla and beat until incorporated. Reduce speed to low and add flour mixture in 2 additions until just combined, scraping down bowl as needed. Form dough into 6-inch disk. Wrap disk in plastic wrap and refrigerate for at least 1 hour or up to 24 hours.

2 Adjust oven racks to upper-middle and lower-middle positions and heat oven to 350 degrees. Line 2 baking sheets with parchment paper. Break 5 chocolate bars crosswise along their 3 seams to yield 4 rectangles. (You should have 20 chocolate pieces total.) Roll dough into 20 by 8-inch rectangle on lightly floured counter. Cut dough into twenty 4 by 2-inch rectangles. Working with 1 dough rectangle at a time, place 1 chocolate piece crosswise across dough so chocolate overhangs edges and fold dough around chocolate. Place cookies seam side down, 1½ inches apart, on prepared sheets (10 per sheet). Brush with egg and sprinkle with sanding sugar.

3 Bake until cookies are golden brown, 18 to 20 minutes, switching and rotating sheets halfway through baking. Let cookies cool on sheets for 5 minutes, then transfer to wire rack and let cool completely.

4 Break remaining 1 chocolate bar into pieces and microwave in bowl at 50 percent power, stirring occasionally, until melted, about 1 minute. Drizzle chocolate over tops of cookies. Let chocolate set for at least 30 minutes before serving.

ULTIMATE CHOCOLATE CUPCAKES

MAKES 12 CUPCAKES

Why This Recipe Works When it comes to chocolate, a cupcake catch-22 befalls bakery and homemade confections alike: If the cupcakes are packed with enough chocolate to be worthy of their name, their structure usually suffers and they fall apart into a crumbly mess. Conversely, if the cakes strike just the right balance between moisture and tenderness to avoid crumbling, the chocolate flavor is barely discernible. We were loath to compromise the chocolate's intensity, so instead we tried fortifying the structure of the cupcakes, substituting higher-protein bread flour for all-purpose flour. Specifically engineered for gluten development, bread flour turned out a cupcake that was markedly less crumbly yet not tough. But we still needed to reduce the amount of bar chocolate a bit. To compensate, we mixed the bittersweet chocolate and some cocoa powder with hot coffee to intensify their flavors and replaced the butter with neutral-flavored vegetable oil, which allowed the chocolate flavor to dominate. Just a couple teaspoons of distilled white vinegar helped activate the baking soda in our cupcakes without throwing off our carefully constructed ratio of ingredients. For a final bit of decadence, we spooned ganache onto the cupcakes before baking, which sank to the middle for a truffle-like center. Though we highly recommend the ganache filling, you can omit it for a more traditional cupcake.

1 For the filling Microwave chocolate, cream, and sugar in bowl at 50 percent power until mixture is warm to touch, about 30 seconds. Whisk until smooth, then transfer bowl to refrigerator and let sit until filling is just chilled, no longer than 30 minutes.

2 For the cupcakes Adjust oven rack to middle position and heat oven to 350 degrees. Line 12-cup muffin tin with paper or foil liners. Place chocolate and cocoa in large heatproof bowl. Pour hot coffee over mixture and let sit, covered, for 5 minutes. Whisk chocolate mixture gently until smooth, then transfer to refrigerator and let cool completely, about 20 minutes.

3 Whisk flour, sugar, salt, and baking soda together in bowl. Whisk oil, eggs, vinegar, and vanilla into cooled chocolate mixture until smooth. Add flour mixture and whisk until smooth.

4 Divide batter evenly among prepared muffin cups. Place 1 slightly rounded teaspoon filling on top of each portion of batter. Bake cupcakes until set and just firm to touch, 17 to 19 minutes, rotating muffin tin halfway through baking. Let cupcakes cool in muffin tin on wire rack for 10 minutes. Remove cupcakes from muffin tin and let cool completely on rack, about 1 hour. (Unfrosted cupcakes can be stored at room temperature for up to 24 hours.) Spread or pipe frosting evenly on cupcakes. Serve.

FILLING

- 2 ounces bittersweet chocolate, chopped fine
- ¼ cup heavy cream
- 1 tablespoon confectioners' sugar

CUPCAKES

- 3 ounces bittersweet chocolate, chopped fine
- ⅓ cup (1 ounce) unsweetened cocoa powder
- ¾ cup brewed coffee, hot
- ¾ cup (4⅛ ounces) bread flour
- ¾ cup (5¼ ounces) granulated sugar
- ½ teaspoon table salt
- ½ teaspoon baking soda
- 6 tablespoons vegetable oil
- 2 large eggs
- 2 teaspoons distilled white vinegar
- 1 teaspoon vanilla extract

- 3 cups Chocolate Buttercream (page 346)

BLACK-BOTTOM CUPCAKES

MAKES 24 CUPCAKES

1 pound cream cheese, softened

1¾ cups (12¼ ounces) sugar, divided

¾ teaspoon table salt, divided

2 large egg whites, room temperature

2 tablespoons plus ¾ cup sour cream, room temperature, divided

⅓ cup (2 ounces) mini semisweet chocolate chips

1½ cups (7½ ounces) all-purpose flour

½ cup (1½ ounces) Dutch-processed cocoa powder

1¼ teaspoons baking soda

1⅓ cups water

8 tablespoons unsalted butter, melted and slightly cooled

1 teaspoon vanilla extract

Why This Recipe Works Black-bottom cupcakes are best known—and loved—for their creamy centers of tangy cheesecake studded with chocolate chips. But all too often the cupcake itself is neglected and devoid of rich chocolate flavor. We wanted cake with big chocolate flavor that would be sturdy enough to support the cheesecake filling. The cake portion of black-bottom cupcakes traditionally gets its color and chocolate flavor from cocoa powder. A mere ½ cup was all we needed, and using Dutch-processed cocoa rather than natural cocoa deepened the color and boosted the flavor further. Adding a little sour cream to the batter accentuated the chocolate and added richness. Black-bottom cupcakes are usually made with oil, but we used melted butter instead to make our cupcakes appealingly dense and fudgy; it also gave them enough structure to support the filling. With our tangy cheesecake center, you can forget about frosting. Do not substitute regular chocolate chips for the miniature chips; regular chips are much heavier and will sink to the bottom of the cupcakes.

1 Adjust oven racks to upper-middle and lower-middle positions and heat oven to 400 degrees. Line two 12-cup muffin tins with paper or foil liners. Using stand mixer fitted with paddle, beat cream cheese, ½ cup sugar, and ¼ teaspoon salt on medium speed until smooth, about 30 seconds. Beat in egg whites and 2 tablespoons sour cream until combined, about 30 seconds. Stir in chocolate chips and set aside.

2 Whisk flour, cocoa, baking soda, remaining 1¼ cups sugar, and remaining ½ teaspoon salt together in large bowl. Whisk in water, melted butter, vanilla, and remaining ¾ cup sour cream until just combined.

3 Divide batter evenly among prepared muffin cups and top each with 1 rounded tablespoon cream cheese mixture. Bake until tops of cupcakes just begin to crack, 23 to 25 minutes, switching and rotating muffin tins halfway through baking. Let cupcakes cool in muffin tins on wire rack for 10 minutes. Remove cupcakes from muffin tins and let cool completely before serving. (Cupcakes can be refrigerated for up to 2 days.)

VEGAN DARK CHOCOLATE CUPCAKES

MAKES 12 CUPCAKES

Why This Recipe Works Dark chocolate cupcakes should be rich and tender and feature deep chocolate flavor. To make vegan cupcakes that fit this description, we relied on aquafaba, the liquid found in canned chickpeas, in place of egg whites; whipped to stiff peaks and folded into the batter, it gave our cupcakes a light, fluffy crumb. Creating complex chocolate flavor was easily achieved with bittersweet chocolate. But when we added enough to satisfy our chocolate craving, the cupcakes developed a chalky texture. To fortify the flavor without overloading our cupcakes with the cocoa butter that gave us that chalky texture, we replaced some of the chocolate with a generous ½ cup of cocoa powder, which kept our cupcakes tender. Use organic sugar if you're a strict vegan. Not all brands of bittersweet chocolate are vegan, so check ingredient lists carefully. For an accurate measurement of aquafaba, start by shaking the unopened can of chickpeas well. Drain the chickpeas though a fine mesh strainer over a bowl and reserve the beans for another use. Whisk the aquafaba liquid and then measure out the desired amount. Do not use the liquid from Progresso brand chickpeas; we found it does not consistently reach a foam. Do not use the liquid from chickpeas cooked at home. These cupcakes are best served the day they're made.

1⅓ cups (6⅔ ounces) all-purpose flour

1 cup (7 ounces) sugar

¾ teaspoon baking powder

¼ teaspoon baking soda

½ teaspoon table salt

1 cup water

½ cup (1½ ounces) unsweetened cocoa powder

1 ounce bittersweet chocolate, chopped

¼ cup coconut oil

¾ teaspoon vanilla extract

¼ cup aquafaba

1 teaspoon cream of tartar

2 cups Creamy Vegan Chocolate Frosting (page 347)

1 Adjust oven rack to middle position and heat oven to 400 degrees. Line 12-cup muffin tin with paper or foil liners. Whisk flour, sugar, baking powder, baking soda, and salt together in large bowl.

2 Microwave water, cocoa, chocolate, oil, and vanilla in second bowl at 50 percent power, whisking occasionally, until melted and smooth, about 2 minutes; set aside to cool slightly.

3 Meanwhile, using stand mixer fitted with whisk attachment, whip aquafaba and cream of tartar on high speed until stiff foam that clings to whisk forms, 3 to 9 minutes. Using rubber spatula, stir chocolate mixture into flour mixture until batter is thoroughly combined and smooth (batter will be thick). Stir one-third of whipped aquafaba into batter to lighten, then gently fold in remaining aquafaba until no white streaks remain.

4 Divide batter evenly among prepared muffin cups. Bake until tops are set and spring back when pressed lightly, 16 to 20 minutes, rotating muffin tin halfway through baking. Let cupcakes cool in muffin tin on wire rack for 10 minutes. Remove cupcakes from muffin tin and let cool completely on rack, about 1 hour. Spread frosting evenly on cupcakes. Serve.

FUDGY BROWNIES

MAKES 36 BROWNIES

5 ounces bittersweet or semisweet chocolate, chopped

2 ounces unsweetened chocolate, chopped

8 tablespoons unsalted butter, cut into 4 pieces

3 tablespoons unsweetened cocoa powder

1¼ cups (8¾ ounces) sugar

3 large eggs

2 teaspoons vanilla extract

½ teaspoon table salt

1 cup (5 ounces) all-purpose flour

Why This Recipe Works Brownies are a controversial territory to chart: Some like them cakey and light in flavor—more of a snack than a rich dessert; some like them moist and chewy; and others, the biggest chocoholics, like them to be purely decadent—almost as dense as fudge and deliciously dark. We wanted to make sinfully rich brownies that would be a chocolate lover's dream, so we started by using three forms of chocolate: unsweetened chocolate for intensity, cocoa powder for complexity, and bittersweet or semisweet chocolate for moisture and well-rounded flavor. Melting butter along with the chocolate was the key to a fudgy texture, and a generous three eggs contributed richness and structure. In addition to providing a clean sweetness, granulated sugar gave the baked brownies a delicate, shiny, crackly top crust. We found it best to cut these brownies into small bites rather than big bake-sale squares—a little goes a long way. Tasters preferred the more complex flavor of bittersweet chocolate over semisweet, but either type works well here, as does 5 ounces of bittersweet or semisweet chocolate chips in place of the bar chocolate. Be sure to use a metal baking pan and not a glass baking dish in this recipe.

1 Adjust oven rack to middle position and heat oven to 350 degrees. Make foil sling for 8-inch square baking pan by folding 2 long sheets of aluminum foil so each is 8 inches wide. Lay sheets of foil in pan perpendicular to each other, with extra foil hanging over edges of pan. Push foil into corners and up sides of pan, smoothing foil flush to pan. Grease foil.

2 Microwave bittersweet and unsweetened chocolates in bowl at 50 percent power for 2 minutes. Stir in butter and continue to microwave, stirring often, until melted and smooth. Whisk in cocoa and let mixture cool slightly.

3 Whisk sugar, eggs, vanilla, and salt in large bowl until combined. Whisk chocolate mixture into sugar mixture until smooth. Using rubber spatula, stir in flour until no dry streaks remain. Transfer batter to prepared pan and smooth top. Bake until toothpick inserted in center comes out with few moist crumbs attached, 35 to 40 minutes, rotating pan halfway through baking.

4 Let brownies cool completely in pan on wire rack, about 2 hours. Using foil overhang, remove brownies from pan. (Uncut brownies can be refrigerated for up to 3 days.) Cut into 36 pieces. Serve.

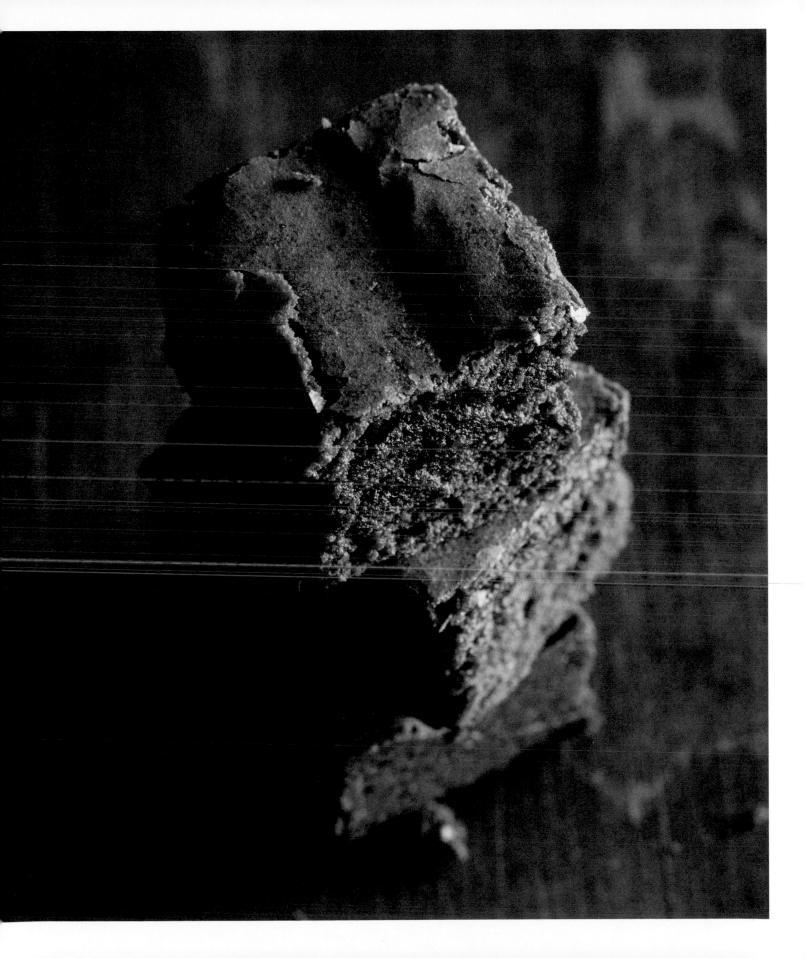

VEGAN FUDGY BROWNIES

MAKES 24 BROWNIES

Why This Recipe Works Chewy, fudgy, ultrachocolaty brownies take little work for an immensely satisfying reward. Could we make decadent brownies without butter and eggs? Happily, we found we could whip up a batch of fudgy vegan brownies just as easily as we do conventional ones. Neutral-flavored vegetable oil was a quick swap for the butter. We typically don't add chemical leavener to a fudgy brownie; however, we found that a small amount of baking powder gave our brownies the perfect amount of lift and structure and eliminated the need to find a replacement for eggs. A combination of unsweetened chocolate and cocoa powder—bloomed in boiling water to unlock their flavor compounds—contributed intensity. Finally, a scattering of chocolate chips created pockets of gooey goodness. Use organic sugar if you're a strict vegan. Not all chocolate chips are vegan, so check ingredient lists carefully. It's important to let the brownies cool thoroughly before cutting. For an accurate measurement of boiling water, bring a full kettle of water to a boil and then measure out the desired amount. Be sure to use a metal baking pan and not a glass baking dish in this recipe.

2 cups (10 ounces) all-purpose flour

1 teaspoon baking powder

¾ teaspoon table salt

1 cup boiling water

3 ounces unsweetened chocolate, chopped fine

¾ cup (2¼ ounces) unsweetened cocoa powder

1½ teaspoons instant espresso powder (optional)

2½ cups (17½ ounces) sugar

½ cup vegetable oil

1 tablespoon vanilla extract

½ cup (3 ounces) bittersweet or semisweet chocolate chips

1 Adjust oven rack to lowest position and heat oven to 350 degrees. Make foil sling for 13 by 9-inch baking pan by folding 2 long sheets of aluminum foil; first sheet should be 13 inches wide and second sheet should be 9 inches wide. Lay sheets of foil in pan perpendicular to each other, with extra foil hanging over edges of pan. Push foil into corners and up sides of pan, smoothing foil flush to pan. Grease foil.

2 Whisk flour, baking powder, and salt together in bowl. Whisk boiling water; unsweetened chocolate; cocoa; and espresso powder, if using, in large bowl until well combined and chocolate is melted. Whisk in sugar, oil, and vanilla. Using rubber spatula, stir flour mixture into chocolate mixture until combined; fold in chocolate chips.

3 Scrape batter into prepared pan and smooth top. Bake until toothpick inserted halfway between edge and center comes out with few moist crumbs attached, 30 to 35 minutes, rotating pan halfway through baking. Let brownies cool in pan on wire rack for 2 hours.

4 Using foil overhang, lift brownies from pan. Return brownies to wire rack and let cool completely, about 1 hour. Cut into 24 pieces. Serve. (Brownies can be stored at room temperature for up to 4 days.)

CHEWY BROWNIES

MAKES 24 BROWNIES

⅓ cup (1 ounce) unsweetened cocoa powder

1½ teaspoons instant espresso powder (optional)

½ cup plus 2 tablespoons boiling water

2 ounces unsweetened chocolate, chopped fine

½ cup plus 2 tablespoons vegetable oil

4 tablespoons unsalted butter, melted

2 large eggs plus 2 large yolks

2 teaspoons vanilla extract

2½ cups (17½ ounces) sugar

1¾ cups (8¾ ounces) all-purpose flour

¾ teaspoon table salt

6 ounces bittersweet chocolate, cut into ½-inch pieces

Why This Recipe Works While box-mix brownies may not offer superior chocolate flavor, there's no denying their chewy appeal. We were determined to crack the code for perfectly chewy brownies, and while we were at it we wanted to amp up this crowd-pleaser's chocolate allure. In terms of chewiness, we discovered that the key was fat—specifically, the right proportions of saturated and unsaturated fats. After much testing, we decided that an almost 1:3 ratio of saturated fat (butter) to unsaturated fat (vegetable oil) produced the chewiest brownies. Two whole eggs plus two extra yolks emulsified the batter, preventing the brownies from turning greasy. For full, well-rounded chocolate flavor, we whisked unsweetened cocoa, along with a little espresso powder, into boiling water and then stirred in unsweetened chocolate. The heat unlocked the chocolate's flavor compounds, boosting its impact. Chunks of bittersweet chocolate, folded in before baking, provided a final boost of chocolate intensity. For the chewiest texture, it's important to let the brownies cool thoroughly before cutting. For an accurate measurement of boiling water, bring a full kettle of water to a boil and then measure out the desired amount. Be sure to use a metal baking pan and not a glass baking dish in this recipe.

1 Adjust oven rack to lowest position and heat oven to 350 degrees. Make foil sling for 13 by 9-inch baking pan by folding 2 long sheets of aluminum foil; first sheet should be 13 inches wide and second sheet should be 9 inches wide. Lay sheets of foil in pan perpendicular to each other, with extra foil hanging over edges of pan. Push foil into corners and up sides of pan, smoothing foil flush to pan. Grease foil.

2 Whisk cocoa; espresso powder, if using; and boiling water in large bowl until smooth. Add unsweetened chocolate and whisk until chocolate is melted. Whisk in oil and melted butter (mixture may look curdled). Whisk in eggs and yolks and vanilla until smooth and homogeneous. Whisk in sugar until fully incorporated. Using rubber spatula, stir in flour and salt until combined. Fold in bittersweet chocolate.

3 Transfer batter to prepared pan and smooth top. Bake until toothpick inserted halfway between edge and center comes out with few moist crumbs attached, 30 to 35 minutes, rotating pan halfway through baking. Let brownies cool in pan on wire rack for 1½ hours. Using foil overhang, remove brownies from pan. Transfer to wire rack and let cool completely, about 1 hour. Cut into 24 pieces. (Brownies can be stored at room temperature for up to 4 days.)

S'MORES BROWNIES

MAKES 16 BROWNIES

Why This Recipe Works We can never get enough s'more-themed desserts and loved the idea of incorporating the components of the campfire treat into a multilayered brownie. We knew the base needed to be sturdy enough to support a hefty topping, and a crust made from crushed graham crackers, butter, and a bit of sugar fit the bill; parbaking it ensured it wouldn't turn soggy once the other layers were added. Next we assembled a basic brownie batter made with unsweetened chocolate which we spread on top of the crust. Once baked, we topped our brownie layer with marshmallows and ran the pan under the broiler until the marshmallows were gooey and kissed with a toasty-brown top. The crisp cracker base, decadent chocolate brownie "filling," and soft toasted marshmallow top gave us the best of this summertime treat in one tidy package. Be sure to use a metal baking pan and not a glass baking dish in this recipe.

1 Adjust oven rack to middle position and heat oven to 350 degrees. Make foil sling for 8-inch square baking pan by folding 2 long sheets of aluminum foil so each is 8 inches wide. Lay sheets of foil in pan perpendicular to each other, with extra foil hanging over edges of pan. Push foil into corners and up sides of pan, smoothing foil flush to pan. Grease foil.

2 **For the crust** Using your fingers, combine graham cracker crumbs, melted butter, and sugar in bowl until evenly moistened. Sprinkle mixture into prepared pan and press firmly into even layer. Bake until firm and lightly browned, 8 to 10 minutes; set aside.

3 **For the brownies** While crust is baking, microwave butter and chocolate in bowl at 50 percent power, stirring often, until melted and smooth, 1 to 3 minutes; let cool slightly.

4 Whisk flour, baking powder, and salt together in second bowl. Whisk sugar, eggs, and vanilla together in large bowl. Whisk chocolate mixture into sugar mixture until combined. Using rubber spatula, stir in flour mixture until just incorporated.

5 Transfer batter to pan with crust and smooth top. Bake until toothpick inserted in center comes out with few moist crumbs attached, 22 to 27 minutes, rotating pan halfway through baking. Remove pan from oven and heat broiler.

6 Sprinkle brownies evenly with single layer of marshmallows. Return brownies to oven and broil until marshmallows are lightly browned, 1 to 3 minutes. (Watch oven constantly; marshmallows will melt slightly but should hold their shape.) Immediately remove pan from oven. Let brownies cool completely in pan on wire rack, about 2 hours.

7 Using foil overhang, remove brownies from pan. Slide foil out from under brownies. Spray knife with vegetable oil spray to prevent marshmallows from sticking. Cut into 16 squares. Serve.

CRUST

- 6 whole graham crackers, crushed into crumbs (¾ cup)
- 4 tablespoons unsalted butter, melted
- 1 tablespoon sugar

BROWNIES

- 8 tablespoons unsalted butter
- 3 ounces unsweetened chocolate, chopped
- ⅔ cup (3⅓ ounces) all-purpose flour
- ½ teaspoon baking powder
- ¼ teaspoon table salt
- 1 cup (7 ounces) sugar
- 2 large eggs
- 1 teaspoon vanilla extract
- 2 cups miniature marshmallows

ULTIMATE TURTLE BROWNIES

MAKES 25 BROWNIES

CARAMEL

- 6 tablespoons heavy cream
- ¼ teaspoon table salt
- ¼ cup water
- 2 tablespoons light corn syrup
- 1¼ cups (8¾ ounces) sugar
- 2 tablespoons unsalted butter
- 1 teaspoon vanilla extract

BROWNIES

- 8 tablespoons unsalted butter, cut into 8 pieces
- 4 ounces bittersweet chocolate, chopped
- 2 ounces unsweetened chocolate, chopped
- ¾ cup (3¾ ounces) all-purpose flour
- ½ teaspoon baking powder
- 2 large eggs, room temperature
- 1 cup (7 ounces) sugar
- 2 teaspoons vanilla extract
- ¼ teaspoon table salt
- ⅔ cup chopped pecans, plus 25 toasted pecan halves, divided
- ⅓ cup (2 ounces) semisweet chocolate chips (optional)

Why This Recipe Works Dark chocolate brownies, rich caramel, and crunchy pecans—this irresistible combination featured in turtle brownies is hard to beat. But many recipes for this treat call for box mixes and jarred caramel sauce; unsurprisingly, these shortcuts yield lackluster and sickly sweet results. For brownies that were reminiscent of the classic turtle candy, we started with a basic recipe: Whole eggs, a modest amount of flour, and baking powder gave us brownies with a structure that was partway between cakey and chewy—perfect for supporting a blanket of caramel. A combination of bittersweet and unsweetened chocolate struck just the right balance. Garnishing each brownie with a pecan half made them look like turtles, but they didn't taste like turtles until we stirred chopped pecans into the brownie batter as well. We wanted a thick, shiny caramel that wouldn't drip off the brownies—but that also wouldn't tug at our teeth. Caramel made with cream, butter, and sugar was pleasantly chewy and gooey, and a little corn syrup prevented it from crystallizing. Swirling some caramel into the batter and pouring more over the top ensured plenty of rich, gooey caramel in every bite. If the caramel is too cool to be fluid, reheat it in the microwave. Be sure to use a metal baking pan and not a glass baking dish in this recipe.

1 For the caramel Combine cream and salt in small bowl; stir well to dissolve salt. Combine water and corn syrup in medium saucepan; pour sugar into center of saucepan, taking care not to let sugar granules touch sides of saucepan. Gently stir with spatula to moisten sugar thoroughly. Cover and bring to boil over medium-high heat and cook, covered and without stirring, until sugar is completely dissolved and liquid is clear, 3 to 5 minutes. Uncover and continue to cook, without stirring, until bubbles show faint golden color, 3 to 5 minutes longer. Reduce heat to medium-low and continue to cook (swirling saucepan occasionally) until caramel is light amber and registers about 360 degrees, 1 to 3 minutes longer. Off heat, carefully add cream mixture to center of saucepan; stir (mixture will bubble and steam vigorously) until cream is fully incorporated and bubbling subsides. Stir in butter and vanilla until combined. Transfer caramel to liquid measuring cup or bowl; set aside.

2 For the brownies Adjust oven rack to lower-middle position and heat oven to 325 degrees. Make foil sling for 9-inch square baking pan by folding 2 long sheets of aluminum foil so each is 9 inches wide. Lay sheets of foil in pan perpendicular to each other, with extra foil hanging over edges of pan. Push foil into corners and up sides of pan, smoothing foil flush to pan. Grease foil.

3 Microwave butter, bittersweet chocolate, and unsweetened chocolate in bowl at 50 percent power, stirring occasionally, until melted and smooth, 2 to 4 minutes; set aside and let cool slightly. Meanwhile, whisk flour and baking powder together in second bowl; set aside. Whisk eggs in large bowl to combine; add sugar, vanilla, and salt and whisk until incorporated. Add cooled chocolate mixture to egg mixture and whisk until combined. Using rubber spatula, stir in flour mixture until almost combined. Stir in chopped pecans and chocolate chips, if using, until incorporated and no flour streaks remain.

4 Spread half of brownie batter in even layer in prepared pan. Using greased ¼-cup dry measuring cup, drizzle ¼ cup caramel over batter. Using spoon, dollop remaining batter in large mounds over caramel layer and spread into even layer. Using butter knife, swirl brownie batter through caramel. Bake until toothpick inserted in center comes out with few moist crumbs attached, 35 to 40 minutes, rotating pan halfway through baking. Let brownies cool completely in pan on wire rack, about 1½ hours.

5 Heat remaining caramel (you should have about ¾ cup) in microwave until warm and pourable but still thick (do not boil), 45 to 60 seconds, stirring once or twice; pour caramel over brownies. Spread caramel to cover surface. Refrigerate brownies, uncovered, for 2 hours.

6 Using foil overhang, remove brownies from pan, loosening sides with paring knife if needed. Using chef's knife, cut brownies into 25 pieces. Press pecan half onto surface of each brownie. Serve chilled or at room temperature. (Brownies can be refrigerated for up to 3 days.)

OATMEAL FUDGE BARS

MAKES 16 BARS

Why This Recipe Works Bar cookies have obvious appeal: They're convenient, easy to transport, and are a platform for displaying multiple delicious layers of flavor. These bars, featuring three distinct layers, are no different: They start with an oatmeal-laced, shortbread-like crust which is followed by a fudgy middle and then finished with a streusel crumb topping. For the shortbread base (which also doubles as the topping), we tried standard, old-fashioned rolled oats, but the resulting crust was hard and crunchy—not what we were looking for here. Replacing the old-fashioned oats with quick oats created a chewy texture, as did swapping out the granulated sugar for brown sugar; plus, the brown sugar's molasses notes played well with the oats. We didn't want to simply fill these bars with chocolate; we wanted a fudgy and dense yet plush, almost custardy, middle. Semisweet chocolate boosted with instant espresso provided plenty of chocolate flavor, and brown sugar again provided a subtle complexity. A scant amount of flour and an egg bound the filling and achieved the sliceable texture we were looking for. Be sure to cool the crust completely before adding the filling in step 5.

1 For the crust and topping Adjust oven rack to middle position and heat oven to 325 degrees. Make foil sling for 8-inch square baking pan by folding 2 long sheets of aluminum foil so each is 8 inches wide. Lay sheets of foil in pan perpendicular to each other, with extra foil hanging over edges of pan. Push foil into corners and up sides of pan, smoothing foil flush to pan. Grease foil.

2 Whisk oats, sugar, flour, baking powder, baking soda, and salt together in large bowl. Stir in melted butter until combined. Reserve ¾ cup oat mixture for topping.

3 Sprinkle remaining oat mixture into prepared pan and press into even layer. Bake until light golden brown, about 8 minutes. Let crust cool completely on wire rack, about 1 hour.

4 For the filling Whisk flour, sugar, espresso powder, and salt together in bowl. Microwave chocolate chips and butter in large bowl at 50 percent power, stirring often, until melted and smooth, 1 to 3 minutes. Let cool slightly. Whisk in egg until combined. Stir in flour mixture until just incorporated.

5 Transfer filling to cooled crust and spread into even layer. Sprinkle evenly with reserved oat topping. Bake until toothpick inserted in center comes out with few moist crumbs attached and filling begins to pull away from sides of pan, 25 to 30 minutes, rotating pan halfway through baking.

6 Let bars cool completely in pan on wire rack, about 2 hours. Using foil overhang, remove bars from pan. Cut into 16 pieces. Serve. (Bars can be refrigerated for up to 3 days.)

CRUST AND TOPPING

- 1 cup (3 ounces) quick-cooking oats
- 1 cup packed (7 ounces) light brown sugar
- ¾ cup (3¾ ounces) all-purpose flour
- ¼ teaspoon baking powder
- ¼ teaspoon baking soda
- ⅛ teaspoon table salt
- 8 tablespoons unsalted butter, melted and cooled

FILLING

- ¼ cup (1¼ ounces) all-purpose flour
- ¼ cup packed (1¾ ounces) light brown sugar
- 2 teaspoons instant espresso powder or instant coffee powder
- ¼ teaspoon table salt
- 1½ cups (9 ounces) semisweet chocolate chips
- 2 tablespoons unsalted butter
- 1 large egg

WHITE CHOCOLATE RASPBERRY BARS

MAKES 16 BARS

1 cup (5 ounces) all-purpose flour

1 teaspoon baking powder

¼ teaspoon table salt

6 ounces white chocolate, divided

4 tablespoons unsalted butter, softened

½ cup (3½ ounces) plus 2 teaspoons sugar, divided

1 large egg

1 teaspoon vanilla extract

5 ounces (1 cup) raspberries

Why This Recipe Works Bittersweet chocolate shouldn't have a monopoly on bar cookies. When stirred into batter and baked, white chocolate infuses these blondie-like bars with a complex, buttery, caramelized flavor that gives dark chocolate brownies a run for their money. These white chocolate bars are satisfyingly chewy—the way a good bar cookie should be—without being heavy. We used just enough white chocolate for a moist, rich-tasting bar but not so much that it was cloyingly sweet. Juicy, bright raspberries are a perfect foil to the silky, mild sweetness of white chocolate, so we punctuated these bars with whole fresh berries. Tossing the raspberries with a little sugar before pressing them into the batter encouraged them to roast and caramelize and tempered their tartness a bit. Baking these bars at a slightly higher temperature than most brownie recipes call for—375 degrees instead of 350—resulted in beautifully browned edges that further enhanced the caramel notes. An elegant drizzle of white chocolate provided just the right finishing touch to these dressed-up bars.

1 Adjust oven rack to middle position and heat oven to 375 degrees. Make foil sling for 8-inch square baking pan by folding 2 long sheets of aluminum foil so each is 8 inches wide. Lay sheets of foil in pan perpendicular to each other, with extra foil hanging over edges of pan. Push foil into corners and up sides of pan, smoothing foil flush to pan. Grease foil.

2 Whisk flour, baking powder, and salt together in bowl. Roughly chop 3 ounces chocolate and microwave in second bowl at 50 percent power, stirring often, until melted, about 1 minute. Chop remaining 3 ounces chocolate into ½-inch pieces.

3 Using stand mixer fitted with paddle, beat butter and ½ cup sugar on medium-high speed until pale and fluffy, about 3 minutes. Add egg and vanilla and beat until combined. Add melted chocolate and mix until incorporated, about 30 seconds. Reduce speed to low and slowly add flour mixture until combined, about 45 seconds. Stir in all but 2 tablespoons chopped chocolate.

4 Transfer batter to prepared pan and spread into even layer. Toss raspberries with remaining 2 teaspoons sugar to coat and gently press into batter, spacing evenly apart. Bake until edges are puffed and golden and toothpick inserted in center comes out with few moist crumbs attached, 25 to 35 minutes, rotating pan halfway through baking.

5 Let bars cool completely in pan on wire rack, about 2 hours. Using foil overhang, remove bars from pan. Microwave reserved 2 tablespoons chocolate in bowl at 50 percent power, stirring occasionally, until melted, about 45 seconds. Drizzle melted chocolate over bars. Cut into 16 pieces and let chocolate set, about 30 minutes, before serving.

MILLIONAIRE'S SHORTBREAD

MAKES 40 BARS

Why This Recipe Works Millionaire's shortbread is a fitting name for this rich British cookie/confectionery hybrid that features a crunchy shortbread base; a chewy, caramel-like filling; and a shiny, snappy chocolate top. We started by making a quick short-bread with melted butter. Sweetened condensed milk was important to the flavor of the filling, and some fresh cream prevented it from breaking. We used our microwave tempering technique (for more information see page 14) for the chocolate topping, and calling for half a pound of bittersweet ensured the chocolate layer would be more than just an afterthought for this rich yet refined cookie.

1 **For the crust** Adjust oven rack to lower-middle position and heat oven to 350 degrees. Make foil sling for 13 by 9-inch baking pan by folding 2 long sheets of aluminum foil; first sheet should be 13 inches wide, and second sheet should be 9 inches wide. Lay sheets of foil in pan perpendicular to each other, with extra foil hanging over edges of pan. Push foil into corners and up sides of pan, smoothing foil flush to pan.

2 Combine flour, sugar, and salt in bowl. Add melted butter and stir with rubber spatula until flour is evenly moistened. Crumble dough evenly over bottom of prepared pan. Using your fingertips and palm of your hand, press and smooth dough into even thickness. Using fork, pierce dough at 1-inch intervals. Bake until light golden brown and firm to touch, 25 to 30 minutes. Transfer pan to wire rack. Using sturdy metal spatula, press on entire surface of warm crust to compress (this will make finished bars easier to cut). Let crust cool until just warm, at least 20 minutes.

3 **For the filling** Stir all ingredients together in large, heavy-bottomed saucepan. Cook over medium heat, stirring frequently, until mixture registers between 236 and 239 degrees (temperature will fluctuate), 16 to 20 minutes. Pour over crust and spread to even thickness (mixture will be very hot). Let cool completely, about 1½ hours.

4 **For the chocolate** Microwave finely chopped chocolate in bowl at 50 percent power, stirring often, until about two-thirds melted, 1 to 2 minutes. (Melted chocolate should not be much warmer than body temperature; check by holding bowl in palm of your hand.) Add grated chocolate and stir until smooth, returning to microwave for no more than 5 seconds at a time to finish melting if necessary. Spread chocolate evenly over surface of filling. Refrigerate shortbread until chocolate is just set, about 10 minutes.

5 Using foil overhang, remove shortbread from pan. Using serrated knife and gentle sawing motion, cut shortbread in half crosswise to create two 6½ by 9-inch rectangles. Cut each rectangle in half to make four 3¼ by 9-inch strips. Cut each strip crosswise into 10 equal pieces. Serve. (Shortbread can be stored at room temperature, between layers of parchment, for up to 1 week.)

CRUST

- 2½ cups (12½ ounces) all-purpose flour
- ½ cup (3½ ounces) granulated sugar
- ¾ teaspoon table salt
- 16 tablespoons unsalted butter, melted

FILLING

- 1 (14-ounce) can sweetened condensed milk
- 1 cup packed (7 ounces) brown sugar
- ½ cup heavy cream
- ½ cup corn syrup
- 8 tablespoons unsalted butter
- ½ teaspoon table salt

CHOCOLATE

- 8 ounces bittersweet chocolate (6 ounces chopped fine, 2 ounces grated), divided

MILK CHOCOLATE REVEL BARS

MAKES 24 BARS

3 cups (9 ounces) old-fashioned rolled oats

2 cups (10 ounces) all-purpose flour

1½ cups packed (10½ ounces) brown sugar

1 cup raw whole almonds, chopped

1 teaspoon baking soda

1¼ teaspoons table salt, divided

16 tablespoons unsalted butter, melted, plus 2 tablespoons unsalted butter, divided

2 large eggs

2 teaspoons vanilla extract

2 cups (12 ounces) milk chocolate chips

1 cup sweetened condensed milk

Why This Recipe Works Chocolate revel bars are a nostalgic treat featuring a layer of rich, dreamy chocolate filling sandwiched between an oatmeal cookie base and a crumbly topping. But making a three-layer bar cookie can be a trying process, one that involves assembling and baking the dessert in stages. We wanted a revel bar we could put together all at once and bake in one go. To streamline the process, we made our dough work double duty by using it to form both the sturdy base and the crumbly topping. A combination of oats and almonds gave these bars a simultaneously chewy and crunchy texture. Turning our attention to the creamy fudge filling, we settled on using milk chocolate chips, which provided the familiar chocolaty sweetness we craved. To the chocolate chips we added sweetened condensed milk and butter for a filling that was easy to incorporate and both sliceable and fudgy. Best of all, these three-layered treats required only one trip to the oven. If all you can find is an 11.5-ounce bag of chocolate chips, there's no need to buy a second bag to make up the extra ½ ounce.

1 Adjust oven rack to middle position and heat oven to 350 degrees. Make foil sling for 13 by 9-inch baking pan by folding 2 long sheets of aluminum foil; first sheet should be 13 inches wide and second sheet should be 9 inches wide. Lay sheets of foil in pan perpendicular to each other, with extra foil hanging over edges of pan. Push foil into corners and up sides of pan, smoothing foil flush to pan. Grease foil.

2 Combine oats, flour, sugar, almonds, baking soda, and 1 teaspoon salt in large bowl. Whisk melted butter, eggs, and vanilla together in second bowl. Stir butter mixture into flour mixture until dough forms. Set aside 1½ cups dough for topping. Press remaining dough into even layer in bottom of prepared pan.

3 Microwave chocolate chips, condensed milk, remaining ¼ teaspoon salt, and remaining 2 tablespoons butter in bowl at 50 percent power, stirring occasionally, until melted and smooth, 2 to 4 minutes. (Mixture will resemble thick fudge.)

4 Transfer chocolate mixture to pan and spread evenly over crust to sides of pan. Crumble reserved dough and sprinkle pieces evenly over chocolate mixture. Bake until topping is golden brown, about 30 minutes, rotating pan halfway through baking. Transfer pan to wire rack and let bars cool until set, about 6 hours. Using foil overhang, remove bars from pan. Cut into 24 pieces. Serve.

DOUBLE CHOCOLATE ÉCLAIRS

MAKES 8 ÉCLAIRS

PASTRY CREAM

2 cups half-and-half

½ cup (3½ ounces) granulated sugar, divided

Pinch table salt

5 large egg yolks

3 tablespoons cornstarch

4 tablespoons unsalted butter, cut into 4 pieces

2 ounces bittersweet chocolate, chopped fine

½ teaspoon vanilla extract

PASTRY

2 large eggs plus 1 large white

6 tablespoons water

5 tablespoons unsalted butter, cut into 10 pieces

2 tablespoons whole milk

1½ teaspoons granulated sugar

¼ teaspoon table salt

½ cup (2½ ounces) all-purpose flour, sifted

GLAZE

2 ounces semisweet or bittersweet chocolate, chopped fine

3 tablespoons half-and-half

1 cup (4 ounces) confectioners' sugar

Why This Recipe Works We wanted our éclairs to feature a double dose of chocolate, so we planned to incorporate it not only into the glaze but also the pastry cream. Using a pastry bag to pipe our pate a choux onto the baking sheet ensured evenly sized pastries. Once baked, we cut a small slit into each pastry and returned them to the turned-off oven until the centers were moist and the surface was crisp. Adding a couple ounces of bittersweet chocolate to a basic pastry cream ensured chocolaty goodness throughout. A decadent chocolate glaze covered the holes we made to fill our pastries with the chocolate cream. Be sure the pastry cream is thoroughly chilled before filling the pastries. The chocolate glaze should still be warm when glazing the éclairs. You will need a large pastry bag with a ½-inch plain tip and a ¼-inch plain tip.

1 **For the pastry cream** Bring half-and-half, 6 tablespoons sugar, and salt to simmer in medium saucepan over medium-high heat, stirring occasionally.

2 Meanwhile, whisk egg yolks, cornstarch, and remaining 2 tablespoons sugar together in bowl until smooth. Slowly whisk 1 cup of hot half-and-half mixture into egg mixture to temper, then slowly whisk tempered egg mixture into remaining half-and-half mixture in saucepan. Reduce heat to medium and cook, whisking constantly, until mixture is thickened, smooth, and registers 180 degrees, about 30 seconds. Off heat, whisk in butter, chocolate, and vanilla. Transfer pastry cream to clean bowl and press plastic wrap directly on surface. Refrigerate until cold and set, at least 3 hours or up to 2 days.

3 **For the pastry** Adjust oven rack to middle position and heat oven to 400 degrees. Line rimmed baking sheet with parchment paper.

4 Beat eggs and white in 2-cup liquid measuring cup until well combined. (You should have about ½ cup egg mixture. Discard excess.) Set aside. Bring water, butter, milk, sugar, and salt to boil in small saucepan over medium heat. Remove from heat and stir in flour until incorporated and mixture clears sides of saucepan. Return saucepan to low heat and cook, stirring constantly using smearing motion, until paste is slightly shiny with wet-sand appearance and tiny beads of fat appear on bottom of saucepan, about 3 minutes (mixture should register 175 to 180 degrees).

5 Immediately transfer hot paste to food processor and process with feed tube open for 5 seconds to cool slightly. With processor running, gradually add reserved egg mixture in steady stream until incorporated. Scrape down sides of bowl and continue to process until smooth, thick, sticky paste forms, about 30 seconds longer.

6 Fit pastry bag with ½-inch plain tip and fill with warm pate a choux. Pipe pate a choux into eight 5 by 1-inch logs spaced about 1 inch apart on prepared sheet. Use your dampened finger or back of wet teaspoon to even out shape and smooth surface of each log.

7 Bake for 15 minutes (do not open oven door), then reduce oven temperature to 350 degrees and continue to bake until pastries are golden brown and fairly firm (pastries should not be soft and squishy), 8 to 10 minutes longer.

8 Remove sheet from oven. Using paring knife, cut ¾-inch slit into side of each pastry to release steam. Return pastries to oven, turn off oven, and prop door open with handle of wooden spoon. Dry pastries in turned-off oven until centers are just moist (not wet) and surfaces are crisp, about 45 minutes. Transfer pastries to wire rack and let cool completely, about 30 minutes.

9 **For the glaze** Using tip of paring knife, cut 3 small Xs along top of each pastry. Fit clean pastry bag with ¼-inch plain tip and fill pastry bag with pastry cream. Pipe pastry cream into pastries through each opening until éclairs are completely filled.

10 Microwave chocolate in bowl at 50 percent power until melted, about 30 seconds. Whisk in half-and-half until smooth. Gradually whisk in sugar until smooth.

11 Transfer éclairs to wire rack set in rimmed baking sheet. Spoon warm glaze evenly over tops, making sure to cover holes completely. Let glaze set, about 20 minutes, before serving.

MAKING DOUBLE CHOCOLATE ÉCLAIRS

1. Fit pastry bag with ½-inch plain tip and fill with warm pate a choux. Pipe pate a choux into eight 5 by 1-inch logs spaced about 1 inch apart on prepared sheet.

2. Use your dampened finger or back of wet teaspoon to even out shape and smooth surface of each log.

3. Bake for 15 minutes, reduce oven temperature to 350 degrees, and continue to bake until golden brown, 8 to 10 minutes longer. Remove sheet from oven and cut ¾-inch slit into side of each pastry with paring knife to release steam.

4. Dry pastries in turned-off oven until centers are just moist (not wet) and surfaces are crisp, about 45 minutes. Once completely cool, use tip of paring knife to cut 3 small Xs along top of each pastry.

5. Fit clean pastry bag with ¼-inch plain tip and fill pastry bag with pastry cream. Pipe pastry cream into pastries through each opening until éclairs are completely filled.

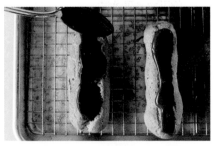

6. Spoon warm glaze evenly over tops of éclairs, making sure to cover holes completely.

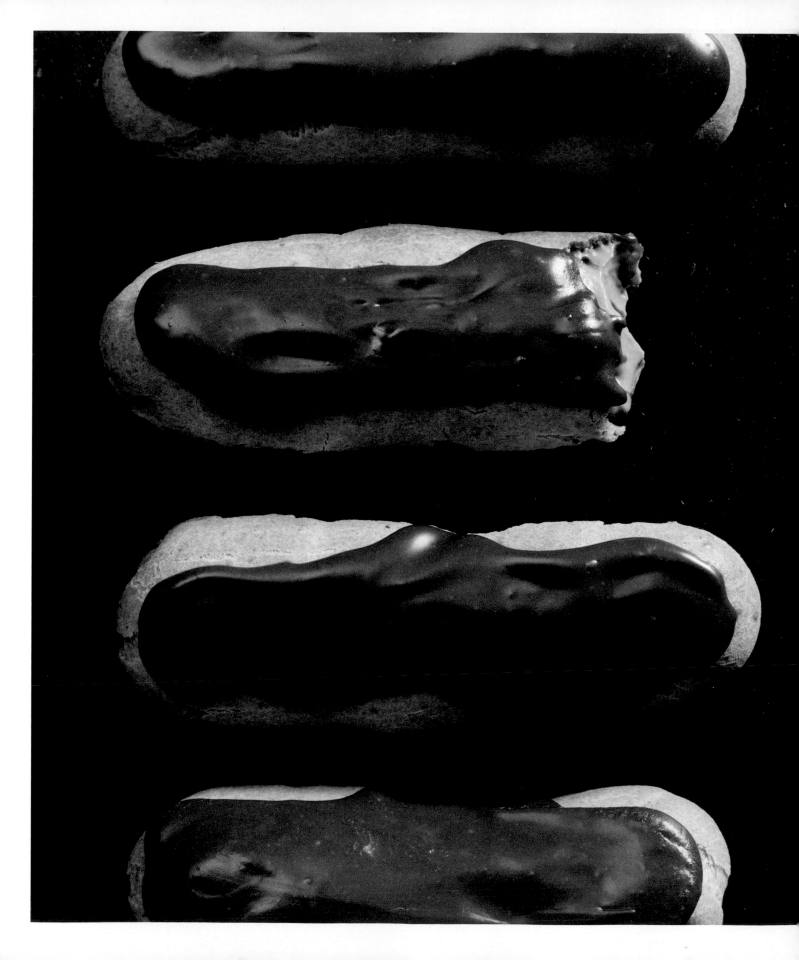

HOMEMADE CHOCOLATE CANNOLI

MAKES 10 CANNOLI

- 12 ounces (1½ cups) whole-milk ricotta cheese
- 12 ounces (1½ cups) mascarpone cheese
- 10 ounces semisweet chocolate (6 ounces chopped fine, 4 ounces finely grated), divided
- ¾ cup (3 ounces) confectioners' sugar
- 1½ teaspoons vanilla extract
- Pinch table salt
- 10 cannoli shells

Why This Recipe Works Cannoli (fried pastry tubes filled with creamy, sweetened ricotta) are featured in almost every Italian American bakery case, but not every bakery offers a chocolate option. We rarely find chocolate optional and made sure to include it in two places in our homemade version: in the filling and as coating for the shells. Instead of draining the ricotta for our filling overnight, we placed the ricotta in cheesecloth and then weighted it with heavy cans to remove maximum moisture in minimal time, resulting in a desirably dense filling in only an hour. Then we stirred in some mascarpone, sugar, vanilla, salt, and, of course, grated chocolate. The fine shards didn't disrupt the texture of the filling like mini chips could and made every creamy bit chocolaty. We dipped each end of the shells in chocolate for an extra touch that was also elegant-looking. We tempered the chocolate for our coating so the chocolate would have shine and snap against the crunchy shells. And to keep the crunch in our shells, we filled them just before serving—prefilled cannoli are always soggy. You can find cannoli shells at most markets in either the international foods aisle, the gourmet cheese section, or the bakery. Make sure to use a high-quality whole-milk ricotta; our favorite is BelGioioso Ricotta con Latte Whole Milk Ricotta Cheese. This recipe yields enough tempered chocolate to easily dip all the cannoli shells; leftover chocolate can be transferred to a small airtight container and stored at room temperature for another use.

1 Line colander with triple layer of cheesecloth and place in sink. Place ricotta in prepared colander, pull edges of cheesecloth together to form pouch, and twist to squeeze out as much liquid as possible. Place taut, twisted cheese pouch in pie plate and set heavy plate on top. Weight plate with 2 large heavy cans and refrigerate for 1 hour.

2 Discard drained ricotta liquid and transfer dry ricotta to bowl. Stir in mascarpone, 2 ounces finely grated chocolate, sugar, vanilla, and salt until well combined. Cover and refrigerate until chilled, at least 1 hour or up to 24 hours.

3 Meanwhile, line rimmed baking sheet with parchment paper. Microwave finely chopped chocolate in bowl at 50 percent power, stirring often, until about two-thirds melted, 2 to 4 minutes. (Melted chocolate should not be much warmer than body temperature; check by holding bowl in palm of your hand.) Add remaining 2 ounces finely grated chocolate and stir until smooth, returning to microwave for no more than 5 seconds at a time to finish melting if necessary. Dip ends of cannoli shells in chocolate, allowing excess to drip off, and transfer to prepared sheet. Let shells sit until chocolate is firm, about 1 hour. (Coated shells can be stored in airtight container at room temperature for up to 1 week.)

4 Transfer chilled cheese mixture into pastry bag or large zipper-lock bag. (If using zipper-lock bag, cut ¾ inch off one bottom corner.) Pipe filling evenly into cannoli shells from both ends, working outward from center. Serve.

MAKING HOMEMADE CHOCOLATE CANNOLI

1. Line colander with triple layer of cheesecloth and place in sink. Place ricotta in prepared colander, pull edges of cheesecloth together to form pouch, and twist to squeeze out as much liquid as possible.

2. Place taut, twisted cheese pouch in pie plate and set heavy plate on top. Weight plate with 2 large heavy cans and refrigerate for 1 hour.

3. Discard drained ricotta liquid and transfer dry ricotta to bowl.

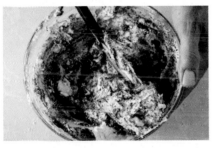

4. Stir in mascarpone, 2 ounces finely grated chocolate, sugar, vanilla, and salt until well combined. Cover and refrigerate until chilled, at least 1 hour or up to 24 hours.

5. Transfer chilled cheese mixture into pastry bag or large zipper-lock bag.

6. Pipe filling evenly into coated cannoli shells from both ends, working outward from center.

cakes from simple TO DECADENT

CHOCOLATE-CARDAMOM CAKE WITH ROASTED PEARS

SERVES 8

PEARS

- 1 tablespoon unsalted butter
- 3 ripe but firm Bartlett or Bosc pears (6 to 8 ounces each), peeled, halved, and cored

CAKE

- ½ cup (2½ ounces) all-purpose flour
- ¼ cup (¾ ounce) unsweetened cocoa powder
- 1 teaspoon ground cardamom
- ¼ teaspoon baking powder
- ¼ teaspoon table salt
- ¾ cup (5¼ ounces) granulated sugar
- 2 large eggs, room temperature
- 8 tablespoons unsalted butter, melted and cooled
- 1 teaspoon vanilla extract
- 2 ounces semisweet chocolate, chopped fine

  Confectioners' sugar

Why This Recipe Works Chocolate and pears might not be the first pairing that comes to mind, but we can assure you they make a fabulous couple. To ensure a happy marriage in an elegant cake, we wanted pears that were as much a star as the chocolate itself. Pears on their own can be quite mild, so lots of caramelization was key to bringing out their floral quality. Before adding them to our cake, we roasted the pears in a 450-degree oven until they were caramelized and tender. We wanted a cake with crumb that was sturdy enough to hold up the pears so they sat pretty on top; this meant using leaner cocoa powder rather than melted chocolate. We ended up with a thick—almost brownie-like—batter that baked up tender and moist with the pears. And we stirred in cardamom to complement the pear's spice notes. Chopped chocolate added surprise gooey pockets. Cakes are often baked at 350 degrees, but we found 325 worked better for slow, even baking from edge to center. When baked at higher temperatures, this cake had hard edges. Fanning the thinly sliced roasted pears over the batter gave this balanced cake a beautiful presentation, no frosting required.

1 For the pears Adjust oven rack to middle position and heat oven to 450 degrees. Melt butter in 12-inch ovensafe skillet over medium-high heat. Arrange pears cut side down in skillet and cook, without moving pears, until just beginning to brown on first side, 3 to 5 minutes. Transfer skillet to oven and roast for 10 minutes. Flip pears and continue to roast until fork easily pierces fruit, 8 to 12 minutes. Remove skillet from oven and transfer pears cut side down to paper towel–lined plate.

2 For the cake Reduce oven temperature to 325 degrees. Grease 9-inch springform pan. Whisk flour, cocoa, cardamom, baking powder, and salt together in bowl. Whisk granulated sugar and eggs in large bowl until pale yellow, about 1 minute. Whisk in melted butter and vanilla until combined. Using rubber spatula, fold in flour mixture until few streaks remain. Fold in chocolate until just combined (don't overmix).

3 Transfer batter to prepared pan and smooth into even layer. Cut 1 pear half crosswise into ¼-inch-thick slices; leave pear intact on cutting board. Discard first 4 slices from narrow end of sliced pear. Slide small offset spatula under pear and gently press pear to fan slices toward narrow end. Slide fanned pear onto batter with narrow end facing center and wide end almost touching edge of pan. Do not press pear into batter. Repeat slicing, fanning, and placing remaining 5 pear halves evenly around pan. Bake until toothpick inserted in center comes out with few moist crumbs attached, 45 to 55 minutes, rotating pan halfway through baking.

4 Let cake cool in pan on wire rack for 20 minutes. Remove sides of pan and let cake cool completely, about 1½ hours. To unmold cake, slide thin metal spatula between cake bottom and pan bottom to loosen, then slide cake onto serving platter. Dust with confectioners' sugar before serving.

PLACING THE PEARS

1. Cut 1 pear half crosswise into ¼-inch-thick slices; leave pear intact on cutting board.

2. Discard first 4 slices from narrow end. Slide small offset spatula under pear and gently press pear to fan slices toward narrow end.

3. Slide fanned pear onto batter with narrow end facing center and wide end almost touching edge of pan. Repeat, placing remaining 5 pear halves evenly around pan.

CHOCOLATE POUND CAKE

SERVES 8

Why This Recipe Works We love pound cake and we love chocolate, but the combination is often a disappointment. That's because most recipes simply add chocolate to a standard pound cake, which mars its finely tuned texture and usually produces lackluster chocolate flavor. We wanted to retool classic pound cake to make it ultrachocolaty without compromising its hallmark velvety-soft crumb. Pound cake recipes can be finicky, requiring the proper emulsion of eggs into the batter, so we sought to make this recipe foolproof by relying on the food processor. We started by blooming cocoa powder in the microwave with butter and bittersweet chocolate for a rich chocolaty base. When we added this mixture to the other liquid ingredients in the food processor, the fast-moving blades emulsified everything before it had a chance to curdle. Cake flour, which has a lower protein content than all-purpose flour, was imperative to make this cake tender and fine-crumbed. Sifting the dry ingredients over our emulsified egg mixture and whisking in three additions ensured that no pockets of flour would affect our final cake. This cake is delicious on its own, but we also like to glaze it with All-Purpose Chocolate Glaze (page 348) or top slices with a scoop of ice cream and fresh berries. The test kitchen's preferred loaf pan measures 8½ by 4½ inches; if you use a 9 by 5-inch loaf pan, start checking for doneness 5 minutes earlier than advised in the recipe.

16 tablespoons unsalted butter

¾ cup (2¼ ounces) unsweetened cocoa powder

2 ounces bittersweet chocolate, chopped fine

1 cup (4 ounces) cake flour

¼ teaspoon baking powder

½ teaspoon table salt

1¼ cups (8¾ ounces) sugar

4 large eggs, room temperature

1½ teaspoons vanilla extract

1 Adjust oven rack to middle position and heat oven to 325 degrees. Grease and flour 8½ by 4½-inch loaf pan. Microwave butter, cocoa, and chocolate in bowl at 50 percent power, stirring occasionally, until melted and smooth; let cool slightly.

2 Whisk flour, baking powder, and salt together in second bowl. Process sugar, eggs, and vanilla in food processor until combined, about 10 seconds, scraping down sides of bowl as needed. Add chocolate mixture and process until incorporated, about 10 seconds; transfer to large bowl.

3 Sift flour mixture over egg mixture in 3 additions, whisking to combine after each addition until few streaks of flour remain. Continue to whisk batter gently until almost no lumps remain (do not overmix).

4 Transfer batter to prepared pan, smooth top with rubber spatula, and gently tap pan on counter to settle batter. Bake until toothpick inserted in center comes out with few moist crumbs attached, 1 hour 5 minutes to 1 hour 15 minutes, rotating pan halfway through baking.

5 Let cake cool in pan on wire rack for 10 minutes. Run thin knife around edge of pan, remove cake from pan, and let cool completely on rack, about 2 hours. Serve.

CHOCOLATE SHEET CAKE WITH MILK CHOCOLATE FROSTING

SERVES 12 TO 15

CAKE

- 1½ cups (10½ ounces) sugar
- 1¼ cups (6¼ ounces) all-purpose flour
- ½ teaspoon baking soda
- ½ teaspoon table salt
- 1 cup whole milk
- 8 ounces bittersweet chocolate, chopped fine
- ¾ cup (2¼ ounces) Dutch-processed cocoa powder
- ⅔ cup vegetable oil
- 4 large eggs
- 1 teaspoon vanilla extract

FROSTING

- 1 pound milk chocolate, chopped
- ⅔ cup heavy cream
- 16 tablespoons unsalted butter, cut into 16 pieces and softened

Why This Recipe Works When the results are good, chocolate sheet cake yields great reward—tender chocolate cake and appealing swirls of frosting—for relatively minimal effort. But most chocolate sheet cakes we've made disappoint: They're dry and crumbly with barely a whisper of chocolate flavor, or are so dense that they veer into brownie territory. For a cake that boasted deep chocolate flavor and color, we used a combination of Dutch-processed cocoa and melted bittersweet chocolate; the cocoa offered assertive chocolate flavor and an appealingly dark color, while the bittersweet chocolate contributed complexity as well as the right amount of fat and sugar. We knew we wanted a milk chocolate frosting to offset the intense flavor of the cake, but we needed to get the texture just right: To make it thicker, richer, and creamier than the norm, we added plenty of softened butter to a milk chocolate ganache. The best part: This cake comes together with everyday staples and basic equipment—no mixers or food processors needed. If you want to take the entire cake out of the pan, grease the pan, line with parchment paper, grease the parchment, and then flour the pan.

1 For the cake Adjust oven rack to middle position and heat oven to 325 degrees. Lightly spray 13 by 9-inch baking pan with vegetable oil spray. Whisk sugar, flour, baking soda, and salt together in bowl; set aside.

2 Combine milk, chocolate, and cocoa in large saucepan. Place saucepan over low heat and cook, whisking frequently, until chocolate is melted and mixture is smooth. Remove from heat and let cool slightly, about 5 minutes. Whisk oil, eggs, and vanilla into chocolate mixture (mixture may initially look curdled) until smooth and homogeneous. Add sugar mixture and whisk until combined, making sure to scrape corners of saucepan.

3 Transfer batter to prepared pan. Bake until firm in center when lightly pressed and toothpick inserted in center comes out with few crumbs attached, 30 to 35 minutes, rotating pan halfway through baking. Let cake cool completely in pan on wire rack, about 2 hours.

4 For the frosting While cake is baking, combine chocolate and cream in large heatproof bowl set over saucepan filled with 1 inch barely simmering water, making sure that water does not touch bottom of bowl. Whisk mixture occasionally until chocolate is uniformly smooth and glossy, 10 to 15 minutes. Remove bowl from saucepan. Add butter, whisking once or twice to break up pieces. Let mixture stand for 5 minutes to finish melting butter, then whisk until completely smooth. Refrigerate frosting, without stirring, until cooled and thickened, 30 minutes to 1 hour.

5 Once cool, whisk frosting until smooth. (Whisked frosting will lighten in color slightly and should hold its shape on whisk.) Spread frosting evenly over top of cake. Serve. (Cake can be refrigerated for up to 2 days.)

TEXAS SHEET CAKE

SERVES 12 TO 15

Why This Recipe Works Texas sheet cake, the official cake of the Lone Star State, is no ordinary sheet cake: It's a sheet pan–size, pecan-topped chocolate cake with three distinct layers of chocolaty goodness. A diverse range of textures is created when the sweet chocolate icing is poured over the cake that's still hot from the oven. Once the cake has cooled, you're left with a layer of icing on top, a fudgy middle layer where the icing and hot cake have melded, and a bottom layer of moist chocolate cake. For the cake, we relied on a combination of butter and vegetable oil for fat, which produced a dense, brownie-like texture. We wanted the cake's fudgy chocolate flavor to match its fudgy texture, so we used both cocoa powder and melted semisweet chocolate for a cake that was ultrachocolaty yet still moist and dense. The icing was the final element, and getting its texture right was key to this cake's success—replacing milk with heavy cream gave it more body, while adding corn syrup produced a lustrous finish. Using the traditional frosting method ensured a cake with the signature fudge-like layer between the icing and cake: We spread the warm icing over the cake straight out of the oven, smoothed it with a spatula, and let it soak into the hot cake.

1 For the cake Adjust oven rack to middle position and heat oven to 350 degrees. Grease 18 by 13-inch rimmed baking sheet. Whisk flour, sugar, baking soda, and salt together in large bowl. Whisk eggs and yolks, sour cream, and vanilla in second bowl until smooth.

2 Heat chocolate, oil, water, cocoa, and butter in large saucepan over medium heat, stirring occasionally, until smooth, 3 to 5 minutes. Whisk chocolate mixture into flour mixture until incorporated. Whisk egg mixture into batter. Transfer batter to prepared sheet. Bake until toothpick inserted in center comes out clean, 18 to 20 minutes, rotating sheet halfway through baking. Transfer sheet to wire rack.

3 For the icing About 5 minutes before cake is done baking, heat butter, cream, cocoa, and corn syrup in large saucepan over medium heat, stirring occasionally, until smooth, about 4 minutes. Off heat, whisk in sugar and vanilla. Spread warm icing evenly over hot cake and sprinkle with pecans. Let cake cool completely in pan on wire rack, about 1 hour, then refrigerate until icing is set, about 1 hour longer. Serve.

CAKE

- 2 cups (10 ounces) all-purpose flour
- 2 cups (14 ounces) granulated sugar
- ½ teaspoon baking soda
- ½ teaspoon table salt
- 2 large eggs plus 2 large yolks
- ¼ cup sour cream
- 2 teaspoons vanilla extract
- 8 ounces semisweet chocolate, chopped
- ¾ cup vegetable oil
- ¾ cup water
- ½ cup (1½ ounces) unsweetened cocoa powder
- 4 tablespoons unsalted butter

ICING

- 8 tablespoons unsalted butter
- ½ cup heavy cream
- ½ cup (1½ ounces) unsweetened cocoa powder
- 1 tablespoon light corn syrup
- 3 cups (12 ounces) confectioners' sugar
- 1 tablespoon vanilla extract
- 1 cup pecans, toasted and chopped

CHOCOLATE-ORANGE ANGEL FOOD CAKE

SERVES 12

¾ cup (3 ounces) cake flour

1½ cups (10½ ounces) sugar, divided

12 large egg whites, room temperature

1 teaspoon cream of tartar

¼ teaspoon table salt

1 tablespoon Grand Marnier

2 teaspoons grated orange zest

½ teaspoon vanilla extract

2 ounces bittersweet chocolate, finely grated

Why This Recipe Works Angel food cake has a downy soft and incredibly light texture, as well as a mild sweetness that makes it an ideal canvas for flavorful additions, including our favorite: chocolate. We wanted to give this cake an elegant upgrade by incorporating a classic combination of chocolate and orange. We tried simply mixing in chopped bittersweet chocolate, but that was a failure: The chunks of chocolate disrupted the ultradelicate structure of the egg white–leavened cake. Finely grated chocolate worked much better and was easier to distribute evenly through-out the batter. A couple teaspoons of fresh orange zest added fragrance, while a splash of orange liqueur amped up the citrus flavor further. If your tube pan has a removable bottom, you do not need to line it with parchment. Do not grease the pan; greasing prevents the cake from climbing up and clinging to the sides as it bakes, and a greased pan will produce a disappointingly short cake. Finely grating the chocolate is key here; use either a Microplane grater or the fine holes of a box grater.

1 Adjust oven rack to lower-middle position and heat oven to 325 degrees. Line 16-cup tube pan with parchment paper but do not grease. Whisk flour and ¾ cup sugar together in bowl; set aside.

2 Using stand mixer fitted with whisk attachment, whip egg whites, cream of tartar, and salt on medium-low speed until foamy, about 1 minute. Increase speed to medium-high and whip to soft, billowy mounds, about 1 minute. Gradually add remaining ¾ cup sugar and whip until soft, glossy peaks form, 1 to 2 minutes. Add Grand Marnier, orange zest, and vanilla and whip until just blended.

3 Sift flour mixture over whites, about 3 tablespoons at a time, gently folding mixture into whites after each addition with large rubber spatula. Gently fold in chocolate.

4 Gently transfer batter to prepared pan and smooth top with rubber spatula. Bake until golden brown and top springs back when pressed firmly, 50 minutes to 1 hour, rotating pan halfway through baking.

5 If pan has prongs around rim for elevating cake, invert pan on them. If not, invert pan over neck of bottle or funnel so that air can circulate all around it. Let cake cool completely in pan, 2 to 3 hours.

6 Run thin knife around edge of pan to loosen cake, then gently tap pan upside down on counter to release cake. Peel off parchment and turn cake right side up onto platter. Serve. (Cake can be stored at room temperature for up to 2 days or refrigerated for up to 4 days.)

OLD-FASHIONED CHOCOLATE CAKE

SERVES 10 TO 12

Why This Recipe Works Over the years, chocolate cakes have become dense, rich, and squat. We wanted a traditional chocolate layer cake with a tender, airy, open crumb—like one from birthday parties past. And of course filled and covered with luxurious chocolate frosting. We turned to a popular old-fashioned method called ribboning, in which eggs are whipped with sugar until they double in volume before the butter, dry ingredients, and milk are added. This process of aerating the eggs gave our cake height and structure, but also made it remarkably tender. To achieve a moist cake with rich chocolate flavor, we once again looked to historical sources, which suggested using buttermilk instead of the milk and making a "pudding" with a mixture of chocolate, hot water, and sugar.

1 Adjust oven rack to middle position and heat oven to 350 degrees. Grease two 9-inch round cake pans, line with parchment paper, grease parchment, and flour pans.

2 Combine chocolate, hot water, and cocoa in heatproof bowl set over saucepan filled with 1 inch barely simmering water, making sure that water does not touch bottom of bowl and stirring with heat-resistant rubber spatula until chocolate is melted, about 2 minutes. Add ½ cup sugar to chocolate mixture and stir until thick and glossy, 1 to 2 minutes. Remove bowl from heat; set aside to cool.

3 Whisk flour, baking soda, and salt together in bowl. Combine buttermilk and vanilla in second bowl. Using stand mixer fitted with whisk attachment, whip eggs and yolks on medium-low speed until combined, about 10 seconds. Add remaining 1¼ cups sugar, increase speed to high, and whip until light and fluffy, 2 to 3 minutes. Fit stand mixer with paddle. Add cooled chocolate mixture to egg mixture and mix on medium speed until thoroughly combined, 30 to 45 seconds, scraping down bowl as needed. Add butter, 1 piece at a time, mixing for about 10 seconds after each addition. Add flour mixture in 3 additions, alternating with buttermilk mixture in 2 additions, mixing until incorporated after each addition (about 15 seconds) and scraping down bowl as needed. Reduce speed to medium-low and mix until batter is thoroughly combined, about 15 seconds. Give batter final stir by hand.

4 Divide batter evenly between prepared pans and smooth tops with rubber spatula. Bake until toothpick inserted in center comes out with few moist crumbs attached, 25 to 30 minutes, rotating pans halfway through baking. Let cakes cool in pans on wire rack for 10 minutes. Remove cakes from pans, discarding parchment, and let cool completely on rack, about 2 hours. (Cooled cake layers can be stored at room temperature for up to 24 hours or frozen for up to 1 month; defrost cake layers at room temperature.)

5 Line edges of cake platter with 4 strips of parchment paper to keep platter clean. Place 1 cake layer on platter. Spread 1½ cups frosting evenly over top, right to edge of cake. Top with second cake layer, press lightly to adhere, then spread remaining frosting evenly over top and sides of cake. Carefully remove parchment strips before serving.

4 ounces unsweetened chocolate, chopped

½ cup hot water

¼ cup (¾ ounce) Dutch-processed cocoa powder

1¾ cups (12¼ ounces) sugar, divided

1¾ cups (8¾ ounces) all-purpose flour

1½ teaspoons baking soda

1 teaspoon table salt

1 cup buttermilk

2 teaspoons vanilla extract

4 large eggs plus 2 large yolks, room temperature

12 tablespoons unsalted butter, cut into 12 pieces and softened

5 cups Chocolate Frosting (page 345)

CHOCOLATE–PEANUT BUTTER CAKE

SERVES 12

FROSTING

- 22 tablespoons (2¾ sticks) unsalted butter, cut into 22 pieces and softened
- 1⅓ cups creamy peanut butter
- 3 tablespoons heavy cream
- 2 teaspoons vanilla extract
- ⅛ teaspoon table salt
- 2 cups (8 ounces) confectioners' sugar

CAKE

- 3 (8-inch) Chocolate Cake Layers (page 349)

GLAZE

- 4 ounces bittersweet chocolate, chopped
- 4 tablespoons unsalted butter, cut into 4 pieces
- 2 tablespoons light corn syrup

  Candied Nuts (page 347)

Why This Recipe Works Beyond the peanut butter cup, the combination of chocolate and peanut butter often appears in casual affairs—cookies, brownies, and the like. We love these treats but also think the duo deserves a grand platform; we envisioned a towering confection featuring rich, moist chocolate cake layered with swirls of decadent peanut butter frosting. We started with our chocolate cake layers, which have a tender crumb yet are sturdy enough to support a generous amount of frosting. Wanting to keep our cake as streamlined as possible, we opted for an easy-to-prepare buttercream frosting with plenty of butter, confectioners' sugar, a little heavy cream, and a whopping 1⅓ cups of creamy peanut butter. Our frosting was decadent, full of peanut flavor, and easy to spread onto the cake layers. For a final dose of chocolaty goodness, we crowned our cake with a bittersweet chocolate ganache and allowed it to drip invitingly down the sides. A garnish of crunchy candied peanuts was a festive finishing touch. Use peanuts in the Candied Nuts.

1 For the frosting Using stand mixer fitted with paddle, beat butter, peanut butter, cream, vanilla, and salt on medium-high speed until smooth, about 1 minute. Reduce speed to medium-low, slowly add sugar, and beat until incorporated and smooth, about 4 minutes. Increase speed to medium-high and beat until frosting is light and fluffy, about 5 minutes. (Frosting can be refrigerated for up to 3 days; let soften at room temperature, about 2 hours, then rewhip on medium speed until smooth, 2 to 5 minutes.)

2 For the cake Line edges of cake platter with 4 strips of parchment paper to keep platter clean. Place 1 cake layer on platter. Spread 1 cup frosting evenly over top, right to edge of cake. Repeat with 1 more cake layer, pressing lightly to adhere, and 1 cup frosting. Top with remaining cake layer, pressing lightly to adhere. Spread remaining frosting evenly over top and sides of cake.

3 For the glaze Microwave chocolate, butter, and corn syrup in bowl at 50 percent power until melted and smooth, about 1 minute, stirring with rubber spatula halfway through microwaving. Stir mixture until fully combined and smooth. Let cool until slightly thickened, about 5 minutes. Pour ¼ cup chocolate glaze in center of cake and spread evenly over top with offset spatula. Drizzle ¼ cup glaze along top edge of cake, allowing it to drip down sides. Pour remaining glaze over top of cake and smooth into even layer with offset spatula. Arrange 1-tablespoon clusters of candied peanuts around top edge of cake. Let sit until glaze sets, about 20 minutes. Carefully remove parchment strips before serving.

GLAZING WITH CHOCOLATE

Frosting covers cakes and other treats with whimsical cloud-like billows; glaze is sleeker and shinier, with a more intense chocolate flavor. You can find glazes in recipes throughout this book and an all-purpose option on page 348—it's the perfect consistency for cakes of all kinds. It's a cinch to make, and dries nicely. Here are our tips for making glazes look as smooth as they taste.

Cool Down—but Not Too Much

For most desserts, glaze is too fluid when first whisked together; the warm melted chocolate will run right off the cake, leaving a too-thin layer that doesn't carry impact. We found that glaze should rest for 30 minutes before coating most cakes. At this point, the glaze is still pourable but not runny. An exception is for tortes: For these cakes, we typically want a thin coating with a mirror-like sheen enveloping every millimeter of the cake, and that's achieved with not-yet-thickened glaze.

Try a Liquid Measuring Cup

It's tempting to avoid dirtying another vessel, but if you have a shaky hand, using a liquid measuring cup can help make your cakes shine. The handle allows for a steady pour, and the lip ensures an uninterrupted flow of chocolate. Our favorites are by **Pyrex**.

Don't Make a Mess

We like to glaze cakes on a wire rack set in a rimmed baking sheet. The wire rack allows chocolate drips to fall freely rather than pooling at the bottom of a cake, and the baking sheet contains the mess. You can also cool the cake right on this setup. Our favorite wire rack, the **Checkered Chef Cooling Rack** ($17), fits inside our favorite rimmed baking sheet, the **Nordic Ware Baker's Half Sheet** ($14.97). For tall layer cakes built on a platter, we place parchment strips below the cake. When you remove the strips they take errant glaze and messy drips with them.

Glazing Loaf Cakes

A loaf cake should have a cloak of glaze from end to end, with natural drips and dribbles coming down the sides. **Example:** Chocolate Pound Cake (page 149)

1. Starting at 1 short end of the loaf, carefully begin pouring the glaze.

2. Slowly move down the length of the loaf until cake is covered, letting glaze drip naturally down the sides.

Glazing Bundt Cakes

Bundt cakes should feature a glaze that alluringly works its way down the cake's natural ridges. **Example:** Chocolate-Stout Bundt Cake (page 168)

1. Starting at the top of the Bundt, pour the glaze so that it flows down the ridges of the cake.

2. Slowly move around the cake.

Glazing Tortes

Tortes gain elegance from an even layer of glaze coating the top and sides. **Example:** Chocolate-Raspberry Torte (page 216)

1. Pour glaze onto the center of the torte.

2. Using an offset spatula, spread the glaze evenly over the top of the torte, letting it flow down the sides.

3. Spread the glaze along the sides of the torte to coat evenly.

Glazing Layer Cakes

Usually glaze for a layer cake tops a buttercream, and we often want it thick enough to have presence and to drip attractively down the straight sides, so we give it a double-dose. **Example:** Chocolate–Peanut Butter Cake (page 159)

1. Pour ¼ cup chocolate glaze in the center of the cake.

2. Spread the glaze evenly over the top with an offset spatula.

3. Drizzle ¼ cup glaze along the top edge of the cake, allowing it to drip down the sides.

4. Pour the remaining glaze over the top of the cake and smooth into an even layer.

Dipping Doughnuts

We love doughnuts with glaze on both sides, not just the top. **Example:** Chocolate Cake Doughnuts (page 81)

1. Dip 1 side of the doughnut into the glaze in a bowl.

2. Dip the second side of the doughnut into the glaze and shake off any excess.

WHITE CHOCOLATE–MACADAMIA NUT CAKE WITH MANGO

SERVES 12

FILLING

12 ounces frozen chopped mango, thawed

½ cup water

¼ cup (1¾ ounces) sugar

1 tablespoon lemon juice

CAKE

1½ cups roasted unsalted macadamia nuts, divided

4 ounces white chocolate, grated

1 cup (7 ounces) sugar

1¼ cups (5 ounces) cake flour

1½ teaspoons baking powder

½ teaspoon table salt

3 large eggs, separated, plus 2 large whites

½ cup vegetable oil

¼ cup water

2½ teaspoons vanilla extract

¼ teaspoon cream of tartar

1 ripe but firm mango, peeled, pitted, and sliced very thin lengthwise

FROSTING

8 ounces white chocolate, chopped

½ cup (3½ ounces) granulated sugar

3 large egg whites

⅛ teaspoon table salt

16 tablespoons unsalted butter, cut into 16 pieces and softened

Why This Recipe Works White chocolate's creamy, rich sweetness makes it a lovely foil for the often tart, punchy flavors of tropical fruit. Chocolate-enhanced layer cakes are usually of the deep, dark variety; we decided to make something different, a stunning layer cake that featured a pairing of mango and too-often-overlooked white chocolate. Macadamia nuts are another friend of the two, so we decided to make layers of macadamia nut cake to hold white chocolate and mango components. For light, airy layers with full macadamia flavor, we ground roasted nuts with sugar to make a fine nut flour and used it for a portion of the cake flour in a chiffon cake batter. We sandwiched the layers with a jammy filling that we made by cooking pieces of frozen mango on the stove, mashing them with a potato masher to help them break down but also maintain some texture. We decorated the cake with rich, mellowing, and ultracreamy white chocolate buttercream. We chose a Swiss Meringue–style buttercream in which egg whites and sugar are heated over a double boiler, whipped with knobs of butter, and then, in this case, enhanced with a half-pound of melted white chocolate. A side coating of chopped macadamia nuts brought everything together and added welcome crunch and visual appeal. For even more glamour on this very special layer cake, we garnished the top with easy-to-make mango roses. The melted chocolate should be cooled to between 85 and 100 degrees before being added to the frosting.

1 For the filling Bring mango, water, and sugar to a boil in medium saucepan over medium heat and cook, stirring occasionally, until mango is softened. Mash mango with potato masher until broken down and continue to cook until mixture has thickened, about 5 minutes. Off heat, stir in lemon juice. Transfer filling to bowl, let cool slightly, then cover and refrigerate until completely chilled, about 1 hour. (Filling can be refrigerated for up to 3 days.)

2 For the cake Adjust oven rack to middle position and heat oven to 350 degrees. Line two 9-inch round cake pans with parchment paper; grease parchment but not pan sides.

3 Pulse 1 cup macadamia nuts in food processor until chopped, about 10 pulses. Transfer to bowl and stir in chocolate; set aside for decorating. Add remaining ½ cup macadamia nuts and sugar to now-empty processor and process until finely ground, about 20 seconds. Add flour, baking powder, and salt and pulse to combine, about 5 pulses; transfer to large bowl. Whisk egg yolks, oil, water, and vanilla together in second bowl. Whisk egg yolk mixture into flour mixture until smooth batter forms.

4 Using stand mixer fitted with whisk attachment, whip egg whites and cream of tartar on medium-low speed until foamy, about 1 minute. Increase speed to medium-high and whip until soft peaks form, 1 to 2 minutes. Gently whisk one-third of whites into batter. Using rubber spatula, gently fold remaining whites into batter until no white streaks remain.

5 Divide batter evenly between prepared pans. Gently tap pans on counter to release air bubbles. Bake until tops are light golden brown and cakes spring back when pressed lightly in center, 25 to 28 minutes, switching and rotating pans halfway through baking.

6 Let cakes cool in pans on wire rack for 15 minutes. Run thin knife around edges of pans. Remove cakes from pan, discarding parchment, and let cool completely on rack, about 1 hour.

7 **For the frosting** Microwave chocolate in bowl at 50 percent power, stirring occasionally, until melted and smooth, 2 to 4 minutes; let cool. Combine sugar, egg whites, and salt in clean, dry bowl of stand mixer. Set bowl over saucepan filled with 1 inch of barely simmering water, making sure that water does not touch bottom of bowl. Cook, whisking constantly, until mixture registers 150 degrees, about 3 minutes. Remove bowl from heat and transfer to stand mixer fitted with whisk attachment. Whip warm egg mixture on medium speed until it has consistency of shaving cream and has cooled slightly, about 5 minutes. Add butter, 1 piece at a time, and whip until smooth and creamy, about 2 minutes. (Frosting may look curdled after half of butter has been added; it will smooth out with additional butter.)

8 Add melted chocolate and mix until combined. Increase speed to medium-high and whip until light and fluffy, about 30 seconds, scraping down sides of bowl as needed. If frosting seems too soft after adding chocolate, chill it briefly in the refrigerator, then rewhip until creamy. (Frosting can be refrigerated for up to 24 hours; warm frosting briefly in microwave until just slightly softened, 5 to 10 seconds, then stir until creamy.)

9 Line edges of cake platter with 4 strips of parchment to keep platter clean. Place 1 cake layer on platter. Spread mango filling evenly over top, right to edge of cake. Top with remaining cake layer and spread frosting evenly over top and sides of cake. Press reserved chopped macadamia nuts onto sides of cake. Refrigerate cake until set, about 30 minutes. (Frosted cake can be refrigerated for up to 24 hours; bring to room temperature before serving.)

10 Before serving, remove parchment strips. Shingle 3 mango slices on cutting board or counter, overlapping each slice by about ½ inch. Starting at 1 end, roll up slices to form rose shape; place on top of cake. Repeat, arranging mango roses decoratively over top of cake.

MAKING THE MANGO ROSES

1. Shingle 3 mango slices on cutting board or counter, overlapping each slice by about ½ inch.

2. Working from your left to right, roll up slices to form rose shape; place on top of cake.

BOSTON CREAM PIE

SERVES 10 TO 12

PASTRY CREAM

2	cups half-and-half
6	large egg yolks, room temperature
½	cup (3½ ounces) sugar
	Pinch table salt
¼	cup (1¼ ounces) all-purpose flour
4	tablespoons unsalted butter, cut into 4 pieces and chilled
1½	teaspoons vanilla extract

CAKE

1½	cups (7½ ounces) all-purpose flour
1½	teaspoons baking powder
¾	teaspoon table salt
¾	cup whole milk
6	tablespoons unsalted butter
1½	teaspoons vanilla extract
3	large eggs, room temperature
1½	cups (10½ ounces) sugar

GLAZE

½	cup heavy cream
2	tablespoons light corn syrup
4	ounces bittersweet chocolate, chopped fine

Why This Recipe Works Legend has it that Boston cream pie was invented in the 1850s at Boston's landmark Parker House hotel. A creative baker produced a wildly popular dessert by pouring a rich chocolate glaze onto a cream-filled cake. So why is this dessert called a pie? Food historians theorize that home cooks transferred the concept to the most common form of bakeware in the mid-19th-century kitchen: a pie plate. These days, Boston cream pie is rarely made at home, owing to its reputation as an intimidating recipe with multiple tricky components. That's too bad because when it hits all the right marks, this dessert is supremely satisfying. A hot-milk sponge cake made a good base for our Boston cream pie; it doesn't call for separating eggs or require any finicky folding techniques, making it a streamlined choice. Adding extra egg yolks to the pastry cream thickened it just enough to prevent it from oozing out of the uncoated sides of our cake. For the crowning touch, we combined melted bittersweet chocolate, heavy cream, and a little corn syrup for an incredibly simple, smooth glaze that clung to the top of our pie and dripped invitingly down its sides.

1 For the pastry cream Heat half-and-half in medium saucepan over medium heat until just simmering. Meanwhile, whisk egg yolks, sugar, and salt in bowl until smooth. Add flour and whisk until incorporated. Whisk about ½ cup half-and-half into yolk mixture to temper, then slowly whisk tempered yolk mixture back into remaining half-and-half in saucepan. Continue to cook, whisking constantly, until mixture thickens slightly, about 1 minute. Reduce heat to medium-low and continue to simmer, whisking constantly, for 8 minutes.

2 Increase heat to medium and cook, whisking vigorously, until bubbles burst on surface, 1 to 2 minutes. Off heat, whisk in butter and vanilla until incorporated. Strain pastry cream through fine-mesh strainer set over bowl. Press plastic wrap directly on surface. Refrigerate pastry cream until set, at least 2 hours or up to 24 hours.

3 For the cake Adjust oven rack to middle position and heat oven to 325 degrees. Grease two 9-inch round cake pans, line with parchment paper, and grease parchment. Whisk flour, baking powder, and salt together in bowl. Heat milk and butter in small saucepan over low heat until butter is melted. Remove from heat, add vanilla, and cover to keep warm.

4 Using stand mixer fitted with whisk attachment, whip eggs and sugar on high speed until light and airy, about 5 minutes. Add hot milk mixture and whisk by hand until incorporated. Add flour mixture and whisk by hand until incorporated.

5 Divide batter evenly between prepared pans. Bake until tops of cakes are light brown and toothpick inserted in center comes out clean, 20 to 22 minutes, rotating pans halfway through baking. Let cakes cool completely in pans on wire rack, about 2 hours. Run thin knife around edges of pans, remove cakes from pans, discarding parchment, and let cool completely on rack.

6 Place 1 cake layer on platter. Whisk pastry cream briefly, then spoon onto center of cake. Using offset spatula, spread evenly to edge. Place second layer on pastry cream, bottom side up, and press lightly on cake to level. Refrigerate cake while preparing glaze.

7 **For the glaze** Bring cream and corn syrup to simmer in small saucepan over medium heat. Remove from heat, add chocolate, and let sit, covered, for 5 minutes. Whisk mixture gently until smooth.

8 Pour glaze onto center of cake. Using offset spatula, spread glaze to edge of cake, letting excess drip down sides. Refrigerate cake for at least 3 hours before serving. (Cake can be refrigerated for up to 24 hours; bring to room temperature before serving.)

Demystifying Corn Syrup

Is Karo corn syrup the same thing as the high-fructose corn syrup ubiquitous in soft drinks and other processed foods? In a word, no. Corn syrup (the most popular brand being Karo, introduced in 1902) is made by adding enzymes to a mixture of cornstarch and water to break the long starch strands into glucose molecules. It's valuable in candy making because it discourages crystallization; it also helps baked goods retain moisture. And corn syrup makes an excellent addition to glazes; it's less sweet than granulated sugar, and it contributes body and sticking power. High-fructose corn syrup (HFCS) is a newer product that came on the market in the 1960s. It's made by putting regular corn syrup through an additional enzymatic process that converts a portion of the glucose molecules into fructose, boosting its sweetness to a level even higher than that of cane sugar. Because HFCS is considerably less expensive than cane sugar, it's widely used in processed foods, but it's not sold directly to consumers. Corn syrup comes in light and dark varieties, with dark corn syrup having a deeper flavor. Manufacturers turn light corn syrup into dark by adding caramel color and a molasses-like product.

CHOCOLATE-STOUT BUNDT CAKE

SERVES 12

CAKE

- ¾ cup (2¼ ounces) natural unsweetened cocoa powder, plus 1 tablespoon for pan
- 12 tablespoons unsalted butter, softened, plus 1 tablespoon melted, for pan
- ¾ cup stout, such as Guinness
- 6 ounces bittersweet chocolate, chopped
- 1 cup sour cream
- 1 tablespoon vanilla extract
- 1¾ cups (8¾ ounces) all-purpose flour
- 1 teaspoon table salt
- 1 teaspoon baking soda
- 2 cups packed (14 ounces) light brown sugar
- 5 large eggs, room temperature

GLAZE

- 6 ounces bittersweet chocolate, chopped
- ½ cup heavy cream
- ¼ cup stout, such as Guinness

Why This Recipe Works Wine or beer and chocolate pairings have become as popular as cheese pairings, and stout, in particular, tastes great with chocolate—it has notes of chocolate itself, after all. We wanted to take the chocolate off the plate and the beer out of the flight glass and bring the two together in a fine-crumbed, moist, rich chocolate cake enhanced by the slightly bitter, malty, roasted flavors of stout. A Bundt cake seemed like the right choice as it could also be an attractive vehicle for displaying a chocolate-stout glaze, which we knew would boost the flavor of the cake itself. We used both bittersweet chocolate and cocoa powder, dissolving them in boiling stout to bloom their flavor. Brown sugar and sour cream both provided moisture and the latter contributed a subtle tang that enlivened the other flavors. Coating the Bundt pan with a paste made from cocoa and melted butter ensured a clean release from the pan's ridges. We cut some of the heavy cream from the glaze with beer to give our cake a substantial glossy coating with a real hit of stout. We prefer natural cocoa here; Dutch-processed cocoa will result in a compromised rise. When measuring the beer, do not include the foam.

1 For the cake Adjust oven rack to lower-middle position and heat oven to 350 degrees. Stir 1 tablespoon cocoa and melted butter into paste in small bowl. Using pastry brush, thoroughly coat interior of 12-cup nonstick Bundt pan with paste.

2 Microwave stout, chocolate, and remaining ¾ cup cocoa in bowl at 50 percent power, stirring occasionally, until melted and smooth, about 3 minutes. Let chocolate mixture cool for 5 minutes, then whisk in sour cream and vanilla.

3 Whisk flour, salt, and baking soda together in second bowl. Using stand mixer fitted with paddle, beat remaining 12 tablespoons butter and sugar on medium-high speed until pale and fluffy, about 3 minutes. Add eggs, one at a time, and beat until combined. Reduce speed to low and add flour mixture in 3 additions, alternating with chocolate mixture in 2 additions, scraping down sides of bowl as needed. Give batter final stir by hand.

4 Transfer batter to prepared pan and smooth top with rubber spatula. Bake until skewer inserted in center comes out clean, 45 to 50 minutes, rotating pan halfway through baking.

5 Let cake cool in pan on wire rack for 10 minutes. Invert cake onto wire rack set in rimmed baking sheet, remove pan, and let cool completely, about 3 hours.

6 For the glaze Microwave chocolate, cream, and stout in bowl at 50 percent power, stirring occasionally, until melted and smooth, about 3 minutes; let cool for 30 minutes. Drizzle glaze over cake and let set for at least 15 minutes before serving.

WELLESLEY CHOCOLATE FUDGE CAKE

SERVES 10 TO 12

Why This Recipe Works Roughly 100 years ago, the founder of Wellesley College held that "pies, lies, and doughnuts should never have a place in Wellesley College." (The girls were expected to stick to "plain" food and avoid sweets.) But students held secret fudge-making parties in their dorm rooms and within 10 years, several tearooms were known for their Wellesley fudge cake, a chocolate layer cake filled and frosted with a thick layer of confectionery fudge frosting. The frostings we tested were alternately hard and grainy, thin and soupy, or too darn difficult. For our version, we started with a base of evaporated milk, butter, brown sugar, and chopped bittersweet chocolate, which created a deeply fudgy frosting with the slight crystalline crunch that marks real fudge—no candy thermometer required. Adding some confectioners' sugar and allowing the mixture to cool ensured our frosting had a thick, luscious texture with a spreadable and sliceable consistency.

1 For the cake Adjust oven rack to middle position and heat oven to 350 degrees. Grease two 8-inch square cake pans, line with parchment paper, grease parchment, and flour pans. Whisk flour, baking soda, baking powder, and salt together in bowl. Whisk hot water and cocoa in small bowl until smooth. Using stand mixer fitted with paddle, beat butter and sugar on medium-high speed until pale and fluffy, about 3 minutes. Add eggs, one at a time, and beat until combined. Reduce speed to low and add flour mixture in 3 additions, alternating with buttermilk in 2 additions, scraping down bowl as needed. Slowly add cocoa mixture and vanilla and mix until incorporated. Give batter final stir by hand.

2 Divide batter evenly between prepared pans and smooth tops with rubber spatula. Bake until toothpick inserted in center comes out with few crumbs attached, 25 to 30 minutes, rotating pans halfway through baking. Let cakes cool in pans on wire rack for 15 minutes. Remove cakes from pans, discarding parchment, and let cool completely on rack, about 2 hours.

3 For the frosting Heat brown sugar, ½ cup evaporated milk, 4 tablespoons butter, and salt in large saucepan over medium heat until small bubbles appear around perimeter of pan, 4 to 8 minutes. Reduce heat to low and simmer, stirring occasionally, until large bubbles form and mixture has thickened and turned deep golden brown, about 6 minutes; transfer to large bowl. Stir in remaining ½ cup evaporated milk and remaining 4 tablespoons butter until mixture is slightly cool. Add chocolate and vanilla and stir until smooth. Whisk in confectioners' sugar until incorporated. Let cool completely, stirring occasionally, about 1 hour.

4 Line edges of cake platter with 4 strips of parchment to keep platter clean. Place 1 cake layer on platter. Spread 1 cup frosting evenly over top, right to edge of cake. Top with second cake layer, press lightly to adhere, then spread remaining frosting evenly over top and sides of cake. Refrigerate cake until frosting is set, about 1 hour. Carefully remove parchment strips before serving.

CAKE

- 2½ cups (12½ ounces) all-purpose flour
- 2 teaspoons baking soda
- 1 teaspoon baking powder
- ½ teaspoon table salt
- ¾ cup hot water
- ½ cup (1½ ounces) unsweetened cocoa powder
- 16 tablespoons unsalted butter, cut into 16 pieces and softened
- 2 cups (14 ounces) granulated sugar
- 2 large eggs
- 1 cup buttermilk, room temperature
- 2 teaspoons vanilla extract

FROSTING

- 1½ cups packed (10½ ounces) light brown sugar
- 1 cup evaporated milk, divided
- 8 tablespoons unsalted butter, cut into 8 pieces and softened, divided
- ½ teaspoon table salt
- 8 ounces bittersweet chocolate, chopped
- 1 teaspoon vanilla extract
- 3 cups (12 ounces) confectioners' sugar, sifted

GERMAN CHOCOLATE CAKE

SERVES 10 TO 12

FILLING

- 4 large egg yolks
- 1 (12-ounce) can evaporated milk
- 1 cup (7 ounces) granulated sugar
- 6 tablespoons unsalted butter, cut into 6 pieces
- ¼ cup packed (1¾ ounces) light brown sugar
- ⅛ teaspoon table salt
- 2 teaspoons vanilla extract
- 2⅓ cups (7 ounces) sweetened shredded coconut
- 1½ cups pecans, toasted and chopped fine

CAKE

- 4 ounces semisweet or bittersweet chocolate, chopped fine
- ¼ cup (¾ ounce) unsweetened cocoa powder
- ½ cup boiling water
- 2 cups (10 ounces) all-purpose flour
- ¾ teaspoon baking soda
- 12 tablespoons unsalted butter, softened
- 1 cup (7 ounces) granulated sugar
- ⅔ cup packed (4⅔ ounces) light brown sugar
- ¾ teaspoon table salt
- 4 large eggs
- 1 teaspoon vanilla extract
- ¾ cup sour cream

Why This Recipe Works German chocolate cake is a distinctly American invention—it gets its name from Baker's German's Sweet Chocolate—and most recipes are similar, if not identical, to the one on the back of the box. The result is a cake that's too sweet, with weak chocolate flavor and a filling so wet and heavy it ruins the texture of the cake. We wanted a German chocolate cake that was just sweet enough, with an unmistakable chocolate presence and a thick—but not dense—coconut-pecan filling that could support the layers of cake. We quickly realized that the chocolate for which this cake is named was simply much too sweet. Using both cocoa powder and semisweet or bittersweet chocolate improved matters, and mixing them with boiling water intensified their flavors. A combination of brown and white sugars gave this cake the right level of caramel-like sweetness we loved from the original and also contributed to a tender texture. The filling's base of egg yolks, evaporated milk, sugar, and butter is typically simmered, but we found this resulted in a loose consistency. Boiling the filling ensured it thickened properly. We stirred sweetened shredded coconut into the filling before chilling (refrigerating the filling helped it firm up), but we waited until it was time to assemble the cake before adding the toasted pecans to preserve their crunch. For an accurate measurement of boiling water, bring a full kettle of water to a boil and then measure out the desired amount.

1 **For the filling** Whisk egg yolks in medium saucepan, then gradually whisk in evaporated milk. Whisk in granulated sugar, butter, brown sugar, and salt and cook over medium-high heat, whisking constantly, until mixture is boiling, frothy, and slightly thickened, about 6 minutes. Transfer mixture to bowl, whisk in vanilla, then stir in coconut. Let cool until just warm, then refrigerate until cool, at least 2 hours or up to 3 days. (Pecans are added later.)

2 **For the cake** Adjust oven rack to lower-middle position and heat oven to 350 degrees. Grease two 9-inch round cake pans, line with parchment paper, grease parchment, and flour pans. Combine chocolate and cocoa in bowl, add boiling water, cover, and let sit for 5 minutes. Whisk chocolate mixture until smooth, then let cool completely. Whisk flour and baking soda together in second bowl.

3 Using stand mixer fitted with paddle, beat butter, granulated sugar, brown sugar, and salt on medium-high speed until light and fluffy, about 3 minutes. Add eggs, one at a time, and beat until combined. Add vanilla and beat until light and fluffy, about 45 seconds. Reduce speed to low, add chocolate mixture, then increase speed to medium and beat until combined, about 30 seconds, scraping down bowl once (batter may look curdled). Reduce speed to low, add flour mixture in 3 additions, alternating with sour cream in 2 additions, scraping down bowl as needed. Give batter final stir by hand (batter will be thick).

4 Divide batter evenly between prepared pans and smooth tops with rubber spatula. Gently tap pans on counter to settle batter. Bake until toothpick inserted in center comes out clean, about 30 minutes, rotating pans halfway through baking.

5 Let cakes cool in pans on wire rack for 10 minutes. Remove cakes from pans, discarding parchment, and let cool completely on rack, about 2 hours.

6 Using long serrated knife, cut 1 horizontal line around sides of each layer; then, following scored lines, cut each layer into 2 even layers. Stir toasted pecans into chilled filling.

7 Place 1 cake layer on platter. Spread 1 cup filling evenly over top, right to edge of cake. Repeat with remaining cake layers, aligning cuts so layers are even and pressing lightly to adhere (leave sides unfrosted). Serve. (Frosted cake can be refrigerated for up to 24 hours; bring to room temperature before serving.)

FALLEN CHOCOLATE CAKES

SERVES 8

Unsweetened cocoa powder, for ramekins

8 ounces semisweet chocolate, chopped

8 tablespoons unsalted butter, cut into 8 pieces

4 large eggs plus 1 large yolk, room temperature

½ cup (3½ ounces) granulated sugar

1 teaspoon vanilla extract

¼ teaspoon table salt

2 tablespoons all-purpose flour

Confectioners' sugar

Why This Recipe Works Fallen chocolate cake, also known as molten chocolate cake, is superlatively decadent with its undercooked center that pours seductively out of a mound of rich chocolate cake. We wanted to turn this restaurant-menu standard into a practical recipe for home cooks. Beating the egg whites and yolks separately and then folding them together as some recipes instruct resulted in a cottony cake; we found that beating the eggs with sugar to a foam and then folding them into melted chocolate delivered cakes with the rich, moist texture we wanted. A mere 2 tablespoons of flour did an able job of holding the soufflé-like cakes together—any more and the cakes were dry, with no fluid center. Finally, we wanted to ensure that these decadent desserts would arrive at the table hot and still molten; happily, we found that we could prepare the batter ahead of time, refrigerate the filled ramekins until ready to use, and then place them in the oven to bake during dinner. You can substitute bittersweet chocolate for the semisweet; the flavor will be slightly more intense. Serve the cakes with Whipped Cream (page 340) or ice cream and/or berries, if desired.

1 Adjust oven rack to middle position and heat oven to 400 degrees. Grease eight 6-ounce ramekins and dust with cocoa. Arrange ramekins on rimmed baking sheet. Microwave chocolate and butter in large bowl at 50 percent power, stirring occasionally, until melted and smooth, 2 to 4 minutes; set aside.

2 Using stand mixer fitted with whisk attachment, whip eggs, yolk, granulated sugar, vanilla, and salt on high speed until eggs are pale yellow and have nearly tripled in volume. (Egg foam will form ribbon that sits on top of mixture for 5 seconds when dribbled from whisk.) Scrape egg mixture over chocolate mixture, then sprinkle flour on top. Using rubber spatula, gently fold egg mixture and flour into chocolate until mixture is uniformly colored.

3 Divide batter evenly among prepared ramekins. (Unbaked cakes can be refrigerated for up to 8 hours. Return to room temperature for 30 minutes before baking.) Bake until cakes have puffed about ½ inch above rims of ramekins, have thin crust on top, and jiggle slightly at center when ramekins are shaken very gently, 12 to 13 minutes. Run thin knife around edges of ramekins to loosen cakes. Invert each ramekin onto plate and let sit until cakes release themselves from ramekins, about 1 minute. Lift off ramekins, dust with confectioners' sugar, and serve.

Fallen Orange-Chocolate Cakes

Fold 2 tablespoons orange liqueur and 1 tablespoon grated orange zest into chocolate with egg mixture and flour at the end of step 2.

TORTA CAPRESE

SERVES 12 TO 14

Why This Recipe Works A simple yet elegant dessert with origins along the Amalfi Coast, *torta caprese* is a chocolate-almond cake with all the richness and depth of flourless chocolate cake, but it features finely ground almonds that subtly break up the fudgy crumb, making it a lighter final course. And with no layers to assemble or frosting to prepare, this cake is easy to make. Bittersweet chocolate provided a solid chocolate base, and some cocoa powder added complexity. To aerate the heavy batter and provide enough structure and lift, we beat the whites and yolks separately. We also discovered that commercial almond flour worked just as well as nuts we had ground ourselves, which saved us the trouble of using two appliances. This cake tastes great the next day, so it's an excellent make-ahead dessert for entertaining. Either almond flour or almond meal will work in this recipe; we used Bob's Red Mill Almond Flour. We like the cake with Orange Whipped Cream (page 340).

12 tablespoons unsalted butter, cut into 12 pieces

6 ounces bittersweet chocolate, chopped

1 teaspoon vanilla extract

4 large eggs, separated

1 cup (7 ounces) granulated sugar, divided

2 cups (7 ounces) almond flour

2 tablespoons unsweetened cocoa powder

½ teaspoon table salt

Confectioners' sugar (optional)

1 Adjust oven rack to middle position and heat oven to 325 degrees. Lightly spray 9-inch springform pan with vegetable oil spray.

2 Microwave butter and chocolate in bowl at 50 percent power, stirring occasionally, until melted and smooth, 1½ to 2 minutes. Stir in vanilla and set aside.

3 Using stand mixer fitted with whisk attachment, whip egg whites on medium-low speed until foamy, about 1 minute. Increase speed to medium-high and whip, slowly adding ½ cup granulated sugar, until glossy, stiff peaks form, about 4 minutes. Transfer whites to large bowl.

4 Add egg yolks and remaining ½ cup granulated sugar to now-empty mixer bowl and whip on medium-high speed until thick and pale yellow, about 3 minutes, scraping down bowl as needed. Add chocolate mixture and mix on medium speed until incorporated, about 15 seconds. Add almond flour, cocoa, and salt and mix until incorporated, about 30 seconds.

5 Remove bowl from mixer and stir batter few times with large rubber spatula, scraping bottom of bowl to ensure almond flour is fully incorporated. Add one-third of whipped whites to bowl, return bowl to mixer, and mix on medium speed until no streaks of white remain, about 30 seconds, scraping down bowl halfway through mixing. Transfer batter to bowl with remaining whites. Using large rubber spatula, gently fold whites into batter until no streaks of white remain. Transfer batter to prepared pan and smooth top with spatula. Place pan on rimmed baking sheet and bake until toothpick inserted in center comes out with few moist crumbs attached, about 50 minutes, rotating sheet halfway through baking. Let cake cool in pan on wire rack for 20 minutes. Remove side of pan and let cake cool completely, about 2 hours. (Cake can be stored at room temperature for up to 3 days.)

6 Dust top of cake with confectioners' sugar, if using. Using offset spatula, transfer cake to serving platter. Cut into wedges and serve.

CHOCOLATE BLACKOUT CAKE

SERVES 10 TO 12

PUDDING

2	cups half-and-half
1	cup whole milk
1¼	cups (8¾ ounces) granulated sugar
¼	cup (1 ounce) cornstarch
½	teaspoon table salt
6	ounces unsweetened chocolate, chopped
2	teaspoons vanilla extract

CAKE

1½	cups (7½ ounces) all-purpose flour
2	teaspoons baking powder
½	teaspoon baking soda
½	teaspoon table salt
8	tablespoons unsalted butter
¾	cup (2¼ ounces) Dutch-processed cocoa powder
1	cup brewed coffee
1	cup buttermilk
1	cup packed (7 ounces) light brown sugar
1	cup (7 ounces) granulated sugar
2	large eggs
1	teaspoon vanilla extract

Why This Recipe Works When the Ebinger's chain of bakeries closed its doors more than 45 years ago, Brooklyn residents went into mourning over the loss of their beloved blackout cake, a tender, decadent chocolate cake layered with a pudding-like filling and covered with cake crumbs. We set out to create our own version. Using an ample amount of cocoa powder—Dutch-processed was essential for its dark hue—in the batter and blooming it in butter were the first steps toward making a cake worthy of the name. The addition of some brewed coffee and brown sugar further underscored the chocolate notes. A generous amount of unsweetened chocolate kept the sweetness of the pudding in check, and some cornstarch thickened it to the proper consistency so it would cling to the sides of the cake. A combination of milk and half-and-half gave the pudding a velvety, lush quality that complemented the dark, rich cake.

1 For the pudding Whisk half-and-half, milk, sugar, cornstarch, and salt together in large saucepan. Add chocolate and whisk constantly over medium heat until chocolate melts and mixture begins to bubble, 2 to 4 minutes. Off heat, stir in vanilla. Transfer pudding to large bowl and press plastic wrap directly on surface. Refrigerate pudding until cold, at least 4 hours or up to 24 hours.

2 For the cake Adjust oven rack to middle position and heat oven to 325 degrees. Grease two 8-inch round cake pans, line with parchment paper, grease parchment, and flour pans. Whisk flour, baking powder, baking soda, and salt together in bowl.

3 Melt butter in large saucepan over medium heat. Stir in cocoa and cook until fragrant, about 1 minute. Off heat, whisk in coffee, buttermilk, brown sugar, and granulated sugar until sugars are dissolved. Whisk in eggs and vanilla, then slowly whisk in flour mixture.

4 Divide batter evenly between prepared pans. Bake until toothpick inserted in center comes out clean, 30 to 35 minutes, rotating pans halfway through baking. Let cakes cool in pans on wire rack for 15 minutes. Remove cakes from pans, discarding parchment, and let cool completely on rack, about 2 hours.

5 Using long serrated knife, cut 1 horizontal line around sides of each layer; then, following scored lines, cut each layer into 2 even layers. Crumble 1 cake layer into medium crumbs and set aside. Line edges of cake platter with 4 strips of parchment to keep platter clean. Place 1 cake layer on platter. Spread 1 cup pudding evenly over top, right to edge of cake. Repeat with 1 more cake layer, pressing lightly to adhere, and 1 cup pudding. Top with remaining cake layer, pressing lightly to adhere. Spread remaining pudding evenly over top and sides of cake. Sprinkle cake crumbs evenly over top and sides of cake, pressing lightly to adhere. Carefully remove parchment strips before serving. (Cake can be refrigerated for up to 2 days.)

MAGIC CHOCOLATE FLAN CAKE

SERVES 12

Why This Recipe Works Magic chocolate flan cake is a showy, all-in-one dessert featuring a layer of fudgy chocolate cake topped with creamy, vanilla-scented flan, all dripping with gooey caramel. The magic happens in the oven: After lining the bottom of a pan (often a Bundt pan) with caramel, the cake batter is poured in followed by the flan batter. As the cake bakes, the flan sinks and the cake rises, so when you flip the whole thing out of the pan, the caramel-lined flan sits on top. There's also magic in the contrast of dense, deep chocolate; smooth, light flan; and sweet, sticky caramel. Hoping to streamline this multicomponent dessert, we started with a simple chocolate cake recipe—no mixer required—featuring both unsweetened cocoa and bittersweet chocolate. We needed to make the cake drier to accommodate the added moisture from the flan, so we removed some of the buttermilk and reduced the sugar; the result was a cake that was fudgy and luscious, like an exceptionally rich brownie. To help our flan stand tall—not slump—when sliced, we used whole eggs in addition to the yolks and added cream cheese. It's worth using good-quality caramel sauce here. If your blender doesn't hold 2 quarts, process the flan in two batches. The cake needs to chill for at least 8 hours before you can unmold it.

1 **For the cake** Adjust oven rack to middle position and heat oven to 350 degrees. Grease 12-cup nonstick Bundt pan. Microwave caramel until easily pourable, about 30 seconds, then pour into prepared pan to coat bottom. Whisk flour, cocoa, baking soda, and salt together in bowl.

2 Microwave chocolate and butter in large bowl at 50 percent power, stirring occasionally, until melted and smooth, 2 to 4 minutes. Whisk in buttermilk, sugar, eggs, and vanilla until incorporated. Stir in flour mixture until just combined. Pour batter over caramel in prepared pan and wipe away any drips.

3 **For the flan** Process all ingredients in blender until smooth, about 1 minute. Gently pour flan over cake batter. Place Bundt pan in large roasting pan. Place roasting pan on oven rack and pour warm water into roasting pan until it reaches halfway up sides of Bundt pan. Bake until toothpick inserted in center of cake comes out clean and flan registers 180 degrees, 1¼ to 1½ hours. Transfer Bundt pan to wire rack and let cool completely, about 2 hours. Refrigerate until set, at least 8 hours. (Remove roasting pan from oven once water has cooled.)

4 Place bottom third of Bundt pan in bowl of hot tap water for 1 minute. Invert completely flat cake platter, place platter over top of Bundt pan, and gently turn platter and pan upside down. Slowly remove pan, allowing caramel to drizzle over top of cake. Serve.

CAKE

- ½ cup caramel sauce or topping
- ½ cup plus 2 tablespoons (3⅛ ounces) all-purpose flour
- ⅓ cup (1 ounce) unsweetened cocoa powder
- ½ teaspoon baking soda
- ⅛ teaspoon table salt
- 4 ounces bittersweet chocolate, chopped
- 6 tablespoons unsalted butter
- ½ cup buttermilk
- ½ cup (3½ ounces) sugar
- 2 large eggs
- 1 teaspoon vanilla extract

FLAN

- 2 (14-ounce) cans sweetened condensed milk
- 2½ cups whole milk
- 6 ounces cream cheese
- 6 large eggs plus 4 large yolks
- 1 teaspoon vanilla extract

CHOCOLATE MALTED CAKE

SERVES 12

FROSTING

- 6 ounces milk chocolate, chopped
- 1 cup (4½ ounces) malted milk powder
- ⅓ cup heavy cream
- 1 teaspoon vanilla extract
- 24 tablespoons (3 sticks) unsalted butter, softened
- ¼ teaspoon table salt
- 3 cups (12 ounces) confectioners' sugar

CAKE

- 2 (5-ounce) boxes malted milk balls, divided
- 3 (8-inch) Chocolate Cake Layers (page 349)

Why This Recipe Works Grain-based malted milk powder gives old-fashioned malted milkshakes their toffee-like sweetness, but its powers don't have to be limited to ice cream. For a dessert with nostalgic ice cream parlor flavor in every bite, we created a multilayer malted chocolate cake with lots of retro appeal. A full cup of malted milk powder in the frosting provided plenty of that familiar nutty sweetness. We opted for milk chocolate in our frosting, which underscored the malted milk powder's dairy notes and contributed a creamy texture. The addition of some heavy cream further ensured a smooth, silky consistency. Crushed malted milk ball candies sprinkled between the frosted cake layers provided a crunchy surprise and reinforced the flavor of our frosting. Whole malted milk balls arranged around the top and bottom edges of the cake were a decorative finishing touch that made the cake pretty for a pedestal. Malted milk powder is a mixture of malted barley, wheat flour, and evaporated whole milk. It can be found in the baking section of most grocery stores.

1 For the frosting Microwave chocolate in bowl at 50 percent power, stirring occasionally, until melted, 1 to 3 minutes. Let cool completely. Stir malted milk powder, cream, and vanilla in second bowl until thoroughly combined. Using stand mixer fitted with whisk attachment, whip butter and salt on medium-high speed until smooth, about 1 minute. Reduce speed to medium-low, slowly add sugar, and mix until smooth, 1 to 2 minutes. Add malted milk mixture, increase speed to medium-high, and whip until light and fluffy, about 3 minutes. Add chocolate mixture and whip until thoroughly combined.

2 For the cake Place 1 cup malted milk balls in 1-gallon zipper-lock bag and crush coarse with rolling pin. Line edges of cake platter with 4 strips of parchment paper to keep platter clean. Place 1 cake layer on platter. Spread 1 cup frosting evenly over top. Sprinkle half of crushed malted milk balls evenly over frosting. Repeat with 1 more cake layer, 1 cup frosting, and remaining crushed malted milk balls. Top with remaining cake layer, pressing lightly to adhere. Spread remaining frosting evenly over top and sides of cake. Arrange whole malted milk balls around top and bottom edges of cake. Arrange 5 malted milk balls in center of cake. Carefully remove parchment strips before serving.

TUNNEL OF FUDGE CAKE

SERVES 12

Why This Recipe Works Tunnel of fudge is a retro cake that's exactly what it sounds like: an ultrachocolaty moist-crumbed cake with a rich, fudgy interior section. We wanted to resurrect this old-school favorite—and chocolate lover's dream—but the original relied on the most unusual ingredient to achieve the creamy, fudgelike tunnel: powdered frosting mix. To create our own (all-natural) chocolaty tunnel without a mix we used Dutch-processed cocoa and confectioners' sugar in the cake batter—both key ingredients in the frosting mix. Adding melted chocolate as well made our cake moister; replacing some of the granulated sugar with brown sugar and cutting back on the flour and butter provided the perfect environment for the fudgy interior to form. Slightly underbaking the cake was the final essential step to achieving the ideal consistency for the man-made chocolate tunnel. For an accurate measurement of boiling water, bring a full kettle of water to a boil and then measure out ½ cup. Do not use a cake tester, toothpick, or skewer to test the cake—the fudgy interior won't give an accurate reading. Instead, remove the cake from the oven when the sides just begin to pull away from the pan and the surface of the cake springs back when pressed gently with your finger.

1 Adjust oven rack to lower-middle position and heat oven to 350 degrees. Mix 1 tablespoon cocoa and melted butter for pan into paste in small bowl. Using pastry brush, thoroughly coat interior of 12-cup nonstick Bundt pan. Pour boiling water over chocolate in bowl and whisk until smooth. Let cool completely. Whisk flour, pecans, confectioners' sugar, salt, and remaining ¾ cup cocoa together in large bowl. Whisk eggs and vanilla in 4-cup liquid measuring cup.

2 Using stand mixer fitted with paddle, beat softened butter, granulated sugar, and brown sugar on medium-high speed until fluffy, about 2 minutes. Reduce speed to low and add egg mixture until combined, about 30 seconds. Add chocolate mixture and mix until incorporated, about 30 seconds. Add flour mixture and mix until just combined, about 30 seconds.

3 Transfer batter to prepared pan and smooth top with rubber spatula. Bake until edges are beginning to pull away from pan, about 45 minutes, rotating pan halfway through baking. Let cake cool in pan on wire rack set in rimmed baking sheet for 1½ hours. Invert cake onto rack, remove pan, and let cool completely, at least 2 hours. Drizzle glaze over cooled cake and let set for at least 10 minutes before serving. (Cake can be stored at room temperature for up to 2 days.)

¾ cup (2¼ ounces) Dutch-processed cocoa powder, plus 1 tablespoon for pan

20 tablespoons (2½ sticks) unsalted butter, cut into 20 pieces and softened, plus 1 tablespoon, melted, for pan

½ cup boiling water

2 ounces bittersweet chocolate, chopped

2 cups (10 ounces) all-purpose flour

2 cups pecans or walnuts, chopped fine

2 cups (8 ounces) confectioners' sugar

1 teaspoon table salt

5 large eggs, room temperature

1 tablespoon vanilla extract

1 cup (7 ounces) granulated sugar

¾ cup packed (5¼ ounces) light brown sugar

1 recipe All-Purpose Chocolate Glaze (page 348)

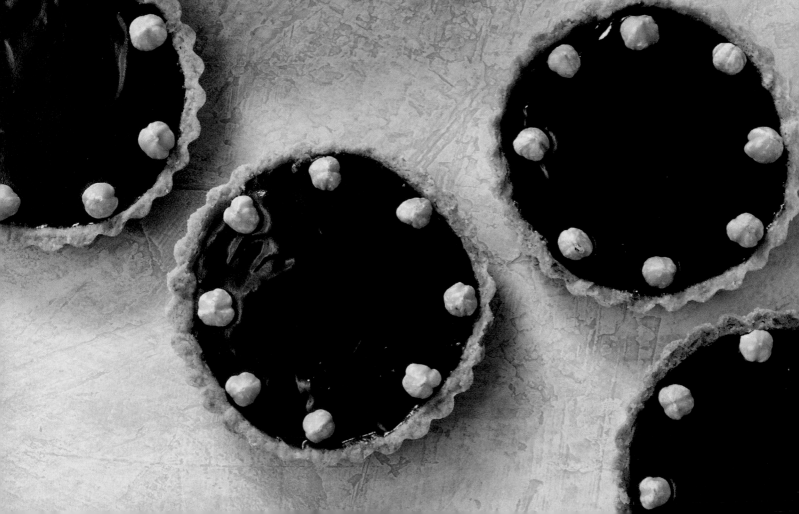

sublime
SLICES

RICH CHOCOLATE TART

SERVES 10 TO 12

1 recipe Chocolate Tart Dough
(page 201)

FILLING

9 ounces bittersweet chocolate,
chopped fine

1¼ cups heavy cream

½ teaspoon instant espresso
powder

¼ teaspoon table salt

4 tablespoons unsalted butter,
sliced thin and softened

2 large eggs, room temperature

GLAZE

3 tablespoons heavy cream

1 tablespoon light corn syrup

2 ounces bittersweet chocolate,
chopped fine

1 tablespoon hot water

Why This Recipe Works To us, the real draw of a rich chocolate tart is its simple confidence: The best versions boast a flawlessly smooth, truffle-like texture; unadulterated chocolate flavor; and a sophisticated polish. As chocolate is the sole filling, we wanted a custard-style mixture here—one that would be dense and rich, but not as dense as ganache; and not as plush, so we could eat more than a couple bites. The ganache we saved for a thin glaze to give the top a pristine sheen. The tart can be garnished with chocolate curls (see page 266) or a flaky sea salt, such as Maldon. Chocolate pairs well with so many flavors that we also wanted to give our tart an intriguing variation. Chocolate and peanut butter are a classic combination but we wanted something distinctly grown-up, so we turned to nutty tahini. Its slight bitterness allowed its flavor to come through all that chocolate. A topping of sesame seed brittle reinforced the sesame flavor and made for a stunning geometric finish to this artistic tart.

1 Roll dough into 11-inch circle on floured counter, then transfer to parchment paper–lined rimmed baking sheet; cover loosely with plastic wrap and refrigerate until firm but pliable, about 10 minutes.

2 Loosely roll dough around rolling pin and gently unroll it onto 9-inch tart pan with removable bottom, letting excess dough hang over edge. Ease dough into pan by gently lifting edge of dough with your hand while pressing into corners and fluted sides of pan with your other hand. Run rolling pin over top of pan to remove any excess dough. Wrap loosely in plastic, place on large plate, and freeze until fully chilled and firm, about 30 minutes. (Dough-lined tart pan can be frozen for up to 1 month.) Adjust oven rack to middle position and heat oven to 375 degrees.

3 Line chilled tart shell with double layer of aluminum foil and fill with pie weights. Bake on foil-lined rimmed baking sheet until tart shell is golden brown and set, about 30 minutes, rotating sheet halfway through baking. Remove foil and weights and continue to bake tart shell until it is fully baked and golden, 5 to 10 minutes longer. Transfer sheet to wire rack and let cool completely, about 1 hour.

4 **For the filling** Reduce oven temperature to 250 degrees. Place chocolate in large bowl. Bring cream, espresso powder, and salt to simmer in small saucepan over medium heat, whisking to dissolve espresso powder and salt, then pour over chocolate. Cover and let sit until chocolate is softened, about 5 minutes, then whisk to combine. Whisk in butter until smooth, then add eggs and whisk until combined and glossy.

5 Pour filling into cooled tart shell and spread into even layer with rubber spatula, popping any large bubbles with toothpick. Bake tart on sheet until edge of filling is just set but center jiggles slightly and very faint cracks appear on surface, 30 to 35 minutes. Let tart cool completely on sheet on wire rack, about 2 hours. Refrigerate, uncovered, until filling is chilled and set, at least 3 hours. (Tart can be refrigerated for up to 18 hours.)

6 **For the glaze** Remove tart from refrigerator and let sit at room temperature for 30 minutes. Bring cream and corn syrup to simmer in small saucepan over medium heat, stirring occasionally. Off heat, add chocolate, cover, and let sit until chocolate is softened, about 5 minutes. Whisk to combine, then whisk in hot water (glaze should be homogeneous, shiny, and pourable). Working quickly, pour glaze onto center of tart and tilt tart to allow glaze to run to edge. Pop any large bubbles with toothpick. Let sit at room temperature until glaze is set, at least 1 hour or up to 3 hours.

7 Remove outer ring of tart pan, slide thin metal spatula between tart and tart pan bottom, and carefully slide tart onto serving platter or cutting board. Serve.

Chocolate-Tahini Tart

Be mindful of how you plan to cut the tart when arranging the brittle over the top.

In filling, reduce chocolate to 5 ounces and cream to ¾ cup. Add ¼ cup sugar to saucepan with espresso powder in step 4, whisking until sugar is dissolved. Add ¾ cup tahini to saucepan with butter in step 4, whisking until smooth. Arrange 1 recipe Sesame Brittle (page 348) over finished tart before serving.

CHOCOLATE CARAMEL-WALNUT TART

SERVES 8 TO 10

1 recipe Classic Tart Dough
(page 201)

CARAMEL-WALNUT FILLING

¼ cup water

1 cup (7 ounces) sugar

⅔ cup heavy cream

3 tablespoons unsalted butter,
cut into 3 pieces

½ teaspoon vanilla extract

½ teaspoon lemon juice

⅛ teaspoon table salt

16–18 walnut halves, plus 1 cup
walnuts, toasted and
chopped, divided

CHOCOLATE FILLING

2 large egg yolks

1 tablespoon plus ⅓ cup heavy
cream, divided

⅓ cup whole milk

5 ounces semisweet chocolate,
chopped fine

2 tablespoons unsalted butter,
cut into 4 pieces

Why This Recipe Works Holding rich chocolate, deep caramel, and earthy walnuts, this tart is truly something special. To make certain each of its elements received the proper emphasis, we took a layered approach to tart building: First a simple prebaked tart crust, then a layer of toasted walnuts draped with soft caramel, and finally a topping of smooth chocolate ganache—the filling firm enough to slice neatly but neither dense nor overpowering. For the layer of ganache, we tested various ratios of chocolate, cream, and butter, but tasters repeatedly noted that the chilled ganache was too dense—more confection than tart filling—and overshadowed the flavor of the walnuts and caramel. Efforts to lighten it by increasing the quantities of cream and butter resulted in a ganache that was too soft to slice. The answer was to switch to a custard filling that we baked on top of the caramel-walnut layer. To slice, dip a sharp knife in very hot water and wipe dry before each cut.

1 Roll dough into 11-inch circle on floured counter, then transfer to parchment paper–lined rimmed baking sheet; cover loosely with plastic wrap and refrigerate until firm but pliable, about 10 minutes.

2 Loosely roll dough around rolling pin and gently unroll it onto 9-inch tart pan with removable bottom, letting excess dough hang over edge. Ease dough into pan by gently lifting edge of dough with your hand while pressing into corners and fluted sides of pan with your other hand. Run rolling pin over top of pan to remove any excess dough. Wrap loosely in plastic, place on large plate, and freeze until fully chilled and firm, about 30 minutes. (Dough-lined tart pan can be frozen for up to 1 month.) Adjust oven rack to middle position and heat oven to 375 degrees.

3 Line chilled tart shell with double layer of aluminum foil and fill with pie weights. Bake on foil-lined rimmed baking sheet until tart shell is golden brown and set, about 30 minutes, rotating sheet halfway through baking. Remove foil and weights and continue to bake tart shell until it is fully baked and golden, 5 to 10 minutes. Transfer sheet to wire rack and let tart shell cool completely, about 1 hour. Reduce oven temperature to 300 degrees.

4 **For the caramel-walnut filling** While crust is cooling, add water to medium saucepan, then pour sugar into center of saucepan, taking care not to let sugar granules hit sides of pan. Gently stir sugar with clean spatula to moisten sugar thoroughly. Bring mixture to boil over medium-high heat and cook, without stirring, until sugar has dissolved completely and liquid has faint golden color and registers about 300 degrees, 6 to 10 minutes.

5 Reduce heat to medium-low and continue to cook, stirring occasionally, until caramel has dark amber color and registers about 350 degrees, 1 to 3 minutes. Off heat, slowly whisk in cream until combined (mixture will bubble and steam vigorously). Stir in butter, vanilla, lemon juice, and salt until combined. Stir in walnut halves to coat. Let caramel mixture sit until slightly thickened, about 8 minutes.

6 Set wire rack over large sheet of parchment paper. Using slotted spoon, transfer caramel-coated walnuts to rack, flip nuts right side up, and let cool completely. Stir chopped walnuts into remaining caramel, then pour caramel mixture into cooled crust. Refrigerate tart, uncovered, until caramel is firm and does not run when pan is tilted, about 20 minutes.

7 For the chocolate filling Meanwhile, whisk egg yolks and 1 tablespoon cream together in bowl. Bring milk and remaining ⅓ cup cream to simmer over medium heat in small saucepan. Off heat, stir in chocolate and butter, cover saucepan, and let stand until chocolate is mostly melted, about 2 minutes. Gently stir mixture until smooth, then stir in egg yolk mixture.

8 Pour chocolate filling evenly over chilled caramel and smooth into even layer to cover caramel by tilting pan. Bake tart on rimmed baking sheet until tiny bubbles are visible on surface and chocolate layer is just set, about 25 minutes, rotating sheet halfway through baking.

9 Transfer sheet to wire rack, arrange caramel-coated walnut halves around edge of tart to garnish, and let tart cool slightly on sheet for 30 minutes; then refrigerate, uncovered, until chocolate is firm, about 3 hours. Remove outer ring of tart pan, slide thin metal spatula between tart and tart pan bottom, and carefully slide tart onto serving platter or cutting board. Serve.

CHOCOLATE-HAZELNUT TART

SERVES 8 TO 10

TART DOUGH

- 1 cup (4 ounces) confectioners' sugar
- ½ cup blanched hazelnuts, toasted
- ⅛ teaspoon table salt
- 1 large egg yolk
- 2 teaspoons heavy cream
- 4 tablespoons unsalted butter, cut into 8 pieces and chilled
- ¾ cup plus 2 tablespoons (4⅜ ounces) all-purpose flour

CHOCOLATE FILLING

- 4 cups ice cubes
- 5⅓ ounces bittersweet chocolate (70 percent cacao or higher), chopped
- 3 tablespoons plus 1 teaspoon granulated sugar
- ⅛ teaspoon table salt

HAZELNUT WHIPPED CREAM

- 1 cup heavy cream
- ¼ teaspoon table salt
- ¼ cup blanched hazelnuts, toasted and chopped

Why This Recipe Works For this dressy tart we took inspiration from one of the best desserts out there: a spoonful of Nutella. The tart features a hazelnut crust, hazelnut whipped cream, and hazelnut sugar on top, but it's the unique layer of chocolate ganache that is the real standout. We employed a technique that French chemist Hervé This developed in the 1990s to make a dairy-free chocolate Chantilly, or whipped chocolate. Here, bittersweet chocolate is melted with a generous amount of water and then whipped to achieve a mousse-like texture. Without the cream found in a typical ganache to mask the chocolate flavor, the result is a filling that is intensely chocolaty and decadent—one that won't fade into the background no matter what it is paired with. After melting the chocolate in the water—along with a little sugar and a bit of salt—we rapidly cooled the mixture by stirring it vigorously over an ice bath. This partially crystallized the cocoa butter, formed a stable emulsion, and trapped a small amount of air for a ganache layer that was cohesive and firm enough to slice but also not too dense. This recipe requires chocolate with a high ratio of cocoa solids and cocoa butter. We found that using chocolate with a lower cacao percentage resulted in a loose, grainy chocolate layer.

1 For the tart dough Process sugar, hazelnuts, and salt in food processor until fine and powdery, about 1 minute. Measure out ⅔ cup plus 2 tablespoons sugar mixture and set aside. Whisk egg yolk and cream together in small bowl and set aside. Add butter to remaining sugar mixture in food processor and process until smooth and creamy, scraping down sides of bowl as needed, about 1 minute. Gradually add egg mixture and process until smooth and combined, scraping down sides of bowl as needed, about 1 minute. Add flour and process until mixture forms cohesive dough, about 30 seconds. Transfer dough to counter and briefly knead until smooth. Roll dough between 2 large sheets of parchment paper into 12-inch round. Transfer dough, still between parchment, to baking sheet and freeze for 15 minutes or refrigerate for 30 minutes, until dough is firm.

2 Transfer dough to counter, discard top sheet of parchment, and lightly dust dough with flour. Let dough sit until slightly pliable, 1 to 3 minutes. Loosely roll dough around rolling pin, peeling away bottom sheet of parchment, and gently unroll it onto 9-inch tart pan with removable bottom, letting excess dough hang over edge. Ease dough into pan by gently lifting edge of dough with your hand while pressing into corners and fluted sides of pan with your other hand. Run rolling pin over top of pan to remove any excess dough. Wrap loosely in plastic, place on large plate, and refrigerate for at least 30 minutes or up to 3 days. (Dough-lined tart pan can be frozen for up to 1 month.)

3 Adjust oven rack to middle position and heat oven to 325 degrees. Remove dough-lined tart pan from refrigerator and, using skewer, poke 30 small holes, evenly spaced, in dough on bottom. Bake tart shell on rimmed baking sheet until edges just begin to brown, 20 to 25 minutes, rotating sheet halfway through baking. Transfer sheet to wire rack and let cool completely.

4 **For the chocolate filling** Fill large bowl with 2 cups water and ice cubes. Place chocolate, ½ cup plus 1 tablespoon water, sugar, and salt in heatproof bowl over saucepan filled with 1 inch barely simmering water. Cook, stirring frequently with rubber spatula, until chocolate is fully melted and smooth, about 5 minutes. Transfer bowl to ice bath and chill, stirring constantly, until mixture is slightly thickened and registers between 75 and 80 degrees, 30 seconds to 1 minute. Remove bowl from ice bath and continue to stir 30 seconds longer. Transfer filling to cooled tart shell and tap baking sheet lightly on counter to release air bubbles; refrigerate tart until set, about 1 hour. (Tart can refrigerated for up to 24 hours.)

5 **For the hazelnut whipped cream** In bowl of stand mixer fitted with whisk attachment, whip cream and salt on high speed until frothy and slightly thickened, about 1 minute. Add ⅔ cup reserved sugar mixture and whip on high speed until stiff peaks form, 1 to 3 minutes. Remove tart from refrigerator. Remove outer ring of tart pan, slide thin metal spatula between tart and tart pan bottom, and carefully slide tart onto serving platter or cutting board. Spread or pipe whipped cream evenly over chocolate layer. Using fine-mesh strainer, dust tart with remaining 2 tablespoons reserved sugar mixture. Sprinkle with hazelnuts and serve.

CHOCOLATE-PEAR TART

SERVES 8 TO 10

1 recipe Chocolate Tart Dough
  (page 201)

CHOCOLATE FILLING

4 ounces bittersweet chocolate,
  chopped

4 tablespoons butter, cut into
  4 pieces

2 large eggs, room temperature

⅓ cup (2⅓ ounces) sugar

Pinch table salt

1 tablespoon all-purpose flour

POACHED PEARS

3 cups ruby port

½ cup (3½ ounces) sugar

4 (2-inch) strips orange zest

1 cinnamon stick

1 teaspoon black peppercorns

½ teaspoon whole cloves

3 ripe but firm pears, such as Bosc
  or Bartlett, peeled, halved
  lengthwise, and cored

2 tablespoons apple jelly, melted

Why This Recipe Works Adorning a chocolate tart with fruit turns a simple yet elegant dessert into a real showstopper. But it's rare to see chocolate paired with any fruit other than fresh raspberries or strawberries; for a chocolate-and-fruit tart with interest, we added a layer of juicy, ripe pears poached in spiced ruby port. Instead of custard or ganache, we made a filling of nearly flourless chocolate cake, which was incredibly rich and decadent and also sturdy enough to support the heavy fruit. Whipped eggs lightened the batter, but they also created a filling that souffles so dramatically in the oven that it rises up and over the pears. Chilling the filling for an hour caused the chocolate and butter to firm up and resulted in a more moderate puff. Poaching the pears in port scented with orange zest, cinnamon, cloves, and black pepper added an elegant, complex layer of flavor and ensured they baked evenly. A buttery chocolate tart crust was the perfect complement to the filling. The pears should be ripe but firm, the flesh near the stem giving slightly when gently pressed with your finger. This tart is best when served with a dollop of Whipped Cream (page 340).

1 Roll dough into 11-inch circle on floured counter, then transfer to parchment paper–lined rimmed baking sheet; cover loosely with plastic wrap and refrigerate until firm but pliable, about 10 minutes.

2 Loosely roll dough around rolling pin and gently unroll it onto 9-inch tart pan with removable bottom, letting excess dough hang over edge. Ease dough into pan by gently lifting edge of dough with your hand while pressing into corners and fluted sides of pan with your other hand. Run rolling pin over top of pan to remove any excess dough. Wrap loosely in plastic, place on large plate, and freeze until fully chilled and firm, about 30 minutes. (Dough-lined tart pan can be frozen for up to 1 month.) Adjust oven rack to middle position and heat oven to 375 degrees.

3 Line chilled tart shell with double layer of aluminum foil and fill with pie weights. Bake on foil-lined rimmed baking sheet until tart shell is golden brown and set, about 30 minutes, rotating sheet halfway through baking. Remove foil and weights and continue to bake tart shell until it is fully baked and golden, 5 to 10 minutes. Transfer sheet to wire rack and let cool while making filling. Reduce oven temperature to 325 degrees.

4 **For the chocolate filling** While crust is cooling, microwave chocolate and butter in bowl at 50 percent power, stirring occasionally, until melted and smooth, about 1 minute. Set aside to cool slightly.

5 Using stand mixer fitted with whisk attachment, whip eggs, sugar, and salt together on medium-high speed until pale yellow and thick, about 3 minutes. Fold one-third of egg mixture into chocolate mixture until combined, then fold in remaining egg mixture. Sift flour over chocolate mixture and gently fold until combined. Cover bowl with plastic and refrigerate filling for 1 hour.

6 **For the poached pears** Bring port, sugar, orange zest, cinnamon, peppercorns, and cloves to boil in medium saucepan over high heat, stirring occasionally, until sugar dissolves. Reduce heat to low, add pears, and simmer, covered, until pears are nearly tender, about 10 minutes. Remove from heat and let cool completely, about 1 hour. (Pears can be refrigerated in poaching liquid for up to 3 days.)

7 Using slotted spoon, remove pears from liquid, pat dry, and cut each into eighths; discard liquid. Spread chilled filling over cooled crust. Arrange pear slices in concentric circles on top of filling, overlapping them slightly. Bake tart on sheet until filling has puffed up and center feels firm to touch, 45 to 55 minutes, rotating sheet halfway through baking. Let tart cool on wire rack for at least 1 hour. Brush pears with melted jelly. Remove outer ring of tart pan, slide thin metal spatula between tart and tart pan bottom, and carefully slide tart onto serving platter or cutting board. Serve warm or at room temperature.

CHOCOLATE PASSION FRUIT TART

SERVES 8

1 recipe Chocolate Tart Dough (page 201)

1¼ pounds passion fruit, halved

½ cup (3½ ounces) granulated sugar

6 large egg yolks

2 tablespoons lemon juice

1 tablespoon cornstarch

⅛ teaspoon table salt

4 tablespoons unsalted butter, cut into 4 pieces

½ cup heavy cream

Why This Recipes Works Maybe you're not familiar with passion fruit. Maybe you've never seen it in a tart. More likely still, maybe you've never had a passion fruit and chocolate tart. Passion fruit packs a tropical punch that, even in the middle of winter, transports us to the beach on a hot, sunny day, while chocolate is rich, dreamy, and a little moody. It's these contrasts that make a chocolate and passion fruit tart work. We made a smooth passion fruit curd to fill a buttery, chocolaty shortbread tart shell for a harmonious blend of sweet, tangy, and rich flavors. The addition of lemon juice ensured that the curd retained its pleasantly tart edge against the rich chocolate crust, while a small amount of cornstarch helped firm it up. A moderate amount of whipped cream folded into the curd gave it a plush texture. You can substitute ½ cup frozen passion fruit puree, thawed, for the fresh in this recipe (skip step 4). Do not use passion fruit concentrate, which contains additional sugar. You need only to lightly flour the counter when rolling out this supple dough. Serve with Cocoa Whipped Cream (page 340), if desired.

1 Roll dough into 11-inch circle on floured counter, then transfer to parchment paper–lined rimmed baking sheet; cover loosely with plastic wrap and refrigerate until firm but pliable, about 10 minutes. Loosely roll dough around rolling pin and gently unroll it onto 9-inch tart pan with removable bottom, letting excess dough hang over edge. Ease dough into pan by gently lifting edge of dough with your hand while pressing into corners and fluted sides of pan with your other hand. Run rolling pin over top of pan to remove any excess dough. Wrap loosely in plastic, place on large plate, and freeze until fully chilled and firm, about 30 minutes. (Dough-lined tart pan can be frozen for up to 1 month.) Adjust oven rack to middle position and heat oven to 375 degrees.

2 Line chilled tart shell with double layer of aluminum foil and fill with pie weights. Bake on foil-lined rimmed baking sheet until tart shell is set and fragrant, about 30 minutes, rotating sheet halfway through baking. Remove foil and weights and continue to bake 5 minutes longer. Transfer sheet to wire rack and let cool completely, about 30 minutes.

3 Meanwhile, scrape pulp (including seeds) from passion fruit into clean, dry bowl of food processor. Pulse until seeds are separated from pulp, about 4 pulses. Strain puree through fine-mesh strainer into bowl, discarding solids. Measure out ½ cup puree, reserving any remaining puree for another use.

4 Whisk puree, sugar, egg yolks, lemon juice, cornstarch, and salt together in large saucepan until combined. Cook over medium-low heat, stirring constantly with rubber spatula, until mixture thickens slightly and registers 160 degrees, 10 to 12 minutes. Off heat, whisk in butter until smooth. Strain curd through clean fine-mesh strainer into large bowl, cover with plastic wrap, and refrigerate until chilled, about 1½ hours.

5 Using stand mixer fitted with whisk attachment, whip cream on medium-low speed until foamy, about 1 minute. Increase speed to high and whip until soft peaks form, about 2 minutes. Gently whisk one-third whipped cream into chilled puree mixture to lighten it. Using rubber spatula, gently fold in remaining whipped cream until homogenous. Spread curd over cooled crust, smoothing with clean spatula into even layer. Refrigerate until set, at least 8 hours or up to 24 hours, before serving.

NUTELLA TARTLETS

SERVES 6

CRUST

2 cups (10 ounces) all-purpose flour

½ cup (3½ ounces) sugar

¾ teaspoon table salt

14 tablespoons unsalted butter, melted

FILLING

1 cup hazelnuts, toasted and skinned

1½ cups Nutella

½ cup plus 1 tablespoon heavy cream

3 ounces bittersweet chocolate, chopped

3 tablespoons unsalted butter

Why This Recipe Works Nutella makes an ideal tartlet filling: With just a couple more simple ingredients, you can create a decadent—and easy—dessert. In order to transform the chocolate-hazelnut spread into a creamy filling, we knew we'd have to amp up its richness and transform its thick texture. We started with 1½ cups of Nutella—just the right amount for six individual tarts—and then added heavy cream and butter for richness and creaminess, as well as a few ounces of bittersweet chocolate for a deeper, more intense chocolate flavor. We then microwaved the mixture, stirring it often, until it formed a homogeneous filling—essentially a ganache that just needed some time in the fridge to set up. Once chilled, the luscious truffle-like filling perfectly complemented the crisp, buttery crust. But we wanted even more contrast: A sprinkling of chopped hazelnuts in the bottom of each tart shell added welcome crunch to the smooth, creamy filling, while adorning the top with whole hazelnuts hinted at what was inside. You will need six 4-inch tart pans with removable bottoms for this recipe.

1 **For the crust** Adjust oven racks to middle and lowest positions and heat oven to 350 degrees. Spray six 4-inch tart pans with removable bottoms with vegetable oil spray. Whisk flour, sugar, and salt together in bowl. Add melted butter and stir with wooden spoon until dough forms. Divide dough into 6 equal pieces. Working with 1 piece of dough at a time, press two-thirds of dough into bottom of 1 prepared pan using your fingers. Press remaining dough into fluted sides of pan. Press and smooth dough with your fingers to even thickness.

2 Line tart pans with double layer of aluminum foil, covering edges to prevent burning, and fill with pie weights. Place pans on rimmed baking sheet and bake on lower rack until edges are beginning to turn golden, about 25 minutes. Carefully remove foil and weights, rotate sheet, and continue to bake until crusts are golden brown and firm to touch, 10 to 15 minutes; transfer tart pans to wire rack and let shells cool completely, about 1 hour.

3 **For the filling** Reserve 48 whole hazelnuts for garnish, then chop remaining hazelnuts. Sprinkle chopped hazelnuts evenly among cooled tart shells.

4 Microwave Nutella, cream, chocolate, and butter together in covered bowl at 30 percent power, stirring often, until mixture is melted, smooth, and glossy, about 1 minute (do not overheat). Divide warm Nutella filling evenly among cooled tart shells, smoothing tops with clean rubber spatula into even layer.

5 Refrigerate tarts until filling is just set, about 15 minutes. Arrange reserved whole hazelnuts evenly around edge of tarts and continue to refrigerate until filling is firm, about 1½ hours. Remove outer ring of tart pans, slide thin metal spatula between tartlets and tart pan bottoms, and carefully slide tartlets onto serving platter or individual plates. Serve.

FORMING THE CRUSTS FOR TARTLETS

1. Whisk flour, sugar, and salt together in bowl. Add melted butter and stir with wooden spoon until dough forms.

2. Divide dough into 6 equal pieces. Working with 1 piece of dough at a time, press two-thirds of dough into bottom of 1 prepared pan using your fingers.

3. Press remaining dough into fluted sides of pan. Press and smooth dough with your fingers to even thickness.

FOOLPROOF ALL-BUTTER PIE DOUGH

MAKES ENOUGH FOR ONE 9-INCH PIE

10 tablespoons unsalted butter, chilled, divided

1¼ cups (6¼ ounces) all-purpose flour, divided

1 tablespoon sugar

½ teaspoon table salt

¼ cup (2 ounces) ice water, divided

Why This Recipe Works This is our go-to dough: It's supremely supple and extremely easy to roll out. Even better, it bakes up buttery, tender, and flaky. How did we do it? First we used the food processor to mix two-thirds of the flour with butter, creating a water-resistant pastelike mixture. Next we broke that paste into pieces, coated the pieces with the remaining flour, and tossed in grated butter. By doing this, the water we folded in was absorbed only by the dry flour that coated the butter-flour chunks. Since gluten can develop only when flour is hydrated, this resulted in a crust that was supertender but had enough structure to support flakes. After a 2-hour chill, the dough was completely hydrated and easy to roll out. Be sure to weigh the flour. This dough will be moister than most pie doughs, but it will absorb a lot of excess moisture as it chills. Roll out the dough on a well-floured counter.

1 Grate 2 tablespoons butter on large holes of box grater and place in freezer. Cut remaining 8 tablespoons butter into ½-inch cubes.

2 Pulse ¾ cup flour, sugar, and salt in food processor until combined, about 2 pulses. Add cubed butter and process until homogeneous paste forms, about 30 seconds. Using your hands, carefully break paste into 2-inch chunks and redistribute evenly around processor blade. Add remaining ½ cup flour and pulse until mixture is broken into pieces no larger than 1 inch (most pieces will be much smaller), 4 to 5 pulses. Transfer mixture to bowl. Add grated butter and toss until butter pieces are separated and coated with flour.

3 Sprinkle 2 tablespoons ice water over mixture. Toss with rubber spatula until mixture is evenly moistened. Sprinkle remaining 2 tablespoons ice water over mixture and toss to combine. Press dough with spatula until dough sticks together. Transfer dough to sheet of plastic wrap. Draw edges of plastic over dough and press firmly on sides and top to form compact, fissure-free mass. Wrap in plastic and form into 5-inch disk. Refrigerate dough for at least 2 hours or up to 2 days. Let chilled dough sit on counter to soften slightly, about 10 minutes, before rolling. (Wrapped dough can be frozen for up to 1 month. If frozen, let dough thaw completely on counter before rolling.)

Nut Pie Dough

Do not use toasted nuts in this recipe.

Reduce cubed butter to 6 tablespoons and reduce first addition of flour to 6 tablespoons (1¾ ounces). Add ½ cup pecans, walnuts, hazelnuts, almonds, or peanuts, chopped and frozen, to food processor with flour, sugar, and salt and process until finely ground, about 30 seconds.

CLASSIC TART DOUGH

MAKES ENOUGH FOR ONE 9-INCH TART

Why This Recipe Works While regular pie crust is tender and flaky, classic tart crust should be fine-textured, buttery-rich, crisp, and crumbly. (It's often described as shortbread-like.) A tart typically features less filling than a traditional pie, so we needed a top-notch crust that could handle the spotlight. We found that using a whole stick of butter made tart dough that tasted great and was easy to handle, yet still had a delicate crumb. Instead of using the hard-to-find superfine sugar and pastry flour that many recipes call for, we used confectioners' sugar (the finest of the fine) combined with all-purpose flour to achieve a crisp texture. The result was a dough that was easy to roll and fit into the tart pan, and ample enough to patch any holes. You need only to lightly flour the counter when rolling out this supple dough.

1 | large egg yolk
1 | tablespoon heavy cream
½ | teaspoon vanilla extract
1¼ | cups (6¼ ounces) all-purpose flour
⅔ | cup (2⅔ ounces) confectioners' sugar
¼ | teaspoon table salt
8 | tablespoons unsalted butter, cut into ¼-inch pieces and chilled

1 Whisk egg yolk, cream, and vanilla together in bowl. Process flour, sugar, and salt together in food processor until combined, about 5 seconds. Scatter butter over top and pulse until mixture resembles coarse cornmeal, about 15 pulses. With processor running, add egg yolk mixture and continue to process until dough just comes together around processor blade, about 12 seconds.

2 Transfer dough to sheet of plastic wrap and form into 6-inch disk. Wrap tightly in plastic and refrigerate for at least 1 hour or up to 2 days. Let chilled dough sit on counter to soften slightly, about 10 minutes, before rolling. (Wrapped dough can be frozen for up to 1 month. If frozen, let dough thaw completely on counter before rolling.)

Chocolate Tart Dough

Increase heavy cream to 2 tablespoons, confectioners' sugar to ¾ cup, and butter to 10 tablespoons. Add ¼ cup cocoa powder with flour.

CHOCOLATE CREAM PIE

SERVES 8 TO 10

1 recipe Foolproof All-Butter
   Pie Dough (page 200)

⅓ cup (2⅓ ounces) sugar

¼ cup (1 ounce) cornstarch

2 tablespoons unsweetened
   cocoa powder

¼ teaspoon table salt

3 cups whole or 2 percent
   low-fat milk

6 ounces bittersweet chocolate,
   chopped fine

3 tablespoons unsalted butter,
   cut into 3 pieces

2 teaspoons vanilla extract

1 recipe Whipped Cream
   (page 340)

Why This Recipe Works Chocolate cream pie—with its generous layer of fluffy chocolate filling tucked beneath a towering mound of whipped cream—nearly always looks inviting, but its flavor and texture usually disappoint. All too often the chocolate cream filling is gluey, overly sweet, and impossible to slice. We wanted a voluptuously creamy pie, with well-balanced chocolate flavor somewhere between milkshake and candy bar. For a filling that wasn't overly rich, we ditched the cream and used milk instead; a modest amount of sugar kept the sweetness in check and some cornstarch ensured a sliceable consistency. For the best flavor we used two types of chocolate: a couple tablespoons of cocoa powder along with 6 ounces of bittersweet chocolate contributed complexity and depth to our pudding base. A few tablespoons of butter guaranteed a silky filling once it was poured into the prebaked pie shell and refrigerated, and a topping of lightly sweetened whipped cream provided the finishing touch. We developed this recipe with whole milk, but you can use 2 percent low-fat milk, if desired. Avoid using 1 percent low-fat or skim milk, as the filling will be too thin.

1 Roll dough into 12-inch circle on floured counter. Loosely roll dough around rolling pin and gently unroll it onto 9-inch pie plate, letting excess dough hang over edge. Ease dough into plate by gently lifting edge of dough with your hand while pressing into plate bottom with your other hand.

2 Trim overhang to ½ inch beyond lip of plate. Tuck overhang under itself; folded edge should be flush with edge of plate. Crimp dough evenly around edge of plate. Wrap dough-lined plate loosely in plastic wrap and refrigerate until firm, about 30 minutes. Adjust oven rack to middle position and heat oven to 350 degrees.

3 Line chilled pie shell with double layer of aluminum foil, covering edges to prevent burning, and fill with pie weights. Bake on foil-lined rimmed baking sheet until edges are set and just beginning to turn golden, 25 to 30 minutes, rotating sheet halfway through baking. Remove foil and weights, rotate sheet, and continue to bake crust until golden brown and crisp, 10 to 15 minutes. Transfer sheet to wire rack and let cool completely, about 30 minutes.

4 Whisk sugar, cornstarch, cocoa, and salt together in large saucepan. Whisk in milk until incorporated, making sure to scrape corners of saucepan. Place saucepan over medium heat; cook, whisking constantly, until mixture is thickened and bubbling over entire surface, 8 to 10 minutes. Cook 30 seconds longer; remove from heat. Add chocolate and butter and whisk until melted and fully incorporated. Whisk in vanilla. Pour filling into cooled pie crust. Press lightly greased parchment paper against surface of filling and let cool completely, about 1 hour. Refrigerate until filling is firmly set, at least 2½ hours or up to 24 hours. Spread whipped cream attractively over chilled pie. Serve.

CHOCOLATE CHESS PIE

SERVES 8 TO 12

Why This Recipe Works You may be familiar with chess pie, a popular custard pie in the South. The beauty of this rich, sweet pie lies in its simplicity: It's easy to prepare and calls for everyday ingredients most cooks are likely to have on hand. While lemon is the most common flavor of choice, we wanted to introduce smooth, silky chocolate for a more luxurious spin. Melted unsweetened chocolate (rather than cocoa powder) and cream (instead of the buttermilk or too-thick evaporated milk that we found in some recipes) lent the right amount of chocolate intensity and richness, while four eggs plus two additional yolks created a silky, creamy texture. Just 3 tablespoons of flour was all we needed to help bind the ingredients and ensure neat slicing. We tried mixing the filling in a food processor, but this aerated the mixture, making the baked filling foamy, so we simply whisked it together by hand. We baked this pie in a moderate 325-degree oven to yield a soft but fully cooked custard. An even coat of granulated sugar over the top provided a crunchy textural contrast to the rich, fudgy filling.

1 recipe Foolproof All-Butter Pie Dough (page 200)

12 tablespoons unsalted butter, cut into 12 pieces

3 ounces unsweetened chocolate, chopped

1½ cups (10½ ounces) plus 1 teaspoon sugar, divided

3 tablespoons all-purpose flour

½ teaspoon table salt

4 large eggs plus 2 large yolks

¼ cup heavy cream

1½ teaspoons vanilla extract

1 Roll dough into 12-inch circle on floured counter. Loosely roll dough around rolling pin and gently unroll it onto 9-inch pie plate, letting excess dough hang over edge. Ease dough into plate by gently lifting edge of dough with your hand while pressing into plate bottom with your other hand.

2 Trim overhang to ½ inch beyond lip of plate. Tuck overhang under itself; folded edge should be flush with edge of plate. Crimp dough evenly around edge of plate. Wrap dough-lined plate loosely in plastic wrap and refrigerate until firm, about 30 minutes. Adjust oven rack to middle position and heat oven to 425 degrees.

3 Line chilled pie shell with double layer of aluminum foil, covering edges to prevent burning, and fill with pie weights. Bake on foil-lined rimmed baking sheet until pie dough looks dry and is pale in color, about 15 minutes. Remove foil and weights and continue to bake until center begins to look opaque and slightly drier, 3 to 6 minutes. Transfer sheet to wire rack and let cool completely, about 45 minutes.

4 Reduce oven temperature to 325 degrees. Microwave butter and chocolate in bowl at 50 percent power, stirring occasionally, until melted and smooth, about 2 minutes. Whisk 1½ cups sugar, flour, and salt in second bowl until combined. Whisk eggs and yolks, cream, and vanilla into sugar mixture until combined. Whisk chocolate mixture into sugar-egg mixture until fully incorporated and no streaks remain.

5 With pie shell still on sheet, pour filling into cooled crust and sprinkle remaining 1 teaspoon sugar evenly over filling. Bake until center of pie is just set and registers 180 degrees, 35 to 40 minutes, rotating sheet halfway through baking. (Slight crust will have formed on top.) Let pie cool completely on wire rack, about 4 hours. Serve. (Pie can be refrigerated for up to 4 days. Bring to room temperature before serving.)

MISSISSIPPI MUD PIE

SERVES 10 TO 12

CRUST

- 16 Oreo cookies, broken into rough pieces
- 4 tablespoons unsalted butter, melted and cooled

BROWNIE LAYER

- 4 ounces bittersweet chocolate, chopped fine
- 3 tablespoons unsalted butter
- 3 tablespoons vegetable oil
- 1½ tablespoons Dutch-processed cocoa powder
- ⅔ cup packed (4⅔ ounces) dark brown sugar
- 2 large eggs
- 2 teaspoons vanilla extract
- ¼ teaspoon table salt
- 3 tablespoons all-purpose flour

TOPPING

- 10 chocolate wafer cookies (2 ounces)
- 2 tablespoons confectioners' sugar
- 1 tablespoon Dutch-processed cocoa powder
- ⅛ teaspoon table salt
- 2 tablespoons unsalted butter, melted

MOUSSE

- 6 ounces milk chocolate, chopped fine
- 1 cup heavy cream, chilled, divided
- 2 tablespoons Dutch-processed cocoa powder
- 2 tablespoons confectioners' sugar
- ⅛ teaspoon table salt

Why This Recipe Works The layers of this intense—and we mean intense—chocolate pie are said to be named for the Mississippi River's silty bottom, but there's nothing muddy about the pie's flavor or texture—it's pure chocolate and boasts crunch, chew, and creaminess. We started with a chocolate cookie crust and baked a chewy brownie layer in it. To achieve the perfect gooey texture for this layer, we relied on a mixture of melted bittersweet chocolate and moisture-rich dark brown sugar and baked it until it was slightly underdone. Once this layer was fully chilled, we added the mousse—essentially a mixture of melted and cooled milk chocolate, sugar, and cocoa powder folded into whipped cream. We discovered that two steps were essential for a fluffy yet sliceable mousse: We replaced granulated sugar with starchier confectioners' sugar for more stability, and we made sure to let the chocolate cool to between 90 and 100 degrees before incorporating it—any warmer and it deflated the mousse. For a crunchy topping, we toasted chocolate wafer cookie pieces with melted butter, cocoa, and sugar and sprinkled them over the mousse layer to form a cookie streusel. Be sure to use milk chocolate in the mousse, as bittersweet chocolate will make it too firm.

1 For the crust Adjust oven rack to middle position and heat oven to 325 degrees. Pulse cookies in food processor until coarsely ground, about 15 pulses, then process to fine, even crumbs, about 15 seconds. Sprinkle melted butter over crumbs and pulse to incorporate, about 5 pulses.

2 Sprinkle mixture into 9-inch pie plate. Using bottom of dry measuring cup, press crumbs into even layer on bottom and up sides of pie plate. Bake until crust is fragrant and appears set, 13 to 18 minutes; transfer to wire rack.

3 For the brownie layer Combine chocolate, butter, oil, and cocoa in bowl and microwave at 50 percent power, stirring often, until melted and smooth, about 1½ minutes. Whisk sugar, eggs, vanilla, and salt in second bowl until smooth. Whisk in chocolate mixture until incorporated. Whisk in flour until just combined.

4 Pour brownie batter into crust. Bake pie until edges begin to set and toothpick inserted in center comes out with thin coating of batter attached, about 15 minutes. Transfer to wire rack and let cool for 1 hour, then refrigerate until fully chilled, about 1 hour longer.

5 For the topping Meanwhile, line rimmed baking sheet with parchment paper. Place cookies in zipper-lock bag, press out air, and seal bag. Using rolling pin, crush cookies into ½- to ¾-inch pieces. Combine sugar, cocoa, salt, and crushed cookies in bowl. Stir in melted butter until mixture is moistened and clumps begin to form. Spread crumbs in even layer on prepared sheet and bake until fragrant, about 10 minutes, shaking sheet to break up crumbs halfway through baking. Transfer sheet to wire rack and let cool completely.

6 **For the mousse** Once brownie layer has fully chilled, microwave chocolate in large bowl at 50 percent power, stirring often, until melted, 1½ to 2 minutes. Let cool until just barely warm and registers between 90 and 100 degrees, about 10 minutes.

7 Microwave 3 tablespoons cream in small bowl until it registers between 105 and 110 degrees, about 15 seconds. Whisk in cocoa until combined. Combine cocoa-cream mixture, sugar, salt, and remaining cream in bowl of stand mixer. Fit mixer with whisk attachment and whip cream mixture on medium speed until beginning to thicken, about 30 seconds, scraping down bowl as needed. Increase speed to high and whip until soft peaks form, 30 seconds to 1 minute.

8 Using whisk, fold one-third of whipped cream mixture into melted chocolate to lighten it. Using rubber spatula, fold in remaining whipped cream mixture until no dark streaks remain. Spoon mousse into chilled pie and spread evenly from edge to edge. Sprinkle with cooled topping and refrigerate for at least 3 hours or up to 8 hours. Serve.

CHOCOLATE PECAN PIE

SERVES 8 TO 10

Why This Recipe Works It's not that we don't love classic pecan pie—we just love chocolate pecan pie more. But we weren't looking for the type that simply has some chocolate chips floating in the filling; we wanted to fully lean into the chocolate aspect of chocolate pecan pie by achieving a creamy, smooth, sliceable chocolate-amped custard filling (not brownie-like in texture nor a pooling puddle of syrup). Pecan pie filling is sweet enough so we added 2 ounces of pure unsweetened chocolate, which showcased the complex, slightly bitter, rich notes of chocolate. When combined with melted butter and the base of eggs, sugar, and corn syrup, the melted chocolate made a luxurious, cohesive filling. We toasted the nuts so they didn't turn soggy within the filling and provided crunchy textural contrast, and we chopped them so we could cut neat slices. Toast the pecans on a rimmed baking sheet in a 300-degree oven for 7 to 10 minutes, stirring occasionally. We like to serve the pie with Bourbon Whipped Cream (page 340).

1 recipe Foolproof All-Butter Pie Dough (page 200)

6 tablespoons unsalted butter

2 ounces unsweetened chocolate, chopped fine

¾ cup light corn syrup

¾ cup packed (5¼ ounces) brown sugar

3 large eggs

1 tablespoon vanilla extract

½ teaspoon table salt

2 cups pecans, toasted and chopped coarse

1 Roll dough into 12-inch circle on floured counter. Loosely roll dough around rolling pin and gently unroll it onto 9-inch pie plate, letting excess dough hang over edge. Ease dough into plate by gently lifting edge of dough with your hand while pressing into plate bottom with your other hand.

2 Trim overhang to ½ inch beyond lip of plate. Tuck overhang under itself; folded edge should be flush with edge of plate. Crimp dough evenly around edge of plate. Wrap dough-lined plate loosely in plastic wrap and refrigerate until firm, about 30 minutes. Adjust oven rack to lowest position and heat oven to 375 degrees.

3 Line chilled pie shell with double layer of aluminum foil, covering edges to prevent burning, and fill with pie weights. Bake on wire rack set in rimmed baking sheet until edges are dry and pale, about 45 minutes. Remove foil and weights, rotate sheet, and continue to bake until center of crust is light golden brown, 20 to 25 minutes longer. Remove sheet from oven. Reduce oven temperature to 325 degrees.

4 Melt butter and chocolate in bowl at 50 percent power, stirring halfway through microwaving, until melted and smooth, about 2 minutes. Add corn syrup, sugar, eggs, vanilla, and salt to chocolate mixture and whisk until combined. Stir in pecans.

5 Transfer pie shell to foil–lined rimmed baking sheet. Pour filling into crust and spread evenly with rubber spatula. Bake until pecan layer that forms on top begins to crack and filling in center of pie registers 185 to 190 degrees (filling will jiggle slightly when pie is shaken), 1 hour to 1 hour 5 minutes, rotating sheet halfway through baking. Let pie cool on wire rack until set, about 4 hours. Serve.

FLOURLESS CHOCOLATE CAKE

SERVES 10 TO 12

12 ounces bittersweet chocolate, broken into 1-inch pieces

16 tablespoons unsalted butter

6 large eggs

1 cup (7 ounces) sugar

½ cup water

1 tablespoon cornstarch

1 tablespoon vanilla extract

1 teaspoon instant espresso powder

½ teaspoon table salt

Why This Recipe Works Incredibly rich and impossibly smooth, flourless chocolate cake is elegant, refined, and universally beloved. But recipes for this intense, deeply chocolate dessert typically require complicated techniques. Our take on this indulgent cake minimizes fuss without sacrificing flavor or texture. We began by gently melting bittersweet chocolate and butter in the microwave before incorporating the remaining ingredients. In the absence of flour, we called on eggs for structure, cornstarch for body, and water for a moist, smooth texture. Vanilla and espresso powder underscored the chocolate flavor and deepened its impact. Ensuring a crack-free surface was as easy as straining and resting the batter before tapping out bubbles that rose to the surface. Baking the cake in a low oven produced a perfectly smooth top. This cake needs to chill for at least 6 hours, so we recommend making it the day before serving. An accurate oven thermometer is essential here. To slice the cake, dip a sharp knife in very hot water and wipe dry before each cut.

1 Adjust oven rack to middle position and heat oven to 275 degrees. Spray 9-inch springform pan with vegetable oil spray. Microwave chocolate and butter in bowl at 50 percent power, stirring occasionally, until melted and smooth, about 4 minutes. Let chocolate mixture cool for 5 minutes.

2 Whisk eggs, sugar, water, cornstarch, vanilla, espresso powder, and salt in large bowl until thoroughly combined, about 30 seconds. Whisk in chocolate mixture until smooth and slightly thickened, about 45 seconds. Strain batter through fine-mesh strainer into prepared pan, pressing against strainer with rubber spatula or back of ladle to help batter pass through. Gently tap pan on counter to release air bubbles; let sit on counter for 10 minutes to allow air bubbles to rise to top. Use tines of fork to gently pop any air bubbles that have risen to surface. Bake until edges are set and center jiggles slightly when cake is shaken gently, 45 to 50 minutes.

3 Let cake cool in pan on wire rack for 5 minutes; run thin knife around edge of pan to loosen cake. Let cake cool on rack until barely warm, about 30 minutes. Cover cake tightly with plastic wrap, poke small hole in top, and refrigerate until cold and firmly set, at least 6 hours or up to 2 days. Remove sides of pan and slide thin metal spatula between cake bottom and pan bottom to loosen, then slide cake onto platter. Let cake stand at room temperature for 30 minutes before serving.

CHOCOLATE-PECAN TORTE

SERVES 10 TO 12

Why This Recipe Works Sweets featuring chocolate with peanuts, almonds, or hazelnuts are fairly common, but the richness and pleasant bitterness of dark chocolate is also a great match for sweet pecans in an elegant dessert. Here: a sleek torte. Don't let the simplicity of the ingredients fool you—this cake is pure decadence. A generous amount of bittersweet chocolate provided the deep, dark richness we associate with this type of cake, and plenty of ground pecans gave the cake a buttery sweetness. The addition of a little cinnamon and some spiced rum contributed warm notes which complemented both the chocolate and the nuts. While the pecans added both flavor and structure to the cake, we decided to add some flour too; a moderate amount ensured our cake wouldn't collapse and sink, as flourless chocolate cakes have a tendency to do. We were careful to whip the egg whites just to soft peaks so they were easy to incorporate into the batter. A glaze in the form of a rich ganache made by pouring hot cream over chopped bittersweet chocolate—and adding a little corn syrup for a luxurious, glossy sheen—was an elegant and inviting finishing touch.

1 For the cake Adjust oven rack to middle position and heat oven to 300 degrees. Grease 9-inch springform pan and line with parchment paper. Microwave chocolate and butter in bowl at 50 percent power, stirring occasionally, until melted and smooth, 1 to 2 minutes; let cool slightly. Process 1½ cups pecans, flour, cinnamon, and salt in food processor until finely ground, about 30 seconds.

2 Using stand mixer fitted with whisk attachment, whip egg whites on medium-low speed until foamy, about 1 minute. Increase speed to medium-high and whip whites to soft, billowy mounds, about 1 minute. Gradually add ¼ cup sugar and whip until glossy, soft peaks form, 1 to 2 minutes.

3 Whisk egg yolks, vanilla, and remaining ¾ cup sugar in large bowl until pale and thick, about 30 seconds. Slowly whisk in chocolate mixture until combined. Slowly whisk in rum until combined. Using whisk, fold in one-third of whipped whites. Using rubber spatula, gently fold in half of pecan mixture. Repeat with half of remaining whites and remaining pecan mixture, finishing with remaining whites. Transfer batter to prepared pan and bake until toothpick inserted in center comes out clean, 45 to 50 minutes, rotating pan halfway through baking. Let cake cool completely in pan on wire rack, about 2 hours. Run thin knife around edge of pan to loosen cake, then remove sides of pan. Invert cake onto wire rack set over rimmed baking sheet, discarding parchment.

4 For the glaze Place chocolate in bowl. Heat cream in small saucepan over medium-high heat until just simmering. Pour over chocolate and let sit for 5 minutes. Gently whisk mixture, starting in center and working outward, until melted and smooth. Gently stir in corn syrup and salt until combined. Immediately pour glaze evenly over top and sides of cake. Refrigerate until set, about 30 minutes. Transfer cake to platter. Arrange pecan halves along bottom edge. Serve.

CAKE

- **8** ounces bittersweet chocolate, chopped
- **6** tablespoons unsalted butter, cut into 3 pieces
- **1½** cups pecans, plus about 35 pecans for decorating, divided
- **1** cup (5 ounces) all-purpose flour
- **¾** teaspoon ground cinnamon
- **½** teaspoon table salt
- **4** large eggs, separated
- **1** cup packed (7 ounces) light brown sugar, divided
- **2** teaspoons vanilla extract
- **⅓** cup spiced rum

GLAZE

- **8** ounces bittersweet chocolate, chopped
- **1** cup heavy cream
- **2** tablespoons corn syrup

  Pinch table salt

MILK CHOCOLATE CHEESECAKE

SERVES 12 TO 16

16   Oreo cookies, broken into rough pieces

1   tablespoon plus ½ cup (3½ ounces) sugar, divided

2   tablespoons unsalted butter, melted

8   ounces milk chocolate, chopped, divided

⅓   cup heavy cream

2   tablespoons unsweetened cocoa powder

¼   teaspoon table salt

1½   pounds cream cheese, cut into pieces and softened

4   large eggs, room temperature

2   teaspoons vanilla extract

Why This Recipe Works While chocolate typically makes everything better, in cheesecake it can prove problematic. The sharp edge of bittersweet chocolate—our go-to—is a poor match for the tang of cream cheese. Adding cream helped soften the sharpness, but only slightly. Similarly, swapping in semisweet chocolate was an improvement, but only a modest one. After making dozens of cheesecakes, we figured out that mild-mannered milk chocolate was the secret to a sweet, creamy cheesecake with just the right balance of chocolate and cheese. Milk chocolate's gentle, milky character delivered almost no bitterness, but our cake now needed a deeper, rounder chocolate flavor. Luckily, the fix was easy: Adding a bit of cocoa powder provided complexity without compromising the texture or welcoming back the bitterness. For a solid base, we used Oreo cookies to create an easy, crunchy, chocolaty crust.

1 Adjust oven rack to middle position and heat oven to 350 degrees. Grease bottom and sides of 9-inch springform pan. Process cookies and 1 tablespoon sugar in food processor until finely ground, about 30 seconds. Add melted butter and pulse until crumbs are evenly moistened, about 6 pulses. Using your hands, press crumb mixture evenly into pan bottom. Using bottom of dry measuring cup, firmly pack crust into pan. Bake until fragrant and set, about 10 minutes. Let crust cool completely on wire rack, about 30 minutes.

2 Reduce oven temperature to 250 degrees. Combine 6 ounces chocolate and cream in bowl and microwave at 50 percent power, stirring occasionally, until melted and smooth, 60 to 90 seconds. Let cool for 10 minutes. Whisk cocoa, salt, and remaining ½ cup sugar in second bowl until no lumps remain. Using stand mixer fitted with paddle, beat cream cheese and cocoa mixture on medium speed until creamy and smooth, about 3 minutes, scraping down bowl as needed. Reduce speed to medium-low, add chocolate mixture, and beat until combined. Gradually add eggs, one at a time, until incorporated, scraping down bowl as needed. Add vanilla and give batter final stir by hand until no streaks of chocolate remain.

3 Pour filling into cooled crust and smooth top with spatula. Gently tap pan on counter to release air bubbles. Cover pan tightly with aluminum foil (taking care not to touch surface of cheesecake with foil) and place on rimmed baking sheet. Bake for 1 hour, then remove foil. Continue to bake until edges are set and center registers 150 degrees and jiggles slightly when shaken, 30 to 45 minutes. Let cheesecake cool completely in pan on wire rack. Wrap cheesecake tightly in plastic wrap and refrigerate until cold, at least 8 hours or up to 4 days.

4 To unmold cheesecake, remove sides of pan and slide thin metal spatula between crust and pan bottom to loosen, then slide cheesecake onto platter. Microwave remaining 2 ounces chocolate in small bowl at 50 percent power, stirring occasionally, until melted, 60 to 90 seconds. Let cool for 5 minutes. Transfer to small zipper-lock bag, cut small hole in corner, and pipe chocolate in thin zigzag pattern across top of cheesecake. Let cheesecake sit at room temperature for 30 minutes before serving.

CHOCOLATE-RASPBERRY TORTE

SERVES 12 TO 16

CAKE

- **8** ounces bittersweet chocolate, chopped fine
- **12** tablespoons unsalted butter, cut into ½-inch pieces
- **2** teaspoons vanilla extract
- **¼** teaspoon instant espresso powder
- **1¾** cups sliced almonds, toasted, divided
- **¼** cup (1¼ ounces) all-purpose flour
- **½** teaspoon salt
- **5** large eggs, room temperature
- **¾** cup (5¼ ounces) sugar
- **2** (9-inch) cardboard rounds

FILLING

- **2½** ounces (½ cup) raspberries, plus 16 raspberries for garnishing
- **¼** cup seedless raspberry jam

GLAZE

- **5** ounces bittersweet chocolate, chopped fine
- **½** cup plus 1 tablespoon heavy cream

Why This Recipe Works In theory, Sacher torte—a traditional Viennese dessert featuring rich chocolate cake layered with apricot jam and enrobed in a refined chocolate glaze—makes a lavish finish to an elegant meal. In reality, however, this torte always sounds more appealing than it actually tastes: Dry cake, an overly sweet jam with little fruity complexity, and a thin, sugary coating are common pitfalls. We set out to improve this classic dessert, but decided to give it our own unique spin by pairing the rich chocolate cake with tangy raspberries. We wanted a decadent, fudgy base, so we started by baking two thin layers of flourless chocolate cake. But when we tried to stack the layers, the dense cake tore and fell apart. Adding ground almonds (along with a small amount of flour) gave our cake the structure it needed and provided a good flavor boost. The winning approach for our raspberry filling was to combine jam with lightly mashed fresh berries for a sweet-tart mixture that clung to the cake. For the glaze, we kept things simple, melting bittersweet chocolate with heavy cream to create a rich, glossy ganache.

1 **For the cake** Adjust oven rack to middle position and heat oven to 325 degrees. Grease two 9-inch round cake pans, line with parchment paper, grease parchment, and flour pans. Melt chocolate and butter in large heatproof bowl set over saucepan filled with 1 inch barely simmering water, making sure that water does not touch bottom of bowl and stirring occasionally until smooth. Let cool completely, about 30 minutes. Stir in vanilla and espresso powder.

2 Pulse ¾ cup almonds in food processor until coarsely chopped, 6 to 8 pulses; transfer to bowl and set aside for garnish. Process remaining 1 cup almonds until very finely ground, about 45 seconds. Add flour and salt and continue to process until combined, about 15 seconds. Transfer almond mixture to second bowl. Process eggs in now-empty processor until lightened in color and almost doubled in volume, about 3 minutes. With processor running, slowly add sugar and process until thoroughly combined, about 15 seconds. Using whisk, gently fold egg mixture into chocolate mixture until some streaks of egg remain. Sprinkle half of ground almond mixture over chocolate mixture and gently whisk until just combined. Sprinkle with remaining ground almond mixture and gently whisk until just combined.

3 Divide batter evenly between prepared pans and smooth tops with rubber spatula. Bake until centers are firm and toothpick inserted in center comes out with few moist crumbs attached, 14 to 16 minutes, rotating pans halfway through baking. Let cakes cool completely in pans on wire rack, about 30 minutes.

4 Run thin knife around edges of pans to loosen cakes, then invert onto cardboard rounds, discarding parchment. Using wire rack, turn 1 cake right side up, then slide from rack back onto cardboard round.

5 **For the filling** Place ½ cup raspberries in bowl and mash coarse with fork. Stir in jam until just combined.

6 Spread raspberry mixture onto cake layer that is right side up. Top with second cake layer, leaving it upside down. Transfer assembled cake, still on cardboard round, to wire rack set in rimmed baking sheet.

7 For the glaze Melt chocolate and cream in heatproof bowl set over saucepan filled with 1 inch barely simmering water, making sure that water does not touch bottom of bowl and stirring occasionally until smooth. Off heat, gently whisk until very smooth. Pour glaze onto center of assembled cake. Using offset spatula, spread glaze evenly over top of cake, letting it drip down sides. Spread glaze along sides of cake to coat evenly.

8 Using fine-mesh strainer, sift reserved chopped almonds to remove any fine bits. Gently press sifted almonds onto cake sides. Arrange remaining 16 raspberries on top around outer edge. Refrigerate cake on rack until glaze is set, at least 1 hour or up to 24 hours. (If refrigerated for more than 1 hour, let cake sit at room temperature for about 30 minutes before serving.) Transfer cake to platter and serve.

celebrating
THE HOLIDAYS

HOLIDAY CHOCOLATE BUTTER COOKIES

MAKES ABOUT 48 COOKIES

20 tablespoons unsalted butter, softened, divided

½ cup (1½ ounces) unsweetened cocoa powder

1 teaspoon instant espresso powder

1 cup (7 ounces) sugar

¼ teaspoon table salt

2 large egg yolks

1 tablespoon vanilla extract

2¼ cups (11¼ ounces) all-purpose flour

Why This Recipe Works On the holiday cookie plate, the chocolate butter cookie, with its rich, dark color, is often the most alluring of the bunch. Sadly, though, a cookie that looks like it's made from chocolate doesn't necessarily taste like it's made from chocolate. So we tried doubling the amount of cocoa found in most recipes and blooming it in hot melted butter, along with a teaspoon of espresso powder, before adding it to the dough. However, such a generous amount of cocoa powder resulted in dry cookies. To restore moisture, we cut back on the flour and added two egg yolks. Do not reroll the scraps more than once. Serve the cookies plain or dust with confectioners' sugar or glaze with All-Purpose Chocolate Glaze (page 348) before serving.

1 Melt 4 tablespoons butter in medium saucepan over medium heat. Add cocoa and espresso powder; stir until mixture forms smooth paste. Let cool for 15 to 20 minutes.

2 Using stand mixer fitted with paddle, beat remaining 16 tablespoons butter, sugar, salt, and cooled cocoa mixture on high speed until well combined and fluffy, about 1 minute, scraping down bowl as needed. Reduce speed to medium, add egg yolks and vanilla, and mix until thoroughly combined, about 30 seconds. Scrape down bowl. Reduce speed to low and add flour in 3 additions, waiting until each addition is incorporated before adding next and scraping down bowl after each addition. Continue to mix until dough forms cohesive ball, about 5 seconds. Transfer dough to counter and divide into 3 equal pieces. Form each piece into 4-inch disk, wrap disks tightly in plastic wrap, and refrigerate until dough is firm yet malleable, 45 minutes to 1 hour.

3 Adjust oven rack to middle position and heat oven to 375 degrees. Line 2 baking sheets with parchment paper. Working with 1 disk of dough at a time, roll ³⁄₁₆ inch thick between 2 large sheets of parchment. If dough becomes too soft and sticky to work with, slide rolled dough on parchment onto baking sheet and refrigerate until firm, about 10 minutes.

4 Remove top parchment. Using 2-inch cookie cutter, cut dough into shapes; space shapes about 1 inch apart on prepared sheets. Bake, 1 sheet at a time, until cookies show slight resistance to touch, 10 to 12 minutes, rotating sheet halfway through baking. (If cookies begin to darken on edges, they have overbaked.) Let cookies cool on sheets for 5 minutes, then transfer to wire rack. Let cookies cool completely before serving. (Cookies can be stored at room temperature for up to 3 days.)

Chocolate–Orange Butter Cookies with Chocolate–Brandy Glaze

Beat 2 teaspoons grated orange zest with butter, sugar, and salt in step 2. Substitute 1 teaspoon brandy for vanilla extract. While cookies are cooling, make All-Purpose Chocolate Glaze (page 348), substituting 1 teaspoon brandy for vanilla. Glaze cooled cookies and let dry for at least 20 minutes before serving.

Glazed Chocolate–Mint Butter Cookies
Substitute 2 teaspoons mint extract for vanilla extract. Glaze cookies with All-Purpose Chocolate Glaze (page 348) and let dry for at least 20 minutes. Melt 1 cup white chocolate chips and drizzle over glazed cookies. Let set for at least 20 minutes before serving.

Mexican Chocolate Butter Cookies
Toast ½ cup sliced almonds, 1 teaspoon ground cinnamon, and ⅛ teaspoon cayenne in 10-inch skillet over medium heat until fragrant, about 3 minutes; transfer to small bowl and let cool completely. Process cooled mixture in food processor until very fine, about 15 seconds. Whisk almond-spice mixture into flour before adding flour to dough in step 2. Sprinkle cookies evenly with ½ cup Demerara, turbinado, or sanding sugar before baking.

Salted Chocolate–Caramel Butter Cookies
While cookies are cooling, heat 14 ounces soft caramels and ¼ cup heavy cream in medium saucepan over medium-low heat, stirring until melted and smooth. Spread each cookie with 1 heaping teaspoon caramel, sprinkle evenly with ½ teaspoon flake sea salt, and let caramel set for at least 30 minutes before serving.

NUTTY CHOCOLATE-RASPBERRY THUMBPRINTS

MAKES ABOUT 36 COOKIES

Why This Recipe Works For many, buttery, colorful thumbprint cookies are a must in the holiday cookie lineup. While variations are endless, the signature feature of this cookie is the indentation in the center, which holds a filling—most commonly a bright-flavored jam—that provides an irresistible (and beautiful) contrast to the buttery dough surrounding it. Instead of using the more common butter cookie base, we wanted to use a chocolate dough and fill the center with raspberry jam for a rich and festive treat. With its high proportion of cocoa solids, cocoa powder provided a big hit of chocolate flavor without disturbing the shortbread-like snap typical of these cookies. For a complementary nutty flavor and satisfying texture we rolled the balls of dough in chopped toasted pecans. Despite the cookies' name, we kept our thumbs out of these thumbprints; we found that the underside of a rounded teaspoon measure made a perfectly sized, more even divot for the jam. Once filled with jam and baked, we finished our thumbprints with a final decorative dose of chocolate, drizzling melted white chocolate over the tops to create striking stripes.

1 Adjust oven racks to upper-middle and lower-middle positions and heat oven to 350 degrees. Line 2 baking sheets with parchment paper. Whisk flour, cocoa, baking powder, baking soda, and salt together in bowl. Using handheld mixer set at medium-high speed, beat butter and sugar until light and fluffy, about 2 minutes. Add egg and vanilla and mix until incorporated. Reduce speed to low, add flour mixture, and mix until just combined.

2 Spread pecans in shallow dish. Working with 1 tablespoon dough at a time, roll into balls, then roll in pecans, pressing to adhere. Space balls 2 inches apart on prepared baking sheets. Using teaspoon measure, make indentation in center of each ball. Fill each dimple with ½ teaspoon jam. Bake cookies until set, about 10 minutes, switching and rotating sheets halfway through baking. Let cookies cool on sheets for 5 minutes, then transfer to wire rack and let cool completely.

3 Microwave white chocolate chips in bowl at 50 percent power, stirring occasionally, until melted, 30 seconds to 1 minute. Drizzle cookies with melted chocolate and let sit until chocolate hardens, about 15 minutes. (Cookies can be stored at room temperature for up to 3 days.)

1½ cups (7½ ounces) all-purpose flour

½ cup (1½ ounces) unsweetened cocoa powder

¼ teaspoon baking powder

¼ teaspoon baking soda

¼ teaspoon table salt

8 tablespoons unsalted butter, softened

1 cup (7 ounces) sugar

1 large egg

1½ teaspoons vanilla extract

1 cup pecans, toasted and chopped fine

6 tablespoons seedless raspberry jam

½ cup (3 ounces) white chocolate chips

CHOCOLATE-HAZELNUT BISCOTTI

MAKES 30 COOKIES

1¼ cups hazelnuts, toasted and skinned, divided

1¼ cups (6¼ ounces) all-purpose flour

½ cup (1½ ounces) unsweetened cocoa powder

2 teaspoons baking powder

1 teaspoon instant espresso powder

¼ teaspoon table salt

2 large eggs, plus 1 large white beaten with pinch salt, divided

1 cup (7 ounces) sugar

4 tablespoons unsalted butter, melted and cooled

½ teaspoon vanilla extract

Vegetable oil spray

Why This Recipe Works Biscotti, the Italian cookies that are baked twice, should be twice as nice if chocolate-flavored. But chocolate biscotti usually fall short in terms of flavor due to the extra time drying in the oven—and they're often as hard as jawbreakers. Our goal was to develop intensely chocolaty biscotti with a crumb that didn't require hot coffee to soften. To get chocolate into the dough, we started with cocoa powder (plus some espresso powder) because it carries intense chocolate flavor and was easy to incorporate. For a nutty element, we chose complementary hazelnuts. Lightly toasting the nuts gave them roasty flavor to balance the chocolate. In addition, we ground some of the nuts to a fine meal; dispersed throughout the dough, they helped minimize gluten development and therefore that tough, hard texture. Before baking, we brushed the loaves with an egg white, which left a shiny, crackly sheen. These cookies were so rich in flavor, the typical chocolate dip was unnecessary.

1 Adjust oven rack to middle position and heat oven to 325 degrees. Using ruler and pencil, draw two 8 by 3-inch rectangles, spaced 4 inches apart, on piece of parchment paper. Grease baking sheet and place parchment on it, marked side down.

2 Pulse 1 cup hazelnuts in food processor until coarsely chopped, 8 to 10 pulses; transfer to bowl and set aside. Process remaining ¼ cup hazelnuts in now-empty processor until finely ground, about 45 seconds. Add flour, cocoa, baking powder, espresso powder, and salt and process until combined, about 15 seconds. Transfer flour mixture to second bowl.

3 Process 2 eggs in again-empty processor until lightened in color and almost doubled in volume, about 3 minutes. With processor running, slowly add sugar until thoroughly combined, about 15 seconds. Add melted butter and vanilla and process until combined, about 10 seconds. Transfer egg mixture to bowl. Sprinkle half of flour mixture over egg mixture and, using spatula, gently fold until just combined. Add remaining flour mixture and chopped hazelnuts and gently fold until just combined.

4 Divide dough in half. Using your floured hands, form each half into 8 by 3-inch rectangle, using lines on parchment as guide. Spray each loaf lightly with oil spray. Using rubber spatula lightly coated with oil spray, smooth tops and sides of rectangles. Gently brush tops of rectangles with egg white wash. Bake until loaves are set and beginning to crack on top, 25 to 30 minutes, rotating sheet halfway through baking.

5 Let loaves cool on baking sheet for 30 minutes. Transfer loaves to cutting board. Using serrated knife, slice each loaf on slight bias into ½-inch-thick slices. Lay slices cut side down, about ¼ inch apart on wire rack set in rimmed baking sheet. Bake until crisp on both sides, about 35 minutes, flipping slices halfway through baking. Let biscotti cool completely on wire rack, about 1 hour, before serving. (Biscotti can be stored in airtight container at room temperature for up to 1 month.)

BACI DI DAMA
MAKES 32 SANDWICH COOKIES

Why This Recipe Works *Baci di Dama*, tiny, bulbous chocolate-filled hazelnut cookies that translate as "lady's kisses," might just be the world's cutest cookie—until you try to make them. The rich, fragile dough easily softens and crumbles when you roll it, and the chocolate filling tends to ooze out the sides. We had a special trick: Leaving bits of skin on the nuts firmed up the dough and added complex flavor and attractive color. Precisely portioning the dough usually requires scooping and weighing dozens of individual pieces. Our method was much faster: We pressed the dough into a baking pan, briefly froze it to firm it up, and cut a "portion grid" out of the resulting dough block. Then we rolled each square into even balls. Finding the right bittersweet chocolate to glue these cookies together was a challenge. Neither ganache nor Nutella firmed up enough. Melted chocolate became set and snappy but ran down the sides when we sandwiched the heavy cookies. Letting the chocolate cool and thicken before spooning it onto cookies ensured that it didn't drip off. Gently pressing the second cookie on top spread the filling just to the edges. For these cookies, toast the hazelnuts on a rimmed baking sheet in a 325-degree oven until fragrant, 13 to 15 minutes, shaking the sheet halfway through toasting. To skin them, gather the warm hazelnuts in a dish towel and rub to remove some of the skins. A square-cornered metal baking pan works best for shaping the dough.

¾ cup hazelnuts, toasted and partially skinned

⅔ cup (3⅓ ounces) all-purpose flour

⅓ cup (2⅓ ounces) sugar

⅛ teaspoon table salt

6 tablespoons unsalted butter, cut into ½-inch pieces and chilled

2 ounces bittersweet chocolate, chopped

1 Adjust oven rack to middle position and heat oven to 325 degrees. Line two rimmed baking sheets with parchment paper. Line bottom of 8-inch square baking pan with parchment. Process hazelnuts, flour, sugar, and salt in food processor until hazelnuts are very finely ground, 20 to 25 seconds. Add butter and pulse until dough just comes together, 20 to 25 pulses.

2 Transfer dough to counter, knead briefly to form smooth ball, place in prepared pan, and press into even layer that covers bottom of pan. Freeze for 10 minutes. Run knife or bench scraper between dough and edge of pan to loosen. Transfer dough to counter and discard parchment. Cut dough into 64 squares (8 rows by 8 rows). Roll dough squares into balls and evenly space 32 dough balls on each prepared sheet. Bake, 1 sheet at a time, until cookies look dry and are fragrant (cookies will settle but not spread), about 20 minutes, rotating sheet halfway through baking. Transfer sheet to wire rack and let cookies cool completely, about 30 minutes.

3 Microwave chocolate in small bowl at 50 percent power, stirring every 20 seconds, until melted, 1 to 2 minutes. Allow chocolate to cool at room temperature until it is slightly thickened and registers 80 degrees, about 10 minutes. Invert half of cookies on each sheet. Using ¼-teaspoon measure, spoon chocolate onto flat surfaces of all inverted cookies. Top with remaining cookies, pressing lightly to adhere. Let chocolate set for at least 15 minutes before serving. (Cookies can be stored in airtight container at room temperature for up to 10 days.)

CHOCOLATE RUM BALLS

MAKES ABOUT 48 BALLS

1 cup granulated sugar

5 cups (12 ounces) chocolate wafer cookies

1¼ cups pecans, toasted

1 cup (4 ounces) confectioners' sugar

6 tablespoons dark rum

¼ cup light corn syrup

⅛ teaspoon table salt

Why This Recipe Works Chocolate rum balls were originally made (or so the story goes) as a way for Depression-era bakeries to use up their leftover cake and cookie scraps. They'd mix them with rum and a binder and sell them as adult-only trifles. The no-bake treats became a popular holiday dessert as they're a direct delivery system for two things we crave at holiday time: chocolate and booze—and ease. They're the perfect thing to make to give or enjoy during a busy season. There was no need to make our own chocolate cookies or cake for the base; wafer cookies are dark and ultrachocolaty and were perfect for making up the bulk of our rum balls. The other dry ingredient: pecans. Toasting them boosted their flavor and provided extra-nutty depth. Just ¼ cup of corn syrup stuck everything together without making the balls too sweet. Rum balls often contain vanilla extract, but it can taste boozy when raw and was adding sharpness when coupled with the rum. Ditching the vanilla allowed us to increase the rum to 6 tablespoons for more flavor—no chaser needed. We prefer the bold flavor of dark rum here, but you can substitute golden or spiced rum, if desired.

1 Place granulated sugar in shallow dish. Process cookies and pecans in food processor until finely ground, about 20 seconds. Transfer to large bowl. Stir in confectioners' sugar, rum, corn syrup, and salt until fully combined.

2 Working with 1 tablespoon at a time, shape mixture into balls. Transfer balls to dish with granulated sugar and roll to evenly coat; transfer to large plate. Refrigerate rum balls until firm, at least 1 hour. Serve. (Rum balls can be refrigerated for up to 1 week.)

PEPPERMINT MERINGUE KISSES

MAKES ABOUT 72 COOKIES

Why This Recipe Works Crisp and light as a feather, sweet peppermint-flavored meringue makes an ideal foil—in both flavor and texture—to a rich, creamy chocolate base in these easy, adorable holiday treats. Beating the egg whites with sugar until stiff peaks form produced cookies with a delicate texture. We beat the whites at a lower speed to start to lend the egg white mixture stability, and then we added the sugar slowly to ensure glossy, stiff peaks for a meringue that stood tall once baked—like little Santa hats. Before piping the meringue onto the baking sheets, we incorporated mini chocolate chips and crushed peppermint candies for festive holiday flair. Once fully cooled, we dipped the bottom of our kisses in melted chocolate chips. Try to work as quickly as possible when shaping the kisses; they'll deflate if they're left to sit for too long before baking. You will need about seven round peppermint candies to make 3 tablespoons crushed candy.

2 large egg whites

⅛ teaspoon cream of tartar

⅛ teaspoon table salt

⅔ cup (4⅔ ounces) sugar

½ teaspoon vanilla extract

2 cups (12 ounces) mini semisweet chocolate chips, divided

3 tablespoons crushed peppermint candies

2 teaspoons vegetable oil

1 Adjust oven racks to upper-middle and lower-middle positions and heat oven to 275 degrees. Line 2 baking sheets with parchment paper.

2 Using stand mixer fitted with whisk attachment, whip egg whites, cream of tartar, and salt on medium-low speed until foamy, about 1 minute. Increase speed to medium-high and whip whites to soft, billowy mounds, about 1 minute. Gradually add sugar and vanilla and whip until glossy, stiff peaks form, 2 to 3 minutes. Using rubber spatula, gently fold in 1 cup chocolate chips and crushed peppermints.

3 Using spoon or pastry bag fitted with ½-inch tip, dollop or pipe 1-teaspoon mounds of meringue, about 1 inch high, onto prepared sheets, spacing them about 1 inch apart. Bake until exterior begins to crack and turn light golden brown, 25 to 30 minutes, switching and rotating sheets halfway through baking. Transfer sheets to wire rack and let cookies cool completely on sheets.

4 Microwave remaining 1 cup chocolate chips in bowl at 50 percent power, stirring occasionally, until melted, about 1 minute. Stir in oil until incorporated. Dip bottoms of cookies in melted chocolate, scrape off excess, and place cookies on freshly lined baking sheet. Let chocolate set for at least 1 hour before serving.

CHOCOLATE CHIP PANETTONE

SERVES 8

¾ cup warm milk (110 degrees)

2 large eggs plus 2 large yolks, divided

3 tablespoons light corn syrup

1 teaspoon vanilla extract

½ teaspoon almond extract

2¾ cups (13¾ ounces) all-purpose flour

2¼ teaspoons instant or rapid-rise yeast

1 teaspoon table salt

8 tablespoons unsalted butter, cut into 8 pieces and softened

1 cup (6 ounces) mini semisweet chocolate chips

3 ounces finely chopped candied orange peel

Why This Recipe Works Panettone—a beautiful sweetened bread enriched with egg yolks and plenty of butter and studded with dried and candied fruits—is a northern Italian specialty popular during the Christmas season. We wanted to go a chocolaty route by using chocolate chips along with a modest amount of aromatic candied orange peel—and skipping the rest of the cloying fruit—for a version that was sure to please the whole family. And since the holidays are a busy time, we hoped to speed up the rising process. To do so, we used warm milk and corn syrup; yeast acts faster in warm environments and can metabolize invert sugars (such as corn syrup) faster than white sugar. Using mini chocolate chips—a full cup—ensured even distribution. To avoid having to special-order the customary panettone mold, we found that using an 8-inch cake pan produced the signature dome shape. Use an instant-read thermometer to make sure the milk is the correct temperature. If using a traditional 6 by 4-inch paper panettone mold, extend the baking time after tenting in step 5 by 10 minutes.

1 Whisk milk, 1 egg and 2 yolks, corn syrup, vanilla, and almond extract in 2-cup liquid measuring cup until combined. Using stand mixer fitted with dough hook, mix flour, yeast, and salt on medium-low speed until combined, about 5 seconds. With mixer running, slowly add milk mixture and knead until cohesive dough forms and no dry flour remains, 3 to 5 minutes, scraping down bowl and dough hook as needed.

2 With mixer running, add butter, 1 piece at a time, until incorporated. Increase speed to medium-high and knead until dough pulls away from sides of bowl but still sticks to bottom, about 10 minutes. Reduce speed to low, add chocolate chips and orange peel, and knead until fully incorporated, about 2 minutes.

3 Turn out dough onto lightly floured counter and knead until smooth, about 1 minute. Form dough into tight ball and transfer to greased large bowl. Cover with plastic wrap and let rise at room temperature (about 70 degrees) until doubled in size, about 2 hours.

4 Grease 8-inch cake pan. Pat dough into 12-inch disk on lightly floured counter. Working around circumference of dough, fold edges of dough toward center to form rough square. Flip dough over and, applying gentle pressure, move your hands in small circular motions to form dough into smooth, taut ball. Transfer ball, seam side down, to prepared pan. Cover loosely with greased plastic and let rise at room temperature until center is about 2 inches above lip of pan, 2 to 2½ hours.

5 Adjust oven rack to middle position and heat oven to 350 degrees. Lightly beat remaining egg and brush over dough. Bake until golden brown, 15 to 20 minutes. Rotate pan, tent with aluminum foil, and continue to bake until center of loaf registers 190 degrees, 30 to 40 minutes longer. Transfer pan to wire rack and let cool for 15 minutes. Remove loaf from pan and let cool completely on wire rack, about 3 hours. Serve.

CHOCOLATE CANDY CANE CAKE

SERVES 10 TO 12

Why This Recipe Works With creamy white chocolate frosting, refreshing crushed peppermint candies, and whimsical decorating, decadent chocolate cake layers get a wintry touch for the holiday season in this recipe. But while the icing provided another layer of chocolate flavor and a smooth, rich complement to the peppermint, it wasn't thick enough to support a coating of crushed candies. To get a frosting with the right amount of body, we simply stirred some melted white chocolate into our go-to vanilla frosting. But we added white chocolate to only half of the frosting, which we used to spread on the top and sides of the cake; to the rest we added a generous amount of ground peppermint candies and used this frosting to fill the cake. To finish, we piped beautiful rosettes of white chocolate icing around the top of the cake and topped each one with a single round peppermint candy. For this recipe, we used about 76 round peppermint candies: six for the garnish and 70 for the cake's two other peppermint uses (the filling and the coating).

8   ounces white chocolate, chopped

1   pound (4 sticks) unsalted butter, each stick cut into quarters and softened

¼   cup heavy cream

1   tablespoon vanilla extract

¼   teaspoon table salt

4   cups (16 ounces) confectioners' sugar

1¾   cups finely ground peppermint candies, divided, plus 6 whole candies for garnish

3   (8-inch) Chocolate Cake Layers (page 349)

1 Microwave chocolate in bowl at 50 percent power, stirring occasionally, until melted, 1 to 3 minutes; let cool. Using stand mixer fitted with paddle, beat butter, cream, vanilla, and salt on medium-high speed until smooth, about 1 minute. Reduce speed to medium-low, slowly add sugar, and beat until incorporated and smooth, about 4 minutes.

2 Increase speed to medium-high and beat until frosting is light and fluffy, about 5 minutes. Divide frosting evenly between 2 bowls. Stir white chocolate into 1 portion of frosting. Stir ¾ cup ground peppermints into remaining frosting.

3 Line edges of cake platter with 4 strips of parchment paper to keep platter clean. Place 1 cake layer on platter. Spread half of peppermint frosting evenly over top, right to edge of cake. Repeat with 1 more cake layer, press lightly to adhere, and then spread with remaining peppermint frosting. Top with remaining cake layer, pressing lightly to adhere.

4 Set aside ¾ cup white chocolate frosting; spread remaining white chocolate frosting evenly over top and sides of cake. Gently press remaining 1 cup ground peppermints onto cake sides and sprinkle evenly over top. Carefully remove parchment strips. Using remaining white chocolate icing, pipe ring of dots around base of cake and pipe 6 rosettes on top of cake. Place 1 whole peppermint candy on each rosette. Serve.

YULE LOG

SERVES 8 TO 10

BARK

12 ounces semisweet chocolate
(9 ounces chopped fine,
3 ounces grated), divided

GANACHE

6 ounces semisweet chocolate,
chopped

¾ cup heavy cream

2 tablespoons unsalted butter

1 tablespoon cognac

FILLING

6 tablespoons (1½ ounces)
confectioners' sugar

2 tablespoons heavy cream

1 teaspoon instant espresso
powder

1 pound (2 cups) mascarpone
cheese, room temperature

CAKE

6 ounces semisweet chocolate,
chopped fine

2 tablespoons unsalted butter,
cut into 2 pieces

2 tablespoons water

¼ cup (1¼ ounces) all-purpose
flour

¼ cup (¾ ounce) unsweetened
cocoa powder

¼ teaspoon baking powder

⅛ teaspoon table salt

6 large eggs, separated, room
temperature

⅛ teaspoon cream of tartar

⅓ cup (2⅓ ounces) granulated
sugar

1 teaspoon vanilla extract

Why This Recipe Works If it's a showcase holiday dessert you want, it's hard to top *bûche de Noël*. The chocolate-frosted roulade (rolled) shape of this classic French dessert mimics that of the yule logs burned in fireplaces on Christmas Day, and its whimsical appearance makes it a festive centerpiece. For a not-too-sweet roulade with a velvety texture, we used semisweet chocolate, plenty of eggs, and cocoa and flour for structural support. A filling of whipped mascarpone cheese flavored with espresso and a chocolate ganache coating complemented the rich cake. For a modern twist on decorating, we made a chocolate bark using our easy tempering technique (see page 267 for more information) and broke it into shards to cover our log. You can use bittersweet chocolate in place of semisweet for the cake, ganache, and bark. We used BelGioioso Mascarpone; some mascarpones are runnier, and you may have to whisk them vigorously before using. To serve, cut into diagonal slices with a serrated knife.

1 **For the bark** Adjust oven rack to upper-middle position and heat oven to 400 degrees. Line rimmed baking sheet with parchment paper. Microwave finely chopped chocolate in bowl at 50 percent power, stirring often, until about two-thirds melted, 2 to 4 minutes. (Melted chocolate should not be much warmer than body temperature; check by holding bowl in palm of your hand.) Add grated chocolate and stir until smooth, returning to microwave for no more than 5 seconds at a time to finish melting if necessary. Pour chocolate directly onto prepared sheet and spread to edges using small offset spatula. Drag tines of fork through warm chocolate to make abstract bark pattern. Refrigerate until chocolate is set, at least 30 minutes.

2 **For the ganache** Microwave chocolate, cream, butter, and cognac in bowl at 50 percent power, stirring occasionally, until melted and smooth, about 2 minutes. Measure out 3 tablespoons into small bowl and set aside to cool slightly. Set aside remaining ganache and let cool completely, about 30 minutes.

3 **For the filling** Whisk sugar, cream, espresso powder, and reserved 3 tablespoons ganache together in bowl. Stir mascarpone with rubber spatula in second bowl until softened and smooth, then stir in confectioners' sugar mixture; refrigerate until needed.

4 **For the cake** Grease 18 by 13-inch rimmed baking sheet, line with parchment paper, and grease parchment. Microwave chocolate, butter, and water in large, shallow bowl at 50 percent power, stirring occasionally, until melted, smooth, and glossy, about 1 minute; set aside to cool slightly.

5 Whisk flour, cocoa, baking powder, and salt together in small bowl; set aside. Using stand mixer fitted with whisk attachment, whip egg whites and cream of tartar on medium-low speed until foamy, about 1 minute. Increase speed to medium-high and whip whites to soft, billowy mounds, about 1 minute. Gradually add sugar and vanilla and whip until glossy, stiff peaks form, 2 to 3 minutes. Do not overwhip.

6 While whites are whipping, stir egg yolks into cooled chocolate-water mixture. Whisk one-quarter of whites into chocolate-water mixture. Using rubber spatula, gently fold remaining whites into chocolate mixture until almost no white streaks remain. Sprinkle cocoa mixture over top of batter and fold in quickly but gently until just incorporated and no dry flour remains. Pour batter into prepared sheet and, working quickly, level surface and smooth batter into sheet corners with offset spatula. Bake until center of cake springs back when touched, 8 to 10 minutes, rotating sheet halfway through baking. Invert second baking sheet, grease bottom lightly, and line with parchment.

7 Immediately run thin knife around edge of baking sheet to loosen cake. Working quickly while cake is warm, place second baking sheet on top, parchment side down, and gently flip pans over, discarding parchment attached to cake. Starting from long side, roll cake and bottom parchment into log. Let cake cool, seam side down, for 15 minutes.

8 Gently unroll cake. Stir filling to loosen, then spread evenly over cake, leaving 1-inch border along bottom edge. Reroll cake around filling, leaving parchment behind as you roll. Using long slicing knife, trim both uneven ends of cake on diagonal; set aside. Line edges of platter with 4 strips of parchment paper to keep platter clean. Transfer cake to platter. Dollop 1 tablespoon ganache off-center on top of log and place 1 cut end piece flat edge down on top of log. Using small offset spatula, gently spread remaining ganache over all of cake, covering ends of log, but leaving top stump edge exposed.

9 Gently break chilled chocolate bark into 1- to 3-inch shards. Press shards gently into ganache, overlapping slightly, covering entire cake. Refrigerate, uncovered, until ganache has set, about 20 minutes, before serving. (Cake can be refrigerated for up to 24 hours; let cake stand at room temperature for 30 minutes before serving.)

ASSEMBLING THE YULE LOG

1. Using long slicing knife, trim both uneven ends of cake on diagonal; set aside. Dollop 1 tablespoon ganache off-center on top of log. Place 1 cut end piece flat edge down on top of log.

2. Using small offset spatula, gently spread remaining ganache over all of cake, covering ends of log, but leaving top stump edge exposed.

3. Gently break chilled chocolate bark into 1- to 3-inch shards. Press shards gently into ganache, overlapping slightly, covering entire cake.

WHITE CHOCOLATE–RASPBERRY BOMBE

SERVES 8 TO 10

CAKE

- ½ cup whole milk, room temperature
- 3 large egg whites, room temperature
- 1 teaspoon vanilla extract
- 1 cup plus 2 tablespoons (4½ ounces) cake flour
- ¾ cup plus 2 tablespoons (6⅛ ounces) sugar
- 2 teaspoons baking powder
- ½ teaspoon table salt
- 6 tablespoons unsalted butter, cut into 6 pieces and softened

MOUSSE AND TOPPING

- ¼ cup raspberry liqueur, such as Chambord
- ¼ cup raspberry-flavored gelatin
- ⅛ teaspoon table salt
- 1 pound white chocolate, chopped fine, divided
- 2 cups heavy cream, divided
- 10 ounces (2 cups) raspberries
- White chocolate curls (see page 266)

Why This Recipe Works White chocolate and raspberries explode with flavor in this stunning dessert, making it an ideal grand finale to a celebratory New Year's Eve meal. The showy affair known as a bombe typically features layers of ice cream with a center of custard or fruit, all molded into a half-sphere shape. But bombes are notoriously time-consuming to prepare, as each layer must harden before the next can be added. We wanted to keep the elegant shape but hoped to speed up the process by ditching the layers of ice cream; instead, we envisioned a giant truffle-like display featuring a base of delicate cake topped with a dome of rich white chocolate mousse, all encased in a shell of silky white chocolate. Infusing our mousse with raspberry liqueur gave it a bright taste and pink hue; raspberry gelatin added another layer of flavor and ensured our mousse set up to a sliceable consistency. A sprinkling of whole raspberries throughout the mousse added pops of freshness. Garnishing the coating with curls of more white chocolate put the finishing touch on this impressive cake.

1 For the cake Adjust oven rack to middle position and heat oven to 350 degrees. Grease 9-inch round cake pan, line with parchment paper, grease parchment, and flour pan. Whisk milk, egg whites, and vanilla together in 2-cup liquid measuring cup.

2 Using stand mixer fitted with paddle, mix flour, sugar, baking powder, and salt on low speed until combined. Add butter, 1 piece at a time, until only pea-size pieces remain, about 1 minute. Add half of milk mixture, increase speed to medium-high, and beat until light and fluffy, about 1 minute. Reduce speed to medium-low, add remaining milk mixture, and mix until fully incorporated, about 30 seconds (batter may look curdled). Give batter final stir by hand.

3 Transfer batter to prepared pan and spread into even layer with rubber spatula. Bake until toothpick inserted in center comes out clean, 21 to 25 minutes, rotating pan halfway through baking.

4 Let cake cool in pan on wire rack for 10 minutes. Remove cake from pan, discarding parchment, and let cool completely on rack, about 2 hours.

5 For the mousse and topping Bring liqueur to simmer in small saucepan over medium-high heat. Stir in gelatin and salt until dissolved; remove from heat. Microwave 8 ounces chocolate and ½ cup cream in bowl at 50 percent power, stirring occasionally, until melted and smooth, about 2 minutes. Stir in gelatin mixture and let cool completely, about 30 minutes. Using stand mixer fitted with whisk attachment, whip remaining 1½ cups cream on medium-low speed until foamy, about 1 minute. Increase speed to high and whip until soft peaks form, 1 to 3 minutes. Gently fold one-third of whipped cream into chocolate mixture. Fold in remaining whipped cream until incorporated.

6 Line 10-cup mixing bowl with plastic wrap. Transfer one-third of mousse to prepared bowl and stud with one-third of raspberries. Repeat twice with remaining mousse and raspberries. Invert cake round on top of mousse, trimming cake to fit if necessary. Cover with plastic and refrigerate until mousse is set, at least 4 hours or up to 24 hours.

7 Unmold bombe onto cake platter, discarding plastic. Microwave remaining 8 ounces chocolate in bowl at 50 percent power, stirring occasionally, until melted, about 2½ minutes. Gently spread melted chocolate over mousse and cake, press chocolate curls into melted chocolate, and serve.

FORMING WHITE CHOCOLATE–RASPBERRY BOMBE

1. Line 10-cup mixing bowl with plastic wrap. Transfer one-third of mousse to prepared bowl and stud with one-third of raspberries.

2. Repeat twice with remaining mousse and raspberries.

3. Invert cake round on top of mousse, trimming cake to fit if necessary. Cover with plastic and refrigerate until mousse is set, at least 4 hours or up to 24 hours.

4. Unmold bombe onto cake platter, discarding plastic.

5. Gently spread melted chocolate over mousse and cake.

6. Press chocolate curls into melted chocolate.

CHOCOLATE-RASPBERRY HEART CAKE

SERVES 10 TO 12

CAKE

1¼ cups (6¼ ounces) all-purpose flour

¾ cup (2¼ ounces) unsweetened cocoa powder

½ teaspoon baking soda

¼ teaspoon table salt

8 ounces semisweet chocolate, chopped

12 tablespoons unsalted butter, cut into 12 pieces

1½ cups (10½ ounces) sugar

1 cup buttermilk

4 large eggs

1 teaspoon vanilla extract

FROSTING

7½ ounces (1½ cups) fresh or thawed frozen raspberries, plus about 20 fresh raspberries, divided

8 ounces white chocolate, chopped

1½ cups (10½ ounces) sugar

6 large egg whites

⅛ teaspoon table salt

24 tablespoons unsalted butter, cut into 24 pieces and softened

Why This Recipe Work We wanted to create a special, heart-shaped cake for Valentine's Day featuring the flavors of chocolate and raspberry. And we wanted to put our love into this dessert with pans we already had at home—while we knew we could probably find a flimsy heart-shaped cake pan at a craft store, we generally avoid purchasing single-use kitchen items. For a cake with undeniable chocolaty richness, we used a generous amount of both cocoa and semisweet chocolate; some buttermilk added a mild tang. We poured the batter into one 8-inch square and one 8-inch round pan. Once baked, we leveled the round cake to ensure both were the same height and simply cut the round cake in half vertically to create two ears to attach to two adjacent sides of the square. For the frosting, we opted for a Swiss meringue buttercream; less sweet than other frostings, it helped balance the richness of the cake, and its ultrasatiny texture added an elegant decadence. Fresh raspberry puree gave our buttercream a lovely pink hue as well a note of bright berry flavor, while mixing in some melted white chocolate contributed a silky richness. Piping pink roses over the cake and dotting it with whole fresh raspberries were beautiful finishing touches.

1 For the cake Adjust oven rack to middle position and heat oven to 325 degrees. Grease 8-inch square baking pan and 8-inch round cake pan, line each with parchment paper, grease parchment, and flour pans.

2 Sift flour, cocoa, baking soda, and salt together in bowl. Microwave chocolate and butter in second bowl at 50 percent power, stirring occasionally, until melted and smooth, 2 to 4 minutes. Whisk sugar, buttermilk, eggs, and vanilla together in third large bowl.

3 Whisk chocolate mixture into sugar mixture until combined. Whisk in flour mixture until smooth. Divide batter evenly between prepared pans and bake until toothpick inserted in center of each cake comes out clean, 35 to 45 minutes, rotating pans halfway through baking. Let cakes cool in pans on wire rack for 10 minutes. Run thin knife around edge of pans, remove cakes from pans, discarding parchment, and let cool completely on rack, about 1 hour.

4 For the frosting Process 1½ cups raspberries in food processor until smooth, about 30 seconds. Strain puree through fine-mesh strainer into bowl; discard solids and set aside puree. Microwave chocolate in bowl at 50 percent power, stirring occasionally, until melted, 1 to 2 minutes; let cool slightly. Combine sugar, egg whites, and salt in bowl of stand mixer. Set bowl over saucepan filled with 1 inch barely simmering water, making sure that water does not touch bottom of bowl. Cook, whisking constantly,

until mixture reaches 160 degrees, 5 to 8 minutes. Remove bowl from heat and transfer to stand mixer fitted with whisk attachment. Whip warm egg mixture on medium-high speed until stiff peaks form, about 5 minutes. Reduce speed to medium-low, add butter 1 piece at a time, and whip until smooth and creamy, about 2 minutes. Add melted chocolate and mix until just combined. Slowly add raspberry puree and mix until incorporated.

5 Place 1 corner of square cake against lower edge of large (about 16-inch diameter) cake platter. Using serrated knife, shave domed top from round cake to make it level with square cake; discard top. Cut round cake in half. Place halves, with cut sides facing in, against top 2 edges of square cake to form heart shape. Spread 2½ cups frosting over top and sides of cake in thin, even layer. Fill pastry bag fitted with star tip with remaining frosting and pipe roses (spiraling from inside out) over top and sides of cake. Place fresh raspberries between roses. Serve.

CHOCOLATE-STRAWBERRY CAKE

SERVES 12

TOPPING

20 fresh strawberries, hulled

¼   cup strawberry jam

1   teaspoon water

FROSTING

9   ounces (2 cups) frozen
    strawberries, thawed

1¼ pounds (5 sticks) unsalted
    butter, softened

5   cups (20 ounces) confectioners'
    sugar

1   tablespoon vanilla extract

⅛   teaspoon table salt

2   (9-inch) Chocolate Cake Layers
    (page 349)

Why This Recipe Works Chocolate-covered strawberries are a classic Valentine's Day sweet treat; for a full-scale dessert that celebrates this combination, we wanted to make a decadent chocolate cake featuring smooth, creamy strawberry frosting. Frozen strawberries were a convenient option to flavor the frosting; we used the food processor to create a strawberry puree, which we added to the frosting once the butter and confectioners' sugar had been whipped to a light, fluffy consistency. The pale pink hue of the frosting provided a striking contrast to the deep, dark layers of chocolate. But while frozen strawberries were fine in the frosting, fresh were essential for the cake's topping. We glazed fresh berries with strawberry jam and arranged them atop the cake, putting a bright, glistening crown on this Valentine's Day showstopper. Let the frozen strawberries thaw in the refrigerator overnight.

1 **For the topping** Reserve 1 whole strawberry. Halve remaining 19 strawberries. Place jam and water in large bowl and microwave until bubbling, about 2 minutes. Add whole and halved strawberries to jam mixture and toss until evenly coated. Transfer strawberries to parchment paper–lined baking sheet and spread into single layer. Set aside.

2 **For the frosting** Drain strawberries in fine-mesh strainer, pressing firmly on fruit with rubber spatula (discard juice). Transfer strawberry solids to food processor and process until smooth, about 1 minute.

3 Using stand mixer fitted with whisk attachment, whip butter on medium-high speed until smooth, about 20 seconds. Add sugar and whip on medium-low speed until most of sugar is moistened, about 45 seconds. Scrape down bowl. Add vanilla, salt, and strawberry puree and whip on medium-high speed until light and fluffy, about 4 minutes, scraping down bowl as needed.

4 Line edges of cake platter with 4 strips of parchment paper to keep platter clean. Place 1 cake layer on platter. Spread 1½ cups frosting evenly over top, right to edge of cake. Top with second cake layer, pressing lightly to adhere. Spread remaining frosting evenly over top and sides of cake.

5 Place whole glazed strawberry in center of cake. Arrange 5 glazed strawberry halves, stem end down and cut side facing in, around whole strawberry. Repeat in concentric circular pattern 2 times, angling tips of strawberries outward at 45 degrees and alternating orientation of cut side and round side of strawberries. Arrange remaining strawberry halves in circle, cut side down, at base of subsequent rings of strawberries, with points facing outward. Carefully remove parchment strips before serving.

CHOCOLATE SHADOW CAKE

SERVES 12

Why This Recipe Works This cake's name, inspired by its bewitching dark glaze dripping over a stark white backdrop of fluffy seven-minute icing, invokes the spirit of Halloween, but there's nothing scary about making this rich chocolate butter cake. We already had a great recipe for layers of rich chocolate cake, so we focused our attention on the frosting and glaze. Sweet seven-minute icing is an old-fashioned thick, glossy frosting with a marshmallow-y taste that gets its name from the time it takes to beat the ingredients—egg whites, sugar, water, and cream of tartar—over simmering water. We found we could speed up the cooling process by removing the mixture from the heat once stiff peaks had formed and continuing to beat until it had cooled to room temperature. We made an intense chocolate glaze with bittersweet chocolate, butter, and light corn syrup; the corn syrup ensured it had a glossy texture, allowing it to cling tightly to the cake and drip invitingly down the sides to create a scary shadow.

4 large egg whites

3 tablespoons water

1¼ cups (8¾ ounces) sugar

1 teaspoon cream of tartar
Pinch table salt

1 teaspoon vanilla extract

3 (8-inch) Chocolate Cake Layers (page 349)

4 ounces bittersweet chocolate, chopped

4 tablespoons unsalted butter

2 tablespoons light corn syrup

1 Whisk egg whites, water, sugar, cream of tartar, and salt in large heatproof bowl set over medium saucepan filled with 1 inch barely simmering water, making sure that water does not touch bottom of bowl. Using handheld mixer set at medium-high speed, carefully beat egg white mixture to stiff peaks, 6 to 8 minutes. Remove bowl from heat, add vanilla, and continue to beat until icing is very thick and stiff and cooled to room temperature, about 8 minutes.

2 Line edges of cake platter with 4 strips of parchment paper to keep platter clean. Place 1 cake layer on platter. Spread 1 cup icing evenly over top, right to edge of cake. Repeat with 1 more cake layer and 1 cup icing. Top with remaining cake layer and spread remaining icing evenly over top and sides of cake.

3 Place chocolate, butter, and corn syrup in large heatproof bowl set over medium saucepan filled with 1 inch barely simmering water, making sure that water does not touch bottom of bowl. Stir until melted and smooth, then remove bowl from heat and let cool 5 minutes. Spoon ¼ cup chocolate mixture over top of cake and then drizzle remaining glaze along top edge of cake, allowing it to drip about halfway down the sides. Carefully remove parchment strips before serving.

dazzling
DESSERTS

CHOCOLATE PAVLOVA WITH BERRIES AND WHIPPED CREAM

SERVES 10

MERINGUE

1½ cups (10½ ounces) sugar

¾ cup (6 ounces) egg whites (5 to 7 large eggs)

1½ teaspoons distilled white vinegar

1½ teaspoons cornstarch

1 teaspoon vanilla extract

2 ounces bittersweet chocolate, grated

TOPPING

2 pounds (5 cups) blackberries, blueberries, and/or raspberries

3 tablespoons sugar, divided

Pinch table salt

2 ounces bittersweet chocolate, chopped fine

2 cups heavy cream, chilled

Why This Recipe Works If you associate chocolate decadence only with the ultrafudgy and dense, this ethereal chocolate pavlova will expand your chocolate horizons—in a glamorous display. Pavlova is a large meringue base for billowy whipped cream and a topping. But unlike uniformly crunchy meringue cookies, pavlova offers a range of textures: a crisp outer shell; a tender, marshmallowy interior; and a pleasant chew where the two meet. Chocolate pavlova was particularly intriguing to us: The richness of bar chocolate would balance some of the sweetness of the meringue. Instead of Italian meringue, which calls for the unnerving task of drizzling hot sugar syrup into egg whites, our pavlova is baked from a Swiss meringue: Sugar is dissolved in the whites as they're heated over simmering water and then whipped. Chopped chocolate weighed down the meringue, interrupting the delicate structure and texture. We were able to fold in finely grated bittersweet chocolate to flavor every bite. Lightly sweetened whipped cream and berries brought things further into balance and made for a beautiful presentation of colors and textures. The chocolate gave the meringue plenty of flavor, but we couldn't resist a generous drizzle on top. The showstopping dessert was light in texture but not in chocolate flavor, making it the perfect ending to a rich meal. Because eggs can vary in size, measuring the egg whites by weight or volume is essential to ensure that you are working with the correct ratio of egg whites to sugar. Open the oven door as infrequently as possible while the meringue is inside. Do not worry if the meringue cracks; it's part of the dessert's charm.

1 For the meringue Adjust oven rack to middle position and heat oven to 250 degrees. Using pencil, draw 10-inch circle in center of 18 by 13-inch piece of parchment paper. Combine sugar and egg whites in bowl of stand mixer; place bowl over saucepan filled with 1 inch simmering water, making sure that water does not touch bottom of bowl. Whisking gently but constantly, heat until sugar is dissolved and mixture registers 160 to 165 degrees, 5 to 8 minutes.

2 Fit stand mixer with whisk attachment and whip mixture on high speed until meringue forms stiff peaks, is smooth and creamy, and is bright white with sheen, about 4 minutes (bowl may still be slightly warm to touch). Stop mixer and scrape down bowl with spatula. Add vinegar, cornstarch, and vanilla and whip on high speed until combined, about 10 seconds. Remove bowl and, using rubber spatula, fold in grated chocolate.

3 Spoon about ¼ teaspoon meringue onto each corner of rimmed baking sheet. Press parchment, marked side down, onto sheet to secure. Pile meringue in center of circle on parchment. Using circle as guide, spread and smooth meringue with back of spoon or spatula from center outward, building 10-inch disk that is slightly higher around edges. Finished disk should measure about 1 inch high with ¼-inch depression in center.

4 Bake meringue until exterior is dry and crisp and meringue releases cleanly from parchment when gently lifted at edge with thin metal spatula, 1 to 1½ hours. Meringue should be quite pale (a hint of creamy color is OK). Turn off oven, prop door open with wooden spoon, and let meringue cool in oven for 1½ hours. Remove from oven and let cool completely before topping, about 15 minutes. (Cooled meringue can be wrapped tightly in plastic wrap and stored at room temperature for up to 1 week.)

5 **For the topping** Toss berries with 1 tablespoon sugar and salt in large bowl. Set aside for 30 minutes. Meanwhile, microwave chocolate in bowl at 50 percent power, stirring occasionally, until melted, about 1 minute. Set aside to cool slightly.

6 Before serving, whip cream and remaining 2 tablespoons sugar in clean, dry bowl of stand mixer fitted with whisk attachment on medium-low speed until foamy, about 1 minute. Increase speed to high and whip until soft peaks form, 1 to 3 minutes.

7 Carefully peel meringue away from parchment and place on large serving platter. Spoon whipped cream into center of meringue. Spoon berries in even layer over whipped cream, then drizzle with melted chocolate. Let sit for at least 5 minutes or up to 1 hour. Slice and serve.

MAKING CHOCOLATE PAVLOVA WITH BERRIES AND WHIPPED CREAM

1. Whip hot egg white mixture on high speed until meringue forms stiff peaks, is smooth and creamy, and is bright white with sheen, about 4 minutes.

2. Scrape down bowl with spatula. Add vinegar, cornstarch, and vanilla and whip on high speed until combined, about 10 seconds. Fold in grated chocolate.

3. Pile meringue in center of circle on prepared parchment.

4. Spread and smooth meringue with back of spoon or spatula from center outward, building 10-inch disk that is slightly higher around edges.

5. Carefully peel baked meringue away from parchment and place on large serving platter. Spoon whipped cream into center of meringue.

6. Spoon berries in even layer over whipped cream. Drizzle with melted chocolate. Slice and serve.

CHOCOLATE PROFITEROLES

MAKES 10 PROFITEROLES

2 large eggs plus 1 large white

½ cup (2½ ounces) all-purpose flour

2 tablespoons unsweetened cocoa powder

5 tablespoons unsalted butter

2 tablespoons whole milk

6 tablespoons water

1½ teaspoons sugar

¼ teaspoon table salt

4 cups ice cream

1 cup Classic Hot Fudge Sauce (page 340)

Why This Recipe Works On its own, pate a choux, the temperamental pastry dough that's glazed, filled, or coated for desserts like éclairs, cream puffs, and even churros, is buttery, rich, and crisp but a bit plain. We wanted to make it chocolate for our ice cream–filled profiteroles recipe—and disassociate it from the word "temperamental." To turn the dough chocolate, we cut back on some of the flour and replaced it with cocoa powder. The inconsistency in pate a choux results is due largely to the variation in egg size—an exacting ratio of eggs to the other ingredients is necessary for success. To prevent problems for these most delicate pastry shells, we came up with a cup equivalent for eggs, whisking together the eggs and measuring out the perfect amount to ensure successful results every time. Traditionally the eggs are incorporated by hand in arm-straining fashion. We turned to the food processor, adding the eggs to the dough gradually to incorporate fully. For classic pate a choux, there are visual clues as to when the dough can come off the stove, but the cocoa powder makes this dough dark in color, so we encourage using a digital thermometer. With the traditional drizzle of hot fudge over the ice cream–filled puffs, we turned profiteroles into a double-chocolate experience (triple if you choose chocolate ice cream). In step 4, the dough can be piped using a pastry bag fitted with a ½-inch plain tip.

1 Adjust oven rack to upper-middle position and heat oven to 425 degrees. Line rimmed baking sheet with parchment paper and nest it in second rimmed baking sheet. Beat eggs and white in 2-cup liquid measuring cup until well combined. (You will use ½ cup egg mixture. Discard excess.) Set aside.

2 Sift flour and cocoa together into bowl. Heat butter, milk, water, sugar, and salt in small saucepan over medium heat. When mixture begins to simmer, reduce heat to low and immediately stir in flour mixture using wooden spoon. Cook, stirring constantly using smearing motion, until paste is slightly shiny with wet-sand appearance and tiny beads of fat appear on bottom of saucepan (temperature of paste should register 175 to 180 degrees), about 3 minutes.

3 Immediately transfer hot paste to food processor and process with feed tube open for 5 seconds to cool slightly. With processor running, gradually add reserved ½ cup egg mixture in steady stream until incorporated. Scrape down sides of bowl and continue to process until smooth, thick, sticky paste forms, about 30 seconds longer.

4 Using 2 spoons, scoop 2 heaping tablespoons of dough onto prepared sheet. Repeat with remaining dough, spacing mounds 2 inches apart (you should have 10 portions). Using back of spoon lightly coated with vegetable oil spray, shape each portion of dough into 2-inch-wide, 1-inch-tall mound and smooth away any creases and large peaks.

5 Bake puffs for 15 minutes (do not open oven door), then reduce oven temperature to 375 degrees and continue to bake until puffs are fairly firm (puffs should not be soft and squishy), 6 to 8 minutes. Turn off oven and remove sheet.

6 Using paring knife, cut ¾-inch slit into side of each puff to release steam. Return puffs to turned-off oven and prop door open with handle of wooden spoon. Dry puffs until centers are just moist (not wet) and surfaces are crisp, about 40 minutes. Transfer puffs to wire rack and let cool completely, about 30 minutes. (Cooled puffs can be stored at room temperature for up to 24 hours or frozen in zipper-lock plastic bag for up to 1 month. Before serving, crisp room temperature puffs in 300-degree oven for 5 to 8 minutes, or thawed frozen puffs for 8 to 10 minutes.)

7 Meanwhile, line second rimmed baking sheet with parchment; freeze until cold, about 20 minutes. Using 2-inch ice cream scoop (about same diameter as puffs), scoop 10 portions of ice cream onto cold sheet and freeze until firm. Cover with plastic wrap and keep frozen until ready to serve, or up to 1 week.

8 When ready to serve, use paring knife to split open puffs about ⅜ inch from bottom. Set bottoms on individual serving plates. Place scoop of ice cream on each bottom and gently press tops into ice cream. Pour hot fudge over profiteroles and serve immediately.

MAKING THE CHOCOLATE PATE A CHOUX

1. Heat butter, milk, water, sugar, and salt in small saucepan over medium heat. When mixture begins to simmer, reduce heat to low and immediately stir in flour-cocoa mixture using wooden spoon.

2. Cook, stirring constantly using smearing motion, until mixture is slightly shiny with wet-sand appearance and tiny beads of fat appear on bottom of saucepan (temperature of paste should register 175 to 180 degrees), about 3 minutes.

3. Immediately transfer mixture to food processor and process with feed tube open for 5 seconds to cool slightly. With processor running, gradually add reserved ½ cup egg mixture in steady stream until incorporated.

4. Scrape down sides of bowl and continue to process until smooth, thick, sticky paste forms, about 30 seconds.

5. Using 2 spoons, scoop 2 heaping tablespoons of dough onto prepared sheet. Repeat with remaining dough, spacing mounds 2 inches apart (you should have 10 portions).

6. Using back of spoon lightly coated with vegetable oil spray, shape each portion of dough into 2-inch-wide, 1-inch-tall mound and smooth away any creases and large peaks.

WHITE CHOCOLATE–PINK PEPPERCORN PANNA COTTA

SERVES 6

2 cups heavy cream

3 tablespoons pink peppercorns, cracked, plus extra for serving

2 teaspoons unflavored gelatin

6 ounces white chocolate, chopped

3 tablespoons sugar

⅛ teaspoon salt

1 cup buttermilk

White Chocolate Curls (see page 266)

Why This Recipe Works Panna cotta is tailor-made for entertaining, not only because it's a cool and creamy finishing course but because it can be made ahead. Always wanting to impress our guests, we traded the traditional vanilla panna cotta for a spiced-up (literally) one with buttery white chocolate balancing slightly pungent pink peppercorns. These berries from a tropical evergreen tree (not a true pepper) are fruity and floral so they take well to dessert. We infused the cream with peppercorns and incorporated white chocolate to melt it into the mix. To balance the spiciness from the pepper and richness from the chocolate, we added some tangy buttermilk. This dessert hits all the right flavor notes, especially after being garnished with beautiful chocolate curls and more peppercorns. Buttermilk is temperature sensitive, so stir it in only after the base has cooled to 50 degrees. To serve unmolded, you'll need six 4- to 5-ounce ramekins. Panna cotta may also be chilled and served in wineglasses. If you'd like to make the panna cotta a day ahead, reduce the amount of gelatin by ½ teaspoon and chill the filled ramekins for at least 18 hours or up to 24 hours.

1 Bring cream and peppercorns to simmer in medium saucepan over medium heat. Off heat, sprinkle surface of cream mixture with gelatin and let sit until flavors meld and gelatin softens, about 10 minutes.

2 Return cream mixture to medium heat and cook, stirring constantly, until gelatin is dissolved and mixture registers 135 degrees, 1 to 2 minutes. Off heat, stir in chocolate, sugar, and salt and let sit for 3 minutes. Whisk mixture until smooth and chocolate is fully melted.

3 Fill large bowl halfway with ice and water. Set six 4- to 5-ounce ramekins on rimmed baking sheet. Transfer cream mixture to bowl, set over prepared ice bath, and let sit, stirring often, until slightly thickened and registers 50 degrees, about 20 minutes. Stir in buttermilk. Strain mixture through fine-mesh strainer into 4-cup liquid measuring cup, then divide evenly among ramekins. Cover ramekins with plastic wrap and refrigerate until panna cottas are just set (mixture should wobble when shaken gently), at least 4 hours or up to 12 hours.

4 To unmold, run paring knife around perimeter of each ramekin. (If shape of ramekin makes this difficult, quickly dip ramekin into hot water bath to loosen panna cotta.) Hold serving plate over top of each ramekin and invert; set plate on counter and gently shake ramekin to release panna cotta. Sprinkle with chocolate curls and extra pink peppercorns before serving.

TRIPLE CHOCOLATE MOUSSE CAKE

SERVES 12 TO 16

BOTTOM LAYER

- 6 tablespoons unsalted butter, cut into 6 pieces
- 7 ounces bittersweet chocolate, chopped fine
- ¾ teaspoon instant espresso powder
- 4 large eggs, separated
- 1½ teaspoons vanilla extract
  - Pinch cream of tartar
  - Pinch table salt
- ⅓ cup packed (2⅓ ounces) light brown sugar

MIDDLE LAYER

- 5 tablespoons hot water
- 2 tablespoons unsweetened cocoa powder
- 7 ounces bittersweet chocolate, chopped fine
- 1½ cups heavy cream, chilled
- 1 tablespoon granulated sugar
- ⅛ teaspoon table salt

TOP LAYER

- ¾ teaspoon unflavored gelatin
- 1 tablespoon water
- 1 cup (6 ounces) white chocolate chips
- 1½ cups heavy cream, chilled, divided

  Chocolate curls (see page 266) (optional)

Why This Recipe Works Triple chocolate mousse cake is a triple-decker stunner that becomes incrementally lighter in texture and richness from bottom to top. For a base layer with the heft to support the upper two tiers, we chose a nicely aerated flourless chocolate cake instead of the typical mousse cake. For the middle layer, we started with a traditional chocolate mousse but found it a little heavy; removing the eggs resulted in a lighter layer. And for the top tier, we made an easy white chocolate mousse by folding whipped cream into melted white chocolate. To prevent the soft top mousse from oozing during slicing, we added a little gelatin. This recipe requires a springform pan that is at least 3 inches high. For the best results, chill the mixer bowl before whipping the heavy cream in steps 5 and 8. To slice, dip a sharp knife in very hot water and wipe dry before each cut. (If you're making the cake a day in advance, let it sit at room temperature for up to 45 minutes before releasing from the pan and serving.)

1 **For the bottom layer** Adjust oven rack to middle position and heat oven to 325 degrees. Grease 9-inch springform pan. Microwave butter, chocolate, and espresso powder in large bowl at 50 percent power, stirring occasionally, until melted and smooth, 2 to 4 minutes. Let cool slightly, about 5 minutes. Whisk in egg yolks and vanilla; set aside.

2 Using stand mixer fitted with whisk attachment, whip egg whites, cream of tartar, and salt on medium-low speed until foamy, about 1 minute. Add half of sugar and whip until combined, about 15 seconds. Add remaining sugar, increase speed to high, and whip until soft peaks form, about 1 minute longer, scraping down bowl halfway through whipping. Using whisk, fold one-third of whipped whites into chocolate mixture to lighten it. Using rubber spatula, fold in remaining whites until no white streaks remain. Carefully pour batter into prepared pan and smooth top with rubber spatula.

3 Bake until cake has risen, is firm around edges, and center springs back when pressed gently with your finger, 13 to 18 minutes, rotating pan halfway through baking. Let cake cool completely in pan on wire rack, about 1 hour, before filling. (Cake will collapse as it cools.) Do not remove cake from pan.

4 **For the middle layer** Combine hot water and cocoa in small bowl; set aside. Microwave chocolate in large bowl at 50 percent power, stirring occasionally, until melted, 1 to 3 minutes. Let cool slightly, 2 to 5 minutes.

5 Using clean, dry mixer bowl and whisk attachment, whip cream, sugar, and salt on medium-low speed until foamy, about 1 minute. Increase speed to high and whip until soft peaks form, 1 to 3 minutes.

6 Whisk cocoa mixture into melted chocolate until smooth. Using whisk, fold one-third of whipped cream into chocolate mixture to lighten it. Using rubber spatula, fold in remaining whipped cream until no white streaks remain. Spoon

mousse into pan over cooled cake and smooth top with offset spatula. Gently tap pan on counter to release air bubbles. Wipe inside edge of pan with damp cloth to remove any drips. Refrigerate cake for at least 15 minutes.

7 **For the top layer** Sprinkle gelatin over water in small bowl and let sit until gelatin softens, about 5 minutes. Place white chocolate chips in large heatproof bowl. Bring ½ cup cream to simmer in small saucepan over medium-high heat. Remove from heat, add gelatin mixture, and stir until gelatin is fully dissolved. Pour cream mixture over chocolate chips and let sit, covered, for 5 minutes. Whisk mixture gently until smooth. Let cool completely, stirring occasionally (mixture will thicken slightly).

8 Using clean, dry mixer bowl and whisk attachment, whip remaining 1 cup cream on medium-low speed until foamy, about 1 minute. Increase speed to high and whip until soft peaks form, 1 to 3 minutes. Using whisk, fold one-third of whipped cream into white chocolate mixture to lighten it. Using rubber spatula, fold in remaining whipped cream until no white streaks remain. Spoon white chocolate mousse into pan over middle layer and smooth top with offset spatula. Refrigerate cake until set, at least 2½ hours or up to 24 hours.

9 Garnish top of cake with chocolate curls, if using. Run thin knife around edge of pan to loosen cake, then remove sides of pan. Run clean knife along outside of cake to smooth. Serve.

HAZELNUT–CHOCOLATE CRÊPE CAKE

SERVES 10 TO 12

CRÊPES

½ teaspoon vegetable oil

⅔ cup hazelnuts, toasted and skinned

1¼ cups (6¼ ounces) all-purpose flour

1 tablespoon granulated sugar

¼ teaspoon table salt

3 cups whole milk

6 large eggs

4 tablespoons unsalted butter, melted and cooled

FILLING

6 ounces bittersweet chocolate, chopped

16 tablespoons unsalted butter, cut into 16 pieces and softened

¼ teaspoon table salt

⅔ cup (2⅔ ounces) confectioners' sugar

8 ounces marshmallow crème

3 tablespoons unsweetened cocoa powder

1½ teaspoons hazelnut extract

WHIPPED CREAM

½ cup heavy cream, chilled

2 teaspoons granulated sugar

½ teaspoon vanilla extract

2 tablespoons chopped toasted and skinned hazelnuts

Why This Recipe Works A fun departure from traditional cakes, this statuesque dessert is made from more than 20 crêpes, all spread with a luxurious chocolate-hazelnut filling and stacked tall. To underscore the filling's flavor, we substituted ground hazelnuts for a portion of the flour in our crêpes. For the filling, an easy Swiss meringue buttercream made with marshmallow crème was light yet sticky enough to hold the crêpes together. Bittersweet chocolate and cocoa provided complex chocolate flavor to our filling, and hazelnut extract contributed nuttiness without disrupting the smooth texture. The crêpes will give off steam as they cook, but if the skillet begins to smoke, remove it from the heat immediately and turn down the heat. Stacking the crêpes on a wire rack allows steam to escape so they won't stick together. If making the crêpes ahead, microwave them in 2 batches until slightly warm and you can peel them apart, 30 to 45 seconds (45 to 60 seconds if the crêpes are cold). We prefer freshly ground hazelnuts in our crêpes, but ¾ cup hazelnut flour or almond flour may be substituted. We developed this recipe using Fluff brand marshmallow crème. To slice the cake, dip a sharp knife in very hot water and wipe dry before each cut.

1 For the crêpes Heat oil in 8-inch nonstick skillet over low heat for at least 10 minutes. Meanwhile, process hazelnuts in food processor until finely ground, about 1 minute; transfer to large bowl. Whisk in flour, sugar, and salt until combined. Whisk milk and eggs together in second bowl. Add half of milk mixture to hazelnut mixture and whisk until smooth. Add melted butter and whisk until incorporated. Whisk in remaining milk mixture until smooth.

2 Wipe out skillet with paper towel, leaving thin film of oil on bottom and sides of pan. Increase heat to medium and let skillet heat for 1 minute. After 1 minute, test heat of skillet by placing 1 teaspoon batter in center and cooking for 20 seconds. If mini crêpe is golden brown on bottom, skillet is properly heated; if it is too light or too dark, adjust heat accordingly and retest.

3 Pour ¼ cup batter into far side of skillet; tilt and shake gently until batter evenly covers bottom of skillet. Cook crêpe without moving it until top surface is dry and edges are starting to brown, loosening crêpe from sides of skillet with heat-resistant rubber spatula, about 1 minute. Gently slide spatula underneath edge of crêpe, grasp edge with your fingertips, and flip crêpe. Cook until second side is lightly spotted, about 30 seconds. Transfer crêpe, spotted side up, to wire rack. Return skillet to heat and heat for 10 seconds before repeating with remaining batter. (You should have about 24 crêpes.) As crêpes are done, stack on wire rack. Let cool completely. (Crêpes can be stacked, covered with plastic wrap, and refrigerated for up to 24 hours; bring to room temperature before using.)

4 For the filling Microwave chocolate in bowl at 50 percent power, stirring occasionally, until melted, 2 to 4 minutes; let cool slightly. Using stand mixer fitted with paddle, beat butter, melted chocolate, and salt on medium speed until smooth, about 1 minute. Reduce speed to low and slowly add sugar. Increase speed to medium and beat until smooth, about 2 minutes, scraping down bowl as needed. Add marshmallow crème, increase speed to medium-high, and beat until light and fluffy, 3 to 5 minutes. Reduce speed to low, add cocoa and hazelnut extract, and beat to incorporate, about 30 seconds. (Filling can be refrigerated for up to 3 days; let soften at room temperature, about 2 hours, then rewhip on medium speed until smooth, 2 to 5 minutes.)

5 Place small dab of filling in center of cake platter to anchor cake. Lay 1 crêpe on platter. Spread 3 tablespoons filling evenly over top, right to edge of crêpe. Top with 1 crêpe, pressing lightly to adhere. Repeat with remaining crêpes and filling, refrigerating cake for 15 minutes halfway through assembly to set layers and ending with crêpe on top. Refrigerate for at least 30 minutes or up to 12 hours.

6 For the whipped cream Using clean, dry mixer bowl and whisk attachment, whip cream, sugar, and vanilla on medium-low speed until foamy, about 1 minute. Increase speed to high and whip until soft peaks form, 1 to 3 minutes.

7 Spread whipped cream into even layer on top of cake, then garnish with chopped hazelnuts. Let stand at room temperature for 20 minutes before serving.

MAKING THE CRÊPES

1. Heat oil in 8-inch nonstick skillet over low heat for at least 10 minutes. Wipe out skillet with paper towel, leaving thin film of oil on bottom and sides of pan.

2. Increase heat to medium and let skillet heat for 1 minute. Test heat of skillet by placing 1 teaspoon batter in center and cook for 20 seconds. If mini crêpe is golden brown on bottom, skillet is properly heated; if it is too light or too dark, adjust heat and retest.

3. Pour ¼ cup batter into far side of pan and tilt and shake gently until batter evenly covers bottom of pan.

4. Cook crêpe without moving it until top surface is dry and edges are starting to brown, loosening crêpe from sides of pan with heat-resistant rubber spatula, about 1 minute.

5. Gently slide spatula underneath edge of crêpe, grasp edge with your fingertips, and flip crêpe.

6. Cook until second side is lightly spotted, about 30 seconds. Transfer cooked crêpe, spotted side up, to wire rack.

CHOCOLATE-RASPBERRY PETITS FOURS

MAKES 60 PETITS FOURS

FILLING

7½ ounces (1½ cups) raspberries

¾ cup (5¼ ounces) sugar

2 teaspoons lemon juice

1 ounce bittersweet chocolate, chopped

CAKE

1½ cups (10½ ounces) sugar

8 ounces almond paste, cut into 1-inch pieces

7 large eggs

1 teaspoon vanilla extract

½ teaspoon baking powder

½ teaspoon table salt

8 tablespoons unsalted butter, melted and cooled slightly

2 cups (8 ounces) cake flour

TOPPING

2 cups (12 ounces) white chocolate chips

¼ cup (1½ ounces) bittersweet chocolate chips

Why This Recipe Works Petits fours are small confections typically presented at the end of a classic French meal. Although they're often filled with plain jam, we envisioned these bite-size, decorative cakes with a chocolate-raspberry filling to provide a bright yet rich contrast to the delicate cake. And we wanted an easy-to-prepare recipe that would make a statement at any party. We started by baking three thin layers of almond sponge cake, one at a time, in a 13 by 9-inch baking pan. We made a quick raspberry jam, stirring chopped chocolate into the warm puree before cooking it down, for a simple, luscious filling. Rather than bathing the cake pieces in sugary glaze (which tasters thought was outmoded), we simply spread a layer of melted white chocolate over the cake, drizzled dark chocolate in lines over the white, and ran the tines of a fork through the chocolates to create an elegant web-like pattern—and, of course, to add more chocolate.

1 **For the filling** Bring raspberries, sugar, and lemon juice to boil in large saucepan over medium-high heat, stirring often. Boil until raspberries have broken down and released their juices, about 5 minutes.

2 Whisk in chocolate until completely melted, about 1 minute. Continue to boil mixture, stirring and adjusting heat as needed, until jam has thickened and measures 1 cup, 10 to 15 minutes. Remove saucepan from heat. Transfer jam to bowl and let cool completely, about 1 hour.

3 **For the cake** Adjust oven rack to middle position and heat oven to 350 degrees. Grease 13 by 9-inch baking pan, line with parchment paper, and grease parchment.

4 Process sugar and almond paste in food processor until mixture resembles coarse sand, 20 to 30 seconds. Add eggs, vanilla, baking powder, and salt and process until pale yellow and frothy, about 2 minutes. With processor running, slowly add melted butter in steady stream until incorporated, about 10 seconds. Add flour and pulse to combine, 4 to 5 pulses.

5 Transfer 1⅔ cups batter to prepared pan and spread into even layer with offset spatula; set remaining batter aside. Bake until top is set and edges are just starting to brown, 8 to 10 minutes. Let cake cool in pan on wire rack for 5 minutes. Remove cake from pan, discarding parchment, and let cake cool completely on rack. Let pan cool slightly, about 10 minutes. Line now-empty and cooled pan with clean parchment paper, and grease parchment. Transfer 1⅔ cups batter to prepared pan and repeat baking cake and cooling pan. Repeat baking and cooling with remaining 1⅔ cups batter.

6 Transfer one cooled cake layer, bottom side up, to cutting board. Spread ½ cup filling evenly over top, right to edge of cake. Top with second cake layer, bottom side up, and spread remaining ½ cup jam evenly over top. Top with third cake layer, bottom side up.

7 For the topping Microwave white chocolate chips and bittersweet chocolate chips in separate bowls at 50 percent power, stirring occasionally, until melted, 2 to 4 minutes. Using small offset spatula, spread white chocolate evenly over top of cake, right to edge of cake. While white chocolate is still warm, use small spoon to drizzle dark chocolate crosswise in thin parallel lines over white chocolate. Gently run tines of fork lengthwise across top of cake to create delicate, webbed pattern. Let cool until chocolate has set, 1 to 2 hours.

8 Dip serrated knife in very hot water and wipe dry before each cut. Trim away edges. Slice cake lengthwise into 5 equal strips (about 1½ inches wide), and then crosswise into 12 equal strips (about 1 inch wide). Serve. (Petits fours can be refrigerated for up to 24 hours.)

TOPPING PETITS FOURS

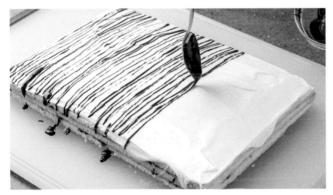

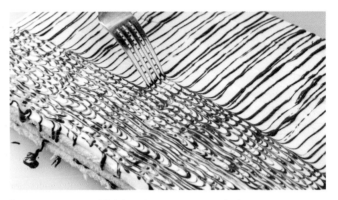

1. Spread white chocolate evenly over cake. Working quickly, use small spoon to drizzle melted dark chocolate crosswise in thin parallel lines.

2. Gently run tines of fork lengthwise across top of cake to create webbed pattern.

DECORATING WITH CHOCOLATE

Sophisticated desserts deserve special decorations. Chocolate is the Silly Putty of the dessert world; it can be played with and molded into nearly anything. Here are some beautiful options beyond drizzling for your elegant desserts—or any time you want another ounce of chocolate on your chocolate dessert.

Making Chocolate Shavings

Want to dress up your dessert without getting crafty? Chocolate shavings are the easiest chocolate decoration to achieve. These flakes of chocolate never go out of style and can be applied with a light or heavy hand. We recommend using white, milk, or semi-sweet chocolate; their lower cacao content makes them softer than bittersweet chocolate. (To use bittersweet, follow the directions for softening chocolate in Making Chocolate Curls.) You can make shavings with a vegetable peeler from our winning chocolates, but it's easiest if you use an 8-ounce block that's at least 1 inch thick. (We recommend Callebaut.)

Using a Y-shaped vegetable peeler, scrape shavings from the block of chocolate.

Making Chocolate Curls

Curls are the fancier cousin to shavings, the chocolate shards turning in like sophisticated scrolls. Once again use an 8-ounce block of chocolate. We soften the chocolate for neat, easy-to-form curls.

1. Soften the chocolate slightly by placing it on a plate and microwaving on the lowest power for about 1 minute. (The chocolate shouldn't melt.)

2. Run the blade of a Y-shaped vegetable peeler along the width of the softened chocolate to create a curl.

Piping Chocolate

Depending on your skill level (or how steady your hand is), you can write practically anything with chocolate. Finishing a sleek ganache-slicked torte with piped chocolate, maybe white for color contrast, can be striking. Alternatively, decorating the tops of cookies is a fun look (and activity).

  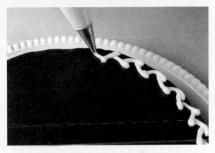

1. Melt chopped chocolate and let it cool slightly. Transfer the chocolate to a piping bag fit with a small round tip or a zipper-lock bag with a small corner snipped off. (Using a very small pastry bag allows for more control.)

2. Grab the base of the bag, twist, and squeeze to pipe out chocolate. Practice your design briefly on a sheet of parchment paper before decorating. Steady pressure with both hands will keep the chocolate flowing at an even rate.

3. Continue the design on your baked good. We like decorating the border of desserts like this torte.

Making Chocolate Shingles

We use chocolate bark to create a proper tree-like surface for our Yule Log (page 236). But without the bark-like ridges, these tempered shingles of chocolate can give cakes, tortes, and tarts of all kind a modern look when applied to frosting or ganache.

1. Pour 12 ounces melted tempered chocolate (see page 14) directly onto the prepared sheet and spread to the edges using a small offset spatula.

2. Refrigerate until the chocolate is set, at least 30 minutes. Gently break the chilled chocolate bark into 1- to 3-inch shards before using.

BLOOD ORANGE–CHOCOLATE TART

SERVES 10 TO 12

1 recipe Chocolate Tart Dough (page 201)

GANACHE

¾ cup heavy cream

1 teaspoon grated blood orange zest

¼ teaspoon table salt

4 ounces bittersweet chocolate, chopped

3 tablespoons unsalted butter, softened

½ teaspoon vanilla extract

GELÉE

1 teaspoon unflavored gelatin

1 teaspoon grated blood orange zest plus 1 cup juice (4 oranges), divided

½ cup (3½ ounces) sugar

¼ teaspoon table salt

1 blood orange

Why This Recipe Works For a beautiful and refined tart that's sure to steal the spotlight at your next dinner party, we paired silky, dark chocolate ganache with a soft but perfectly set jewel-toned blood orange gelée. Starting with our Chocolate Tart Dough as the base ensured the chocolate flavor was prominent. For the filling, we made a standard bittersweet chocolate ganache and added some blood orange zest for fragrant yet understated citrus flavor. To these deeply chocolaty foundations, we added a layer of gelée—nothing more than fresh blood orange juice and zest, sugar, and gelatin cooked until the gelatin dissolved. Layered on top of the ganache, the gelée added a bright, slightly tart flavor which cut through the richness of all that chocolate and added a beautiful glossy sheen. Before serving, we arranged blood orange segments in a pinwheel pattern in the center of the tart for an elegant crowning touch. For the clearest gelée, be sure to first strain the orange juice with a fine-mesh strainer and discard any pulp.

1 Roll dough into 11-inch circle on floured counter, then transfer to parchment paper–lined rimmed baking sheet; cover loosely with plastic wrap and refrigerate until firm but pliable, about 10 minutes.

2 Loosely roll dough around rolling pin and gently unroll it onto 9-inch tart pan with removable bottom, letting excess dough hang over edge. Ease dough into pan by gently lifting edge of dough with your hand while pressing into corners and fluted sides of pan with your other hand. Run rolling pin over top of pan to remove any excess dough. Wrap loosely in plastic, place on large plate, and freeze until fully chilled and firm, about 30 minutes. (Dough-lined tart pan can be frozen for up to 1 month.) Adjust oven rack to middle position and heat oven to 375 degrees.

3 Line chilled tart shell with double layer of aluminum foil and fill with pie weights. Bake on foil-lined rimmed baking sheet until shell is set and fragrant, about 30 minutes, rotating sheet halfway through baking. Remove foil and weights and continue to bake 5 minutes longer. Transfer sheet to wire rack and let cool completely, about 30 minutes.

4 **For the ganache** Bring cream, orange zest, and salt to simmer in small saucepan over medium heat. Off heat, add chocolate, cover, and let sit until chocolate is softened, about 5 minutes, then whisk to combine. Whisk in butter and vanilla until smooth. Pour filling into cooled tart shell, spreading into even layer with rubber spatula. Refrigerate, uncovered, until filling is chilled and set, at least 2 hours or up to 2 days.

5 For the gelée Sprinkle gelatin over ¼ cup orange juice in bowl and let sit until gelatin softens, about 5 minutes. Cook orange zest and remaining ¾ cup juice, sugar, and salt in small saucepan over medium-low heat just until sugar dissolves, about 3 minutes, whisking occasionally. Off heat, add softened gelatin and whisk until dissolved. Strain mixture through fine mesh strainer into bowl and let cool for 15 minutes; discard solids. Slowly pour orange mixture evenly over tart. Refrigerate until gelée is set, about 3 hours. (Tart can be refrigerated for up to 24 hours.)

6 Remove outer ring of tart pan, slide thin metal spatula between tart and tart pan bottom, and carefully slide tart onto serving platter or cutting board. Just before serving, cut away peel and pith from orange. Holding fruit over bowl, use paring knife to slice between membranes to release segments. Arrange orange segments in pinwheel in center of tart. Serve.

CHOCOLATE, MATCHA, AND POMEGRANATE TART

SERVES 8 TO 10

1 recipe Classic Tart Dough (page 201)

CHOCOLATE FILLING

2½ cups plus 1 tablespoon water, divided

4 cups ice cubes

5⅓ ounces bittersweet chocolate (70 percent cacao or higher), chopped

3 tablespoons plus 1 teaspoon granulated sugar

⅛ teaspoon table salt

MATCHA WHIPPED CREAM

1 cup heavy cream

½ cup (2 ounces) confectioners' sugar

⅛ teaspoon table salt

1 tablespoon matcha, plus 1 teaspoon for serving

⅓ cup pomegranate seeds

Why This Recipe Works The flavors of this stunning dessert are amazingly complex: bittersweet, tart, and herbaceous. There's a buttery tart shell, green tea–spiked whipped cream, and pomegranate seeds, but the real star of the show is the layer of chocolate ganache. This was a place to employ our max-chocolate ganache that we turned to for our Chocolate-Hazelnut Tart (page 192); the intense hit of creamy dark chocolate was able to compete with the pleasantly strong flavor and umami notes of the matcha. We adorned the top of the tart with pomegranate seeds for looks but also to provide welcome contrasting tartness and some crunch against the creamy and silky ganache. Be sure to use chocolate containing 70 percent cacao or higher; using chocolate with a lower percentage will result in a loose, grainy chocolate layer. You can make your tart look like the one in the photograph with a piping bag, or you can simply spread the matcha whipped cream over the tart.

1 Roll dough into 11-inch circle on floured counter, then transfer to parchment paper–lined rimmed baking sheet; cover loosely with plastic wrap and refrigerate until firm but pliable, about 10 minutes.

2 Loosely roll dough around rolling pin and gently unroll it onto 9-inch tart pan with removable bottom, letting excess dough hang over edge. Ease dough into pan by gently lifting edge of dough with your hand while pressing into corners and fluted sides of pan with your other hand. Run rolling pin over top of pan to remove any excess dough. Wrap loosely in plastic, place on large plate, and freeze until fully chilled and firm, about 30 minutes. (Dough-lined tart pan can be frozen for up to 1 month.) Adjust oven rack to middle position and heat oven to 375 degrees.

3 Line chilled tart shell with double layer of aluminum foil and fill with pie weights. Bake on foil-lined rimmed baking sheet until tart shell is golden brown and set, about 30 minutes, rotating sheet halfway through baking. Remove foil and weights and continue to bake tart shell until it is fully baked and golden, 5 to 10 minutes longer. Transfer sheet to wire rack and let shell cool completely, about 1 hour.

4 **For the chocolate filling** Fill large bowl with 2 cups water and ice cubes. Place chocolate, ½ cup plus 1 tablespoon water, sugar, and salt in large heatproof bowl over saucepan filled with 1 inch barely simmering water, making sure that water does not touch bottom of bowl. Cook, stirring frequently with rubber spatula, until chocolate is fully melted and smooth, about 5 minutes. Transfer bowl to ice bath and chill, stirring constantly, until mixture is slightly thickened and registers between 75 and 80 degrees, 30 seconds to 1 minute. Remove bowl from ice bath and continue to stir 30 seconds longer. Transfer filling to cooled tart shell and tap baking sheet lightly on counter to release air bubbles; refrigerate tart until set, about 1 hour. (Tart can be refrigerated for up to 24 hours.)

5 **For the matcha whipped cream** Using stand mixer fitted with whisk attachment, whip cream, sugar, and salt on high speed until soft peaks form. Add 1 tablespoon matcha, reduce speed to medium, and whip until stiff peaks form. Remove tart from refrigerator. Remove outer ring of tart pan, slide thin metal spatula between tart and tart pan bottom, and carefully slide tart onto serving platter or cutting board. Spread whipped cream evenly over chocolate layer. Using fine-mesh strainer, dust tart with 1 teaspoon matcha. Sprinkle with pomegranate seeds. Serve.

DECORATING CHOCOLATE, MATCHA, AND POMEGRANATE TART

1. Transfer matcha whipped cream to piping bag fitted with ½-inch tip.

2. Pipe small balls of whipped cream in concentric circles over surface of chocolate layer.

3. Using fine-mesh strainer, dust tart with remaining 1 teaspoon matcha.

4. Sprinkle with pomegranate seeds.

CHOCOLATE-CARAMEL LAYER CAKE

SERVES 10 TO 12

CAKE

1½ cups (7½ ounces) all-purpose flour

¾ cup (2¼ ounces) unsweetened cocoa powder

1½ cups (10½ ounces) granulated sugar

1¼ teaspoons baking soda

¾ teaspoon baking powder

¾ teaspoon table salt

¾ cup buttermilk

½ cup water

¼ cup vegetable oil

2 large eggs

1 teaspoon vanilla extract

CARAMEL FILLING

1¼ cups (8¾ ounces) granulated sugar

¼ cup light corn syrup

¼ cup water

1 cup heavy cream

8 tablespoons unsalted butter, cut into 8 pieces

1 teaspoon vanilla extract

¾ teaspoon table salt

FROSTING

6 ounces bittersweet chocolate, chopped

16 tablespoons unsalted butter, softened

¾ cup (3 ounces) confectioners' sugar

½ cup (1½ ounces) unsweetened cocoa powder

Pinch table salt

½ cup light corn syrup

¾ teaspoon vanilla extract

Flake sea salt (optional)

Why This Recipe Works Chocolate-caramel layer cake is a towering and substantial creation featuring both sweet and salty elements and a sleek, glossy coat of frosting. The cake itself gets its deep, dark flavor from a generous amount of unsweetened cocoa, and a combination of buttermilk, water, and vegetable oil ensures an incredibly moist cake while allowing the chocolate flavor to really shine. But in testing existing chocolate-caramel cake recipes we found that many barely contained enough caramel to merit the name. To ensure rich, salty-sweet caramel flavor in each bite, we planned to sandwich three layers of thick but spreadable caramel filling between the layers of chocolate cake. With visions of our layers slipping and sliding, we cooked the caramel until it was dark (but not burnt) and added both cream and butter to finish. Since butter is solid at room temperature, this ensured that the caramel set up once cooled and didn't ooze. After stacking and filling our layers, we draped our cake in a thick, satiny bittersweet chocolate frosting for a truly decadent affair. And while it's optional, we love the flavor and visual appeal of a sprinkling of coarse flake sea salt to finish. When taking the temperature of the caramel in steps 3 and 4, remove the pot from the heat and tilt the pan to one side. Use your thermometer to stir the caramel back and forth to equalize hot and cool spots and ensure an accurate reading.

1 For the cake Adjust oven rack to middle position and heat oven to 325 degrees. Grease two 9-inch round cake pans, line with parchment paper, grease parchment, and flour pans. Sift flour and cocoa into large bowl. Whisk in sugar, baking soda, baking powder, and salt. Whisk buttermilk, water, oil, eggs, and vanilla together in second bowl. Whisk buttermilk mixture into flour mixture until smooth batter forms. Divide batter evenly between prepared pans and smooth tops with rubber spatula.

2 Bake until toothpick inserted in center comes out clean, 22 to 28 minutes, switching and rotating pans halfway through baking. Let cakes cool in pans on wire rack for 15 minutes. Remove cakes from pans, discarding parchment, and let cool completely on rack, at least 2 hours.

3 For the caramel filling Lightly grease 8-inch square baking pan. Combine sugar, corn syrup, and water in medium saucepan. Bring to boil over medium-high heat and cook, without stirring, until mixture is amber colored, 8 to 10 minutes. Reduce heat to low and continue to cook, swirling saucepan occasionally, until mixture is dark amber and registers 375 to 380 degrees, 2 to 5 minutes.

4 Off heat, carefully stir in cream, butter, vanilla, and salt (mixture will bubble and steam). Return saucepan to medium heat and cook, stirring frequently, until smooth and caramel reaches 240 to 245 degrees, 3 to 5 minutes. Carefully transfer caramel to prepared pan and let cool until just warm to touch (100 to 105 degrees), 20 to 30 minutes.

5 **For the frosting** Microwave chocolate in bowl at 50 percent power, stirring occasionally, until melted, 2 to 4 minutes. Let cool completely. Process butter, sugar, cocoa, and salt in food processor until smooth, about 30 seconds, scraping down sides of bowl as needed. Add corn syrup and vanilla and process until just combined, 5 to 10 seconds. Scrape down sides of processor, then add cooled chocolate and process until smooth and creamy, 10 to 15 seconds. (Frosting can be made 3 hours in advance and kept at room temperature. For longer storage, cover and refrigerate frosting for up to 2 days. Let stand at room temperature for 1 hour before using.)

6 Using long serrated knife, cut 1 horizontal line around sides of each cake layer; then, following scored lines, cut each layer into 2 even layers.

7 Using rubber spatula or large spoon, transfer one-third of caramel to center of 1 cake layer and use small offset spatula to spread over surface, leaving ½-inch border around edge. Repeat with remaining caramel and 2 of remaining cake layers. (Three of your cake layers should be topped with caramel.)

8 Line edges of cake platter with 4 strips of parchment to keep platter clean. Place 1 caramel-covered cake layer on platter. Top with second and third caramel-covered layers. Top with remaining cake layer and spread frosting evenly over top and sides of cake. To smooth frosting, run edge of offset spatula around cake sides and over top. Carefully remove parchment strips. Let cake stand at room temperature for at least 1 hour. (Cake can be made up to 2 days in advance and refrigerated. Let stand at room temperature for at least 5 hours before serving.) Sprinkle with sea salt, if using, and serve.

Salt and Chocolate

Salty-sweet is a desirable attribute in a dessert for a reason: Salt stimulates the palate to want to taste, cuts through rich foods so they're not cloying, and heightens the flavor of just about anything, making sweet treats that much more appealing. With chocolate (and caramel), in particular, salt adds its salinity but also brings out intense dimension.

You can sprinkle just about any chocolate dessert, not just this cake, with finishing flake sea salt. (May we suggest Chocolate Chip Cookies (page 101), Ultimate Chocolate Cupcakes (page 115), Rich Chocolate Tart (page 188), Flourless Chocolate Cake (page 210), and Pots de Crème (page 289)?) In addition to adding sophisticated flavor, an adornment of a finishing salt also adds surprising crunch that makes food pop—and it looks elegant against the dark brown chocolate backdrop. The salt we keep on hand at all times for finishing foods is Maldon Sea Salt because it's affordable and widely available.

Maldon, the town in southeastern England, has been producing salt since at least as far back as 1086. Seawater is collected at high tide, filtered, left to settle in tanks, and then carefully heated until Maldon's characteristic large flake pyramids form. We think Maldon has a clean taste with a mild brininess and round mineral flavor. Its large, light, airy, thin flakes and pyramids have a delicate and shattering texture and soft crunch. So, decorate your desserts with salt!

CHOCOLATE-ESPRESSO DACQUOISE

SERVES 10 TO 12

MERINGUE

- ¾ cup blanched sliced almonds, toasted
- ½ cup hazelnuts, toasted and skinned
- 1 tablespoon cornstarch
- ⅛ teaspoon table salt
- 1 cup (7 ounces) sugar, divided
- 4 large egg whites, room temperature (reserve yolks for buttercream)
- ¼ teaspoon cream of tartar

BUTTERCREAM

- ¾ cup whole milk
- 4 large egg yolks
- ⅓ cup (2⅓ ounces) sugar
- 1½ teaspoons cornstarch
- ¼ teaspoon table salt
- 2 tablespoons amaretto or water
- 1½ tablespoons instant espresso powder
- 16 tablespoons unsalted butter, cut into 16 pieces and softened

GANACHE

- 6 ounces bittersweet chocolate, chopped fine
- ¾ cup heavy cream
- 2 teaspoons corn syrup
- 12 hazelnuts, toasted and skinned
- 1 cup blanched sliced almonds, toasted

Why This Recipe Works It's possible there's no more stunning finale to a meal than a dacquoise, a multilayered showpiece of crisp meringue and rich, silky buttercream elegantly enrobed in a glossy dark chocolate ganache. But preparing one is typically a project to rival all projects. For a more approachable dacquoise, we swapped the individually piped meringue layers for a single sheet that we trimmed into layers; we also shortened the usual 4-plus hours of oven time by increasing the temperature. For the filling, we opted for a German buttercream, which requires no thermometer or tricky hot sugar syrup. Adding a little espresso powder and amaretto to our buttercream contributed another element of sophistication. Making the ganache was simple: We poured warm cream (plus a couple teaspoons of corn syrup for enhanced shine) over finely chopped bittersweet chocolate and stirred the mixture until it was smooth. But a simple coating of ganache wasn't enough; for rich chocolate flavor in every bite, we doubled the amount and not only coated the exterior but also spread some on each layer of meringue, alternating with the buttercream. Toasted hazelnuts and almonds provided a decorative finishing touch. To slice, dip a sharp knife in very hot water and wipe dry before each cut.

1 **For the meringue** Adjust oven rack to middle position and heat oven to 250 degrees. Using ruler, draw 13 by 10½-inch rectangle on piece of parchment paper. Grease baking sheet and place parchment on it, marked side down. Process almonds, hazelnuts, cornstarch, and salt in food processor until nuts are finely ground, 15 to 20 seconds. Add ½ cup sugar and pulse to combine, 1 to 2 pulses.

2 Using stand mixer fitted with whisk attachment, whip egg whites and cream of tartar on medium-low speed until foamy, about 1 minute. Increase speed to medium-high and whip whites to soft, billowy mounds, about 1 minute. Gradually add remaining ½ cup sugar and whip until glossy, stiff peaks form, 2 to 3 minutes. Fold nut mixture into egg whites in 2 batches. Using offset spatula, spread meringue evenly into 13 by 10½-inch rectangle on parchment, using lines on parchment as guide. Using spray bottle, evenly mist surface of meringue with water until glistening. Bake for 1½ hours. Turn off oven and let meringue cool in oven for 1½ hours. (Do not open oven during baking or cooling.) Remove meringue from oven and let cool completely, about 10 minutes. (Meringue can be wrapped tightly in plastic wrap and stored at room temperature for up to 2 days.)

3 **For the buttercream** Bring milk to simmer in small saucepan over medium heat. Meanwhile, whisk egg yolks, sugar, cornstarch, and salt in bowl until smooth. Remove milk from heat and, whisking constantly, add half of milk to yolk mixture to temper. Whisking constantly, return tempered yolk mixture to remaining milk in saucepan. Return saucepan to medium heat and cook, whisking constantly, until mixture is bubbling and thickens to consistency of warm pudding, 3 to 5 minutes. Transfer pastry cream to bowl and press plastic wrap directly on surface. Refrigerate until cold and set, at least 2 hours or up to 24 hours. Warm to room temperature in microwave at 50 percent power, stirring every 10 seconds, before using.

4 Stir together amaretto and espresso powder; set aside. Using stand mixer fitted with paddle, beat butter at medium speed until smooth and light, 3 to 4 minutes. Add pastry cream in 3 batches, beating for 30 seconds after each addition. Add amaretto mixture and continue to beat until light and fluffy, about 5 minutes longer, scraping down bowl thoroughly halfway through mixing.

5 **For the ganache** Place chocolate in heatproof bowl. Bring cream and corn syrup to simmer in small saucepan over medium heat. Pour cream mixture over chocolate; let stand for 1 minute, then stir until smooth. Set aside to cool until chocolate mounds slightly when dripped from spoon, about 5 minutes.

6 Carefully invert meringue and peel off parchment. Reinvert meringue and place on cutting board. Using serrated knife and gentle, repeated scoring motion, trim edges of meringue to form 12 by 10-inch rectangle. Discard trimmings. With long side of rectangle parallel to counter, use ruler to mark both long edges of meringue at 3-inch intervals. Using serrated knife, score surface of meringue by drawing knife toward you from mark on top edge to corresponding mark on bottom edge. Repeat scoring until meringue is fully cut through. Repeat until you have four 10 by 3-inch rectangles. (If any meringues break during cutting, use them as middle layers.)

7 Place 3 rectangles on wire rack set in rimmed baking sheet. Spread ¼ cup ganache evenly over each meringue. Set aside remaining ganache. Refrigerate meringues until ganache is firm, about 15 minutes.

8 Using offset spatula, spread top of remaining meringue rectangle with ½ cup buttercream; place rectangle on wire rack with ganache-coated meringues. Invert 1 ganache-coated meringue, place on top of buttercream, and press gently to level. Repeat, spreading top meringue with ½ cup buttercream and topping with inverted ganache-coated meringue. Spread top with buttercream. Invert final ganache-coated meringue on top of cake. Use your hand to steady top of cake and spread half of remaining buttercream to lightly coat sides of cake, then use remaining buttercream to coat top of cake. Smooth until cake resembles box. Refrigerate until buttercream is firm, about 2 hours. (Once buttercream is firm, assembled cake may be wrapped tightly in plastic and refrigerated for up to 2 days.)

9 Warm remaining ganache in large heatproof bowl set over saucepan filled with 1 inch barely simmering water, making sure that water does not touch bottom of bowl; stir occasionally until mixture is very fluid but not hot. Keeping assembled cake on wire rack, pour ganache over top of cake. Using offset spatula, spread ganache in thin, even layer over top of cake, letting excess flow down sides. Spread ganache over sides in thin layer (top must be completely covered, but some small gaps on sides are OK).

10 Garnish top of cake with hazelnuts. Holding bottom of cake with your hand, gently press almonds onto cake sides with your other hand. Refrigerate on wire rack, uncovered, for at least 3 hours or up to 12 hours. Transfer cake to platter. Serve.

ASSEMBLING CHOCOLATE-ESPRESSO DACQUOISE

1. Using offset spatula, spread ¼ cup ganache evenly over 3 meringue rectangles and refrigerate until firm. Spread top of remaining rectangle with ½ cup buttercream.

2. Invert 1 ganache-coated meringue, place on top of buttercream-coated meringue, and press gently to level. Repeat, spreading top meringue with ½ cup buttercream and topping with inverted ganache-coated meringue.

3. Spread top with buttercream. Invert final ganache-coated meringue on top of cake. Coat sides and top with remaining buttercream.

CHOCOLATE-LAVENDER NAPOLEONS

SERVES 6

PASTRY CREAM

1½	cups half-and-half
⅓	cup (2⅓ ounces) granulated sugar, divided
2	tablespoons unsweetened cocoa powder
1½	teaspoons dried lavender
	Pinch salt
3	large egg yolks
1	tablespoon cornstarch
3	tablespoons unsalted butter, cut into 3 pieces
3	ounces bittersweet chocolate, chopped fine
¾	teaspoon vanilla extract

PASTRY

1	(9½ by 9-inch) sheet puff pastry, thawed

GLAZES

1	ounce bittersweet chocolate, chopped fine
2	tablespoons plus 1 teaspoon milk, divided
1	cup (4 ounces) confectioners' sugar, divided
⅛	teaspoon vanilla extract
18	candied violets (optional)

Why This Recipe Works A traditional Napoleon features layers of buttery, flaky-crisp puff pastry sandwiching cool, dreamy vanilla pastry cream—but we're happy to break tradition if it means adding chocolate to a dessert. And while we were breaking traditions, we decided to create an intriguing flavor profile by also incorporating lavender. Both chocolate and lavender can take over a dessert, so we started by making a balanced chocolate-lavender pastry cream. We found that steeping a small amount of lavender in half-and-half and sugar from the start and straining the lavender out before cooling gave our pastry cream a subtle yet distinctive lavender flavor—no potpourri taste. We added cocoa powder to the custard mixture at the start and melted in bittersweet chocolate at the end. Using store-bought puff pastry made this dessert approachable. We found that the best way to achieve level pastry layers was to bake it topped with a second baking sheet, weighted with a large ovensafe dish. The typical method of making one large Napoleon and then cutting the pastry into individual servings sends filling squirting out the sides. We cut the baked pastry into individual rectangles before filling and stacking. And for the icings, we skip fondant in favor of two simple confectioners' sugar glazes. To thaw frozen puff pastry, let it sit either in the refrigerator for 24 hours or on the counter for 30 minutes to 1 hour. If the dough becomes too soft to work with, cover it with plastic wrap and let it chill in the refrigerator until firm.

1 **For the pastry cream** Bring half-and-half, ¼ cup sugar, cocoa, lavender, and salt to simmer in medium saucepan over medium-high heat, stirring occasionally.

2 Meanwhile, whisk egg yolks, cornstarch, and remaining sugar in bowl until smooth. Whisk about ½ cup hot half-and-half mixture into egg mixture to temper, then slowly whisk tempered egg mixture into remaining half-and-half mixture in saucepan. Reduce heat to medium and cook, whisking constantly, until mixture is thickened, smooth, and registers 180 degrees, about 30 seconds. Off heat, whisk in butter and chocolate until combined and smooth. Strain pastry cream through fine-mesh strainer into clean bowl, then whisk in vanilla. Press plastic wrap directly on surface and refrigerate until cold and set, at least 3 hours or up to 2 days.

3 **For the pastry** Adjust oven rack to middle position and heat oven to 325 degrees. Roll dough into 16 by 12-inch rectangle, about ¼ inch thick, between 2 lightly floured sheets of parchment paper. Remove top sheet of parchment and prick pastry with fork every 2 inches.

4 Replace top sheet of parchment and slide dough onto rimmed baking sheet. Place second rimmed baking sheet on top of dough and weight baking sheet with large oven safe dish. Bake pastry until cooked through and lightly golden, 40 to 50 minutes, rotating sheet halfway through baking.

5 Remove weight, top baking sheet, and top sheet of parchment and continue to bake pastry until golden brown, 5 to 10 minutes. Let pastry cool completely on sheet, about 1 hour. (Pastry will shrink slightly.)

6 Cut cooled pastry in half lengthwise with serrated knife and trim edges as necessary to make them straight. Cut each pastry half crosswise into 3 rectangles, then cut each rectangle crosswise into 3 small rectangles (you will have 18 rectangles). (Puff pastry rectangles can be wrapped tightly in plastic wrap and stored at room temperature for up to 1 day.)

7 For the glazes Microwave chocolate and 2 tablespoons milk in bowl at 50 percent power, stirring occasionally, until melted and smooth, 1 to 2 minutes. Whisk in ¾ cup sugar until smooth. Whisk remaining ¼ cup sugar, remaining 1 teaspoon milk, and vanilla in second bowl until smooth.

8 Lay 6 pastry rectangles on wire rack set over sheet of parchment (for easy cleanup) and spread chocolate glaze evenly over top. Drizzle thin stream of vanilla glaze crosswise over chocolate glaze. Run tip of small knife or toothpick lengthwise through icing to make design. Top with candied violets, if using. Let glaze set for 20 minutes.

9 Spread about 2½ tablespoons pastry cream evenly over 6 more rectangles of pastry. Gently top each with one of remaining 6 rectangles of pastry and spread remaining pastry cream evenly over tops. Top each with glazed rectangle and serve. (Napoleons can be stored at room temperature for up to 4 hours.)

ASSEMBLING CHOCOLATE-LAVENDER NAPOLEONS

1. Cut each pastry half crosswise into 3 rectangles, then cut each rectangle crosswise into 3 small rectangles (you will have 18 rectangles).

2. Lay 6 pastry rectangles on wire rack set over sheet of parchment (for easy cleanup) and spread chocolate glaze evenly over top.

3. Drizzle thin stream of vanilla glaze crosswise over chocolate glaze. Run tip of small knife or toothpick lengthwise through icing to make design. Top with candied violets, if using.

4. Spread about 2½ tablespoons of pastry cream evenly over 6 more rectangles of pastry.

5. Gently top each with one of remaining 6 rectangles of pastry and spread remaining pastry cream evenly over tops.

6. Top with glazed pastry rectangles.

a spoonful
OF HEAVEN

CHOCOLATE–PEANUT BUTTER CRÈME BRÛLÉE

SERVES 8

2¾ cups heavy cream, divided

½ cup granulated sugar

4 ounces bittersweet chocolate, chopped fine

¼ cup creamy peanut butter

1 cup whole milk

10 large egg yolks

3 tablespoons turbinado sugar or Demerara sugar

1 recipe Candied Nuts (page 347)

Why This Recipe Works We love the creaminess and textural contrasts of crème brûlée, but ubiquitous and flavored only with vanilla bean, the dessert can be a bit, well, vanilla. We reinvented the classic French dessert by giving it a very American chocolate-peanut profile. We added ¼ cup of creamy peanut butter to our custard base in addition to 4 ounces of bittersweet chocolate, which made the custard chocolaty without adversely affecting the texture or obscuring the peanut butter flavor. We've found that the key to a soft, supple crème brûlée, rather than a bouncy one, is to use just egg yolks rather than whole eggs. We replaced a portion of the cream with milk to prevent the custard from becoming overly rich from the added fat from the chocolate and peanut butter. The traditional sugar crust provided a nice crunch against the creamy custard but we doubled down on the crunch for this new spin, topping the caramelized sugar with toasty, sweet-salty candied peanuts that reinforced the flavor of the peanut butter. You will need eight 6-ounce ramekins (or shallow fluted dishes) for this recipe. Use peanuts in the Candied Nuts.

1 Adjust oven rack to lower-middle position and heat oven to 300 degrees. Place dish towel in bottom of large baking dish or roasting pan. Set eight 6-ounce ramekins (or shallow fluted dishes) on towel. Bring kettle of water to boil.

2 Combine 2 cups cream and granulated sugar in medium saucepan. Bring mixture to boil over medium heat, stirring occasionally to dissolve sugar. Off heat, whisk in chocolate and peanut butter until melted and smooth. Stir in remaining ¾ cup heavy cream and milk. Meanwhile, whisk egg yolks in large bowl until uniform. Whisk about 1 cup chocolate mixture into yolks; repeat with 1 cup more chocolate mixture. Whisk in remaining chocolate mixture until thoroughly combined. Strain custard through fine-mesh strainer into 4-cup liquid measuring cup; discard solids. Divide custard evenly among ramekins.

3 Set baking dish on oven rack. Taking care not to splash water into ramekins, pour enough boiling water into dish to reach two-thirds up sides of ramekins. Bake until centers of custards are just barely set and register 170 to 175 degrees, 25 to 35 minutes depending on ramekin type, checking temperature 5 minutes early. Transfer ramekins to wire rack and let cool completely, about 2 hours. Set ramekins on baking sheet, cover tightly with plastic wrap, and refrigerate until cold, at least 4 hours or up to 3 days.

4 Uncover ramekins and gently blot tops dry with paper towels. Sprinkle each with 1 to 1½ teaspoons turbinado sugar (depending on ramekin type). Tilt and tap each ramekin to distribute sugar evenly, then dump out excess sugar and wipe rims of ramekins clean. Caramelize sugar with torch until deep golden brown, continually sweeping flame about 2 inches above ramekin. Rechill custards for 30 minutes. Sprinkle with candied peanuts before serving.

DARK CHOCOLATE MOUSSE

SERVES 6 TO 8

8 ounces bittersweet chocolate, chopped fine

5 tablespoons water

2 tablespoons unsweetened cocoa powder

1 tablespoon brandy

1 teaspoon instant espresso powder

2 large eggs, separated, divided

1 tablespoon sugar, divided

⅛ teaspoon table salt

1 cup plus 2 tablespoons heavy cream, chilled

Why This Recipe Works Rich, ganache-like chocolate mousse is utterly delicious—for about two spoonfuls. Yet light and silky versions often lack decent chocolate flavor. We wanted a recipe for chocolate mousse that would give us the best of both worlds. Eliminating the butter lightened the texture considerably, as did whipping the cream to soft peaks and folding it into the mix. Reducing the number of egg whites prevented our mousse from having a marshmallow-like quality. Moving on to the star ingredient, we found semisweet chocolate too sweet and one-dimensional. Bittersweet chocolate was a much better choice, and the addition of a couple tablespoons of cocoa powder gave the mousse a fuller flavor profile. We loved the intense flavor that a whopping half pound of bittersweet chocolate provided, but with all that chocolate the texture of our mousse suffered. To eliminate any grittiness, we needed to incorporate a liquid component; but rather than add more cream, we opted for water, which allowed the chocolate flavor to really shine. A little espresso powder and a tablespoon of brandy added just the right amount of complexity to this rich yet light and silky mousse. If making the mousse a day in advance, let it sit at room temperature for 10 minutes before serving.

1 Combine chocolate, water, cocoa, brandy, and espresso powder in large heatproof bowl set over saucepan filled with 1 inch barely simmering water, making sure that water does not touch bottom of bowl and stirring frequently until chocolate is melted and smooth, about 10 minutes. Remove from heat.

2 Whisk egg yolks, 1½ teaspoons sugar, and salt in second large bowl until mixture lightens in color and thickens slightly, about 30 seconds. Pour melted chocolate mixture into egg yolk mixture and whisk until combined. Let cool until just warmer than room temperature, 3 to 5 minutes.

3 Using stand mixer fitted with whisk attachment, whip egg whites at medium-low speed until foamy, about 1 minute. Add remaining 1½ teaspoons sugar, increase speed to medium-high, and whip until soft peaks form, about 1 minute. Using whisk, stir about one-quarter of whipped egg whites into chocolate mixture to lighten it. Using rubber spatula, gently fold in remaining egg whites until few white streaks remain.

4 In now-empty bowl, whip cream on medium speed until it begins to thicken, about 30 seconds. Increase speed to high and whip until soft peaks form, about 15 seconds longer. Using rubber spatula, fold whipped cream into mousse until no white streaks remain. Spoon mousse into 6 to 8 individual serving dishes. Cover with plastic wrap and refrigerate until set and firm, at least 2 hours or up to 24 hours. Serve.

Chocolate-Orange Mousse

For the best flavor, the orange zest needs to steep in the heavy cream overnight, so plan accordingly. Garnish each serving of mousse with a thin strip of orange zest, if desired.

Start by bringing heavy cream to simmer in medium saucepan. Remove from heat and transfer to liquid measuring cup. Add 3 (2-inch) strips orange zest and cool until just warm. Cover and refrigerate overnight. Remove and discard zest; add more heavy cream, if necessary, to equal 1 cup plus 2 tablespoons. Continue with step 1, reducing amount of water to 4 tablespoons and omitting brandy. Once chocolate is melted, stir in 2 tablespoons Grand Marnier and proceed as directed in step 2.

Chocolate-Raspberry Mousse

Chambord is our preferred brand of raspberry-flavored liqueur for this recipe. Serve the mousse with fresh raspberries, if desired.

Reduce amount of water to 4 tablespoons and omit brandy. Once chocolate is melted at end of step 1, stir in 2 tablespoons raspberry-flavored liqueur.

POTS DE CRÈME

SERVES 8

Why This Recipe Works Classic *pots de crème* are incredibly silky and pack an intense hit of chocolate. But making these petite chocolate custards can be a finicky process: Traditional recipes call for a water bath, which is cumbersome and threatens to splash the custards every time the pan is moved. For a more user-friendly pot de crème, we moved the dish out of the oven and took an unconventional approach: cooking the custard on the stovetop and then pouring it into ramekins. We skipped right over semisweet chocolate, which was too mild for our dark chocolate dreams. Bittersweet chocolate, and lots of it—50 percent more than most recipes—gave our custards the rich flavor we sought. We prefer pots de crème made with 60 percent cacao bittersweet chocolate, but 70 percent bittersweet chocolate can also be used—you will need to reduce the amount of chocolate to 8 ounces.

1 For the pots de crème Place chocolate in bowl and set fine-mesh strainer over top. Combine vanilla, water, and espresso powder in second bowl.

2 Whisk egg yolks, sugar, and salt together in third bowl until combined. Whisk in cream and half-and-half. Transfer cream mixture to medium saucepan and cook over medium-low heat, stirring constantly and scraping bottom of pot with wooden spoon, until thickened and silky and registers 175 to 180 degrees, 8 to 12 minutes. (Do not let custard overcook or simmer.)

3 Immediately pour custard through fine-mesh strainer over chocolate. Let mixture stand to melt chocolate, about 5 minutes. Add espresso mixture and whisk until smooth. Divide chocolate custard evenly among eight 5-ounce ramekins. Gently tap ramekins against counter to remove air bubbles.

4 Let pots de crème cool completely, then cover with plastic wrap and refrigerate until chilled, at least 4 hours or up to 3 days. (Before serving, let pots de crème stand at room temperature for 20 to 30 minutes.)

5 For the whipped cream Using stand mixer fitted with whisk attachment, whip cream, sugar, and vanilla on medium-low speed until foamy, about 1 minute. Increase speed to high and whip until stiff peaks form, 1 to 3 minutes. Dollop each pot de crème with about 2 tablespoons whipped cream and garnish with cocoa and/or chocolate shavings, if using. Serve.

Milk Chocolate Pots de Crème

Milk chocolate behaves differently in this recipe than bittersweet chocolate, and more of it must be used to ensure that the custard sets. And because of the increased amount of chocolate, it's necessary to cut back on the amount of sugar so that the custard is not overly sweet.

Substitute 12 ounces milk chocolate for bittersweet chocolate and reduce sugar in pots de crème to 2 tablespoons.

POTS DE CRÈME

- 10 ounces bittersweet chocolate, chopped fine
- 1 tablespoon vanilla extract
- 1 tablespoon water
- ½ teaspoon instant espresso powder
- 5 large egg yolks
- 5 tablespoons (2¼ ounces) sugar
- ¼ teaspoon table salt
- 1½ cups heavy cream
- ¾ cup half-and-half

WHIPPED CREAM

- ½ cup heavy cream, chilled
- 2 teaspoons sugar
- ½ teaspoon vanilla extract

  Cocoa powder and/or chocolate shavings (see page 266) (optional)

CHOCOLATE AVOCADO PUDDING

SERVES 6

1 cup water

¾ cup (5¼ ounces) sugar

¼ cup (¾ ounce) unsweetened cocoa powder

1 tablespoon vanilla extract

1 teaspoon instant espresso powder (optional)

¼ teaspoon table salt

2 large ripe avocados (8 ounces each), halved and pitted

3½ ounces bittersweet chocolate (70 percent cacao or higher), chopped

Why This Recipe Works Making a luscious chocolate pudding by substituting healthful avocados for the cream and eggs has become trendy. But more often than not, these puddings are a far cry from the silky-smooth, ultrachocolaty pudding we want, yielding a grainy texture and lackluster chocolate flavor that doesn't conceal the vegetal notes. We knew we could do better without making the recipe too complicated. Rather than simply blending everything together, we started by creating a simple hot cocoa syrup in a saucepan (with a touch of espresso powder, vanilla, and salt to enhance the chocolate flavor). Meanwhile, we processed the flesh of two large avocados for a full 2 minutes until they were absolutely smooth. Next, with the food processor running, we carefully streamed in the cocoa syrup until the mixture was velvety and glossy. We finished by blending in a moderate amount of melted dark chocolate to give our pudding a wonderfully full chocolate flavor and additional richness.

1 Combine water, sugar, cocoa, vanilla, espresso powder (if using), and salt in small saucepan. Bring to simmer over medium heat and cook, stirring occasionally, until sugar and cocoa dissolve, about 2 minutes. Remove saucepan from heat and cover to keep warm.

2 Scoop flesh of avocados into food processor bowl and process until smooth, about 2 minutes, scraping down sides of bowl as needed. With processor running, slowly add warm cocoa mixture in steady stream until completely incorporated and mixture is smooth and glossy, about 2 minutes.

3 Microwave chocolate in bowl at 50 percent power, stirring occasionally, until melted, 2 to 4 minutes. Add to avocado mixture and process until well incorporated, about 1 minute. Transfer pudding to bowl, cover, and refrigerate until chilled and set, at least 2 hours or up to 24 hours. Serve.

CHOCOLATE SOUFFLÉ

SERVES 6 TO 8

Why This Recipe Works Ethereally light and rising to impressively tall heights, a well-made chocolate soufflé is a thing of beauty—and good taste. But classic recipes would lead you to believe that preparing one is a high-wire act likely to end in an embarrassing collapse. The reality is that making a soufflé isn't all that complicated if you've got the right recipe; we wanted to create a foolproof chocolate soufflé, one that would offer decadent chocolate flavor without compromising the requisite light, creamy texture and dramatic rise. We began with a béchamel base (a classic French sauce made with equal amounts of butter and flour and whisked with milk over heat) and eggs. But we found that the milk and flour muted the chocolate flavor, so the béchamel had to go. We separated the eggs, first beating the yolks with sugar and then whipping the whites. The result was a rich base with plenty of volume, but we thought the chocolate flavor could be more intense still. Luckily, the solution was easy: Increasing the amount of chocolate to a full half pound and reducing the butter slightly resulted in a soufflé with rich, complex chocolate flavor. Soufflé waits for no one, so be ready to serve it immediately.

4 tablespoons unsalted butter, cut into ½-inch pieces, plus 1 tablespoon, softened, divided

⅓ cup (2⅓ ounces) plus 1 tablespoon sugar, divided

8 ounces bittersweet or semisweet chocolate, chopped

1 tablespoon orange-flavored liqueur, such as Grand Marnier

½ teaspoon vanilla extract

⅛ teaspoon table salt

6 large eggs, separated, plus 2 large whites

¼ teaspoon cream of tartar

1 Adjust oven rack to lower-middle position and heat oven to 375 degrees. Grease 2-quart soufflé dish with 1 tablespoon softened butter, then coat dish evenly with 1 tablespoon sugar; refrigerate until ready to use.

2 Microwave chocolate and remaining 4 tablespoons butter in large bowl at 50 percent power, stirring occasionally, until melted and smooth, 2 to 4 minutes. Stir in liqueur, vanilla, and salt; set aside.

3 Using stand mixer fitted with paddle, beat egg yolks and remaining ⅓ cup sugar on medium speed until thick and pale yellow, about 3 minutes. Fold into chocolate mixture.

4 Using clean, dry mixer bowl and whisk attachment, whip egg whites and cream of tartar on medium-low speed until foamy, about 1 minute. Increase speed to medium-high and whip until stiff peaks form, 3 to 4 minutes.

5 Using rubber spatula, vigorously stir one-quarter of whipped whites into chocolate mixture. Gently fold remaining whites into chocolate mixture until just incorporated. Transfer mixture to prepared dish. Bake until fragrant, fully risen, and exterior is set but interior is still a bit loose and creamy, about 25 minutes. (Use 2 large spoons to gently pull open top and peek inside.) Serve immediately.

Individual Chocolate Soufflés

Omit 2-quart soufflé dish. Grease eight 8-ounce ramekins with 1 tablespoon butter, then coat dishes evenly with 1 tablespoon sugar. In step 5, transfer soufflé mixture to ramekins, making sure to completely fill each ramekin and wipe rims with wet paper towel. Reduce baking time to 16 to 18 minutes.

CHOCOLATE FONDUE

SERVES 8 TO 10

12 ounces chocolate, chopped

1⅓ cups heavy cream

Pinch table salt

1 tablespoon corn syrup

Why This Recipe Works Chocolate fondue offers a special kind of bliss: Dipping an enormous red strawberry into a pot of warm melted chocolate is guaranteed to make just about anybody happy. But despite its short ingredient list—primarily just chocolate and cream—getting chocolate fondue right can take some finessing, and we quickly learned that nailing the ratios was the key to a rich, velvety fondue. With too much chocolate, the fondue's texture was thick and difficult to dip accompaniments into. With too much cream, however, the chocolate's flavor was muted and the fondue's texture was drippy. We found that a little more chocolate than cream delivered optimal results, while a tablespoon of corn syrup provided our fondue with a glossy finish. Chocolate fondue stays true to the flavor of the chocolate used to make it; therefore, use a high-quality chocolate you like straight from the package. (For our favorite chocolates, see pages 3–4.) Milk chocolate will produce a mild and sweet fondue, and bittersweet chocolate will present a pronounced bitter and even slightly acidic flavor. If you'd like just a touch of bitterness, we suggest combining milk chocolate with bittersweet chocolate. You will need a real fondue pot (with a heat source) to keep the chocolate mixture warm and fluid. We like to dip fruit or cubes of angel food or pound cake into the fondue.

1 Place chocolate in bowl. Bring cream and salt just to boil in small saucepan over medium heat and pour hot cream over chocolate. Cover bowl and let chocolate soften for 3 minutes. Whisk chocolate mixture until smooth, then add corn syrup and whisk to incorporate.

2 Transfer chocolate mixture to fondue pot, warm pot over Sterno flame for 5 minutes, and serve immediately.

Five-Spice Chocolate Fondue

Add 2 teaspoons ground cinnamon, 5 whole cloves, 1 teaspoon black peppercorns, 2 star anise pods, and one 1-inch piece fresh ginger, peeled and cut in half, to cream and salt mixture. Bring cream, salt, and spices to boil. Cover, remove from heat, and let mixture steep for 10 minutes. Pour cream through fine-mesh strainer into bowl; discard spices. Return cream to saucepan and bring back to simmer before adding corn syrup.

Orange Chocolate Fondue

Add 1 tablespoon grated orange zest to cream and salt mixture. Bring cream, salt, and zest to boil. Cover, remove from heat, and let mixture steep for 10 minutes. Pour cream through fine-mesh strainer into bowl; discard zest. Return cream to saucepan and bring back to simmer. Add 2 tablespoons orange liqueur, such as Grand Marnier or Cointreau, with corn syrup.

CARAMELIZED WHITE CHOCOLATE MOUSSE

SERVES 6

8 ounces white chocolate, chopped

5 tablespoons water

2 large eggs, separated

⅛ teaspoon salt

1 cup heavy cream, chilled

Why This Recipe Works White chocolate has a relatively mild, sweet, milky vanilla flavor that often complements and blends in with the flavors it's paired with. But by applying heat to white chocolate, its plentiful sugars and milk solids caramelize, and it becomes a different confection entirely—bold, less sweet, rich with butterscotch notes, and appropriate for a starring role. (This is similar to the way sweetened condensed milk transforms into dulce de leche.) To caramelize the chocolate, we roast it in a relatively low oven (300 degrees) until it slowly turns from a creamy white hue, to beige, to, finally, light brown—stirring all along the way for even cooking. The color of the roasted chocolate should resemble peanut butter once fully caramelized, and the texture will become more dry and crumbly (almost startlingly so) as it cooks. We whisk the water for the mousse into the skillet of caramelized chocolate and cook it on the stovetop just until the chocolate is mostly smooth again; any remaining small lumps are easily strained out. Folding whipped egg whites and whipped cream into the chocolate and egg yolks gives the creamy mousse a light, buoyant texture. We like serving the mousse with berries; their tartness balances the sweetness. If the interior of your nonstick skillet is very dark, start checking the caramelized white chocolate for doneness 5 minutes earlier.

1 Adjust oven rack to middle position and heat oven to 300 degrees. Place chocolate in 10-inch ovensafe nonstick skillet. Transfer skillet to oven and bake until chocolate is melted, about 10 minutes. Stir chocolate and spread into even layer. Continue to bake, stirring and spreading into even layer every 10 minutes, until golden brown, 30 to 35 minutes. (Chocolate will become dry and crumbly as it bakes.)

2 Transfer skillet to stovetop and set over medium-low heat. Being careful of hot skillet handle, add water to chocolate and cook, whisking constantly, until mixture is fully combined and mostly smooth, about 2 minutes. Strain chocolate mixture through fine-mesh strainer into large bowl, pressing on solids to extract as much chocolate mixture as possible; discard solids. Let cool until just warmer than room temperature, about 10 minutes. Whisk in egg yolks and salt until fully combined.

3 Using stand mixer fitted with whisk attachment, whip egg whites on medium-low speed until foamy, about 1 minute. Increase speed to medium-high and whip until soft peaks form, about 1 minute. Using whisk, stir about one-quarter of whipped egg whites into chocolate mixture to lighten it. Using rubber spatula, gently fold in remaining egg whites until few white streaks remain.

4 Return now-empty bowl to mixer and whip cream on medium-low speed until foamy, about 1 minute. Increase speed to high and whip until soft peaks form, about 1 minute. Using rubber spatula, fold whipped cream into mousse until no white streaks remain. Spoon mousse into 6 individual serving dishes. Cover with plastic wrap and refrigerate until set and firm, at least 2 hours or up to 24 hours. Serve.

CARAMELIZING WHITE CHOCOLATE

1 Place chocolate in 10-inch ovensafe nonstick skillet. Transfer skillet to oven and bake until chocolate is melted, about 10 minutes.

2 Stir chocolate and spread into even layer.

3 Continue to bake, stirring and spreading into even layer every 10 minutes, until golden brown, 30 to 35 minutes.

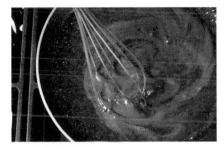

4 Transfer skillet to stovetop and set over medium-low heat.

5 Being careful of hot skillet handle, add water to chocolate and cook, whisking constantly, until mixture is fully combined and mostly smooth.

6 Strain chocolate mixture through fine-mesh strainer into large bowl, pressing on solids to extract as much chocolate mixture as possible.

CHOCOLATE SEMIFREDDO WITH CHERRY SAUCE

SERVES 12

SEMIFREDDO

- 8 ounces bittersweet chocolate, chopped fine
- 1 tablespoon vanilla extract
- ½ teaspoon instant espresso powder
- 3 large eggs
- 5 tablespoons (2¼ ounces) sugar
- ¼ teaspoon table salt
- 2 cups heavy cream, chilled, divided
- ¼ cup water

CHERRY SAUCE

- 12 ounces frozen sweet cherries
- ¼ cup (1¾ ounces) sugar
- 2 tablespoons kirsch
- 1½ teaspoons cornstarch
- 1 tablespoon lemon juice

Why This Recipe Works We love chocolate ice cream (see page 305), but serving a scoop to cap off the evening can seem too casual for certain occasions. Enter *semifreddo*, a classic Italian dessert that's often described as a frozen mousse. (Though it's fully frozen, its name roughly translates as "half-frozen.") It starts with a custard base, which is then lightened with whipped cream and/or beaten egg whites before being frozen in a loaf pan until solid, unmolded, and cut into neat slices. For a chocolate semifreddo that was rich and creamy but not overly complicated, we cooked our custard directly on the stovetop (rather than over a fussy water bath) and then poured it over 8 ounces of finely chopped bittersweet chocolate. This melted the chocolate so we could skip the step of melting it beforehand. The chocolate flavor was where we wanted it, but the semifreddo was too rich. Balancing fat and water—without decreasing the chocolate—was key. Using whole eggs instead of yolks and cutting the cream in the custard base with a bit of water ensured a cold, refreshing semifreddo that wasn't overly rich. A brilliant cherry sauce provided a bright contrast to the rich chocolate and made this an ultra-elegant dessert. If frozen overnight, the semifreddo should be tempered before serving for the best texture: Place slices on individual plates or a large tray and refrigerate for 30 minutes. For some crunch, sprinkle each serving with Candied Nuts (page 347). If you are freezing the semifreddo for longer than 6 hours before unmolding and serving, wrap the pan in a second layer of plastic wrap.

1 For the semifreddo Lightly spray loaf pan with vegetable oil spray and line with plastic wrap, leaving 3-inch overhang on all sides. Place chocolate in large heatproof bowl; set fine-mesh strainer over bowl and set aside. Stir vanilla and espresso powder in second bowl until espresso powder is dissolved.

2 Whisk eggs, sugar, and salt in third bowl until combined. Heat ½ cup cream (keep remaining 1½ cups chilled) and water in medium saucepan over medium heat until simmering. Slowly whisk hot cream mixture into egg mixture until combined. Return mixture to saucepan and cook over medium-low heat, stirring constantly and scraping bottom of saucepan with rubber spatula, until mixture is very slightly thickened and registers 160 to 165 degrees, about 5 minutes. Do not let mixture simmer.

3 Immediately pour mixture through strainer set over chocolate. Let mixture stand to melt chocolate, about 5 minutes. Whisk until chocolate is melted and smooth, then whisk in vanilla mixture. Let chocolate mixture cool completely, about 15 minutes.

4 Using stand mixer fitted with whisk attachment, whip remaining 1½ cups cream on low speed until bubbles form, about 30 seconds. Increase speed to medium and beat until whisk leaves trail, about 30 seconds. Increase speed to high and continue to beat until nearly doubled in volume and whipped cream forms soft peaks, 30 to 45 seconds.

5 Whisk one-third of whipped cream into chocolate mixture. Using rubber spatula, gently fold remaining whipped cream into chocolate mixture until incorporated and no streaks of whipped cream remain. Transfer mixture to prepared pan and spread evenly with rubber spatula. Fold overhanging plastic over surface. Freeze until firm, at least 6 hours. (Semifreddo can be wrapped tightly in plastic wrap and frozen for up to 2 weeks.)

6 **For the cherry sauce** Combine cherries and sugar in bowl and microwave for 1½ minutes. Stir, then continue to microwave until sugar is mostly dissolved, about 1 minute longer. Combine kirsch and cornstarch in small bowl.

7 Drain cherries in fine-mesh strainer set over small saucepan. Return cherries to bowl and set aside.

8 Bring juice in saucepan to simmer over medium-high heat. Stir in kirsch mixture and bring to boil. Boil, stirring occasionally, until mixture has thickened and appears syrupy, 1 to 2 minutes. Remove saucepan from heat and stir in cherries and lemon juice. Let sauce cool completely. (Sauce can be refrigerated for up to 1 week.)

9 When ready to serve, remove plastic from surface and invert pan onto serving platter. Remove plastic and smooth surface with spatula as necessary. Dip slicing knife in very hot water and wipe dry. Slice semifreddo ¾ inch thick, dipping and wiping knife after each slice. Top individual servings with cherry sauce. Serve immediately.

SERVING CHOCOLATE SEMIFREDDO

1 When ready to serve, remove plastic from surface and invert pan onto serving platter.

2 Remove plastic and smooth surface with spatula as necessary.

3 Dip slicing knife in very hot water and wipe dry. Slice semifreddo ¾ inch thick, wiping knife after each slice.

DOUBLE CHOCOLATE DESSERT WAFFLES WITH ICE CREAM

SERVES 8

2½ ounces semisweet chocolate, chopped

1¼ cups (6¼ ounces) all-purpose flour

½ cup (3½ ounces) sugar, plus extra for cooking waffles

¼ cup (¾ ounce) unsweetened cocoa powder

2 teaspoons baking powder

½ teaspoon table salt

1 cup milk

3 large eggs

4 tablespoons unsalted butter, melted and cooled

1 teaspoon vanilla extract

4 cups ice cream

Why This Recipe Works Everybody loves breakfast for dinner, but what about breakfast for dessert? The honeycombed surface of a waffle makes it the perfect "dish" on which to serve a scoop of ice cream for a fun and unexpected treat. Since this was dessert, we wanted our waffles to be chocolate, and a combination of cocoa powder and semisweet chocolate hit all the right notes. Sprinkling the waffle iron with a bit of sugar before pouring on the batter imparted a sweetly crisped crust that perfectly complemented the creamy ice cream. The recipe may yield a different number of waffles if you have a smaller or larger waffle maker; the recipe makes about 3 cups of waffle batter. If not serving the waffles straight from the waffle iron as they finish cooking, place them on a wire rack, cover with a clean kitchen towel, and keep warm in a 200-degree oven; remove the towel and let the waffles recrisp in the oven for several minutes before serving. The sugar sprinkled onto the waffle iron hardens as it cools, so you'll want to clean the waffle iron while it's still hot. We like to serve the waffles with Classic Hot Fudge Sauce (page 340).

1 Microwave chocolate in bowl at 50 percent power, stirring occasionally, until melted, 30 to 60 seconds. Whisk flour, sugar, cocoa, baking powder, and salt together in bowl. Process melted chocolate, milk, eggs, butter, and vanilla in food processor until smooth, about 5 seconds. Add flour mixture and pulse to combine, about 10 pulses; transfer to bowl.

2 Meanwhile, heat waffle iron according to manufacturer's instructions. Spray hot waffle iron with vegetable oil spray and sprinkle with ½ teaspoon sugar. (If your waffle iron makes 2 waffles at a time, sprinkle ½ teaspoon over each side.) Spread appropriate amount of batter onto hot waffle iron and cook until toasted and crisp, about 3 minutes; transfer to plate. Repeat with remaining batter. Serve waffles hot with ice cream.

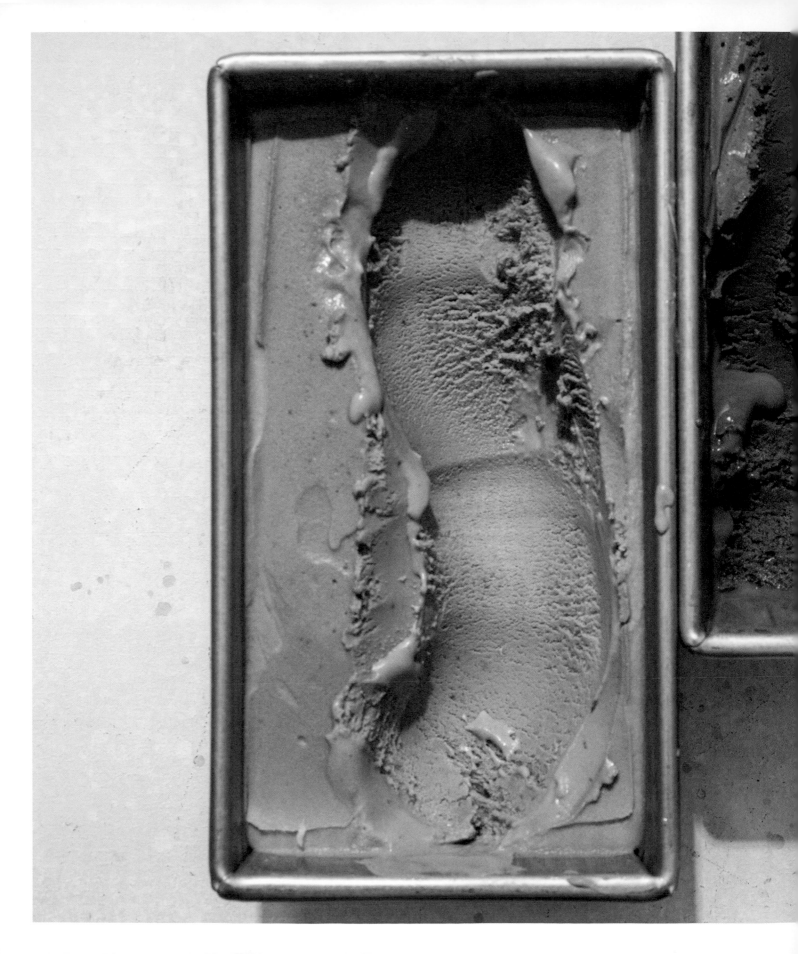

MILK CHOCOLATE NO-CHURN ICE CREAM

SERVES 8 TO 10 (MAKES ABOUT 1 QUART)

Why This Recipe Works Creamy, dreamy milk chocolate ice cream satisfies any time the temperature rises—whether in a cone from the neighborhood scoop shop, as part of an extravagant ice cream sundae, or directly from the freezer carton. What makes it even more satisfying? Making it yourself. An ice cream maker works by churning a mixture (usually a custard of milk, cream, sugar, and egg yolks) as it freezes to inhibit the formation of ice crystals and to incorporate air so that instead of a solid block of frozen milk, you have silky, creamy ice cream. But we learned you don't need a home ice cream maker to make homemade ice cream that will make you melt. We incorporated air ourselves by mixing whipped cream into our no-cook ice cream base. We first processed the cream in a blender to introduce a moderate amount of air. (Cream whipped in a stand mixer gave us a dessert closer to whipped topping.) In addition to the milk, we used sweetened condensed milk in our base, and we sweetened it further with corn syrup. Using two liquid sweeteners kept the ice cream smooth, soft, and scoopable. Melted chocolate blended in easily with the other ingredients for a sweet summer treat. With a blender and some pantry items, you'll be making ice cream in a flash.

6 ounces milk chocolate, chopped

2 cups heavy cream, chilled

1 cup sweetened condensed milk

¼ cup whole milk

¼ cup light corn syrup

2 tablespoons sugar

1 teaspoon vanilla extract

¼ teaspoon table salt

1 Microwave chocolate in bowl at 50 percent power, stirring occasionally, until melted, 2 to 3 minutes.

2 Process cream in blender until soft peaks form, 20 to 30 seconds. Scrape down sides of blender jar and continue to process until stiff peaks form, about 10 seconds longer. Using rubber spatula, stir in condensed milk, melted chocolate, whole milk, corn syrup, sugar, vanilla, and salt. Process until thoroughly combined, about 20 seconds, scraping down sides of blender jar as needed.

3 Pour cream mixture into 8½ by 4½-inch loaf pan. Press plastic wrap flush against surface of cream mixture. Freeze until firm, at least 6 hours or up to 1 week. Serve.

Banana-Walnut Chocolate Chunk No-Churn Ice Cream

Omit milk chocolate and vanilla. Add 2 very ripe bananas with condensed milk. After transferring cream mixture to loaf pan, gently stir in ¼ cup chopped toasted walnuts and ¼ cup coarsely chopped bittersweet chocolate before freezing.

Dark Chocolate No-Churn Ice Cream

Substitute 6 ounces bittersweet chocolate for milk chocolate. Add ½ teaspoon instant espresso powder with condensed milk.

Malted Milk Chocolate No-Churn Ice Cream

Add 6 tablespoons malted milk powder to blender with condensed milk.

CHOCOLATE SORBET

SERVES 8 (MAKES 1 QUART)

2¼ cups water

½ cup (1½ ounces) unsweetened cocoa powder

¾ cup (5¼ ounces) sugar

¼ cup corn syrup

1 teaspoon Sure-Jell for Less or No Sugar Needed Recipes

⅛ teaspoon table salt

8 ounces bittersweet chocolate, chopped fine

½ teaspoon vanilla extract

Why This Recipe Works A perfect chocolate sorbet isn't a watered-down dairy-free alternative to chocolate ice cream—in fact, without the dairy, chocolate sorbet has the potential to be the most chocolaty, deeply bittersweet of the frozen chocolate desserts. So that our sorbet lived up to that potential, we added a whopping half cup of unsweetened cocoa powder to our water base; we simmered it along with sugar and corn syrup to fully bloom and dissolve the cocoa. But that wasn't all: Off heat, we melted in 8 ounces of bittersweet chocolate. Blending the base ensured we had a grit-free chocolate-packed mixture before churning. Super-chilling a cup of the sorbet base in the freezer before reintroducing it to the rest of the chilled base kept ice crystals to a minimum. How? This small amount of base froze rapidly and formed small "seed" crystals that initiated a chain reaction in the larger base, causing a network of small, imperceptible (rather than large and rough) crystals to form immediately. Pectin, in the form of Sure-Jell, is the secret ingredient that slowed melting and also helped preserve a smooth texture. Make certain that you use Sure-Jell engineered for low- or no-sugar recipes (packaged in a pink box) and not regular Sure-Jell (in a yellow box). If using a canister-style ice cream machine, be sure to freeze the empty canister for at least 24 hours and preferably 48 hours before churning. For self-refrigerating machines, prechill the canister by running the machine for 5 to 10 minutes before pouring in the sorbet mixture. Allow the sorbet to sit at room temperature for 5 minutes to soften before serving.

1 Combine water, cocoa, sugar, corn syrup, Sure-Jell, and salt in medium saucepan. Heat over medium-high heat, stirring occasionally, until simmering and sugar and Sure-Jell are fully dissolved, about 5 minutes. Off heat, whisk in chocolate and vanilla until fully combined. Transfer mixture to blender and process until smooth, about 30 seconds.

2 Transfer 1 cup mixture to small bowl and place remaining mixture in large bowl. Cover both bowls with plastic wrap. Place large bowl in refrigerator and small bowl in freezer and let cool completely, at least 4 hours or up to 24 hours. (Small bowl of base will freeze solid.)

3 Remove mixtures from refrigerator and freezer. Scrape frozen base from small bowl into large bowl of base. Stir until frozen base has fully dissolved. Transfer mixture to ice cream machine and churn until mixture has consistency of thick milkshake and color lightens, 15 to 25 minutes.

4 Transfer sorbet to airtight container, pressing firmly to remove any air pockets, and freeze until firm, at least 2 hours. Serve. (Sorbet can be frozen for up to 5 days.)

diy
CONFECTIONS

THREE SUPER-SIMPLE SWEETS

Candy-making isn't always easy—sometimes you need a good instant-read thermometer and patience to get it right—but the gratifying reward is always worth it. You will find foolproof candies of all kinds throughout this chapter, but here are some chocolate confections you can make in minutes and with ease. Instant gratification guaranteed.

1 Chocolate-Covered Strawberries

MAKES 6 STRAWBERRIES

Chocolate-covered strawberries are hugely popular at specialty shops, but they can get quite pricey. Fortunately, it's very easy to make these elegant treats at home. Since you serve the strawberries from the refrigerator there's no need to temper the chocolate: just melt, dunk, and chill. Use strawberries with long stems attached if you can find them—the stem makes a convenient handle. Although strawberries are classic, this recipe also works well with cherries, banana pieces, and pineapple chunks. For fruits without stems, use a skewer to avoid dunking your fingers in the melted chocolate. Once the dipped strawberries are cooled, drizzle them with white chocolate, if desired.

- 8 **ounces bittersweet chocolate, chopped**
- 1 **quart strawberries, rinsed and thoroughly dried**

1. Line baking sheet with parchment paper. Microwave chocolate in bowl at 50 percent power, whisking often, until melted, 2 to 4 minutes.

2. Dip strawberries into chocolate and transfer to prepared baking sheet. Refrigerate strawberries until completely cool, at least 30 minutes or up to 8 hours, before serving.

2 Candy Clusters

MAKES ABOUT 30 CLUSTERS

These treats, studded with candy, pretzels, and peanuts, please with salty and sweet flavors, crunch, and, of course, chocolate. Using white chocolate to bring the ingredients together lets the milk chocolate of the M&M's remain prominent. Salty pretzels keep the sweetness in check as do satisfying peanuts.

- 8 **ounces white chocolate, chopped**
- 3 **ounces thin pretzel sticks, broken into 1-inch pieces (1½ cups)**
- 1 **cup salted dry-roasted peanuts**
- ½ **cup M&M's Minis**

1. Line rimmed baking sheet with parchment paper. Microwave chocolate in bowl at 50 percent power, stirring occasionally, until melted, 2 to 4 minutes. Using rubber spatula, gently fold in pretzels and peanuts until evenly coated.

2. Drop heaping 1-tablespoon mounds of pretzel-peanut mixture onto prepared sheet, spacing them about 1 inch apart. Sprinkle M&M's evenly over clusters. Refrigerate until chocolate is set, about 30 minutes, before serving.

3 White Chocolate Nonpareils

MAKES ABOUT 50 NONPAREILS

If you surprise someone with these sweet little candies, you'll also surprise them if you tell them how fuss-free they are. A pastry bag makes quick work of forming rounds of white chocolate and an easy sprinkle of nonpareils makes them pretty. It is important to use good-quality white chocolate here as its flavor is so prominent. (For our tasting of white chocolate, see page 4.) Use any color or combination of colors you like for the nonpareils.

8 ounces white chocolate, chopped
2 tablespoons nonpareils

1. Line baking sheet with parchment paper. Microwave chocolate in bowl at 50 percent power, stirring occasionally, until melted, 2 to 4 minutes. Let cool slightly.

2. Transfer chocolate to pastry bag, or large zipper-lock bag with small hole cut in bottom corner. Pipe quarter-size rounds of chocolate onto prepared sheet. Sprinkle rounds heavily with nonpareils. Let sit until hardened, about 30 minutes, before serving. (Nonpareils can be stored at room temperature for up to 1 week.)

CHOCOLATE TRUFFLES

MAKES 24 TRUFFLES

¼ cup (¾ ounce) unsweetened cocoa powder

1 tablespoon confectioners' sugar

8 ounces bittersweet chocolate, chopped fine

½ cup heavy cream

Pinch table salt

Why This Recipe Works Chocolate truffles are candy at its most decadent, perfect for a small bite of something sweet after a meal. But making this chocolatier's specialty is often laborious and messy; we wanted an easier, faster stairway to truffle heaven. To make our truffle base—the ganache—we turned to the microwave. Melting the chocolate and cream in the microwave was foolproof and took only a minute. Adding a pinch of salt to the mix amplified the bittersweet chocolate's complex flavors. Careful mixing was essential: The ideal utensil is a rubber spatula as it doesn't incorporate a lot of air the way a whisk does. Some recipes call for cooling the ganache for up to 4 hours before shaping it, but we found that just 45 minutes in the refrigerator was enough time. After portioning out the mixture, another short chill of just 30 minutes was all the ganache needed before being rolled into balls and dusted with cocoa. Wear latex gloves when forming the truffles to keep your hands clean.

1 Sift cocoa and sugar through fine-mesh strainer into pie plate. Microwave chocolate, cream, and salt in bowl at 50 percent power, stirring occasionally with rubber spatula, until melted and smooth, 2 to 4 minutes. Stir chocolate mixture until fully combined; transfer to 8-inch square baking dish and refrigerate until set, about 45 minutes.

2 Using heaping teaspoon measure, scoop chocolate mixture into 24 portions, transfer to large plate, and refrigerate until firm, about 30 minutes. Roll each truffle between your hands to form uniform balls (balls needn't be perfect).

3 Transfer truffles to cocoa mixture and roll to evenly coat. Lightly shake truffles in your hand over pie plate to remove excess coating and transfer to platter. Refrigerate for 30 minutes. Let sit at room temperature for 10 minutes before serving. (Coated truffles can be refrigerated along with excess cocoa mixture in airtight container for up to 1 week. Shake truffles in your hand to remove excess coating and let sit at room temperature for 10 minutes before serving.)

Chocolate-Almond Truffles

Substitute 1 cup sliced almonds, toasted and chopped fine, for cocoa mixture coating. Add ½ teaspoon almond extract to chocolate mixture before microwaving.

Chocolate-Cinnamon Truffles

Sift ¼ teaspoon ground cinnamon with cocoa powder and sugar for coating. Add 1 teaspoon ground cinnamon and ⅛ teaspoon cayenne pepper to chocolate mixture before microwaving.

Chocolate-Ginger Truffles

Add 2 teaspoons ground ginger to chocolate mixture before microwaving.

Chocolate-Lemon Truffles

Add 1 teaspoon grated lemon zest to chocolate mixture before microwaving.

CHOCOLATE TOFFEE

MAKES ABOUT 32 PIECES

Why This Recipe Works Crafting candies at home doesn't have to be a fussy affair, and this chocolate toffee is a great example. Making sure none of the sugar stuck to the sides of the pan guaranteed a smooth consistency, and resisting the urge to agitate the pan prevented crystals from forming. We found it essential to watch the toffee closely, as it can quickly turn from lightly browned to burnt. Once it registered 325 degrees, we added some pecans and poured it into a pan. Coating both sides of the toffee with semisweet chocolate and more pecans guaranteed plenty of rich chocolate flavor and nutty crunch in every bite. When taking the temperature of the toffee in step 2, remove the saucepan from the heat and tilt to one side. Use your thermometer to stir the caramel back and forth to equalize hot and cool spots and make sure you are getting an accurate reading.

8 tablespoons unsalted butter

½ cup water

1 cup (7 ounces) sugar

¼ teaspoon table salt

1½ cups pecans or walnuts, toasted and chopped, divided

8 ounces semisweet chocolate, chopped, divided

1 Make foil sling for 13 by 9-inch baking pan by folding 2 long sheets of aluminum foil; first sheet should be 13 inches wide and second sheet should be 9 inches wide. Lay sheets of foil in pan perpendicular to each other, with extra foil hanging over edges of pan. Push foil into corners and up sides of pan, smoothing foil flush to pan. Grease foil.

2 Heat butter and water in medium saucepan over medium-high heat until butter is melted. Pour sugar and salt into center of saucepan, taking care not to let sugar touch sides of saucepan. Bring mixture to boil and cook, without stirring, until sugar is completely dissolved and syrup is faint golden color and registers 300 degrees, about 10 minutes. Reduce heat to medium-low and continue to cook, gently swirling saucepan, until toffee is amber-colored and registers 325 degrees, 1 to 3 minutes longer. Off heat, stir in ½ cup pecans until incorporated and thoroughly coated. Pour toffee into prepared pan and smooth into even layer with spatula. Refrigerate, uncovered, until toffee has hardened, about 15 minutes.

3 Microwave 4 ounces chocolate in bowl at 50 percent power, stirring occasionally, until melted, 1 to 2 minutes. Pour chocolate over hardened toffee and smooth with spatula, making sure to cover toffee layer evenly and completely. Sprinkle with ½ cup pecans and press lightly to adhere. Refrigerate, uncovered, until chocolate has hardened, about 15 minutes. Line rimmed baking sheet with parchment paper. Using foil sling, invert toffee onto prepared sheet. Discard foil.

4 Microwave remaining 4 ounces chocolate in bowl at 50 percent power, stirring occasionally, until melted, 1 to 2 minutes. Pour chocolate over toffee and smooth with spatula, making sure to cover toffee layer evenly and completely. Sprinkle with remaining ½ cup pecans and press lightly to adhere. Refrigerate, uncovered, until chocolate has hardened, about 15 minutes. Break toffee into rough 2-inch squares and serve. (Toffee can be stored at room temperature for up to 2 weeks.)

CHOCOLATE FUDGE

MAKES 64 PIECES

3 cups packed (21 ounces) light brown sugar

12 tablespoons unsalted butter, cut into 12 pieces

⅔ cup evaporated milk

½ teaspoon table salt

12 ounces bittersweet chocolate, chopped

5 ounces marshmallows

1½ cups walnuts, toasted and chopped (optional)

Why This Recipe Works At its very best, fudge is creamy, rich, and ultrachocolaty—a true chocolate lover's dream. But traditional recipes follow an exhausting formula: Boil butter, sugar, and cream until it reaches a specific temperature, and then add chocolate and stir for upwards of an hour to achieve a smooth consistency. That's fine for a fudge shop with specialty equipment, but we wanted fudge that didn't take hours or an arm workout to put together. Starting with the star ingredient—the chocolate—we found that bittersweet was sweet enough to taste like candy but was also deeply chocolaty. Evaporated milk was the best choice for dairy and gave us consistent results, while light brown sugar contributed complex flavor, more like the nostalgic candy-store quality we were after. Cooking the butter, sugar, and milk to what candymakers call the "softball stage" guaranteed fudge that was firm yet pliable after cooling. And a surprise ingredient—marshmallows—gave our fudge a smooth, creamy texture without all the stirring. You will need a digital or candy thermometer for this recipe. We developed this recipe using Kraft Jet-Puffed Marshmallows. With this brand, 21 marshmallows yield 5 ounces. Be sure to use evaporated milk here, not sweetened condensed milk. Do not use chocolate that's 85 percent cacao or higher. If you're using an electric stove, the mixture will likely take longer than 5 minutes to reach 234 degrees in step 2.

1 Make foil sling for 8-inch square baking pan by folding 2 long sheets of aluminum foil so each is 8 inches wide. Lay sheets of foil in pan perpendicular to each other, with extra foil hanging over edges of pan. Push foil into corners and up sides of pan, smoothing foil flush to pan. Grease foil.

2 Combine sugar, butter, evaporated milk, and salt in large saucepan. Bring to boil over medium-high heat, stirring frequently. Reduce heat to medium-low and simmer, stirring frequently, until mixture registers 234 degrees, 3 to 5 minutes.

3 Off heat, add chocolate and marshmallows and whisk until smooth and all marshmallows are fully melted, about 2 minutes (fudge will thicken to consistency of frosting). Stir in walnuts, if using. Transfer mixture to prepared pan. Let cool completely, about 2 hours. Cover and refrigerate until set, about 2 hours.

4 Using foil overhang, lift fudge out of pan. Cut into 1-inch cubes. Let sit at room temperature for 15 minutes before serving. (Fudge can be stored at room temperature for up to 2 weeks.)

PEANUT BUTTER TRUFFLES

MAKES 20 TRUFFLES

Why This Recipe Works Ohio's favorite candy, the buckeye, is a classic truffle-like treat made with peanut butter and confectioners' sugar that's chilled and partially dipped in chocolate. We wanted to create a more elegant version with peanut butter fully enrobed in chocolate. Adding cream cheese to the filling gave it a richness and pleasant tang; it also kept the sweetness in check. And a few chopped salted, dry-roasted peanuts contributed a subtle crunch that the original lacks. For the coating, milk chocolate was too mild while bittersweet overwhelmed the peanut butter flavor of the truffles; semisweet struck just the right balance. And although this candy typically has a plain matte coating, we wanted to dress ours up with a glossy sheen. This was easily achieved by adding a little vegetable oil to the chocolate; melting these two ingredients together resulted in a satiny chocolate shell. To completely coat our truffles with chocolate, we used a toothpick to dip them—and then covered the hole with a peanut half before the chocolate set. You can use creamy or chunky peanut butter for this recipe. The truffles are best when served chilled.

½ cup (2 ounces) confectioners' sugar

3 tablespoons creamy or chunky peanut butter

1 ounce cream cheese, softened

2 tablespoons salted dry-roasted peanuts, chopped, plus 20 peanut halves, divided

¼ teaspoon vanilla extract

4 ounces semisweet chocolate, chopped

1 tablespoon vegetable oil

1 Line large plate with parchment paper. Stir sugar, peanut butter, cream cheese, chopped peanuts, and vanilla in bowl until uniform. Roll mixture into twenty ½-inch balls; space balls evenly apart on prepared plate. Freeze, uncovered, for 15 minutes.

2 Microwave chocolate and oil in bowl at 50 percent power, stirring occasionally, until melted and smooth, 2 to 4 minutes.

3 Using toothpick, pick up 1 ball and dip into chocolate to coat, letting excess chocolate drip back into bowl. Return ball to plate, remove toothpick, and immediately place peanut half over toothpick hole. Repeat with remaining balls. Freeze balls, uncovered, until chocolate has hardened, about 10 minutes. Serve cold. (Truffles can be refrigerated for up to 1 week.)

NO-BAKE ROCKY ROAD BARS

MAKES 16 BARS

6 whole graham crackers, broken into 1-inch pieces

2½ cups lightly packed miniature marshmallows, divided

1 cup whole almonds, toasted and chopped

4 tablespoons unsalted butter

8 ounces semisweet chocolate, chopped

2 tablespoons light corn syrup

Why This Recipe Works Rich chocolate, crunchy nuts, and gooey marshmallows: These are the ingredients which define all things Rocky Road. But while this mix takes many forms, our favorite is a simple no-bake bar. We wanted a recipe for this nostalgic treat that we could enjoy whenever the craving strikes. Mixing everything together not only gave our bars the requisite cobbled appearance for which they are named, but also made them a cinch to prepare. We melted chopped chocolate with a portion of the marshmallows; this mixture was the glue that held the other ingredients together. Semisweet chocolate was just bitter enough to balance the sweetness of the marshmallows, and toasting the almonds before chopping them deepened their flavor. Some butter and a couple of spoonfuls of corn syrup firmed up the mixture and made the bars easy to slice. A final addition of crumbled graham crackers contributed their familiar flavor and a pleasant crunch. Be careful not to crush the graham crackers into crumbs; break them into large pieces instead. You can substitute peanuts for the almonds.

1 Make foil sling for 8-inch square baking pan by folding 2 long sheets of aluminum foil so each is 8 inches wide. Lay sheets of foil in pan perpendicular to each other, with extra foil hanging over edges of pan. Push foil into corners and up sides of pan, smoothing foil flush to pan. Grease foil.

2 Toss cracker pieces, 1 cup marshmallows, and almonds together in large bowl; set aside. Melt butter in medium saucepan over low heat. Add remaining 1½ cups marshmallows and cook, stirring constantly, until melted and smooth, about 2 minutes. Stir in chocolate and corn syrup and continue to cook, stirring constantly, until incorporated, about 30 seconds.

3 Working quickly, pour chocolate mixture over graham cracker mixture. Gently fold until evenly coated. Transfer mixture to prepared pan and press into even layer with greased spatula. Refrigerate until firm, about 2 hours. Using foil overhang, lift bars out of pan, loosening sides with paring knife, if needed. Using chef's knife, cut into 16 bars. Serve.

BRIGADEIROS
MAKES ABOUT 30 CANDIES

Why This Recipe Works It was a bright, glossy photo that first brought brigadeiros— a gooey, chocolaty, caramel-y Brazilian candy treat—to our attention. And we were happy to discover that the recipe couldn't be easier. Sweetened condensed milk, cocoa powder, and butter are cooked until thick and then poured into a dish and chilled before being rolled into truffle-size nuggets. The last step is simply to coat the brigadeiros in any number of fun toppings. We used more cocoa powder than is traditional as we wanted a candy that emphasized the chocolate. Make sure to stir the cocoa mixture frequently or it will burn. You'll know the mixture is done cooking when it becomes so thick that a spatula dragged through it leaves a trail. Chilling the mixture is essential for easy rolling and decorating. If the dough sticks to your hands when rolling, spray your hands with a bit of vegetable oil spray. The brigadeiros are best enjoyed the day they're made, but they will keep in the refrigerator in an airtight container for up to two weeks.

1 **(14-ounce) can sweetened condensed milk**

½ **cup (1½ ounces) unsweetened cocoa powder**

2 **tablespoons unsalted butter**

Sprinkles, colored sugar, and/ or nonpareils for coating

1 Grease 8-inch square baking dish. Cook condensed milk, cocoa, and butter in medium saucepan over low heat, stirring frequently, until mixture is very thick and rubber spatula leaves distinct trail when dragged across bottom of saucepan, 20 to 25 minutes.

2 Pour mixture into prepared dish and refrigerate until firm, at least 30 minutes or up to 24 hours (cover with plastic wrap if chilling overnight).

3 Pinch mixture into approximately 1 tablespoon–size pieces and roll into 1-inch balls. Place desired coatings in small bowls and roll each candy in coating until covered. Serve. (Brigadeiros can be refrigerated for up to 2 weeks.)

MAKING BRIGADEIROS

1. Cook condensed milk mixture until very thick and rubber spatula leaves distinct trail when dragged across bottom of saucepan, 20 to 25 minutes.

2. Pinch chilled chocolate mixture into approximately 1 tablespoon–size pieces.

3. Roll mixture into 1-inch balls.

CHOCOLATE–PEANUT BUTTER CANDIES

MAKES 36 CANDIES

8 ounces milk chocolate, chopped, divided

2 tablespoons refined coconut oil

1 cup salted dry-roasted peanuts, divided

½ cup creamy peanut butter

4 tablespoons unsalted butter

5 ounces marshmallow crème

4 ounces soft caramels

1–2 tablespoons heavy cream

Why This Recipe Works If you're one who loves a candy bar out of the freezer, these salty-sweet treats, reminiscent of frozen Snickers bars (but even better and prettier to boot) are for you. The base is a mixture of chopped peanuts and melted chocolate; we preferred milk chocolate here for its familiar milky sweetness. We also added some coconut oil to this mix; coconut oil becomes solid at cold temperatures, resulting in a firm base layer with a nice snap. For the easiest-ever peanut butter–nougat filling, we melted peanut butter and butter together and then folded in marshmallow crème before mixing in more peanuts. We spread this plush confection in a thick, even layer over the chocolate base. To finish these candies, we settled on a decorative flourish of caramel and more chocolate. Stirring a little heavy cream into melted store-bought soft caramels (14 candies gave us the 4 ounces we needed) gave them just the right consistency for drizzling in a design you'd never see on a packaged bar. With a rich, chocolaty base; a soft, chewy, crunchy center; and a sweet topping, we may never go for a store-bought candy bar again. For the heavy cream, start with 1 tablespoon and add the second tablespoon if needed. These bars are best served straight from the freezer.

1 Make foil sling for 8-inch square baking pan by folding 2 long sheets of aluminum foil so each is 8 inches wide. Lay sheets of foil in pan perpendicular to each other, with extra foil hanging over edges of pan. Push foil into corners and up sides of pan, smoothing foil flush to pan. Grease foil.

2 Combine 6 ounces chocolate and coconut oil in bowl. Microwave at 50 percent power, stirring occasionally, until melted and smooth, 2 to 3 minutes. Finely chop ½ cup peanuts; add to melted chocolate and stir to combine. Transfer to prepared pan and smooth into even layer. Refrigerate until set, about 30 minutes.

3 Combine peanut butter and butter in bowl and microwave until butter is melted and warm, 30 to 45 seconds. Stir until incorporated. Fold in marshmallow crème and stir until well combined (mixture should lighten in color and may look separated). Fold in remaining ½ cup peanuts. Spread evenly over chocolate layer and refrigerate until firm, about 1 hour.

4 Heat caramels and 1 tablespoon cream in small saucepan over medium-low heat, stirring constantly, until smooth, adding additional 1 tablespoon cream if necessary; set aside. Microwave remaining 2 ounces chocolate in bowl at 50 percent power, stirring occasionally, until melted, about 30 seconds. Drizzle caramel and chocolate over peanut butter layer. Freeze until set, about 30 minutes. Using foil overhang, remove candies from pan. Using greased knife, cut into 36 (1-inch) squares (5 horizontal cuts by 5 vertical cuts) and serve immediately.

DIY CANDY BARS
MAKES 8 BARS

Why This Recipe Works You can always feel like a kid in a candy store when the candy store is your own kitchen. You don't have to be a chocolatier to make candy bars with the sheen, snap, and fun flavor appeal of those made by professionals; you just need to turn to our ultra-simple microwave tempering method (see page 14 for more information). Wanting a candy bar for each type of chocolate, we started sophisticated, with an adult bar that combined tempered bittersweet chocolate with dried fruit and nuts. Moving along to milk chocolate, we made our take on one of our favorites, a Crunch bar. For optimum crunch and a firm but airy structure, we favored Special K cereal over Rice Krispies. A sprinkling of sea salt brought out the chocolate flavor, helped tame the sweetness, and gave the homemade version a definite leg up on the original. And for something sure to satisfy the young and the young at heart, we replicated the flavor of birthday cake by incorporating crushed Nilla Wafers and rainbow sprinkles into white chocolate.

12 ounces bittersweet or semisweet chocolate (9 ounces chopped fine, 3 ounces grated)

½ cup dried cherries, cranberries, or raisins

½ cup whole almonds, shelled pistachios, or walnuts, toasted

1 Make parchment sling for 8-inch square baking pan by folding 2 long sheets of parchment so each is 8 inches wide. Lay sheets of parchment in pan perpendicular to each other, with extra parchment hanging over edges of pan. Push parchment into corners and up sides of pan, smoothing parchment flush to pan.

2 Microwave finely chopped chocolate in bowl at 50 percent power, stirring often, until about two-thirds melted, 2 to 4 minutes. (Melted chocolate should not be much warmer than body temperature; check by holding bowl in palm of your hand.) Add grated chocolate and stir until smooth, returning to microwave for no more than 5 seconds at a time to finish melting if necessary. Stir in cherries and almonds. Transfer mixture to prepared pan, spread to edges, and smooth top. Tap pan firmly on counter to release air bubbles. Let chocolate cool on counter until slightly malleable, about 10 minutes.

3 Using paring knife, score chocolate into eight 4 by 2-inch pieces. Let bars cool until firm, about 1 hour. Using parchment overhang, lift bars from pan and transfer to cutting board; discard parchment. Using serrated knife, separate bars by cutting along scored lines. Serve. (Bars can be stored at room temperature for up to 2 weeks.)

Birthday Cake Bars
Substitute white chocolate for bittersweet chocolate and 1 cup crushed Nilla wafers for cherries and almonds. After tapping pan on counter in step 2, sprinkle chocolate mixture with 2 tablespoons rainbow sprinkles and gently press to adhere.

Milk Chocolate Crunch Bars
Substitute milk chocolate for bittersweet chocolate and 1 cup Special K cereal for cherries and almonds. After tapping pan on counter in step 2, sprinkle chocolate mixture with flake sea salt to taste; press gently to adhere.

POMEGRANATE AND NUT CHOCOLATE COINS

MAKES 12 COINS

⅓ cup pecans, toasted and chopped

¼ cup shelled pistachios, toasted and chopped

2 tablespoons unsweetened flaked coconut, toasted

2 tablespoons pomegranate seeds

3 ounces semisweet chocolate (2½ ounces chopped fine, ½ ounce grated)

Why This Recipe Works With their jewel-like dried fruit toppings and plentiful nuts, chocolate coins are just as sophisticated and gift-worthy as they are easy to make. And of course, with their contrasts in flavor and texture, they're utterly delicious. We found that semisweet chocolate provided deep, rich chocolate flavor without too much bitterness, and a shortcut microwave tempering method gave our chocolate a glossy finish and snappy texture. For our topping, we had fun choosing ingredient combinations. Toasted, chopped pecans and pistachios added satisfying crunch, while toasted coconut offered a pleasant chewy-yet-crisp contrast to the nuts and the silky-smooth chocolate. A sprinkling of pomegranate seeds added pops of sweet-tart juiciness and a sparkling splash of color. We loved these beautiful coins so much that we created two more variations—one with dried cherries, almonds, and walnuts and another with a tropical spin featuring dried mango, cashews, and pepitas.

1 Line rimmed baking sheet with parchment paper. Combine pecans, pistachios, coconut, and pomegranate seeds in bowl.

2 Microwave finely chopped chocolate in bowl at 50 percent power, stirring often, until about two-thirds melted, 45 to 60 seconds. (Melted chocolate should not be much warmer than body temperature; check by holding bowl in palm of your hand.) Add grated chocolate and stir until smooth, returning to microwave for no more than 5 seconds at a time to finish melting if necessary.

3 Working quickly, measure 1 teaspoon melted chocolate onto prepared sheet and spread into 2½-inch-wide circle using back of spoon. Repeat with remaining chocolate, spacing circles 1½ inches apart.

4 Sprinkle pecan mixture evenly over chocolate and press gently to adhere. Refrigerate until chocolate is firm, about 30 minutes. Serve. (Coins can be stored at room temperature for up to 1 week.)

Cherry and Nut Chocolate Coins
Substitute almonds for pecans, walnuts for pistachios, and 4 teaspoons chopped dried cherries for pomegranate seeds.

Mango and Nut Chocolate Coins
Substitute cashews for pecans, pepitas for pistachios, and 4 teaspoons chopped unsweetened dried mango for pomegranate seeds.

NEEDHAMS

MAKES 36 CANDIES

6 tablespoons unsalted butter

3 tablespoons whole milk

¼ teaspoon table salt

¼ cup (½ ounce) plain instant mashed potato flakes

1 teaspoon vanilla extract

1½ cups (6 ounces) confectioners' sugar

1½ cups (4½ ounces) sweetened shredded coconut

1 pound bittersweet chocolate (12 ounces chopped fine, 4 ounces grated)

Why This Recipe Works Also known as potato fudge or potato candy, Needhams are an heirloom chocolate candy from Maine with an unexpected twist: Their creamy, coconut-studded base is built on mashed potatoes. While its flavor is undetectable, the potato does a great job of binding the filling together. Once coated in a silky chocolate shell, the treat is reminiscent of a Mounds candy bar in texture and flavor. To avoid boiling and then mashing only part of one potato, we instead used dried potato flakes: Just ¼ cup mixed with hot milk and melted butter made the perfect amount of unseasoned mashed potatoes for the candy base. We stirred in confectioners' sugar, sweetened shredded coconut, and vanilla and then let the mixture firm up in the refrigerator before cutting it into bite-size squares. For the bittersweet chocolate coating, it was essential to slowly melt the chocolate so it would recrystallize around the candies to form a shiny, snappy shell that wouldn't melt in our hands. For this we used our easy microwave tempering technique, which calls for melting a portion of the chocolate before mixing in the rest.

1 Make foil sling for 8-inch square baking pan by folding 1 long sheet of aluminum foil so it is 8 inches wide. Lay foil sheet in pan with extra foil hanging over edges of pan. Push foil into corners and up sides of pan, smoothing foil flush to pan. Grease foil.

2 Microwave butter, milk, and salt in bowl until butter is melted and mixture is bubbling, about 2 minutes. Stir in potato flakes and vanilla until mixture resembles applesauce, about 30 seconds (mixture will look oily). Stir in sugar and coconut until no dry spots remain and mixture forms loose paste.

3 Transfer coconut mixture to prepared pan and, using rubber spatula, press firmly into thin, even layer reaching into corners of pan. Cover with plastic wrap and refrigerate until firm, at least 2 hours or up to 24 hours.

4 Flip coconut mixture onto cutting board; discard foil. Cut into 36 (1-inch) squares (5 horizontal cuts by 5 vertical cuts). Separate squares into 2 batches and keep half refrigerated while working with other half. Line rimmed baking sheet with parchment paper.

5 Microwave finely chopped chocolate in bowl at 50 percent power, stirring often, until about two-thirds melted, 2 to 4 minutes. (Melted chocolate should not be much warmer than body temperature; check by holding bowl in palm of your hand.) Add grated chocolate and stir until smooth, returning to microwave for no more than 5 seconds at a time to finish melting if necessary.

6 Drop several coconut squares into chocolate. Using 2 forks, gently flip squares to coat on all sides. Lift squares one at a time from chocolate with fork. Tap fork against edge of bowl and then wipe underside of fork on edge of bowl to remove excess chocolate from bottom of candy. Use second fork to slide candy onto prepared sheet.

7 Repeat with remaining coconut squares and remaining chocolate, cleaning forks as needed. (As chocolate begins to set, microwave it at 50 percent power for no more than 5 seconds at a time, stirring at each interval, until fluid. Expect to microwave chocolate at least twice during coating process.)

8 Refrigerate candy until chocolate is set, 25 to 30 minutes. Serve. (Candy can be refrigerated for up to 1 week.)

CHOCOLATE BARK WITH PEPITAS AND GOJI BERRIES

MAKES 16 PIECES

Why This Recipe Works Tired of chocolate barks that feature nuts and little else, we decided to put a fresh spin on this super-easy confection by passing over the workaday whole almonds or crushed candies and incorporating ingredients, flavors, and textures you don't often see in bark, store-bought or homemade. We started with crunchy, earthy roasted pepitas and chewy, sweet-tart dried goji berries, which paired well and made substantial additions to the confection. Once a hard-to-find ingredient, goji berries, native to China, are now widely available in their dried form and have a unique tartness and depth of flavor that shines in dark chocolate. Next we decided to incorporate a couple of spices to liven things up: Cinnamon and chipotle powder added surprising depth and some intriguing heat, while a little sea salt sprinkled on top enhanced all of these unique flavors and finished the bars with a bit of shine and soft crunch.

1   **pound bittersweet chocolate (12 ounces chopped fine, 4 ounces grated)**

2   **teaspoons ground cinnamon**

1   **teaspoon chipotle chile powder**

2   **cups roasted pepitas (1¾ cups left whole, ¼ cup chopped), divided**

1   **cup goji berries, chopped, divided**

1   **teaspoon flake sea salt**

1 Make parchment paper sling for 13 by 9-inch baking pan by folding 2 long sheets of parchment; first sheet should be 13 inches wide and second sheet should be 9 inches wide. Lay sheets in pan perpendicular to each other, with extra parchment hanging over edges of pan. Push parchment into corners and up sides of pan, smoothing parchment flush to pan.

2 Microwave finely chopped chocolate in large bowl at 50 percent power, stirring often, until about two thirds melted, 2 to 4 minutes. (Melted chocolate should not be much warmer than body temperature; check by holding bowl in palm of your hand.) Add grated chocolate, cinnamon, and chile powder and stir until smooth, returning to microwave for no more than 5 seconds at a time to finish melting if necessary.

3 Stir 1¾ cups whole pepitas and ¾ cup goji berries into chocolate mixture. Working quickly, use rubber spatula to spread chocolate mixture evenly into prepared pan. Sprinkle with remaining ¼ cup chopped pepitas and remaining ¼ cup goji berries and gently press topping into chocolate. Sprinkle evenly with salt and refrigerate until chocolate is set, about 30 minutes.

4 Using parchment overhang, lift chocolate out of pan and transfer to cutting board; discard parchment. Using serrated knife and gentle sawing motion, cut bark into 16 even pieces. Serve. (Bark can be stored at room temperature for up to 1 week.)

CHOCOLATE-COVERED CARAMELS

MAKES 64 CARAMELS

1 vanilla bean

1 cup heavy cream

5 tablespoons unsalted butter, cut into ¼-inch pieces

1 teaspoon flake sea salt, plus extra for garnish

1⅓ cups (9⅓ ounces) sugar

¼ cup light corn syrup

¼ cup water

1 pound semisweet chocolate (12 ounces chopped, 4 ounces finely grated)

Why This Recipe Works In the confection world, no candy is quite as sophisticated as the chocolate-cloaked salted caramel. We wanted to crack the caramel code at home and develop our own chewy caramels rounded with aromatic vanilla notes. We started by steeping the heavy cream with a vanilla bean and sea salt for 10 minutes. Meanwhile, we cooked our caramel. We found corn syrup to be key here, as it helped prevent sugar crystals from developing that could later mar the texture of the caramels. We cooked our sugar to 350 degrees and stirred in the vanilla-amped cream mixture until it climbed back to 248 degrees—the exact temperature for caramels that had chew and held their shape but didn't rip our teeth out. After the caramel firmed up, we cut it, dunked the squares in dark chocolate (a pleasantly bitter foil to the sweet caramel), and sprinkled on additional sea salt. When taking the temperature of the caramel in steps 3 and 4, remove the saucepan from the heat and tilt to one side. Use your thermometer to stir the caramel back and forth to equalize hot and cool spots and make sure you are getting an accurate reading. This recipe yields enough tempered chocolate to easily dip all the caramels; leftover chocolate can be transferred to small airtight container and stored at room temperature for another use.

1 Cut vanilla bean in half lengthwise. Using tip of paring knife, scrape out seeds; reserve spent vanilla bean for another use. Bring vanilla bean seeds, cream, butter, and 1 teaspoon sea salt to simmer in small saucepan over medium heat. Off heat, let steep for 10 minutes.

2 Make parchment sling for 8-inch square baking pan by folding 2 long sheets of parchment paper so each is 8 inches wide. Lay sheets of parchment in pan perpendicular to each other, with extra parchment hanging over edges of pan. Push parchment into corners and up sides of pan, smoothing parchment flush to pan. Grease parchment; set aside.

3 Combine sugar, corn syrup, and water in medium saucepan. Bring to boil over medium-high heat and cook, without stirring, until mixture is golden, 8 to 10 minutes. Reduce heat to low and continue to cook, swirling saucepan occasionally, until amber, 2 to 5 minutes. (Caramel should register 350 degrees.)

4 Off heat, carefully stir in cream mixture (it will bubble and steam). Return saucepan to medium-high heat and cook, stirring frequently, until caramel reaches 248 degrees, about 5 minutes.

5 Carefully transfer caramel to prepared pan. Using greased rubber spatula, smooth surface of caramel, and let cool completely, about 1 hour. Transfer to refrigerator and chill until caramel is completely solid and cold to touch, about 1 hour.

6 Using parchment overhang, lift caramel from pan and transfer to lightly greased cutting board; discard parchment. Using greased chef's knife, cut caramel into 1-inch-wide strips, then cut strips crosswise into 1-inch-wide pieces.

7 Microwave finely chopped chocolate in bowl at 50 percent power, stirring often, until about two-thirds melted, 2 to 4 minutes. (Melted chocolate should not be much warmer than body temperature; check by holding bowl in palm of your hand.) Add grated chocolate and stir until smooth, returning to microwave for no more than 5 seconds at a time to finish melting if necessary.

8 Line rimmed baking sheet with parchment. Place 1 caramel in chocolate and, using 2 forks, gently flip to coat all sides. Lift caramel out of chocolate with fork. Tap fork against edge of bowl and then wipe underside of fork on edge of bowl to remove excess chocolate from bottom of caramel. Use second fork to slide caramel onto prepared sheet and sprinkle with sea salt to taste. Repeat with remaining caramels, returning chocolate to microwave for no more than 5 seconds at a time if it becomes too firm. Let caramels sit until chocolate is firm, about 1 hour. Serve. (Caramels can be stored in airtight container, separated by sheets of parchment, at room temperature for up to 2 weeks.)

ICE CREAM BONBONS

MAKES 16 BONBONS

1 pint ice cream

12 ounces bittersweet chocolate, chopped

2 tablespoons vegetable oil

3 tablespoons finely chopped nuts (optional)

3 tablespoons flaked, sweetened coconut (optional)

Why This Recipe Works Coating small scoops of ice cream with chocolate creates ice cream bonbons that deliver a satisfying snap of chocolate giving way to a bite of cool, creamy ice cream. For a playful and super-easy treat, we wanted to create a family-friendly recipe for these bite-size desserts and sprinkle them with fun toppings. We found a small ice cream scoop made quick work of shaping the ice cream into balls, and freezing them for at least an hour ensured they were sufficiently firm so they didn't melt away when we gave them their chocolate coating. Bittersweet chocolate was our choice chocolate: It held its own, contrasting with the sweet dairy flavor of the ice cream. Melting the chocolate with a little vegetable oil ensured that it spread smoothly over the balls of ice cream so we didn't make a mess. The chocolate hardens very quickly, so we found it necessary to add any garnishes as soon as the bonbons were coated. Feel free to use any flavor ice cream without chunks or nuts. We like to dust some bonbons with nuts and others with flaked sweetened coconut for variety.

1 Line 2 large plates with parchment paper or waxed paper. Place plates in freezer for 15 minutes to chill. Using very small ice cream scoop, make about 16 balls, each with about 2 tablespoons ice cream, and place them on chilled plates. Lightly cover plates with plastic wrap and chill until ice cream is very firm, about 1 hour.

2 Microwave chocolate and oil in large bowl at 50 percent power, stirring occasionally, until melted and smooth, 2 to 4 minutes. Let cool completely. Remove 1 plate of ice cream from freezer and, working quickly, use 2 forks to dip and roll 1 ice cream ball in chocolate to coat. Pick up ball by sliding it onto 1 fork and let excess chocolate drip back into bowl. Return bonbon to lined plate. Immediately sprinkle bonbon with 1 teaspoon nuts or coconut, if using.

3 Repeat dipping and garnishing ice cream balls remaining on plate, 1 ball at a time. Return first plate to freezer. Remove second plate of ice cream balls from freezer and repeat process to make 8 more bonbons. Freeze bonbons until firm, at least 1 hour or up to 24 hours, before serving.

toppings, sauces, AND MORE

Using stand mixer fitted with whisk attachment, whip cream, sugar, vanilla, and salt on medium-low speed until foamy, about 1 minute. Increase speed to high and whip until soft peaks form, 1 to 3 minutes. (Whipped cream can be refrigerated in fine-mesh strainer set over small bowl and covered with plastic wrap for up to 8 hours.)

Bourbon Whipped Cream

Substitute 3 tablespoons packed brown sugar for granulated. Reduce vanilla to ½ teaspoon. Add 1 tablespoon bourbon to stand mixer with cream. Mix additional 1 tablespoon bourbon into finished whipped cream to taste.

Cocoa Whipped Cream

Increase sugar to 2 tablespoons. Add 2 tablespoons unsweetened cocoa powder, sifted, to stand mixer with cream before whipping.

Orange Whipped Cream

Substitute 2 tablespoons orange juice for vanilla. Add 1 teaspoon grated orange zest to stand mixer with cream before whipping.

Peanut Butter Whipped Cream

Add ¼ cup creamy peanut butter to stand mixer with cream before whipping. Once mixture is foamy, continue to whip on medium-low speed until soft peaks form, 1 to 3 minutes.

Yogurt Whipped Cream

Omit sugar, vanilla, and salt. Reduce heavy cream to ¾ cup. Add ½ cup plain Greek yogurt to stand mixer with cream before whipping.

WHIPPED CREAM

MAKES ABOUT 2 CUPS

Whipped cream may be a simple topping, but it's often just the right addition to cut through the richness of a decadent chocolate dessert. Whipping the ingredients on medium-low speed to start ensures the sugar, vanilla, and salt are evenly dispersed in the cream before we increase the mixer speed to achieve soft peaks (our preference for a decadent dollop). Lightly sweetened whipped cream goes with just about everything, but occasionally we want to add another layer of flavor: Orange zest and juice add a bright touch, while yogurt offers a thicker, tangier alternative. Incorporating peanut butter requires a slower whipping speed to avoid a curdled mess. Bourbon and brown sugar add a shot and round caramel notes. Finally, we created a cocoa whipped cream for chocolate-on-chocolate experiences.

1   cup heavy cream, chilled

1   tablespoon sugar

1   teaspoon vanilla extract

    Pinch table salt

CLASSIC HOT FUDGE SAUCE

MAKES ABOUT 2 CUPS

Intense and complex, a luxurious chocolate sauce can transform a simple recipe into a decadent dessert. Our classic hot fudge sauce relies on cocoa powder and unsweetened chocolate for complexity, moderate sweetness, and richness. Using milk, rather than cream, helps preserve the intense chocolate flavor, and incorporating cold butter created a thick consistency and imparted an attractive sheen. Pour it over a simple dish of ice cream, make a special sundae out of Double Chocolate Dessert Waffles with Ice Cream (page 303), or spoon it over Frozen Snickers Ice Cream Cake (page 60) for the ultimate in decadence.

Orange Hot Fudge Sauce

Bring milk and 8 (3-inch) strips orange zest to simmer in medium saucepan over medium heat. Off heat, cover and let sit for 15 minutes. Strain milk mixture through fine-mesh strainer into bowl, pressing on orange zest to extract as much liquid as possible. Return milk to now-empty saucepan and proceed with recipe as directed.

Peanut Butter Hot Fudge Sauce

Increase salt to ½ teaspoon. Whisk ¼ cup creamy peanut butter into sauce after butter.

CHOCOLATE–TAHINI SAUCE

MAKES ABOUT 2 CUPS

If you like chocolate with peanut butter and want to branch out, try chocolate with a seed butter, tahini. The pairing is featured in our Chocolate-Tahini Tart (page 189), but the sesame-enriched sauce is also delicious poured over desserts and ice cream (a chocolate sauce for adult tastes). Fans of halvah will recognize its bittersweet flavor; everyone else will appreciate a change from chocolate–peanut butter or Nutella. Stirring in the tahini at the end with the butter guarantees a smooth sauce that's not greasy.

1¼ cups (8¾ ounces) sugar

⅔ cup whole milk

¼ teaspoon table salt

⅓ cup (1 ounce) unsweetened cocoa powder, sifted

3 ounces unsweetened chocolate, chopped fine

4 tablespoons unsalted butter, cut into 8 pieces and chilled

1 teaspoon vanilla extract

1 Heat sugar, milk, and salt in medium saucepan over medium-low heat, whisking gently, until sugar has dissolved and liquid starts to bubble around edges of saucepan, about 6 minutes. Reduce heat to low, add cocoa, and whisk until smooth.

2 Off heat, stir in chocolate and let sit for 3 minutes. Whisk sauce until smooth and chocolate is fully melted. Whisk in butter and vanilla until fully incorporated and sauce thickens slightly. (Sauce can be refrigerated for up to 1 month; gently warm in microwave, stirring every 10 seconds, until pourable before using.)

1¼ cups (8¾ ounces) sugar

⅔ cup whole milk

½ teaspoon table salt

⅓ cup (1 ounce) unsweetened cocoa powder, sifted

3 ounces unsweetened chocolate, chopped fine

4 tablespoons unsalted butter, cut into 8 pieces and chilled

¼ cup tahini

1 teaspoon vanilla extract

1 Heat sugar, milk, and salt in medium saucepan over medium-low heat, whisking gently, until sugar has dissolved and liquid starts to bubble around edges of saucepan, about 6 minutes. Reduce heat to low, add cocoa, and whisk until smooth.

2 Off heat, stir in chocolate and let sit for 3 minutes. Whisk sauce until smooth and chocolate is fully melted. Whisk in butter, tahini, and vanilla until fully incorporated and sauce thickens slightly. (Sauce can be refrigerated for up to 1 month; gently warm in microwave, stirring every 10 seconds, until pourable, before using.)

1¾ cups (12¼ ounces) sugar

½ cup water

¼ cup light corn syrup

1 cup heavy cream

1 teaspoon vanilla extract

¼ teaspoon table salt

1 Bring sugar, water, and corn syrup to boil in large saucepan over medium-high heat. Cook, without stirring, until mixture is straw-colored, 6 to 8 minutes. Reduce heat to low and continue to cook, swirling saucepan occasionally, until caramel is amber-colored, 2 to 5 minutes. (Caramel should register between 360 and 370 degrees.)

2 Off heat, carefully stir in cream, vanilla, and salt; mixture will bubble and steam. Continue to stir until sauce is smooth. Let cool slightly. (Sauce can be refrigerated for up to 2 weeks; gently warm in microwave, stirring every 10 seconds, until pourable, before using.)

Dark Rum Caramel Sauce

Whisk 3 tablespoons dark rum into caramel with cream.

Orange-Espresso Caramel Sauce

Stir 3 tablespoons Kahlúa, 1 tablespoon instant espresso powder, and 2 teaspoons finely grated orange zest in bowl until espresso dissolves. Stir Kahlúa mixture into caramel with cream.

Salted Caramel Sauce

Increase salt to 1 teaspoon.

CLASSIC CARAMEL SAUCE

MAKES ABOUT 2 CUPS

Nutty, buttery caramel sauce adds a layer of complexity to an array of chocolate desserts. But the process of making caramel can intimidate: Too blonde and it lacks flavor; turn away for a second and it's too dark and bitter. We made our recipe foolproof by adding water to ensure that the sugar fully dissolved; this helped us avoid the common pitfalls of burning and crystallization (which occur when the sugar cooks unevenly). We prefer an instant-read thermometer for measuring the temperature of caramel. To ensure an accurate reading, swirl the caramel to even out hot spots and then tilt the pot so that the caramel pools 1 to 2 inches deep. Move the thermometer back and forth for about 5 seconds before taking a reading.

CARAMEL-CHOCOLATE-PECAN SAUCE

MAKES ABOUT 1½ CUPS

The addition of bittersweet chocolate and pecans to caramel creates a turtle-inspired sauce. We prefer an instant-read thermometer for measuring the temperature of caramel. To ensure an accurate reading, swirl the caramel to even out hot spots, then tilt the pot so that the caramel pools 1 to 2 inches deep. Move the thermometer back and forth for about 5 seconds before taking a reading. We love amplifying the flavors and textures in Banana-Walnut Chocolate Chunk No-Churn Ice Cream (page 305) with this nutty sauce.

- 1 cup (7 ounces) sugar
- ⅓ cup water
- 3 tablespoons light corn syrup
- ¾ cup heavy cream
- 2 ounces bittersweet chocolate, chopped
- 1 tablespoon unsalted butter, chilled
- ½ cup pecans, toasted and chopped
- 1 teaspoon vanilla extract
- ⅛ teaspoon table salt

1 Bring sugar, water, and corn syrup to boil in large saucepan over medium-high heat. Cook, without stirring, until mixture is straw-colored, 6 to 8 minutes. Reduce heat to low and continue to cook, swirling saucepan occasionally, until caramel is amber-colored, 2 to 5 minutes. (Caramel should register between 360 and 370 degrees.)

2 Off heat, carefully stir in cream; mixture will bubble and steam. Stir in chocolate and butter and let sit for 3 minutes. Whisk sauce until smooth and chocolate is fully melted. Stir in pecans, vanilla, and salt. Let cool slightly. (Sauce can be refrigerated for up to 2 weeks; gently warm in microwave, stirring every 10 seconds, until pourable, before using.)

CHOCOLATE-PORT SAUCE

MAKES ABOUT ⅔ CUP

To create a sophisticated chocolate sauce for ice cream or fruit, we incorporated ruby port. The brilliant red color of this fortified wine added a subtle but rich hue, and its slightly fruity character balanced the bitter edge of the chocolate. Try a restrained drizzle over Chocolate-Pear Tart (page 194).

- ⅔ cup ruby port
- 3 tablespoons heavy cream
- 3 ounces bittersweet chocolate, chopped fine

1 Bring port to simmer in small saucepan over medium heat and cook until reduced to about ⅓ cup, 5 to 7 minutes. Stir in heavy cream and return to simmer.

2 Off heat, add chocolate and let sit for 3 minutes. Whisk sauce until smooth and chocolate is fully melted. (Sauce can be refrigerated for up to 1 month; gently warm in microwave, stirring every 10 seconds, until pourable, before using.)

PEPPERMINT–WHITE CHOCOLATE SAUCE

MAKES ABOUT ⅔ CUP

For a fun twist on classic chocolate sauce, we used white chocolate and added a dash of peppermint extract, which awoke the rich, vanilla-y white chocolate. Using white chips, rather than bar chocolate, ensured our sauce wasn't grainy and had a smooth, creamy consistency. This sauce is particularly great drizzled over something bittersweet, like brownies or chocolate cake, to offset its flavor.

- ⅔ cup (4 ounces) white chocolate chips
- ¼ cup heavy cream
- Pinch table salt
- ⅛ teaspoon peppermint extract

Microwave chocolate chips, cream, and salt in bowl at 50 percent power, stirring occasionally, until melted and smooth, about 1 minute. Stir in peppermint extract. (Sauce can be refrigerated for up to 1 month; gently warm in microwave, stirring every 10 seconds, until pourable, before using.)

CRÈME ANGLAISE

MAKES ABOUT 1½ CUPS

Crème anglaise is a classic pourable custard sauce that's typically flavored with vanilla bean. It's ideal for upping the elegance of your dessert when you want the creamy richness that ice cream provides but not the icy cold contrast. A vanilla bean gives the deepest flavor, but 1 teaspoon of vanilla extract can be used instead; skip the steeping stage in step 1 after heating the milk mixture and stir the extract into the sauce after straining it in step 2. You can drizzle the custard over refined desserts like Flourless Chocolate Cake (page 210) or serve an elegant slice of Rich Chocolate Tart (page 188) over a shallow pool of it.

- ½ vanilla bean
- 1½ cups whole milk
- Pinch table salt
- 4 large egg yolks
- ¼ cup (1¾ ounces) sugar

1 Cut vanilla bean in half lengthwise. Using tip of paring knife, scrape out seeds. Bring vanilla bean and seeds, milk, and salt to simmer in medium saucepan over medium-high heat, stirring occasionally. Remove from heat, cover, and let steep for 20 minutes.

2 Whisk egg yolks and sugar together in large bowl until smooth, then slowly whisk in hot milk mixture to temper. Return milk mixture to saucepan and cook over low heat, stirring constantly with rubber spatula, until sauce thickens slightly, coats back of spoon, and registers 180 degrees, 5 to 7 minutes. Immediately strain sauce through fine-mesh strainer into clean bowl; discard vanilla bean. Cover custard and refrigerate until cool, about 45 minutes. (Sauce can be refrigerated, with plastic wrap pressed directly on surface, for up to 3 days.)

Coffee Crème Anglaise

Add 1½ teaspoons instant espresso powder to saucepan with vanilla bean and seeds.

Earl Grey Crème Anglaise

Substitute 1 Earl Grey tea bag for vanilla bean. Remove tea bag after steeping in step 1.

Orange Crème Anglaise

Substitute 2 (3-inch) strips orange zest for vanilla bean. Stir 1 tablespoon Grand Marnier into finished sauce after straining.

PEANUT BUTTER SAUCE

MAKES 2 CUPS

There's no shortage of prepared sauces to be found in the supermarket, but homemade versions take just minutes to assemble and taste worlds better. We wanted a rich peanut butter sauce that we could spoon over a dish of Chocolate Sorbet (page 293), a lofty Chocolate Soufflé (page 293), or a slice of Chocolate Cream Pie (page 202). Combining ½ cup creamy peanut butter with a stick of butter ensured plenty of peanutty flavor and a silky consistency. We added sugar, evaporated milk, a little vanilla extract, and a dash of salt and cooked our sauce on the stovetop until thickened and smooth. Evaporated milk helps stabilize the sauce, but you should still take care to cook it over low heat; otherwise the peanut butter will cause the sauce to break.

- 1 cup (7 ounces) sugar
- ¾ cup evaporated milk
- 8 tablespoons unsalted butter
- ½ cup creamy peanut butter
- 1 teaspoon vanilla extract
- ⅛ teaspoon table salt

Bring sugar, milk, butter, peanut butter, vanilla, and salt to simmer in medium saucepan over medium heat. Reduce heat to low and cook, stirring often, until sauce is smooth and thick, about 3 minutes. Serve warm. (Sauce can be refrigerated for up to 1 week; gently warm in microwave, stirring every 10 seconds, until pourable, before using.)

MIXED BERRY COULIS

MAKES ABOUT 1½ CUPS

Sometimes an ultrarich creation—like Milk Chocolate Cheesecake (page 214)—calls for a bright sauce. Coulis, a fruit sauce that's pureed and strained to give it a silky-smooth texture, is perfect. We cooked berries only briefly to release some pectin, which thickened the sauce without dampening the fresh flavor. The type and ripeness of berries used will affect the sweetness; start with 5 tablespoons of sugar, then add more to taste in step 2 if necessary. Stir in additional sugar immediately after straining so that the sugar dissolves.

- 15 ounces (3 cups) fresh or thawed frozen blueberries, blackberries, and/or raspberries
- ¼ cup water, plus extra as needed
- 5 tablespoons sugar, plus extra for seasoning
- ⅛ teaspoon table salt
- 2 teaspoons lemon juice

1 Bring berries, water, sugar, and salt to gentle simmer in medium saucepan over medium heat and cook, stirring occasionally, until sugar is dissolved and berries are heated through, about 1 minute.

2 Process mixture in blender until smooth, about 20 seconds. Strain through fine-mesh strainer into bowl, pressing on solids to extract as much puree as possible. Stir in lemon juice and season with extra sugar as needed. Cover and refrigerate until well chilled, about 1 hour. Adjust consistency with extra water as needed. (Sauce can be refrigerated for up to 4 days; stir to recombine before using.)

Stir vanilla, espresso powder, and salt in small bowl until espresso dissolves. Microwave chocolate and coconut oil in bowl at 50 percent power, stirring occasionally, until melted and smooth, 2 to 4 minutes. Whisk in vanilla mixture and cocoa until combined. Let cool to room temperature, about 30 minutes, before using. (Sauce can be stored at room temperature in airtight container for up to 2 months; gently warm in microwave, stirring every 10 seconds, until pourable but not hot, before using.)

CHOCOLATE FROSTING

MAKES 5 CUPS; ENOUGH FOR 1 TWO-LAYER CAKE

We combined melted chocolate with a hefty amount of cocoa powder—Dutch processed for deeper color and flavor—to create a rich yet versatile chocolate frosting. A combination of confectioners' sugar and corn syrup made it smooth and glossy. To keep the frosting from separating and becoming greasy, we turned to the food processor: The fast-mixing machine eliminated the risk of overbeating, as it blended the ingredients quickly without melting the butter or incorporating too much air. The result is a thick, fluffy foolproof chocolate frosting that spreads like a dream. Bittersweet, semisweet, or milk chocolate can be used in this recipe.

- 12 ounces chocolate, chopped
- 30 tablespoons (3¾ sticks) unsalted butter, softened
- 1½ cups (6 ounces) confectioners' sugar
- 1 cup (3 ounces) Dutch-processed cocoa powder
- ⅛ teaspoon table salt
- 1 cup light corn syrup
- 1½ teaspoons vanilla extract

Microwave chocolate in bowl at 50 percent power, stirring occasionally, until melted, 2 to 4 minutes. Let cool completely. Process butter, sugar, cocoa, and salt in food processor until smooth, about 30 seconds, scraping down sides of bowl as needed. Add corn syrup and vanilla and process until just combined, 5 to 10 seconds. Scrape down sides of bowl, then add chocolate and process until smooth and creamy, 10 to 15 seconds. (Frosting can be kept at room temperature for up to 3 hours or refrigerated for up to 3 days; if refrigerated, let stand at room temperature for 1 hour and stir before using.)

MAGIC CHOCOLATE SHELL

MAKES ABOUT ¾ CUP

Magic shell—a chocolate sauce that forms a thin, brittle shell when poured over ice cream—is a childhood soft-serve stand favorite. You can make the magic at home. The secret ingredient? Coconut oil. Coconut oil's high saturated fat content makes it liquid when warm (74 degrees or higher) but solid as soon as it drops to 70 degrees. Because of this quick transition, our satiny sauce solidifies into a shatteringly thin shell when poured over cold ice cream. We didn't want the overly sweet, anemic coatings we remembered, but very dark chocolate was bitter. Semisweet chocolate, bolstered by espresso powder and cocoa powder and deepened with salt and vanilla, was the perfect balance of nostalgic and mature. Serve over no-churn ice cream (see page 305).

- ¼ teaspoon vanilla extract
- ⅛ teaspoon instant espresso powder
  Pinch salt
- 4 ounces semisweet chocolate, chopped fine
- ⅓ cup coconut oil
- 1 teaspoon unsweetened cocoa powder

Makes 3 cups; enough for 12 cupcakes or 1 sheet cake
Reduce chocolate to 8 ounces, reduce butter to 20 tablespoons (2½ sticks), reduce confectioners' sugar to 1 cup (4 ounces), reduce cocoa powder to ¾ cup (2¼ ounces), reduce corn syrup to ¾ cup, and reduce vanilla to 1 teaspoon.

Makes 6 cups; enough for 1 three-layer cake
Increase chocolate to 1 pound, increase butter to 1¼ pounds (5 sticks), increase confectioners' sugar to 2 cups (8 ounces), and increase cocoa powder to 1½ cups (4½ ounces).

GANACHE FROSTING
MAKES 5 CUPS, ENOUGH FOR 1 TWO-LAYER CAKE

For the most lavish chocolate cake, sometimes only an equally decadent frosting will do. Fortunately, the richest chocolate frosting, ganache, is the easiest to prepare. To make it, we simply brought heavy cream to a boil and then poured it over a pound of chopped chocolate; once the mixture was combined and smooth, we allowed it to cool before whipping it to an airy, mousse-like consistency. This chocolate frosting recipe is very flexible: Bittersweet, milk, or white chocolate can be substituted for the semisweet chocolate if you prefer.

- 1 **pound semisweet chocolate, chopped**
- 2 **cups heavy cream**

1 Place chocolate in large heatproof bowl. Bring cream to boil in small saucepan. Pour boiling cream over chocolate, and let sit, covered, for 5 minutes. Whisk mixture until smooth, then cover with plastic wrap and refrigerate until cool and slightly firm, about 1 hour.

2 Using stand mixer fitted with whisk attachment, whip cooled chocolate mixture on medium speed until fluffy and mousse-like and soft peaks form, about 2 minutes.

Makes 3 cups; enough for 12 cupcakes or 1 sheet cake
Reduce chocolate to 10 ounces and reduce heavy cream to 1¼ cups.

Makes 6 cups; enough for 1 three-layer cake
Increase chocolate to 1¼ pounds and increase heavy cream to 2½ cups. Increase chilling time in step 1 to about 2 hours.

CHOCOLATE BUTTERCREAM
MAKES 5 CUPS, ENOUGH FOR 1 TWO-LAYER CAKE

When we want a more refined chocolate frosting, we opt for a cooked buttercream of the Swiss meringue variety in which egg whites and granulated sugar are heated over a double boiler and then whipped with knobs of softened butter. The result is a rich, creamy chocolate frosting that is the perfect crowning touch for most any chocolate cake. The melted bittersweet chocolate should be cooled to between 85 and 100 degrees before being added to the frosting.

- 14 **ounces bittersweet chocolate, chopped**
- 1 **cup (7 ounces) sugar**
- 5 **large egg whites**
- ⅛ **teaspoon table salt**
- 28 **tablespoons (3½ sticks) unsalted butter, cut into 28 pieces and softened**
- 1¼ **teaspoons vanilla extract**

1 Microwave chocolate in bowl at 50 percent power, stirring occasionally, until melted, 2 to 5 minutes. Let cool completely.

2 Combine sugar, egg whites, and salt in bowl of stand mixer. Set bowl over saucepan filled with 1 inch barely simmering water, making sure that water does not touch bottom of bowl. Cook, whisking constantly, until mixture registers 150 degrees, about 3 minutes.

3 Remove bowl from heat and transfer to stand mixer fitted with whisk attachment. Whip warm egg mixture on medium speed until it has consistency of shaving cream and has cooled slightly, about 5 minutes. Add butter, 1 piece at a time, and whip until smooth and creamy, about 2 minutes. (Frosting may look curdled after half of butter has been added; it will smooth out with additional butter.)

4 Add chocolate and vanilla and mix until combined. Increase speed to medium-high and whip until light and fluffy, about 30 seconds, scraping down bowl as needed. If frosting seems too soft after adding chocolate, chill it briefly in refrigerator, then rewhip until creamy. (Frosting can be refrigerated for up to 24 hours; warm frosting briefly in microwave until just slightly softened, 5 to 10 seconds, then stir until creamy.)

Makes 3 cups; enough for 12 cupcakes or 1 sheet cake
Reduce chocolate to 8 ounces, reduce sugar to ½ cup (3½ ounces), reduce egg whites to 3, and reduce butter to 16 tablespoons.

Makes 6 cups; enough for 1 three-layer cake
Increase chocolate to 1 pound, increase egg whites to 6, increase table salt to ¼ teaspoon, increase butter to 1 pound, and increase vanilla to 1½ teaspoons.

CREAMY VEGAN CHOCOLATE FROSTING

MAKES 2 CUPS, ENOUGH FOR 12 CUPCAKES

For a billowy chocolate frosting to top our Vegan Dark Chocolate Cupcakes (page 119), we began by melting semisweet chocolate with coconut milk. For an extra-rich frosting, we discarded the milky liquid from the cans of coconut milk and used just the layer of cream. Chilling the cans of milk overnight helped separate the cream from the milk. Once cooled, we whipped this thick mixture into a light, mousse-like frosting. But it separated a bit. Using chocolate chips instead of bar chocolate was an easy fix (see page 7). Not all semisweet chocolate chips are vegan, so check ingredient lists carefully. Note that this frosting is made over 2 days.

- 2 (14-ounce) cans coconut milk
- 1⅔ cups (10 ounces) semisweet chocolate chips
- ⅛ teaspoon salt

1 Refrigerate unopened cans of coconut milk for at least 24 hours to ensure that 2 distinct layers form. Skim cream layer from each can and measure out ¾ cup cream (save any extra cream for another use and discard milky liquid).

2 Microwave coconut cream, chocolate chips, and salt in bowl at 50 percent power, whisking occasionally, until melted and smooth, 2 to 4 minutes; transfer to bowl of stand mixer. Press plastic wrap directly on surface of chocolate mixture and refrigerate until cooled completely and texture resembles firm cream cheese, about 3 hours, stirring halfway through chilling. (If mixture has chilled for longer and is very stiff, let stand at room temperature until softened but still cool.) Using stand mixer fitted with whisk attachment, whip at high speed until fluffy, mousse-like soft peaks form, 2 to 4 minutes, scraping down bowl halfway through whipping.

CANDIED NUTS

MAKES ABOUT 1 CUP

Many cakes, pies, or cool and creamy chocolate desserts could benefit from a little crunch to top things off. A very easy way to achieve this is to sprinkle on some toasted nuts, but to take this topping to the next level we like to candy the nuts for a toasty, sweet, salty treat that's much easier to achieve than you'd think. You can use any nut you'd like in this recipe.

- 1 cup nuts, toasted
- ¼ cup (1¾ ounces) sugar
- ¼ cup water
- ½ teaspoon table salt

1 Line rimmed baking sheet with parchment paper. Bring all ingredients to boil in medium saucepan over medium heat. Cook, stirring constantly, until water evaporates and sugar appears dry, opaque, and somewhat crystallized and evenly coats nuts, about 5 minutes.

2 Reduce heat to low and continue to stir nuts until sugar is amber-colored, about 2 minutes. Transfer nuts to prepared sheet and spread in even layer. Let cool completely, about 10 minutes.

CANDIED COFFEE BEANS

MAKES ABOUT ¼ CUP

Nuts aren't the only thing you can candy. Coffee beans make a great alternative accompaniment to a variety of chocolate desserts—not only does their crunch contribute a pleasant texture, but the flavor of the coffee beans highlights and intensifies the flavor of the chocolate. We chopped the beans in the food processor first so they would be easier to eat. These beans are potent—a small amount goes a long way.

¼   cup coffee beans

1   tablespoon sugar

1½   teaspoons water

     Pinch table salt

1 Line rimmed baking sheet with parchment paper. Pulse coffee beans in food processor until coarsely chopped, 6 to 8 pulses. Bring all ingredients to boil in medium saucepan over medium heat. Cook, stirring constantly, until water evaporates and sugar appears dry, opaque, and somewhat crystallized and evenly coats coffee beans, about 5 minutes.

2 Reduce heat to low and continue to stir coffee beans until sugar is amber-colored, about 2 minutes. Transfer coffee beans to prepared sheet and spread in even layer. Let cool completely, about 10 minutes.

SESAME BRITTLE

MAKES ABOUT 2 CUPS

Sesame brittle gives our Chocolate-Tahini Tart (page 189) a stunning patterned top. But you can break this brittle into shards of any size and top your desired chocolate dessert any way you like. The thin brittle tastes of toasted sesame and caramel. When pouring and rolling out the hot mixture, you will need to work quickly to prevent it from setting before it reaches the right thickness. A perfect sundae: Milk Chocolate No-Churn Ice Cream (page 305), Chocolate-Tahini Sauce (page 341), and bite-size pieces of this brittle.

2   tablespoons water

2   tablespoons sugar

2   tablespoons light corn syrup

1   tablespoon unsalted butter

⅓   cup sesame seeds, toasted

⅛   teaspoon table salt

1 Place large sheet parchment on cutting board. Heat water, sugar, corn syrup, and butter in small saucepan over medium-high heat, stirring often, until butter is melted and sugar is fully dissolved, about 1 minute. Bring to boil and cook, without stirring, until mixture has faint golden color and registers 300 degrees, 4 to 6 minutes.

2 Reduce heat to medium-low and continue to cook, gently swirling pan, until syrup is amber-colored and registers 350 degrees, 1 to 2 minutes. Off heat, stir in sesame seeds and salt. Working quickly, transfer mixture to prepared parchment, top with second layer of parchment and carefully smooth into 1/16-inch-thick layer using rolling pin.

3 Remove top sheet parchment and let cool completely, about 45 minutes. Break into rough 1-inch pieces before using. (Brittle can be stored in airtight container at room temperature for up to 1 month.)

ALL-PURPOSE CHOCOLATE GLAZE

MAKES ABOUT 1½ CUPS

We have various glazes embedded in the recipes throughout this book that best serve the given purpose. But if you want to take the lead in glazing other desserts—cakes from unadorned Chocolate Pound Cake (page 149) or Chocolate-Orange Angel Food Cake (page 154) to frosted Chocolate Malted Cake (page 183), or even brownies if you want another layer of decadence—this glaze is perfect. It's shiny-smooth, the right consistency for pouring and dripping decoratively down the ridges of your dessert.

¾   cup heavy cream

¼   cup light corn syrup

8   ounces bittersweet chocolate, chopped

½   teaspoon vanilla extract

Heat cream, corn syrup, and chocolate in small saucepan over medium heat, stirring constantly, until smooth. Stir in vanilla and set aside until slightly thickened, about 30 minutes.

CHOCOLATE CAKE LAYERS

MAKES TWO 9-INCH OR THREE 8-INCH CAKE LAYERS

The cake layers in our classic Old-Fashioned Chocolate Cake (page 156) are too versatile—and too good—to serve just that purpose. They're pleasantly fluffy and light—but not in chocolate flavor. We wanted to use them not just as the base for Chocolate Frosting (page 344) but for the whimsical layer cakes for this book—or any combination you'd like. This recipe makes two or three layers depending on your needs. You can also use any of the frostings in this chapter to fill and coat the layers.

4	ounces unsweetened chocolate, chopped
½	cup hot water
¼	cup (¾ ounce) Dutch-processed cocoa powder
1¾	cups (12¼ ounces) sugar, divided
1¾	cups (8¾ ounces) all-purpose flour
1½	teaspoons baking soda
1	teaspoon table salt
1	cup buttermilk
2	teaspoons vanilla extract
4	large eggs plus 2 large yolks, room temperature
12	tablespoons unsalted butter, cut into 12 pieces and softened

1 Adjust oven rack to middle position and heat oven to 350 degrees. Grease two 9-inch or three 8-inch round cake pans, line with parchment paper, grease parchment, and flour pans.

2 Combine chocolate, hot water, and cocoa in heatproof bowl set over saucepan filled with 1 inch barely simmering water, making sure that water does not touch bottom of bowl and stirring with heat-resistant rubber spatula until chocolate is melted, about 2 minutes. Add ½ cup sugar to chocolate mixture and stir until thick and glossy, 1 to 2 minutes. Remove bowl from heat; set aside to cool.

3 Whisk flour, baking soda, and salt together in bowl. Combine buttermilk and vanilla in second bowl. Using stand mixer fitted with whisk attachment, whip eggs and yolks on medium-low speed until combined, about 10 seconds. Add remaining 1¼ cups sugar, increase speed to high, and whip until light and fluffy, 2 to 3 minutes. Fit stand mixer with paddle. Add cooled chocolate mixture to egg mixture and mix on medium speed until thoroughly combined, 30 to 45 seconds, scraping down bowl as needed. Add butter, 1 piece at a time, mixing for about 10 seconds after each addition. Add flour mixture in 3 additions, alternating with buttermilk mixture in 2 additions, mixing until incorporated after each addition (about 15 seconds) and scraping down bowl as needed. Reduce speed to medium low and mix until batter is thoroughly combined, about 15 seconds. Give batter final stir by hand.

4 Divide batter evenly between prepared pans and smooth tops with rubber spatula. Bake until toothpick inserted in center comes out with few moist crumbs attached, 25 to 30 minutes, rotating pans halfway through baking. Let cakes cool in pans on wire rack for 10 minutes. Remove cakes from pans, discarding parchment, and let cool completely on rack, about 2 hours. (Cooled cake layers can be stored at room temperature for up to 24 hours or frozen for up to 1 month; defrost cake layers at room temperature.)

nutritional information
FOR OUR RECIPES

To calculate the nutritional values of our recipes per serving, we used The Food Processor SQL by ESHA research. When using this program, we entered all the ingredients, using weights for important baking ingredients such as flour for cakes and chocolate for ganache. We also used our preferred brands in these analyses. Any ingredient listed as "optional" was excluded from the analyses. If there is a range in the serving size, we used the highest number of servings to calculate the nutritional values.

	CALORIES	TOTAL FAT (G)	SAT FAT (G)	CHOL (MG)	SODIUM (MG)	TOTAL CARB (G)	DIETARY FIBER (G)	TOTAL SUGARS (G)	PROTEIN (G)
NOSTALGIC TREATS									
Chocolate Fluff Cookies	200	12	5	0	60	26	2	9	2
Nutella and Hazelnut Crispy Rice Cereal Treats	290	14	6	15	160	41	1	21	3
Chocolate Sandwich Cookies	56	2	1	8	23	9	0	5	1
Peanut Butter Sandwich Cookies with Milk Chocolate Filling	223	13	3	13	110	23	1	16	5
Chocolate-Dipped Potato Chip Cookies	138	9	5	18	65	15	1	10	1
Thin Chocolate Mint Cookies	70	3.5	2.5	5	25	9	0	6	1
Chocolate Turtle Cookies	119	7	3	17	35	13	1	8	2
Bergers-Style Cookies	326	16	10	33	100	45	3	30	4
Whoopie Pies	870	39	25	135	510	122	0	77	8
Nanaimo Bars	230	16	9	20	75	23	1	15	2
Midnight Chocolate Cake	209	11	2	6	242	25	1	13	2
Chocolate Cream Cupcakes	340	23	9	54	150	34	2	22	4
Hot Fudge Pudding Cake	288	11	6	40	176	48	3	32	4
Chocolate Éclair Cake	499	28	16	76	335	58	2	41	6
Creamy Chocolate Pudding	418	28	16	155	156	38	1	32	6
Mexican Chocolate Pudding	419	29	17	155	160	39	2	33	6
Mocha Chocolate Pudding	418	28	17	154	155	39	2	32	6
S'mores Molten Microwave Mug Cake	640	33	19	245	370	75	1	39	11
Chocolate Ice Cream Sandwiches	420	21	13	105	170	53	0	36	7
Ultimate Chocolate Milkshakes	360	13	8	47	130	58	2	52	5
Frozen Snickers Ice Cream Cake	670	35	14	50	370	85	2	68	12
WAKE UP WITH CHOCOLATE									
Chocolate-Hazelnut Spread	100	8	0.5	0	910	7	1	5	2
Chewy Granola Bars with Hazelnuts, Cherries, and Cacao Nibs	205	11	1	0	85	24	2	13	3
Make-Ahead Hot Chocolate	248	19	12	33	71	23	2	20	2
Chocolate-Walnut Muffins	490	31	7	60	260	50	1	23	7

	CALORIES	TOTAL FAT (G)	SAT FAT (G)	CHOL (MG)	SODIUM (MG)	TOTAL CARB (G)	DIETARY FIBER (G)	TOTAL SUGARS (G)	PROTEIN (G)
WAKE UP WITH CHOCOLATE (CONT.)									
Chocolate Zucchini Cake	328	16	6	39	191	44	2	27	4
Chocolate Granola	310	20	4	0	65	31	4	8	6
Cherry-Almond Chocolate Granola	330	18	3.5	0	70	38	5	12	7
Coconut-Cashew Chocolate Granola	320	20	6	0	70	34	4	9	6
Chocolate Chip Scones	460	24	15	40	300	55	0	27	7
Chocolate Financiers	104	7	3	13	54	7	0	5	1
Chocolate-Orange Crêpes	411	17	9	164	241	53	2	25	12
Chocolate Bread Pudding	622	43	25	287	210	55	3	32	10
Chocolate Cake Doughnuts	420	15	5	40	200	71	0	46	5
Churros with Mexican Chocolate Sauce	230	10	4.5	30	45	34	0	20	3
Chocolate Brioche Buns	410	19	11	100	320	51	2	11	9
Triple Chocolate Sticky Buns	495	23	14	61	321	67	2	33	7
Chocolate Babka	260	15	9	75	115	28	0	7	5
Chocolate Croissants	370	22	14	65	320	35	1	4	6
BAKERY CASE FAVORITES									
Chocolate Crinkle Cookies	155	5	3	31	95	24	1	16	2
Chocolate Chip Cookies	312	18	9	49	153	36	1	23	3
Chocolate Shortbread	180	11	7	30	75	17	0	3	2
Chocolate-Filled Lace Sandwich Cookies	120	7	3.5	5	20	16	0	14	1
Triple Chocolate Cookies	192	11	7	30	63	23	2	19	2
Chocolate Chunk Oatmeal Cookies	301	16	7	34	141	38	2	25	3
Chocolate Croissant Cookies	172	11	7	31	53	16	0	10	3
Ultimate Chocolate Cupcakes	240	13	4	37	165	29	1	19	3
Black-Bottom Cupcakes	217	13	8	35	174	24	1	17	3
Vegan Dark Chocolate Cupcakes	430	27	22	0	180	49	0	30	5
Fudgy Brownies	100	5	3	20	40	13	0	7	1
Vegan Fudgy Brownies	207	8	2	0	90	34	2	23	2
Chewy Brownies	299	14	5	43	98	41	2	30	3
S'mores Brownies	203	13	8	46	77	20	1	14	2
Ultimate Turtle Brownies	223	12	5	30	63	28	1	23	2
Oatmeal Fudge Bars	154	7	4	26	46	21	1	14	2
White Chocolate Raspberry Bars	150	6	4	20	75	22	1	15	2
Millionaire's Shortbread	195	10	6	25	91	24	0	17	1
Milk Chocolate Revel Bars	353	17	9	43	188	45	2	28	6
Double Chocolate Éclairs	470	29	17	220	160	48	1	30	8
Homemade Chocolate Cannoli	610	38	21	90	135	54	0	36	17
CAKES FROM SIMPLE TO DECADENT									
Chocolate-Cardamom Cake with Roasted Pears	310	16	10	80	105	42	2	29	4
Chocolate Pound Cake	460	28	16	155	200	51	1	31	6
Chocolate Sheet Cake with Milk Chocolate Frosting	778	52	25	131	222	74	4	56	9

	CALORIES	TOTAL FAT (G)	SAT FAT (G)	CHOL (MG)	SODIUM (MG)	TOTAL CARB (G)	DIETARY FIBER (G)	TOTAL SUGARS (G)	PROTEIN (G)
CAKES FROM SIMPLE TO DECADENT *(CONT.)*									
Texas Sheet Cake	388	22	8	39	88	49	2	38	3
Chocolate-Orange Angel Food Cake	170	2	1	0	105	34	0	26	4
Old-Fashioned Chocolate Cake	758	47	28	178	478	81	4	60	9
Chocolate–Peanut Butter Cake	910	62	32	195	550	81	2	54	14
White Chocolate–Macadamia Nut Cake with Mango	690	46	19	85	240	67	2	53	7
Boston Cream Pie	585	29	17	233	322	73	1	52	8
Chocolate-Stout Bundt Cake	580	33	20	130	340	67	2	33	9
Wellesley Chocolate Fudge Cake	763	32	20	99	520	118	3	94	8
German Chocolate Cake	649	37	19	148	317	74	3	57	8
Fallen Chocolate Cakes	342	22	13	146	114	33	1	29	4
Fallen Orange-Chocolate Cakes	285	18	10	117	91	28	1	24	4
Torta Caprese	310	22	9	79	106	26	2	22	5
Chocolate Blackout Cake	541	22	14	69	395	81	4	59	8
Magic Chocolate Flan Cake	244	14	8	120	200	25	1	13	7
Chocolate Malted Cake	950	54	33	200	540	110	0	85	10
Tunnel of Fudge Cake	671	40	19	127	210	79	4	59	8
SUBLIME SLICES									
Rich Chocolate Tart	430	34	21	115	120	33	0	19	5
Chocolate-Tahini Tart	510	37	18	100	150	41	2	17	8
Chocolate Caramel-Walnut Tart	344	23	11	86	60	33	1	25	3
Chocolate-Hazelnut Tart	455	31	14	80	199	43	2	31	4
Chocolate-Pear Tart	480	23	14	100	95	54	2	34	4
Chocolate Passion Fruit Tart	480	28	16	225	140	55	7	30	7
Nutella Tartlets	1180	81	37	110	330	104	3	58	13
Foolproof All-Butter Pie Dough	210	14	9	40	150	18	0	2	2
Nut Pie Dough	200	13	6	25	150	19	1	2	3
Classic Tart Dough	230	12	8	55	75	26	0	9	3
Chocolate Tart Dough	250	16	10	65	75	23	0	11	2
Chocolate Cream Pie	285	20	12	49	102	26	1	21	4
Chocolate Chess Pie	444	28	15	119	242	43	2	31	5
Mississippi Mud Pie	618	39	20	102	325	65	3	44	7
Chocolate Pecan Pie	560	38	15	105	270	54	2	37	7
Flourless Chocolate Cake	415	30	18	147	142	37	2	33	5
Chocolate-Pecan Torte	605	40	18	117	194	59	5	43	8
Milk Chocolate Cheesecake	438	34	19	143	308	26	1	19	8
Chocolate-Raspberry Torte	424	30	14	105	118	37	3	28	6

	CALORIES	TOTAL FAT (G)	SAT FAT (G)	CHOL (MG)	SODIUM (MG)	TOTAL CARB (G)	DIETARY FIBER (G)	TOTAL SUGARS (G)	PROTEIN (G)
CELEBRATING THE HOLIDAYS									
Holiday Chocolate Butter Cookies	108	6	4	22	14	11	0	6	1
Chocolate-Orange Butter Cookies with Chocolate-Brandy Glaze	108	6	4	22	14	11	0	6	1
Glazed Chocolate-Mint Cookies	131	7	4	23	17	14	0	9	1
Mexican Chocolate Butter Cookies	122	7	4	22	14	13	0	8	1
Salted Chocolate-Caramel Butter Cookies	120	6	3.5	20	45	16	0	10	1
Nutty Chocolate-Raspberry Thumbprints	112	6	2	12	33	15	1	9	1
Chocolate-Hazelnut Biscotti	100	5	1.5	15	55	12	0	7	2
Baci di Dama	60	4.5	2	5	10	6	0	2	1
Chocolate Rum Balls	103	4	1	0	69	17	1	12	1
Peppermint Meringue Kisses	45	2	1	0	8	7	0	6	0
Chocolate Chip Panettone	257	12	7	45	179	35	2	15	5
Chocolate Candy Cane Cake	1010	56	35	210	460	118	0	99	9
Yule Log	570	44	25	214	253	39	2	32	9
White Chocolate–Raspberry Bombe	610	38	25	75	310	66	2	55	8
Chocolate-Raspberry Heart Cake	800	47	30	155	210	90	1	74	10
Chocolate-Strawberry Cake	940	56	35	225	420	105	1	83	7
Chocolate Shadow Cake	560	26	16	135	430	77	1	54	9
DAZZLING DESSERTS									
Chocolate Pavlova with Berries and Whipped Cream	400	22	14	55	55	50	5	39	5
Chocolate Profiteroles	430	23	14	95	190	50	1	39	7
White Chocolate–Pink Peppercorn Panna Cotta	470	38	25	95	140	31	1	29	6
Triple Chocolate Mousse Cake	458	36	22	137	94	32	2	28	4
Hazelnut-Chocolate Crêpe Cake	550	36	19	160	190	47	2	23	10
Chocolate-Raspberry Petits Fours	120	5	2.5	25	35	17	0	13	2
Blood Orange–Chocolate Tart	340	23	14	70	150	33	1	19	3
Chocolate, Matcha, and Pomegranate Tart	438	26	14	80	200	51	2	39	3
Chocolate-Caramel Layer Cake	751	41	23	119	483	98	4	78	6
Chocolate-Espresso Dacquoise	503	38	17	124	111	38	3	32	7
Chocolate-Lavender Napoleons	540	32	18	130	210	65	2	33	8
A SPOONFUL OF HEAVEN									
Chocolate–Peanut Butter Crème Brûlée	690	55	27	325	230	41	3	29	14
Dark Chocolate Mousse	282	22	13	92	70	21	2	18	3
Chocolate-Orange Mousse	274	20	12	87	69	21	2	17	3
Chocolate-Raspberry Mousse	280	20	12	87	69	22	2	19	3
Pots de Crème	490	41	25	190	110	31	2	12	6
Milk Chocolate Pots de Crème	510	40	24	195	120	33	0	28	7
Chocolate Avocado Pudding	210	15	5	0	82	19	7	10	3

	CALORIES	TOTAL FAT (G)	SAT FAT (G)	CHOL (MG)	SODIUM (MG)	TOTAL CARB (G)	DIETARY FIBER (G)	TOTAL SUGARS (G)	PROTEIN (G)
A SPOONFUL OF HEAVEN *(CONT.)*									
Chocolate Soufflé	272	19	10	157	101	21	1	18	6
Individual Chocolate Soufflés	306	19	10	157	101	29	1	26	6
Chocolate Fondue	300	25	15	35	25	21	2	3	3
Five-Spice Chocolate Fondue	300	25	15	35	25	21	3	3	3
Orange Chocolate Fondue	310	25	15	35	25	22	2	4	3
Caramelized White Chocolate Mousse	350	27	18	105	110	26	0	25	6
Chocolate Semifreddo with Cherry Sauce	320	23	14	90	75	27	2	15	4
Double Chocolate Dessert Waffles with Ice Cream	430	19	12	120	350	54	0	35	9
Milk Chocolate No-Churn Ice Cream	391	26	16	80	78	37	1	36	5
Banana-Walnut Chocolate Chunk Ice Cream	288	19	11	64	103	30	1	27	3
Dark Chocolate No-Churn Ice Cream	383	26	16	76	125	38	1	37	4
Malted Milk Chocolate No-Churn Ice Cream	401	26	16	81	144	39	1	37	5
Chocolate Sorbet	270	12	7	0	50	44	2	27	3
DIY CONFECTIONS									
Chocolate-Covered Strawberries	127	7	3	1	7	16	1	13	1
Candy Clusters	90	5	2.5	0	55	11	1	7	2
White Chocolate Nonpareils	27	2	1	1	4	3	0	3	0
Chocolate Truffles	66	5	3	7	15	7	1	6	1
Chocolate-Almond Truffles	85	7	3	7	15	7	1	5	1
Chocolate-Cinnamon Truffles	66	5	3	7	15	7	1	6	1
Chocolate-Ginger Truffles	66	5	3	7	15	7	1	6	1
Chocolate-Lemon Truffles	66	5	3	7	15	7	1	6	1
Chocolate Toffee	120	8	3.5	10	20	11	0	10	1
Chocolate Fudge	303	16	9	23	91	43	1	39	2
Peanut Butter Truffles	70	4	1	1	6	7	0	6	1
No-Bake Rocky Road Bars	180	11	4.5	10	15	20	1	15	3
Brigadeiros	70	2.5	1	5	15	11	0	9	1
Chocolate–Peanut Butter Candies	120	8	3.5	5	35	11	1	8	2
DIY Candy Bars	310	21	10	0	0	32	4	8	5
Birthday Cake Bars	280	15	10	0	70	37	0	33	3
Milk Chocolate Crunch Bars	230	13	8	5	160	29	0	21	3
Pomegranate and Nut Chocolate Coins	80	6	2	0	0	6	1	4	1
Cherry and Nut Chocolate Coins	80	6	2	0	0	7	1	4	2
Mango and Nut Chocolate Coins	80	6	2.5	0	0	7	1	4	2
Needhams	119	7	5	5	37	15	1	14	1
Chocolate Bark with Pepitas and Goji Berries	250	20	8	0	150	20	5	11	9
Chocolate-Covered Caramels	80	4	2.5	5	20	10	0	9	1
Ice Cream Bonbons	442	30	15	19	43	48	4	40	5

	CALORIES	TOTAL FAT (G)	SAT FAT (G)	CHOL (MG)	SODIUM (MG)	TOTAL CARB (G)	DIETARY FIBER (G)	TOTAL SUGARS (G)	PROTEIN (G)
TOPPINGS, SAUCES, AND MORE									
Whipped Cream	110	11	7	35	25	2	0	2	1
Bourbon Whipped Cream	57	6	3	20	6	1	0	1	0
Cocoa Whipped Cream	120	11	7	35	25	5	0	4	1
Orange Whipped Cream	110	11	7	35	25	3	0	3	1
Peanut Butter Whipped Cream	160	15	8	35	65	4	0	3	3
Yogurt Whipped Cream	100	10	7	30	10	1	0	1	2
Classic Hot Fudge Sauce	260	12	7	15	85	37	2	32	3
Orange Hot Fudge Sauce	260	12	7	15	85	37	2	32	3
Peanut Butter Hot Fudge Sauce	310	16	8	15	190	39	2	33	4
Chocolate-Tahini Sauce	290	16	8	15	160	39	0	32	4
Classic Caramel Sauce	300	11	7	35	90	53	0	53	1
Dark Rum Caramel Sauce	310	11	7	35	90	53	0	53	1
Orange-Espresso Caramel Sauce	320	11	7	35	90	56	0	55	1
Salted Caramel Sauce	300	11	7	35	310	53	0	53	1
Caramel-Chocolate-Pecan Sauce	290	17	8	30	50	37	1	32	2
Chocolate-Port Sauce	180	13	8	15	5	13	1	1	2
Peppermint–White Chocolate Sauce	190	14	10	15	60	19	0	19	2
Crème Anglaise	80	3.5	1.5	95	40	9	0	8	3
Coffee Crème Anglaise	80	3.5	1.5	95	40	9	0	8	3
Earl Grey Crème Anglaise	80	3.5	1.5	95	40	9	0	8	3
Orange Crème Anglaise	90	3.5	1.5	95	40	9	0	9	3
Peanut Butter Sauce	328	22	10	37	66	31	1	29	5
Mixed Berry Coulis	80	0	0	0	50	19	2	17	0
Magic Chocolate Shell	200	18	15	0	25	12	0	11	1
Chocolate Frosting (enough for 1 two-layer cake)	660	44	28	90	50	69	0	63	4
(enough for 12 cupcakes or 1 sheet cake)	380	25	16	50	40	41	0	37	2
(enough for 1 three-layer cake)	860	64	39	120	30	81	3	33	4
Ganache Frosting (enough for 1 two-layer cake)	390	30	19	55	15	30	0	27	5
(enough for 12 cupcakes or 1 sheet cake)	239	19	11	40	14	18	1	16	1
(enough for 1 three-layer cake)	490	38	24	70	15	38	0	34	6
Chocolate Buttercream (enough for 1 two-layer cake)	580	47	29	85	55	41	3	20	4
(enough for 12 cupcakes or 1 sheet cake)	270	22	14	40	40	18	1	8	2
(enough for 1 three-layer cake)	650	54	33	95	90	44	3	20	5
Creamy Vegan Chocolate Frosting	250	21	17	0	35	17	0	13	3
Candied Nuts	130	9	1.5	0	150	10	2	7	4
Candied Coffee Beans	80	2.5	0	0	85	15	3	6	2
Sesame Brittle	70	4.5	1.5	5	40	9	1	7	1
All Purpose Chocolate Glaze	40	3	2	5	0	4	0	1	0
Chocolate Cake Layers	280	14	8	95	290	37	0	23	5

conversions
AND EQUIVALENTS

Baking is a science and an art, but geography has a hand in it, too. Flours and sugars manufactured in the United Kingdom and elsewhere will feel and taste different from those manufactured in the United States. So we cannot promise that a pie you bake in Canada or England will taste the same as a pie baked in the States, but we can offer guidelines for converting weights and measures. We also recommend that you rely on your instincts when making our recipes. Refer to the visual cues provided. If the dough hasn't "come together in a ball" as described, you may need to add more flour—even if the recipe doesn't tell you to. You be the judge.

The recipes in this book were developed using standard U.S. measures following U.S. government guidelines. The charts below offer equivalents for U.S. and metric measures. All conversions are approximate and have been rounded up or down to the nearest whole number.

EXAMPLE
1 teaspoon = 4.9292 milliliters, rounded up to 5 milliliters
1 ounce = 28.3495 grams, rounded down to 28 grams

VOLUME CONVERSIONS

U.S.	METRIC
1 teaspoon	5 milliliters
2 teaspoons	10 milliliters
1 tablespoon	15 milliliters
2 tablespoons	30 milliliters
¼ cup	59 milliliters
⅓ cup	79 milliliters
½ cup	118 milliliters
¾ cup	177 milliliters
1 cup	237 milliliters
1¼ cups	296 milliliters
1½ cups	355 milliliters
2 cups (1 pint)	473 milliliters
2½ cups	591 milliliters
3 cups	710 milliliters
4 cups (1 quart)	0.946 liter
1.06 quarts	1 liter
4 quarts (1 gallon)	3.8 liters

WEIGHT CONVERSIONS

OUNCES	GRAMS
½	14
¾	21
1	28
1½	43
2	57
2½	71
3	85
3½	99
4	113
4½	128
5	142
6	170
7	198
8	227
9	255
10	283
12	340
16 (1 pound)	454

CONVERSIONS FOR COMMON BAKING INGREDIENTS

Because measuring by weight is far more accurate than measuring by volume, and thus more likely to produce reliable results, in our recipes we provide ounce measures in addition to cup measures for many ingredients. Refer to the chart below to convert these measures into grams.

INGREDIENT	OUNCES	GRAMS
Flour		
1 cup all-purpose flour*	5	142
1 cup cake flour	4	113
1 cup whole-wheat flour	5½	156
Sugar		
1 cup granulated (white) sugar	7	198
1 cup packed brown sugar (light or dark)	7	198
1 cup confectioners' sugar	4	113
Cocoa Powder		
1 cup cocoa powder	3	85
Butter†		
4 tablespoons (½ stick or ¼ cup)	2	57
8 tablespoons (1 stick or ½ cup)	4	113
16 tablespoons (2 sticks or 1 cup)	8	227

* U.S. all-purpose flour, the most frequently used flour in this book, does not contain leaveners, as some European flours do. These leavened flours are called self-rising or self-raising. If you are using self-rising flour, take this into consideration before adding leaveners to a recipe.

† In the United States, butter is sold both salted and unsalted. We recommend unsalted butter. If you are using salted butter, take this into consideration before adding salt to a recipe.

OVEN TEMPERATURE

FAHRENHEIT	CELSIUS	GAS MARK
225	105	¼
250	120	½
275	135	1
300	150	2
325	165	3
350	180	4
375	190	5
400	200	6
425	220	7
450	230	8
475	245	9

CONVERTING TEMPERATURES FROM AN INSTANT-READ THERMOMETER

We include doneness temperatures in many of the recipes in this book. We recommend an instant-read thermometer for the job. Refer to the table above to convert Fahrenheit degrees to Celsius. Or, for temperatures not represented in the chart, use this simple formula:

Subtract 32 degrees from the Fahrenheit reading, then divide the result by 1.8 to find the Celsius reading.

EXAMPLE

"Cook caramel until it registers 160 degrees."

To convert:
160°F − 32 = 128°
128° ÷ 1.8 = 71.11°C, rounded down to 71°C

index

Note: Page references in *italics* indicate photographs.

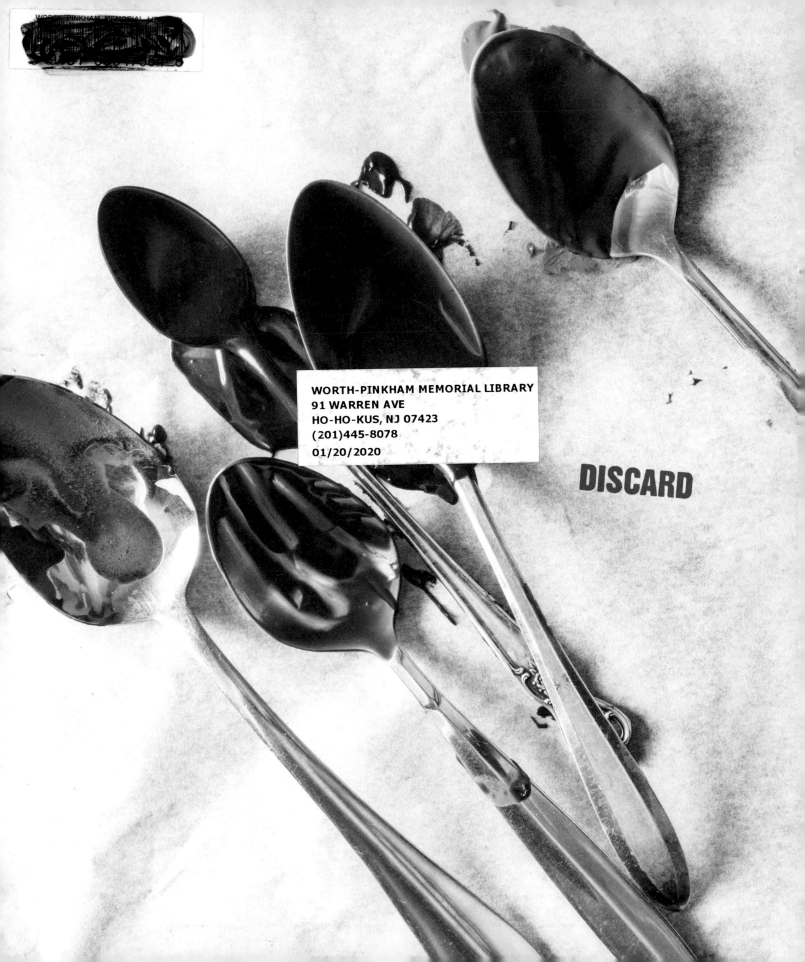